LONGMAN KEYSTONE

A

CALIFORNIA

Anna Uhl Chamot

John De Mado

Sharroky Hollie

Pearson Education, 10 Bank Street, White Plains, NY 10606

Staff credits: The people who made up the Longman Keystone team, representing editorial, production, design, manufacturing, and marketing, are John Ade, Rhea Banker, Liz Barker, Danielle Belfiore, Don Bensey, Virginia Bernard, Kenna Bourke, Brandon Carda, Johnnie Farmer, Maryann Finocchi, Patrice Fraccio, Geraldine Geniusas, Charles Green, Zach Halper, Henry Hild, David L. Jones, Ed Lamprich, Jamie Lawrence, Emily Lippincott, Maria Pia Marrella, Linda Moser, Laurie Neaman, Sherri Pemberton, Liza Pleva, Joan Poole, Edie Pullman, Monica Rodriguez, Tara Rose, Tania Saiz-Sousa, Donna Schaffer, Chris Siley, Lynn Sobotta, Heather St. Clair, Jennifer Stem, Siobhan Sullivan, Jane Townsend, Heather Vomero, Marian Wassner, Lauren Weidenman, Matthew Williams, and Adina Zoltan.

Smithsonian American Art Museum contributors: Project director and writer: Elizabeth K. Eder, Ph.D.; Writer: Mary Collins; Image research assistants: Laurel Fehrenbach, Katherine G. Stilwill, and Sally Otis; Rights and reproductions: Richard H. Sorensen and Leslie G. Green; Building photograph by Tim Hursley.

Text design and composition: Kirchoff/Wohlberg, Inc.

Text font: 11.5/14 Minion
Acknowledgments: See page 473.
Illustration and Photo Credits: See page 474.

Library of Congress Cataloging-in-Publication Data
Chamot, Anna Uhl.
Longman keystone / Anna Uhl Chamot, John De Mado, Sharroky Hollie.
p. cm. -- (Longman keystone ; A)
Includes index.
ISBN 0-13-208600-X (v. A)
1. Language arts (Middle school)--United States. 2. Language arts (Middle school)--Activity programs. 3. Language arts (Secondary)--United States. 4. English language--Study and teaching. I. Demado, John II. Hollie, Sharroky III. Title.
LB1631.C4466 2008
428.0071'2--dc22
2007049279

ISBN-13: 978-0-13-208600-4
ISBN-10: 0-13-208600-X

Printed in the United States of America
2 3 4 5 6 7 8 9 10—DWL—12 11 10 09

About the Authors

Anna Uhl Chamot is a professor of secondary education and a faculty advisor for ESL in George Washington University's Department of Teacher Preparation. She has been a researcher and teacher trainer in content-based second-language learning and language-learning strategies. She co-designed and has written extensively about the Cognitive Academic Language Learning Approach (CALLA) and spent seven years implementing the CALLA model in the Arlington Public Schools in Virginia.

John De Mado has been an energetic force in the field of Language Acquisition for several years. He is founder and president of John De Mado Language Seminars, Inc., an educational consulting firm devoted exclusively to language acquisition and literacy issues. John, who speaks a variety of languages, has authored several textbook programs and produced a series of music CD/DVDs designed to help students acquire other languages. John is recognized nationally, as well as internationally, for his insightful workshops, motivating keynote addresses, and humor-filled delivery style.

Sharroky Hollie is an assistant professor in teacher education at California State University, Dominguez Hills. His expertise is in the field of professional development, African-American education, and second-language methodology. He is an urban literacy visiting professor at Webster University, St. Louis. Sharroky is the Executive Director of the Center for Culturally Responsive Teaching and Learning (CCRTL) and the co-founding director of the nationally acclaimed Culture and Language Academy of Success (CLAS).

Reviewers

Sharena Adebiyi
Fulton County Schools
Stone City, GA

Jennifer Benavides
Garland ISD
Garland, TX

Tracy Bunker
Shearer Charter School
Napa, CA

Dan Fichtner
UCLA Ed. Ext. TESOL Program
Redondo Beach, CA

Trudy Freer-Alvarez
Houston ISD
Houston, TX

Helena K. Gandell
Duval County
Jacksonville, FL

Glenda Harrell
Johnston County School Dist.
Smithfield, NC

Michelle Land
Randolph Middle School
Randolph, NJ

Joseph E. Leaf
Norristown Area High School
Norristown, PA

Ilona Olancin
Collier County Schools
Naples, FL

Jeanne Perrin
Boston Unified School Dist.
Boston, MA

Cheryl Quadrelli-Jones
Anaheim Union High School Dist.
Fullerton, CA

Mary Schmidt
Riverwood High School
Atlanta, GA

Daniel Thatcher
Garland ISD
Garland, TX

Denise Tiffany
West High School
Iowa City, IA

Lisa Troute
Palm Beach County School Dist.
West Palm, FL

Dear Student,

Welcome to LONGMAN KEYSTONE

Longman Keystone has been specially designed to help you succeed in all areas of your school studies. This program will help you develop the English language skills you need for language arts, social studies, math, and science. You will discover new ways to use and build upon your language skills through your interactions with classmates, friends, teachers, and family members.

Keystone includes a mix of many subjects. Each unit has four different reading selections that include literary excerpts, poems, and nonfiction articles about science, math, and social studies. These selections will help you understand the vocabulary and organization of different types of texts. They will also give you the tools you need to approach the content of the different subjects you take in school.

As you use this program, you will discover new words, use your background knowledge of the subjects presented, relate your knowledge to the new information, and take part in creative activities. You will learn strategies to help you understand readings better. You will work on activities that help you improve your English skills in grammar, word study, and spelling. Finally, you will be asked to demonstrate the listening, speaking, and writing skills you have learned through fun projects that are incorporated throughout the program.

Learning a language takes time, but just like learning to skateboard or learning to swim, it is fun! Whether you are learning English for the first time, or increasing your knowledge of English by adding academic or literary language to your vocabulary, you are giving yourself new choices for the future, and a better chance of succeeding in both your studies and in everyday life.

We hope you enjoy *Longman Keystone* as much as we enjoyed writing it for you!

Good luck!

Anna Uhl Chamot
John De Mado
Sharroky Hollie

Learn about Art with the Smithsonian American Art Museum

Dear Student,

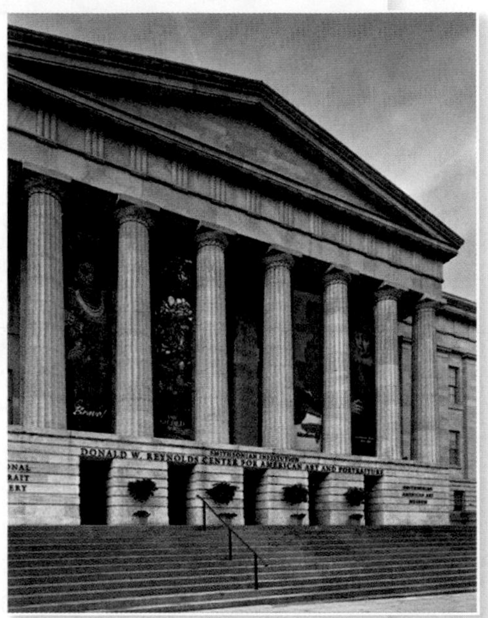

At the end of each unit in this book, you will learn about some artists and artworks that relate to the theme you have just read about. These artworks are all in the Smithsonian American Art Museum in Washington, D.C. That means they belong to you, because the Smithsonian is America's collection. The artworks were created over a period of 300 years by artists who responded to their experiences in personal ways. Their world lives on through their artworks and, as viewers, we can understand them and ourselves in new ways. We discover that many of the things that concerned these artists still engage us today.

Looking at an artwork is different from reading a written history. Artists present few facts or dates. Instead, they offer emotional insights that come from their own lives and experiences. They make their own decisions about what matters, without worrying if others agree or disagree. This is a rare and useful kind of knowledge that we can all learn from. Artists inspire us to respond to our own lives with deeper insight.

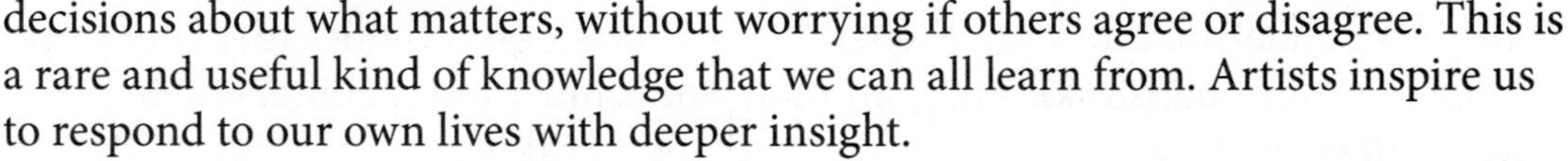

There are two ways to approach art. One way is through the mind—studying the artist, learning about the subject, exploring the context in which the artwork was made, and forming a personal view. This way is deeply rewarding and expands your understanding of the world. The second way is through the senses—letting your imagination roam as you look at an artwork, losing yourself in colors and shapes, absorbing the meaning through your eyes. This way is called "aesthetic." The great thing about art is that an artwork may have many different meanings. You can decide what it means to you.

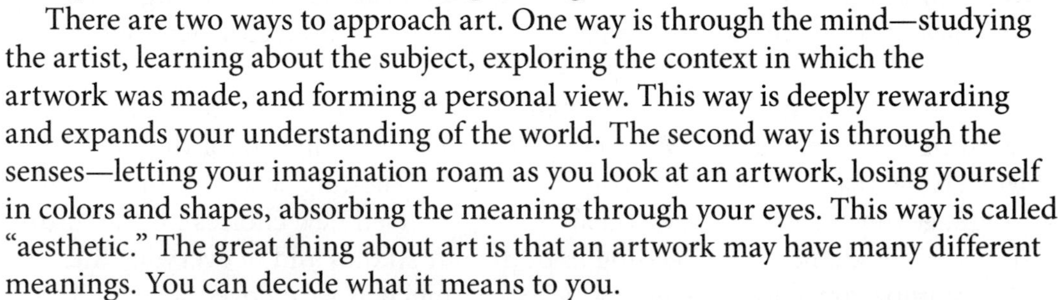

This brief introduction to American art will, I hope, lead to a lifetime of enjoyment and appreciation of art.

Elizabeth Broun
The Margaret and Terry Stent Director
Smithsonian American Art Museum

Glossary of Terms

You will find the following words useful when reading, writing, and talking about art.

abstract a style of art that does not represent things, animals, or people realistically

acrylic a type of paint that is made from ground pigments and certain chemicals

background part of the artwork that looks furthest away from the viewer

brushstroke the paint or ink left on the surface of an artwork by the paintbrush

canvas a type of heavy woven fabric used as a support for painting; another word for a painting

composition the way in which the different parts of an artwork are arranged

detail a small part of an artwork

evoke to produce a strong feeling or memory

figure the representation of a person or animal in an artwork

foreground part of the artwork that looks closest to the viewer

geometric a type of pattern that has straight lines or shapes such as squares, circles, etc.

mixed media different kinds of materials such as paint, fabric, objects, etc. that are used in a single artwork

oil a type of paint that is made from ground pigments and linseed oil

paintbrush a special brush used for painting

perception the way you understand something you see

pigment a finely powdered material (natural or man-made) that gives color to paint, ink, or dye

portrait an artwork that shows a specific person, group of people, or animal

print an artwork that has been made from a sheet of metal or a block of wood covered with a wet color and then pressed onto a flat surface like paper. Types of prints include lithographs, etchings, aquatints, etc.

symbol an image, shape, or object in an artwork that represents an idea

texture the way that a surface or material feels and how smooth or rough it looks

tone the shade of a particular color; the effect of light and shade with color

watercolor a type of paint that is made from ground pigments, gum, and glycerin and/or honey; another word for a painting done with this medium

UNIT 1 Contents

UNIT 2

Contents

How does growing up change us?

UNIT 3 Contents

UNIT 4 Contents

What do we learn through winning and losing?

UNIT 5 Contents

Contents

UNIT 6

What is your vision of life in the future?

California Language Arts Standards

For Intervention and Intervention for English Learners, Grades Four through Eight

Here is a list of the standards so that you can know what you will learn in *Keystone*. You will see that many standards are the same for students in reading programs and students in English language learning programs. However, some standards only apply to reading programs, and others only apply to English language learning programs. The standards for each of these programs are highlighted in a different color. The standards that apply only to Intervention are in **red** (see p. CA-7). The standards that apply only to Intervention for English Learners are in **blue** (see pp. CA-15–CA-17).

READING

Word Analysis, Fluency, and Systematic Vocabulary Development

In this strand of standards, you will learn how to read and use what you know about word origins, relationships, and context clues to learn the meanings of new words.

Concepts About Print In this substrand, you will learn how to read and identify letters, words, and sentences. You will also learn how to match printed words to words you hear. You will learn how to find the title and the author of what you read.

1 1.1 Match oral words to printed words.
1 1.2 Identify the title and author of a reading selection.
1 1.3 Identify letters, words, and sentences.

Phonemic Awareness In this substrand, you will learn how to sound out words and make new words by changing the sounds. You will also learn the relationship between the words you hear and the structure of English.

1 1.4 Distinguish initial, medial, and final sounds in single-syllable words.
1 1.5 Distinguish long- and short-vowel sounds in orally stated single-syllable words (e.g., *bit*/*bite*).
1 1.6 Create and state a series of rhyming words, including consonant blends.
1 1.7 Add, delete, or change target sounds to change words (e.g., change *cow* to *how*; *pan* to *an*).
1 1.8 Blend two to four phonemes into recognizable words (e.g., /*c*/*a*/*t*/ = cat; /*f*/*l*/*a*/*t*/ = flat).
1 1.9 Segment single syllable words into their components (e.g., /c/a/t/ = cat; /s/p/l/a/t/ = splat; /r/i/ch/ = rich).

Decoding and Word Recognition In this substrand, you will learn about the sound structure of words, including syllables, and the relationship between the sounds and the letters. You will also learn to recognize common words. You will learn how to sound out words and read them so they sound natural. You will also learn common abbreviations and how to recognize and use word families.

1 1.10 Generate the sounds from all the letters and letter patterns, including consonant blends and long- and short-vowel patterns (i.e., phonograms), and blend those sounds into recognizable words.
1 1.11 Read common, irregular sight words (e.g., *the, have, said, come, give, of*).
1 1.12 Use knowledge of vowel digraphs and *r*-controlled letter-sound associations to read words.
1 1.13 Read compound words and contractions.
1 1.14 Read inflectional forms (e.g., *-s, -ed, -ing*) and root words (e.g., *look, looked, looking*).
1 1.15 Read common word families (e.g., *-ite, -ate*).
1 1.16 Read aloud with fluency in a manner that sounds like natural speech.
2 1.1 Recognize and use knowledge of spelling patterns (e.g., diphthongs, special vowel spellings) when reading.
2 1.2 Apply knowledge of basic syllabication rules when reading (e.g., vowel-consonant-vowel=*su/per*; vowel-consonant/consonant-vowel=*sup/per*).
2 1.3 Decode two-syllable nonsense words and regular multisyllable words.
2 1.4 Recognize common abbreviations (e.g., *Jan., Sun., Mr., St.*).
2 1.5 Identify and correctly use regular plurals (e.g., *-s, -es, -ies*) and irregular plurals (e.g., *fly/flies, wife/wives*).
2 1.6 Read aloud fluently and accurately and with appropriate intonation and expression.
3 1.1 Know and use complex word families when reading (e.g., *-ight*) to decode unfamiliar words.
3 1.2 Decode regular multisyllabic words.
3 1.3 Read aloud narrative and expository text fluently and accurately and with appropriate pacing, intonation, and expression.

Word Recognition In this substrand, you will learn how to read a text aloud at a normal rate of speed. You will also learn to read at the correct speed, with appropriate intonation and expression.

4 1.1 Read narrative and expository text aloud with grade-appropriate fluency and accuracy and with appropriate pacing, intonation, and expression.
5 1.1 Read aloud narrative and expository text fluently and accurately and with appropriate pacing, intonation, and expression.
6 1.1 Read aloud narrative and expository text fluently and accurately and with appropriate pacing, intonation, and expression.

Vocabulary and Concept Development In this substrand, you will use what you know about word origins, relationships, and context clues to learn the meanings of new words. You will also learn how to recognize root words in order to understand the meanings of unfamiliar words. You will learn how to use reference books to learn the meanings of unfamiliar words and how words relate to one another.

1 1.17 Classify grade-appropriate categories of words (e.g., concrete collections of animals, foods, toys).
2 1.7 Understand and explain common antonyms and synonyms.
2 1.8 Use knowledge of individual words in unknown compound words to predict their meaning.
2 1.9 Know the meaning of simple prefixes and suffixes (e.g., *over-, un-, -ing, -ly*).
2 1.10 Identify simple multiple-meaning words.
3 1.4 Use knowledge of antonyms, synonyms, homophones, and homographs to determine the meanings of words.
3 1.5 Demonstrate knowledge of levels of specificity among grade-appropriate words and explain the importance of these relations (e.g., *dog/mammal/animal/living things*).
3 1.6 Use sentence and word context to find the meaning of unknown words.
3 1.7 Use a dictionary to learn the meaning and other features of unknown words.
3 1.8 Use knowledge of prefixes (e.g., *un-, re-, pre-, bi-, mis-, dis-*) and suffixes (e.g., *-er, -est, -ful*) to determine the meaning of words.
4 1.2 Apply knowledge of word origins, derivations, synonyms, antonyms, and idioms to determine the meaning of words and phrases.
4 1.3 Use knowledge of root words to determine the meaning of unknown words within a passage.
4 1.4 Know common root and affixes derived from Greek and Latin and use this knowledge to analyze the meaning of complex words (e.g., *international*).
4 1.5 Use a thesaurus to determine related words and concepts.
4 1.6 Distinguish and interpret words with multiple meanings.
5 1.2 Use word origins to determine the meaning of unknown words.
5 1.3 Understand and explain frequently used synonyms, antonyms, and homographs.
5 1.4 Know abstract, derived roots and affixes derived from Greek and Latin and use this knowledge to analyze the meaning of complex words (e.g., *controversial*).
5 1.5 Understand and explain the figurative and metaphorical use of words in context.
6 1.2 Identify and interpret figurative language and words with multiple meanings.
6 1.3 Recognize the origins and meanings of frequently used foreign words in English and use these words accurately in speaking and writing.
6 1.4 Monitor expository text for unknown words or words with novel meanings by using word, sentence, and paragraph clues to determine meaning.
6 1.5 Understand and explain "shades of meaning" in related words (e.g., *softly* and *quietly*).

Reading Comprehension

In this strand of standards, you will study new material by connecting important ideas, evaluating structure and organization, and by using what you know about author's purpose to better understand challenging texts.

Structural Features of Informational Materials In this substrand, you will learn how to identify, use, and understand specific structural features that you will see in many types of informational text. You will learn to recognize the sequence of events in texts and you will learn how various types of visuals help you understand the information that you read.

1 2.1 Identify text that uses sequence or other logical order.
2 2.1 Use titles, tables of contents, and chapter headings to locate information in expository text.
3 2.1 Use titles, tables of contents, chapter headings, glossaries, and indexes to locate information in text.
4 2.1 Identify structural patterns found in informational text (e.g., compare and contrast, cause and effect, sequential or chronological order, proposition and support) to strengthen comprehension.
5 2.1 Understand how text features (e.g., format, graphics, sequence, diagrams, illustrations, charts, maps) make information accessible and usable.
5 2.2 Analyze text that is organized in sequential or chronological order.
6 2.1 Identify the structural features of popular media (e.g., newspaper, magazines, online information) and use the features to obtain information.
6 2.2 Analyze text that uses the compare-and-contrast organizational pattern.

Comprehension and Analysis of Grade-Level-Appropriate Text In this substrand, you will learn to use your reading comprehension skills to ask and answer questions, follow instructions, and identify and remember the main ideas in a text. You will also use readings strategies and your own experience and knowledge of a subject to analyze and demonstrate your understanding of a text. You will learn how the author's purpose for writing the text and your purpose for reading both help you understand the information that you read.

1 2.2 Respond to *who, what, when, where,* and *how* questions.
1 2.3 Follow one-step written instructions.
1 2.4 Use context to resolve ambiguities about word and sentence meanings.
1 2.5 Confirm predictions about what will happen next in a text by identifying key words (i.e., signpost words).
1 2.6 Relate prior knowledge to textual information.
1 2.7 Retell the central ideas of simple expository or narrative passages.
2 2.2 State the purpose in reading (i.e., tell what information is sought).
2 2.3 Use knowledge of the author's purpose(s) to comprehend informational text.
2 2.4 Ask clarifying questions about essential textual elements of exposition (e.g., *why, what if, how*).
2 2.5 Restate facts and details in the text to clarify and organize ideas.
2 2.6 Recognize cause-and-effect relationships in text.
2 2.7 Interpret information from diagrams, charts, and graphs.
2 2.8 Follow two-step written instructions.
3 2.2 Ask questions and support answers by connecting prior knowledge with literal information found in, and inferred from, the text.
3 2.3 Demonstrate comprehension by identifying answers in the text.
3 2.4 Recall major points in the text and make and modify predictions about forthcoming information.
3 2.5 Distinguish the main idea and supporting details in expository text.
3 2.6 Extract appropriate and significant information from the text, including problems and solutions.
3 2.7 Follow simple multiple-step written instructions (e.g., how to assemble a product or play a board game).
4 2.2 Use appropriate strategies when reading for different purposes (e.g., full comprehension, location of information, personal enjoyment).

4 2.3 Make and confirm predictions about text by using prior knowledge and ideas presented in the text itself, including illustrations, titles, topic sentences, important words, and foreshadowing clues.

4 2.4 Evaluate new information and hypotheses by testing them against known information and ideas.

4 2.5 Compare and contrast information on the same topic after reading several passages or articles.

4 2.6 Distinguish between cause and effect and between fact and opinion in expository text.

4 2.7 Follow multiple-step instructions in a basic technical manual (e.g., how to use computer commands or video games).

5 2.3 Discern main ideas and concepts presented in texts, identifying and assessing evidence that supports those ideas.

5 2.4 Draw inferences, conclusions, or generalizations about text and support them with textual evidence and prior knowledge.

6 2.3 Connect and clarify main ideas by identifying their relationships to other sources and related topics.

6 2.4 Clarify an understanding of texts by creating outlines, logical notes, summaries, or reports.

6 2.5 Follow multiple-step instructions for preparing applications (e.g., for a public library card, bank savings account, sports club, league membership).

Expository Critique In this substrand, you will learn to distinguish and analyze different features of a text in order to become a critical reader. You will learn to evaluate the facts and opinions in a text so that you can draw conclusions about what you are reading.

5 2.5 Distinguish facts, supported inferences, and opinions in text.

6 2.6 Determine the adequacy and appropriateness of the evidence for an author's conclusions.

6 2.7 Make reasonable assertions about a text through accurate, supporting citations.

6 2.8 Note instances of unsupported inferences, fallacious reasoning, persuasion, and propaganda in text.

Literary Response and Analysis

In this strand of standards, you will learn how to read and respond to historically or culturally significant works of literature that will both reflect and enhance your studies of history and social science.

Structural Features of Literature In this substrand, you will learn ways to identify and understand the similarities and differences between different types of literature. You will also learn why writers choose a particular literary form over another.

3 3.1 Distinguish common forms of literature (e.g., poetry, drama, fiction, nonfiction).

4 3.1 Describe the structural differences of various imaginative forms of literature, including fantasies, fables, myths, legends, and fairy tales.

5 3.1 Identify and analyze the characteristics of poetry, drama, fiction, and nonfiction and explain the appropriateness of the literary forms chosen by an author for a specific purpose.
6 3.1 Identify the forms of fiction and describe the major characteristics of each form.

Narrative Analysis of Grade-Level-Appropriate Text In this substrand, you will learn to identify and understand the narrative elements, language, and structure of different types of literature. You will also learn how and why authors use literary devices such as rhyme, metaphor, and imagery. You will learn how to compare the plots, settings and characters in the books you read, and how to describe the author's message in both fiction and non fiction texts. You will compare and contrast texts from different cultures and understand why authors use a particular literary form.

1 3.1 Identify and describe the elements of plot, setting, and character(s) in a story, as well as the story's beginning, middle, and ending.
1 3.2 Describe the roles of authors and illustrators and their contributions to print materials.
1 3.3 Recollect, talk, and write about books read during the school year.
2 3.1 Compare and contrast plots, settings, and characters presented by different authors.
2 3.2 Generate alternative endings to plots and identify the reason or reasons for, and the impact of, the alternatives.
2 3.3 Compare and contrast different versions of the same stories that reflect different cultures.
2 3.4 Identify the use of rhythm, rhyme, and alliteration in poetry.
3 3.2 Comprehend basic plots of classic fairy tales, myths, folktales, legends, and fables from around the world.
3 3.3 Determine what characters are like by what they say or do and by how the author or illustrator portrays them.
3 3.4 Determine the underlying theme or author's message in fiction and nonfiction text.
3 3.5 Recognize the similarities of sounds in words and rhythmic patterns (e.g., alliteration, onomatopoeia) in a selection.
3 3.6 Identify the speaker or narrator in a selection.
4 3.2 Identify the main events of the plot, their causes, and the influence of each event on future actions.
4 3.3 Use knowledge of the situation and setting and of a character's traits and motivations to determine the causes for that character's actions.
4 3.4 Compare and contrast tales from different cultures by tracing the exploits of one character type and develop theories to account for similar tales in diverse cultures (e.g., trickster tales).
4 3.5 Define figurative language (e.g., simile, metaphor, hyperbole, personification) and identify its use in literary works.
5 3.2 Identify the main problem or conflict of the plot and explain how it is resolved.
5 3.3 Contrast the actions, motives (e.g., loyalty, selfishness, conscientiousness), and appearances of characters in a work of fiction and discuss the importance of the contrasts to the plot or theme.
5 3.4 Understand that *theme* refers to the meaning or moral of a selection and recognize themes (whether implied or stated directly) in sample works.
5 3.5 Describe the function and effect of common literary devices (e.g., imagery, metaphor, symbolism).

6 3.2 Analyze the effect of the qualities of the character (e.g., courage or cowardice, ambition or laziness) on the plot and the resolution of the conflict.
6 3.3 Analyze the influence of setting on the problem and its resolution.
6 3.4 Define how tone or meaning is conveyed in poetry through word choice, figurative language, sentence structure, line length, punctuation, rhythm, repetition, and rhyme.
6 3.5 Identify the speaker and recognize the difference between first- and third-person narration (e.g., autobiography compared with biography).
6 3.6 Identify and analyze features of themes conveyed through characters, actions and images.
6 3.7 Explain the effects of common literary devices (e.g., symbolism, imagery, metaphor) in a variety of fictional and nonfictional texts.

WRITING

Writing Strategies

In this strand of standards, you will learn how to write clear and focused essays. You will learn how to construct essays that contain introductions, supporting details, and conclusions. You will show purpose and demonstrate that you are aware of your audience.

Organization and Focus In this substrand, you will learn to choose the form of writing that best fits your purpose. You will learn to write single and multiple-paragraph compositions that show clear organization of information and ideas. You will also learn how to use appropriate structures, such as sequence, to state your message effectively. You will learn how to get and keep the attention of the person reading your composition by using appropriate language.

1 1.1 Select a focus when writing.
1 1.2 Use descriptive words when writing.
2 1.1 Group related ideas and maintain a consistent focus.
3 1.1 Create a single paragraph:
a. Develop a topic sentence.
b. Include simple supporting facts and details.
4 1.1 Select a focus, an organizational structure, and a point of view based upon purpose, audience, length, and format requirements.
4 1.2 Create multiple-paragraph compositions:
a. Provide an introductory paragraph.
b. Establish and support a central idea with a topic sentence at or near the beginning of the first paragraph.
c. Include supporting paragraphs with simple facts, details, and explanations.
d. Conclude with a paragraph that summarizes the points.
e. Use correct indention.
4 1.3 Use traditional structures for conveying information (e.g., chronological order, cause and effect, similarity and difference, and posing and answering a question).
5 1.1 Create multiple-paragraph narrative compositions:
a. Establish and develop a situation or plot.

b. Describe the setting.
c. Present an ending.

5 1.2 Create multiple-paragraph expository compositions:
a. Establish a topic, important ideas, or events in sequence or chronological order.
b. Provide details and transitional expressions that link one paragraph to another in a clear line of thought.
c. Offer a concluding paragraph that summarizes important ideas and details.

6 1.1 Chose the form of writing (e.g., personal letter, letter to the editor, review, poem, report, narrative) that best suits the intended purpose.

6 1.2 Create multiple-paragraph expository compositions:
a. Engage the interest of the reader and state a clear purpose.
b. Develop the topic with supporting details and precise verbs, nouns, and adjectives to paint a visual image in the mind of the reader.
c. Conclude with a detailed summary linked to the purpose of the composition.

6 1.3 Use a variety of effective and coherent organizational patterns, including comparison and contrast; organization by categories; and arrangement by spatial order, order of importance, or climactic order.

Research In this substrand, you will learn about the purpose, structure, and organization of different reference materials.

2 1.3 Understand the purposes of various reference materials (e.g., dictionary, thesaurus, atlas).

3 1.3 Understand the structure and organization of various reference materials (e.g., dictionary, thesaurus, atlas, encyclopedia).

Research and Technology In this substrand, you will learn to access, evaluate, discard, select, and use information from multiple sources, including reference books and online materials. You will also learn to understand the organization of both electronic and print resources. You will use computer technology to compose electronic documents in the correct format.

4 1.5 Quote or paraphrase information sources, citing them appropriately.

4 1.6 Locate information in reference texts by using organizational features (e.g., prefaces, appendixes).

4 1.7 Use various reference materials (e.g., dictionary, thesaurus, card catalog, encyclopedia, online information) as an aid to writing.

4 1.8 Understand the organization of almanacs, newspapers, and periodicals and how to use those print materials.

4 1.9 Demonstrate basic keyboarding skills and familiarity with computer terminology (e.g., cursor, software, memory, disk drive, hard drive).

5. 1.3 Use organizational features of printed text (e.g., citations, end notes, bibliographic references), to locate relevant information.

5 1.4 Create simple documents by using electronic media and employing organizational features (e.g., passwords, entry and pull-down menus, word searches, the thesaurus, spell checks).

5 1.5 Use a thesaurus to identify alternative word choices and meanings.

6 1.4 Use organizational features of electronic text (e.g., bulletin boards, databases, keyword searches, e-mail addresses) to locate information.

6 1.5 Compose documents with appropriate formatting by using word-processing skills and principles of design (e.g., margins, tabs, spacing, columns, page orientation).

Evaluation and Revision In this substrand, you will learn how to revise and edit your writing. You will learn that by rearranging words, sentences and ideas, you can make your writing more focused. You will also learn how to use a rubric to organize your ideas.

2 1.4 Revise original drafts to improve sequence and provide more descriptive detail.
3 1.4 Revise drafts to improve the coherence and logical progression of ideas by using an established rubric.
4 1.10 Edit and revise selected drafts to improve coherence and progression by adding, deleting, consolidating, and rearranging text.
5 1.6 Edit and revise manuscripts to improve the meaning and focus of writing by adding, deleting, consolidating, clarifying, and rearranging words and sentences.
6 1.6 Revise writing to improve the organization and consistency of ideas within and between paragraphs.

Writing Applications (Genres and their Characteristics)

In this strand of standards, you will learn how to write different types of essays of 500 to 700 words.

1 2.1 Write brief narratives (e.g. fictional, autobiographical) describing an experience.
1 2.2 Write brief expository descriptions of a real object, person, place, or event, using sensory details.
2 2.1 Write brief narratives based on their experiences:
a. Move through a logical sequence of events.
b. Describe the setting, characters, objects, and events in detail.
2 2.2 Write a friendly letter complete with the date, salutation, body, closing, and signature.
3 2.1 Write narratives:
a. Provide a context within which an action takes place.
b. Include well-chosen details to develop the plot.
c. Provide insight into why the selected incident is memorable.
3 2.2 Write descriptions that use concrete sensory details to present and support unified impressions of people, places, things, or experiences.
3 2.3 Write personal and formal letters, thank-you notes, and invitations:
a. Show awareness of the knowledge and interests of the audience and establish a purpose and context.
b. Include the date, proper salutation, body, closing, and signature.
4 2.1 Write narratives:
a. Relate ideas, observations, or recollections of an event or experience.
b. Provide a context to enable the reader to imagine the world of the event or experience.
c. Use concrete sensory details.
d. Provide insight into why the selected event or experience is memorable.

4 2.2 Write responses to literature:
a. Demonstrate an understanding of the literary work.
b. Support judgments through references to both the text and prior knowledge.

4 2.3 Write information reports:
a. Frame a central question about an issue or situation.
b. Include facts and details for focus.
c. Draw from more than one source of information (e.g., speakers, books, newspapers, other media sources).

4 2.4 Write summaries that contain the main ideas of the reading selection and the most significant details.

5 2.1 Write narratives:
a. Establish a plot, point of view, setting, and conflict.
b. Show, rather than tell, the events of the story.

5 2.2 Write responses to literature:
a. Demonstrate an understanding of a literary work.
b. Support judgments through references to the text and to prior knowledge.
c. Develop interpretations that exhibit careful reading and understanding.

5 2.3 Write research reports about important ideas, issues, or events by using the following guidelines:
a. Frame questions that direct the investigation.
b. Establish a controlling idea or topic.
c. Develop the topic with simple facts, details, examples, and explanations.

5 2.4 Write persuasive letters or compositions:
a. State a clear position in support of a proposal.
b. Support a position with relevant evidence.
c. Follow a simple organizational pattern.
d. Address reader concerns.

6 2.1 Write narratives:
a. Establish and develop a plot and setting and present a point of view that is appropriate to the stories.
b. Include sensory details and concrete language to develop plot and character.
c. Use a range of narrative devices (e.g., dialogue, suspense).

6 2.2 Write expository compositions (e.g., description, explanation, comparison and contrast, problem and solution):
a. State the thesis or purpose.
b. Explain the situation.
c. Follow an organizational pattern appropriate to the type of composition.
d. Offer persuasive evidence to validate arguments and conclusions as needed.

6 2.3 Write research reports:
a. Pose relevant questions with a scope narrow enough to be thoroughly covered.
b. Support the main idea or ideas with facts, details, examples, and explanations from multiple authoritative sources (e.g., speakers, periodicals, online information searches).
c. Include a bibliography.

6 2.4 Write responses to literature:
a. Develop an interpretation exhibiting careful reading, understanding and insight.
b. Organize the interpretation around several clear ideas, premises, or images.
c. Develop and justify the interpretation through sustained use of examples and textual evidence.

6 2.5 Write persuasive compositions:
- a. State a clear position on a proposition or proposal.
- b. Support the position with organized and relevant evidence.
- c. Anticipate and address reader concerns and counterarguments.

WRITTEN AND ORAL ENGLISH LANGUAGE CONVENTIONS

Written and Oral English Language Conventions

In this strand of standards, you will learn how to write clear and focused essays. You will learn how to construct essays that contain introductions, supporting details, and conclusions. You will show purpose and demonstrate that you are aware of your audience.

Sentence Structure In this substrand, you will learn to recognize and use important elements of sentence structure both in speaking and in writing. You will also learn how using correct sentence structure and choosing the correct part of speech helps you express your thoughts and ideas more effectively.

1 1.1 Write and speak in complete, coherent sentences.
2 1.1 Distinguish between complete and incomplete sentences.
2 1.2 Recognize and use the correct word order in written sentences.
3 1.1 Understand and be able to use complete and correct declarative, interrogative, imperative, and exclamatory sentences in writing and speaking.
4 1.1 Use simple and compound sentences in writing and speaking.
4 1.2 Combine short, related sentences with appositives, participial phrases, adjectives, adverbs, and prepositional phrases.
5 1.1 Identify and correctly use prepositional phrases, appositives, and independent and dependent clauses; use transitions and conjunctions to connect ideas.
6 1.1 Use simple, compound, and compound-complex sentences; use effective coordination and subordination of ideas to express complete thoughts.

Grammar In this substrand, you will learn to identify and use parts of speech, subject-verb agreement, and verb tenses correctly, both in speaking and in writing.

2 1.3 Identify and correctly use various parts of speech, including nouns and verbs, in writing and speaking.
3 1.2 Identify subjects and verbs that are in agreement and identify and use pronouns, adjectives, compound words, and articles correctly in writing and speaking.
3 1.3 Identify and use past, present, and future verb tenses properly in writing and speaking.
3 1.4 Identify and use subjects and verbs correctly in speaking and writing simple sentences.
4 1.3 Identify and use regular and irregular verbs, adverbs, prepositions, and coordinating conjunctions in writing and speaking.

5 1.2 Identify and correctly use verbs that are often misused (e.g., *lie/lay, sit/set, rise/raise)*, modifiers, and pronouns.
6 1.2 Identify and properly use indefinite pronouns and present perfect, past perfect, and future perfect verb tenses; ensure that verbs agree with compound subjects.

Punctuation In this substrand, you will learn to identify and use the most important features of punctuation in your writing.

1 1.4 Distinguish between declarative, exclamatory, and interrogative sentences.
1 1.5 Use a period, exclamation point, or question mark at the end of sentences.
1 1.6 Use knowledge of the basic rules of punctuation and capitalization when writing.
2 1.4 Use commas in the greeting and closure of a letter and with dates and items in a series.
2 1.5 Use quotation marks correctly.
3 1.5 Punctuate dates, city and state, and titles of books correctly.
3 1.6 Use commas in dates, locations, and addresses and for items in a series.
4 1.4 Use parentheses, commas in direct quotations, and apostrophes in the possessive case of nouns and in contractions.
4 1.5 Use underlining, quotation marks, or italics to identify titles of documents.
5 1.3 Use a colon to separate hours and minutes and to introduce a list; use quotation marks around the exact words of a speaker and titles of poems, songs, short stories, and so forth.
6 1.3 Use colons after the salutation in business letters, semicolons to connect independent clauses, and commas when linking two clauses with a conjunction in compound sentences.

Capitalization In this substrand, you will learn the rules of capitalization in the English language.

1 1.7 Capitalize the first word of a sentence, names of people, and the pronoun *I*.
2 1.6 Capitalize all proper nouns, words at the beginning of sentences and greetings, months and days of the week, and titles and initials of people.
3 1.7 Capitalize geographical names, holidays, historical periods, and special events correctly.
4 1.6 Capitalize names of magazines, newspapers, works of art, musical compositions, organizations, and the first word in quotations when appropriate.
5 1.4 Use correct capitalization.
6 1.4 Use correct capitalization.

Spelling In this substrand, you will learn the spelling rules of the English language and how to spell correctly. You will also learn how to spell irregular and often misspelled words.

1 1.8 Spell three- and four-letter short-vowel words and grade-level-appropriate sight words correctly.
2 1.7 Spell frequently used, irregular words correctly (e.g., *was, were, says, said, who, what, why*).
2 1.8 Spell basic short-vowel, long-vowel *r*-controlled, and consonant-blend patterns correctly.

3 **1.8** Spell correctly one-syllable words that have blends, contractions, compounds, orthographic patterns (e.g., *qu*, consonant doubling, changing the ending of a word from *-y* to *-ies* when forming the plural), and common homophones (e.g., *hair-hare*).
3 **1.9** Arrange words in alphabetic order.
4 **1.7** Spell correctly roots, inflections, suffixes and prefixes, and syllable constructions.
5 **1.5** Spell roots, suffixes, prefixes, contractions, and syllable constructions correctly.
6 **1.5** Spell frequently misspelled words correctly (e.g., *their, they're, there*).

LISTENING AND SPEAKING

Listening and Speaking Strategies

In this strand of standards, you will learn how to listen critically and respond appropriately to oral presentations. You will also learn how to give focused, coherent presentations and how to evaluate the content of presentations.

Comprehension In this substrand, you will learn to listen carefully, to ask and answer questions, to summarize information presented orally, and to analyze the information that you hear. You will also learn to be aware of the musical elements of literary language, as well as tone, pitch, feeling, intonation and nonverbal communication, including gestures.

1 **1.1** Listen attentively.
1 **1.2** Ask questions for clarification and understanding.
1 **1.3** Give, restate, and follow simple two-step directions.
2 **1.1** Determine the purpose or purposes of listening (e.g., to obtain information, to solve problems, for enjoyment).
2 **1.2** Ask for clarification and explanation of stories and ideas.
2 **1.3** Paraphrase information that has been shared orally by others.
2 **1.4** Give and follow three- and four-step oral directions.
3 **1.1** Retell, paraphrase, and explain what has been said by a speaker.
3 **1.2** Connect and relate prior experiences, insights, and ideas to those of a speaker.
3 **1.3** Respond to questions with appropriate elaboration.
3 **1.4** Identify the musical elements of literary language (e.g., rhymes, repeated sounds, instances of onomatopoeia).
4 **1.1** Ask thoughtful questions and respond to relevant questions with appropriate elaboration in oral settings.
4 **1.2** Summarize major ideas and supporting evidence presented in spoken messages and formal presentations.
4 **1.3** Identify how language usages (e.g., sayings, expressions) reflect regions and cultures.
4 **1.4** Give precise directions and instructions.
5 **1.1** Ask questions that seek information not already discussed.
5 **1.2** Interpret a speaker's verbal and nonverbal messages, purposes, and perspectives.
5 **1.3** Make inferences or draw conclusions based on an oral report.

6 1.1 Relate the speaker's verbal communication (e.g., word choice, pitch, feeling, tone) to the nonverbal message (e.g., posture, gesture).
6 1.2 Identify the tone, mood, and emotion conveyed in the oral communication.
6 1.3 Restate and execute multiple-step oral instructions and directions.

Organization and Delivery of Oral Communication In this substrand, you will learnto give organized and coherent oral presentations. You will learn that focus, structure, and lively language are just as important in speaking as they are in writing. You will also learn how to use verbal strategies, such as the pitch of your voice and the rate at which you speak, to make your presentation more effective. You will also learn how to read aloud fluently and at the correct pace.

1 1.4 Stay on the topic when speaking.
1 1.5 Use descriptive words when speaking about people, places, things, and events.
2 1.5 Organize presentations to maintain a clear focus.
2 1.6 Speak clearly and at an appropriate pace for the type of communication (e.g., informal discussion, report to class).
2 1.7 Recount experiences in a logical sequence.
2 1.8 Retell stories, including characters, setting, and plot.
2 1.9 Report on a topic with supportive facts and details.
3 1.5 Organize ideas chronologically or around major points of information.
3 1.6 Provide a beginning, a middle, and an end, including concrete details that develop a central idea.
3 1.7 Use clear and specific vocabulary to communicate ideas and establish the tone.
3 1.8 Clarify and enhance oral presentations through the use of appropriate props (e.g., objects, pictures, charts).
3 1.9 Read prose and poetry aloud with fluency, rhythm, and pace, using appropriate intonation and vocal patterns to emphasize important passages of the text being read.
4 1.5 Present effective introductions and conclusions that guide and inform the listener's understanding of important ideas and evidence.
4 1.6 Use traditional structures for conveying information (e.g., cause and effect, similarity and difference, and posing and answering a question).
4 1.7 Emphasize points in ways that help the listener or viewer to follow important ideas and concepts.
4 1.8 Use details, examples, anecdotes, or experiences to explain or clarify information.
4 1.9 Use volume, pitch, phrasing, pace, modulation, and gestures appropriately to enhance meaning.
5 1.4 Select a focus, organizational structure, and point of view for an oral presentation.
5 1.5 Clarify and support spoken ideas with evidence and examples.
5 1.6 Engage the audience with appropriate verbal cues, facial expressions, gestures.
6 1.4 Select a focus, an organizational structure, and a point of view, matching the purpose, message, occasion, and vocal modulation to the audience.
6 1.5 Emphasize salient points to assist the listener in following the main ideas and concepts.
6 1.6 Support opinions with detailed evidence and with visual or media displays that use appropriate technology.
6 1.7 Use effective rate, volume, pitch, and tone and align nonverbal elements to sustain audience interest and attention.

Analysis and Evaluation of Oral and Media Communications In this substrand, you will learn to analyze and evaluate a speaker or writer's message. You will also identify the purpose of what you see, read, and hear in the media. You will learn to distinguish and understand the purpose of rhetorical – or spoken – devices, such as onomatopoeia.

3 1.10 Compare ideas and points of view expressed in broadcast and print media.
3 1.11 Distinguish between the speaker's opinions and verifiable facts.
4 1.10 Evaluate the role of the media in focusing attention on events and in forming opinions on issues.
5 1.7 Identify, analyze, and critique persuasive techniques (e.g., promises, dares, flattery, glittering generalities); identify logical fallacies used in oral presentations and media messages.
5 1.8 Analyze media as sources for information, entertainment, persuasion, interpretation of events, and transmission of culture.
6 1.8 Analyze the use of rhetorical devices (e.g., cadence, repetitive patterns, use of onomatopoeia) for intent and effect.
6 1.9 Identify persuasive and propaganda techniques used in television and identify false and misleading information.

Speaking Applications (Genres And Their Characteristics)

In this strand of standards, you will learn how to give well-organized presentations, such as narrative, informative, and persuasive presentations. You will also learn important techniques that will help you respond to literature through speech.

1 2.1 Recite poems, rhymes, songs, and stories.
1 2.2 Retell stories using basic story grammar and relating the sequence of story events by answering *who, what, when, where, why,* and *how* questions.
1 2.3 Relate an important life event or personal experience in a simple sequence.
1 2.4 Provide descriptions with careful attention to sensory detail.
2 2.1 Recount experiences or present stories:
a. Move through a logical sequence of events.
b. Describe story elements (e.g., characters, plot, setting).
2 2.2 Report on a topic with facts and details, drawing from several sources of information.
3 2.1 Make brief narrative presentations:
a. Provide a context for an incident that is the subject of the presentation.
b. Provide insight into why the selected incident is memorable.
c. Include well-chosen details to develop character, setting, and plot.
3 2.2 Plan and present dramatic interpretations of experiences, stories, poems, or plays with clear diction, pitch, tempo, and tone.
3 2.3 Make descriptive presentations that use concrete sensory details to set forth and support unified impressions of people, places, things, or experiences.
4 2.1 Make narrative presentations:
a. Relate ideas, observations, or recollections about an event or experience.
b. Provide a context that enables the listener to imagine the circumstances of the event or experience.
c. Provide insight into why the selected event or experience is memorable.

4 2.2 Make informational presentations:
- a. Frame a key question.
- b. Include facts and details that help listeners to focus.
- c. Incorporate more than one source of information (e.g., speakers, books, newspapers, television or radio reports).

4 2.3 Deliver oral summaries of articles and books that contain the main ideas of the event or article and the most significant details.

4 2.4 Recite brief poems (i.e., two or three stanzas), soliloquies, or dramatic dialogues, using clear diction, tempo, volume, and phrasing.

5 2.1 Deliver narrative presentations:
- a. Establish a situation, plot, point of view, and setting with descriptive words and phrases.
- b. Show, rather than tell, the listener what happens.

5 2.2 Deliver informative presentations about an important idea, issue, or event by the following means:
- a. Frame questions to direct the investigation.
- b. Establish a controlling idea or topic.
- c. Develop the topic with simple facts, details, examples, and explanations.

5 2.3 Deliver oral responses to literature:
- a. Summarize significant events and details.
- b. Articulate an understanding of several ideas or images communicated by the literary work.
- c. Use examples or textual evidence from the work to support conclusions.

6 2.1 Deliver narrative presentations:
- a. Establish a context, plot, and point of view.
- b. Include sensory details and concrete language to develop the plot and character.
- c. Use a range of narrative devices (e.g., dialogue, tension, or suspense).

6 2.2 Deliver informative presentations:
- a. Pose relevant questions sufficiently limited in scope to be completely and thoroughly answered.
- b. Develop the topic with facts, details, examples, and explanations from multiple authoritative sources (e.g., speakers, periodicals, online information).

6 2.3 Deliver oral responses to literature:
- a. Develop an interpretation exhibiting careful reading, understanding, and insight.
- b. Organize the selected interpretation around several clear ideas, premises, or images.
- c. Develop and justify the selected interpretation through sustained use of examples and textual evidence.

6 2.4 Deliver persuasive presentations:
- a. Provide a clear statement of the position.
- b. Include relevant evidence.
- c. Offer a logical sequence of information.
- d. Engage the listener and foster acceptance of the proposition or proposal.

6 2.5 Deliver presentations on problems and solutions:
- a. Theorize on the causes and effects of each problem and establish connections between the defined problem and at least one solution.
- b. Offer persuasive evidence to validate the definition of the problem and the proposed solutions.

UNIT 1

THE BIG QUESTION

Can all mysteries be solved?

AEGVPT CAPTA

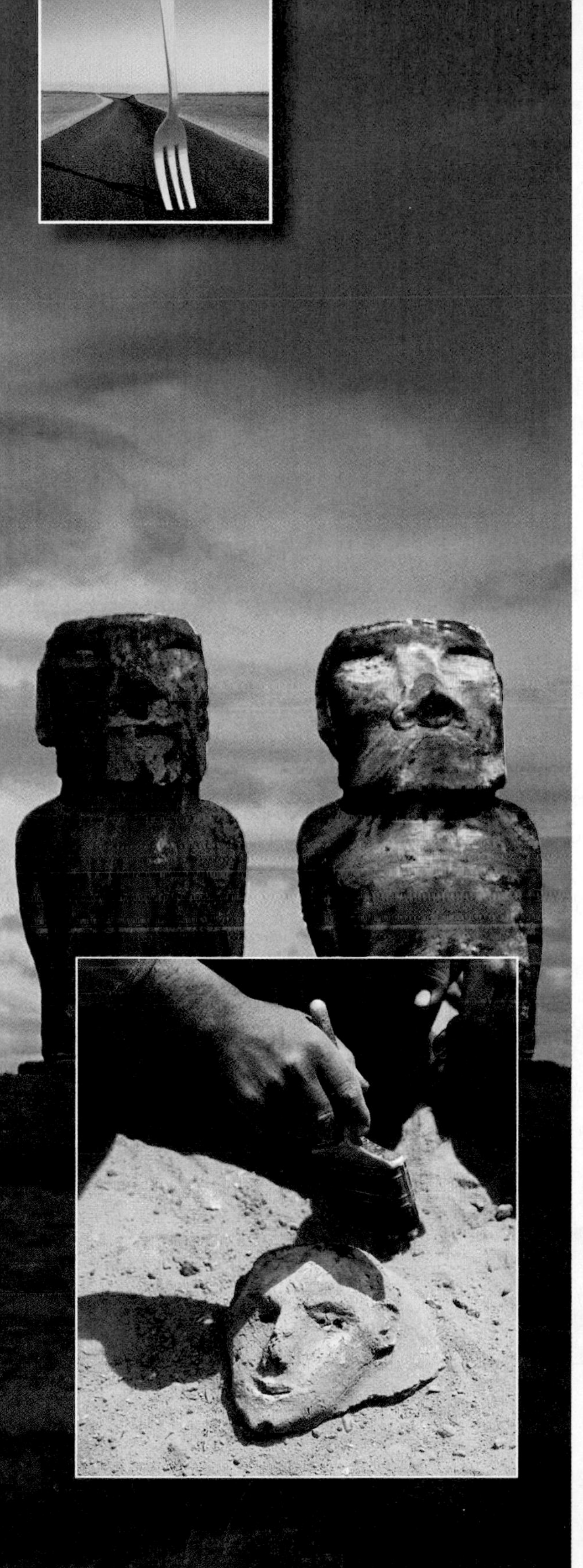

This unit is about real-life and make-believe mysteries. You'll read about crimes, strange events, unusual number patterns, mysterious cities, and monster-like creatures. Exploring these mysteries will help you become a better reader. It will also help you practice the academic and literary language you need to use in school.

READING 1: Novel Excerpt

- From *Chasing Vermeer* by Blue Balliett

READING 2: Math/Science Article

- From *G Is for Googol* by David M. Schwartz

READING 3: Social Studies Article

- "Fact or Fiction?"

READING 4: Two Short Stories

- *Teenage Detectives* by Carol Farley and Hy Conrad

Listening and Speaking

At the end of this unit, you and your classmates will play a **description guessing game**.

Writing

In this unit you will practice **descriptive writing**. This type of writing tells what things look, sound, feel, smell, or taste like. After each reading you will learn a skill to help you write a descriptive paragraph. At the end of the unit, you will use these skills to help you write a descriptive essay.

QuickWrite

In your notebook, write the words *look*, *sound*, and *feel*. Look around your classroom. What do you see, hear, and feel? Write for five minutes.

READING 1 Prepare to Read

What You Will Learn

Reading

- Vocabulary building: *Literary terms, dictionary skills, word study*
- Reading strategy: *Predict*
- Text type: *Literature (novel excerpt)*

Grammar, Usage, and Mechanics
Distinguishing parts of speech

Writing
Describe a character

THE BIG QUESTION

Can all mysteries be solved? Have you ever wondered about what makes something a work of art? Some people think that the nature of art is a mystery. Think about a painting that you know and love. What makes it a work of art? Does it have to be in a museum? Does it have to be created by a famous person? Do you have to like it?

Work with a partner. Study the painting below by the seventeenth-century Dutch painter Johannes Vermeer. It is called *A Lady Writing*. Describe what you see and feel when you look at the picture. Jot down your ideas. Do you think the picture is a work of art? Why or why not?

BUILD BACKGROUND

Chasing Vermeer is a mystery novel about a painting by Vermeer. In real life, there are many mysteries surrounding Vermeer's life and work. For example, one of his paintings was stolen from a museum in Boston, Massachusetts, and it has never been found.

Mysteries are about puzzles and strange events. The people in a mystery novel try to use clues to solve a puzzle. Mysteries are very popular because they are exciting and full of suspense. As the people in the story try to solve the puzzle, so do you.

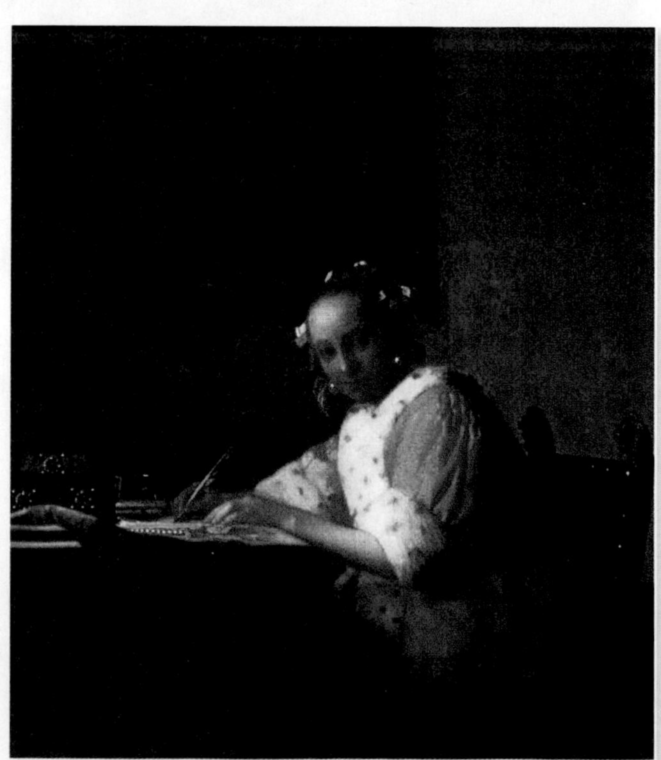

Vermeer painted *A Lady Writing* around 1665–1666. ▶

VOCABULARY

Learn Literary Words

Novels, short stories, and poems are all types of literature. The people or animals in a novel or short story are called **characters**. Like people in real life, the characters in a story have certain qualities, or **character traits**. You can learn about characters and their traits through what the characters say and do and by what happens to them in the story. You can also get to know the characters' personalities, or traits, by paying attention to what other characters say about them.

In the excerpt you are about to read, you will meet several characters, including Petra Andalee and Calder Pillay. You will learn about their traits by the way they speak, act, dress, and think and by what they say about each other. Read this short section from the beginning of the book. What do you learn about Petra and Calder?

Literary Words

characters
character traits

> Calder, at that moment, looked out his front window to see Petra walking by holding a leaf several inches from her nose. He knew he was kind of weird, but she was *exceptionally* weird. She was always by herself at school, and didn't seem to care. She was quiet when other kids were loud. Plus, she had a fierce triangle of hair that made her look like one of those Egyptian queens.
>
> Calder wondered if he was becoming just as much of an oddball. No one had asked him what he was doing after class that day. No one had told him to wait. . . .

Practice

Think of a character from a movie or television show whose character traits you know well. In your notebook, make a copy of the character-traits web below. Fill in the web with traits and examples. Then describe this character to a classmate.

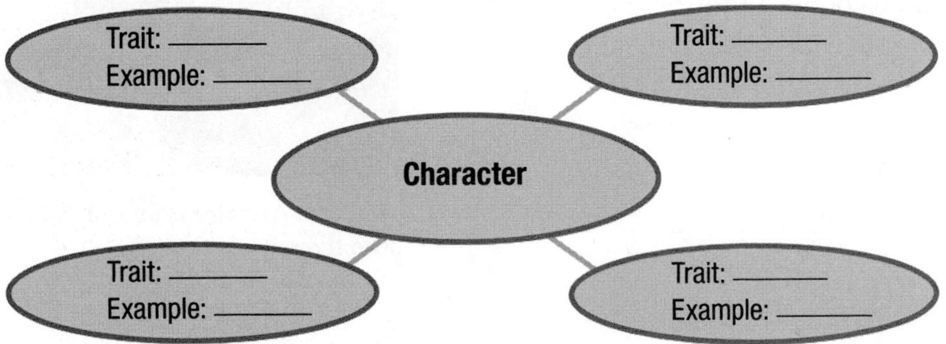

Learn Academic Words

Study the **red** words and their meanings. You will find these words useful when talking and writing about literature. Write each word and its meaning in your notebook. After you read the excerpt from *Chasing Vermeer,* try to use these words to respond to the text.

Academic Words

identify
individual
occur
physical
theory

identify = recognize and name someone or something	➡	The teacher has her students **identify** different examples by pointing at them.
individual = a person, not a group	➡	Petra Andalee is an **individual** in *Chasing Vermeer.* She is one of the characters you will read about.
occur = happen	➡	The main events in *Chasing Vermeer* **occur** in a big city in the United States.
physical = relating to the body or to other things you can see, touch, smell, feel, or taste	➡	Being an artist takes a lot of **physical** effort. The painter is tired from standing and painting all day.
theory = an explanation that may or may not be true	➡	Everyone has a different **theory** about what makes something art. In my opinion, movies are a form of art.

Practice

Work with a partner to answer these questions. Try to include the **red** word in your answer. Write the answers in your notebook.

1. How do you **identify** the artist of an unsigned painting?
2. Where might an **individual** go to study a work of art?
3. Where might a mystery about a stolen painting **occur**?
4. Why do artists have to be in good **physical** shape?
5. What do detectives do to prove a **theory** about a crime?

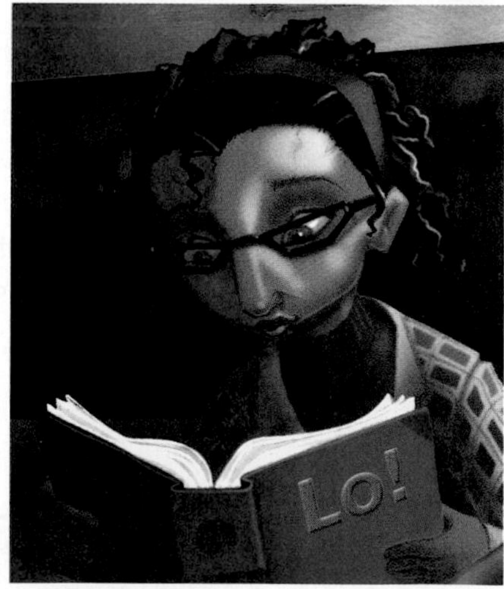

▲ Petra Andalee is an individual who likes art.

Word Study: Prefixes *un-*, *dis-*

A prefix is a word part added to the beginning of a word that changes the word's meaning. Knowing the meanings of prefixes can help you figure out the meanings of many words you read and hear.

The prefixes *un-* and *dis-* occur often in English. *Un-* can mean "not" or "the opposite of." *Dis-* can mean "not," "outside of," or "the opposite of." Look at the examples below. Notice how the meaning of the prefix changes the meaning of each base word.

Prefix	Base Word	New Word
un- +	certain	uncertain ("not certain")
un- +	explained	unexplained ("not explained")
dis- +	approved	disapproved ("opposite of approved")
dis- +	appeared	disappeared ("opposite of appeared")

Practice

Work with a partner. Use what you have learned about prefixes to figure out the meanings of the words below. Then check the meanings in a dictionary. Write the words and definitions in your notebook. Then use each word in a sentence.

disagree	disoriented	unfair	unkind	unknown

Reading Strategy PREDICT

Predicting helps you become a better reader. Before you read, predict (or guess) what the story will be about. To predict, follow these steps:

- Stop after each paragraph. Ask yourself, "What will happen next?"
- Look for clues in the story and illustrations.
- Use the clues from the story and what you already know to predict what will happen.

After you read the first two pages of the excerpt from *Chasing Vermeer*, predict what will happen next. See if you are right.

LITERATURE

NOVEL

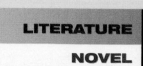

Set a purpose for reading What kind of individual is Petra? How would you describe her? What puzzling object does she find? Read to find out why this object is so appealing to her.

from CHASING VERMEER

Blue Balliett

Ms. Hussey isn't your typical teacher. She asks her students to do unusual projects and investigate mysterious ideas and events. Petra Andalee and Calder Pillay like being in her sixth-grade class. They are about to receive a new assignment from Ms. Hussey that will lead to a mysterious discovery.

By the sixth week of sixth grade, Ms. Hussey still wasn't a disappointment. She had announced on the first day of school that she had no idea what they were going to work on that year, or how. "It all depends on what we get interested in—or what gets interested in us," she had added, as if this was obvious. Calder Pillay was all ears. He had never heard a teacher admit that she didn't know what she was doing. Even better, she was excited about it.

Ms. Hussey's classroom was in the middle school building at the University School, in the neighborhood known as Hyde Park. The school sat on the edge of the University of Chicago campus. John Dewey, an unusual professor, had started it a century earlier as an experiment. Dewey believed in doing, in working on relevant projects in order to learn how to think. Calder had always liked the man's appropriate name. Not all teachers at the U., as it was called, still agreed with Dewey's ideas, but Ms. Hussey obviously did.

They began the year by arguing about whether writing was the most accurate way to communicate. Petra Andalee, who loved to write, said it was. Kids like Calder, who hated it, said it wasn't. What about numbers? What about pictures? What about plain old talking?

Ms. Hussey had told them to investigate. They took piles of books out of the library. They found out about cave art in France, about papyrus scrolls in Egypt, about Mayan petroglyphs in Mexico, and about stone tablets from

---

all ears, very interested in listening to someone
papyrus scrolls, rolls of paper that are made from a plant
petroglyphs, pictures or sets of marks cut into rock
tablets, flat pieces of hard clay or stone that have words cut into them

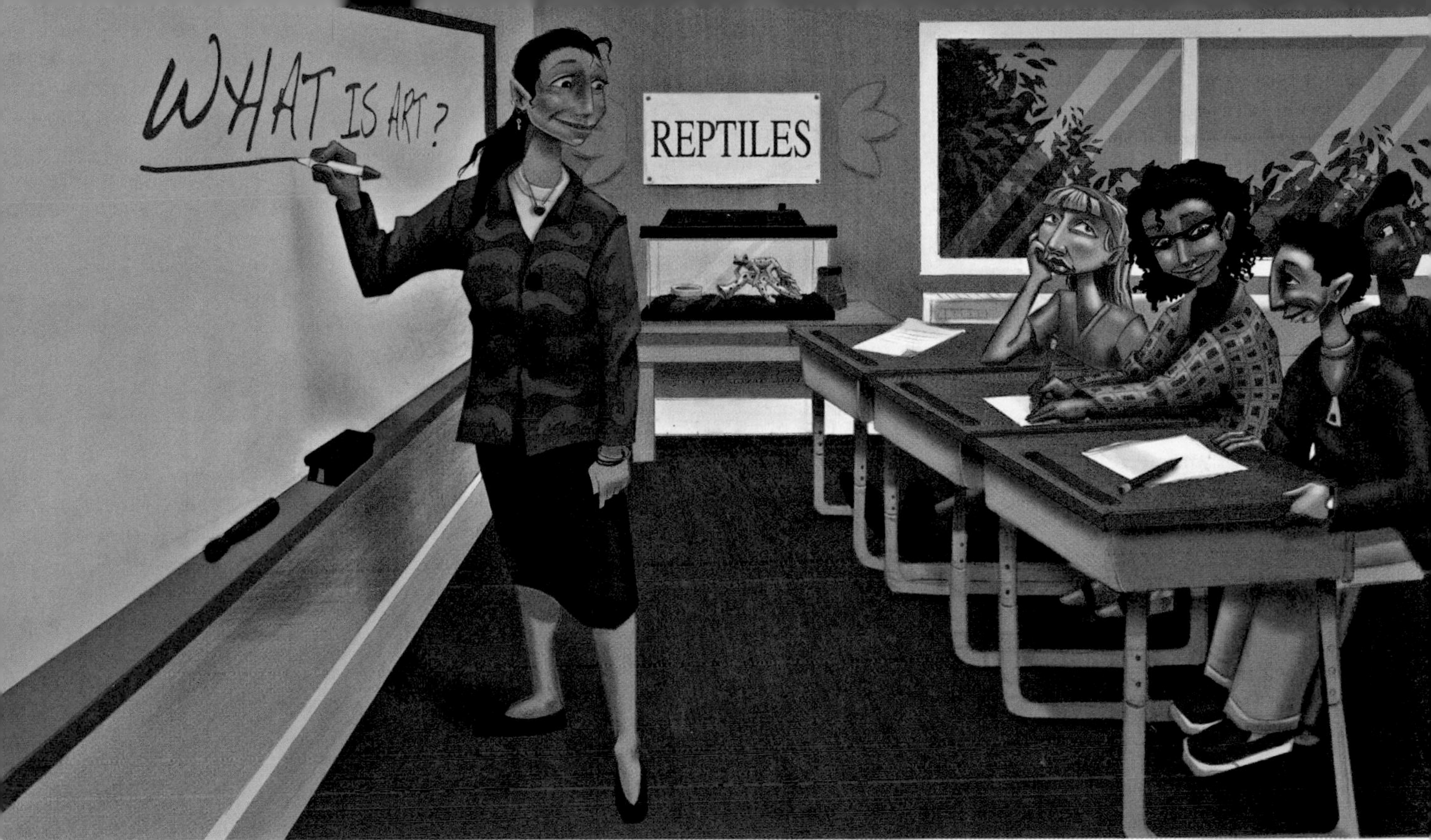

the Middle East. They tried things. They made stamps out of raw potatoes and covered the walls with symbols. They invented a sign language for hands and feet. They communicated for one whole day using nothing but drawings. Now it was almost mid-October. Would they ever study regular subjects, like the other classes did? Calder didn't care. What they were doing was real exploration, real thinking—not just finding out about what a bunch of dead, famous grown-ups believed. Ms. Hussey was cool. . . .

Petra, like Calder, was fascinated by their new teacher. She loved Ms. Hussey's questions and her long ponytail and the three rings in each ear. One earring had a small pearl dangling from a moon, another a high-heeled shoe the size of a grain of rice, another a tiny key. Petra loved how Ms. Hussey listened carefully to the kids' ideas and didn't care about right and wrong answers. She was honest and unpredictable. She was close to perfect. . . .

One day Ms. Hussey ***brought up*** *the nature of art.*

"You know," Ms. Hussey said finally, "Picasso said that art is a lie, but a lie that tells the truth." She was pacing now. "Lies and art . . . it's an ancient problem. So if we work with art," she said slowly, "we'll have to figure out something else first: What makes an object a piece of art?"

Denise rolled her eyes but stayed quiet.

---

brought up, mentioned a subject or started to talk about it

LITERARY CHECK

Which of Ms. Hussey's ***character traits*** *does Petra admire?*

BEFORE YOU GO ON

1. Who is John Dewey and how does Ms. Hussey feel about him?
2. What does Ms. Hussey's class argue about first?

On Your Own
What do you think is the most accurate way to communicate? Why?

"Here's what I want you to do: Start by choosing one item at home that feels like a work of art to you. It can be anything. Don't ask anyone for advice—this has to be your own thinking. Describe this object for us without saying what it is. And this time, I won't let you off the hook." She grinned. "We'll read some of your ideas aloud."

Calder wondered what Picasso had meant. Was it that art wasn't exactly the real world, but it said something real?

He began thinking up other combinations of art, a lie, and the truth that made sense. It worked almost like the logical arrangements of five squares that made up each piece of his set of pentominoes. How about: Art is the truth that tells a lie? Maybe all of life was about rearranging a few simple ideas. Calder, smiling at the chalkboard, now squirmed in his chair with excitement at the thought. If he could just get to those simple ideas, with a little practice, he'd be a cross between Einstein and the mathematician Ramanujan—or maybe Ben Franklin—. . .

There was nothing at home that felt like a piece of art.

Petra considered an embroidered pillow, but it had a big tear in it; she found a silk caterpillar kite, but it had lost one eye; she thought of the stick her mom used to make a bun for her hair, the one with amber on it, but it had been missing for days.

What *was* art anyway? The more she thought about it, the stranger it seemed. What made an invented object special? Why were some manmade things pleasing and others not? Why wasn't a regular mixing bowl or a spoon or a light bulb a piece of art? What made certain objects land in museums and others in the trash?

She guessed that most people who went to museums didn't ask that question. They just believed that they were looking at something valuable or beautiful or interesting. They didn't do any hard thinking about it.

She wasn't going to be that kind of person—*ever.*

She thought about pictures at the Art Institute that made her feel as if she could leave everything predictable behind. She always felt that way when she stood in front of Caillebotte's *Rainy Day* painting—the wet cobblestones underfoot, the people going places in their long skirts and top hats, the inviting turn of the street. This was art that was an adventure. It let her into another world. It made familiar stuff seem mysterious. It sent her back to her life feeling a little different, at least for a few minutes.

Literary Check

*What kind of **character** is Petra? Describe some of her traits.*

---

set of pentominoes, math tool containing twelve pieces, each of which is made up of five squares

embroidered, having beautiful patterns that have been sewed on

amber, a yellowish-brown stone used to make jewelry

Caillebotte, a French painter whose picture *Rainy Day* hangs in the Art Institute of Chicago

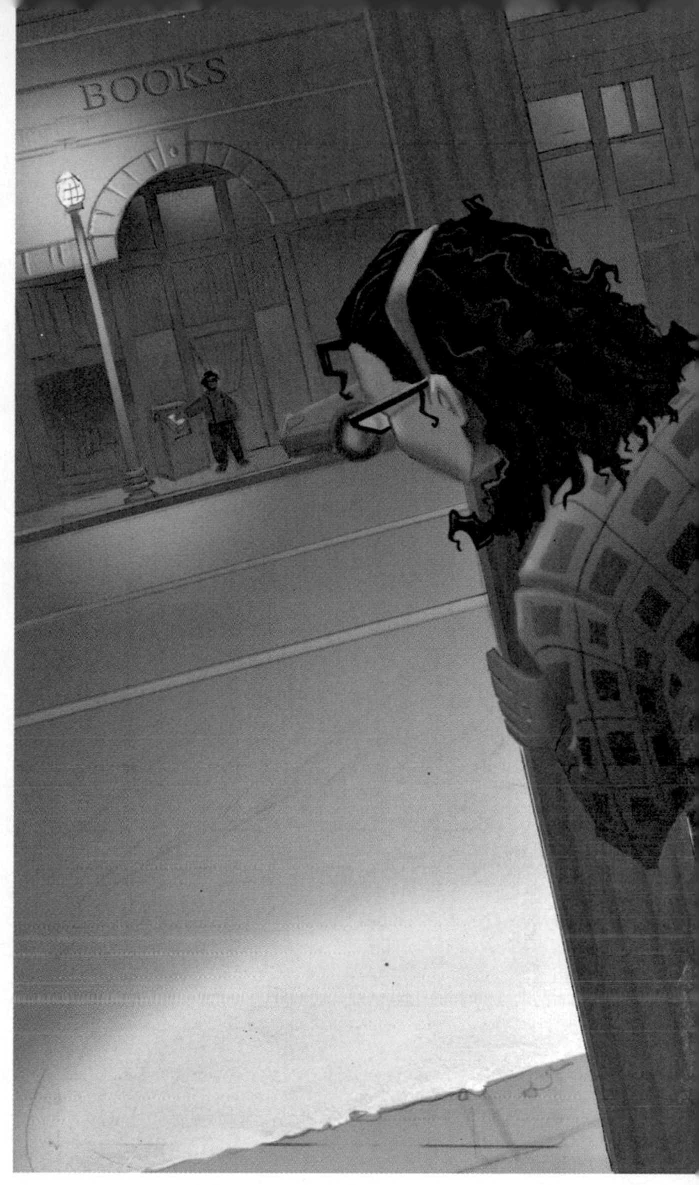

She was still thinking about Caillebotte's Paris street on her way to the grocery store. If he had painted Harper Avenue, would it have looked just as intriguing? As she approached the corner, she noticed a man with **suspenders** . . . step out the front door of Powell's, look around, and drop a book into the giveaway box outside. She sped up.

The book had a cloth cover with several dark stains, and the paper was thick and creamy, soft at the edges. The title jumped out at her: *Lo!* The illustrations were done in black and white—distorted, rubbery figures clutched each other or screamed.

She read a few paragraphs:

TERRIFIED HORSES, UP ON THEIR HIND LEGS, HOOFING A STORM OF FROGS.

FRENZIED **SPRINGBOKS**, CAPERING THEIR EXASPERATIONS AGAINST FROGS THAT WERE TICKLING THEM.

STOREKEEPERS, IN LONDON, GAPING AT FROGS THAT WERE TAPPING ON THEIR WINDOW PANES.

WE SHALL PICK UP AN EXISTENCE BY ITS FROGS.

WISE MEN HAVE TRIED OTHER WAYS. THEY HAVE TRIED TO UNDERSTAND OUR STATE OF BEING, BY GRASPING AT ITS STARS, OR ITS ARTS, OR ITS ECONOMICS. BUT, IF THERE IS AN UNDERLYING ONENESS OF ALL THINGS, IT DOES NOT MATTER WHERE WE BEGIN, WHETHER WITH STARS, OR LAWS OF SUPPLY AND DEMAND, OR FROGS, OR **NAPOLEON BONAPARTE**. ONE MEASURES A CIRCLE, BEGINNING ANYWHERE.

I HAVE COLLECTED 294 RECORDS OF SHOWERS OF LIVING THINGS.

What? Petra flipped back to the front and saw that the book had been written in 1931, by a man named Charles Fort.

She tucked it under her arm.

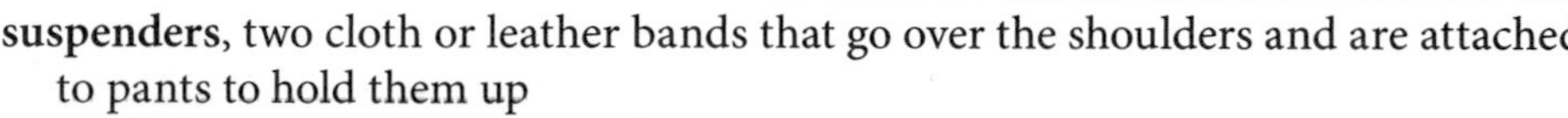

suspenders, two cloth or leather bands that go over the shoulders and are attached to pants to hold them up

springboks, small African deer that can run very fast

Napoleon Bonaparte, the emperor of France (1804–1815) whose armies took control of most of Europe until they were defeated in 1815

BEFORE YOU GO ON

1. Why doesn't Petra want to be like most people who go to museums?
2. What does Petra find in the giveaway box?

On Your Own
If you were in Ms. Hussey's class, what would you choose as a work of art?

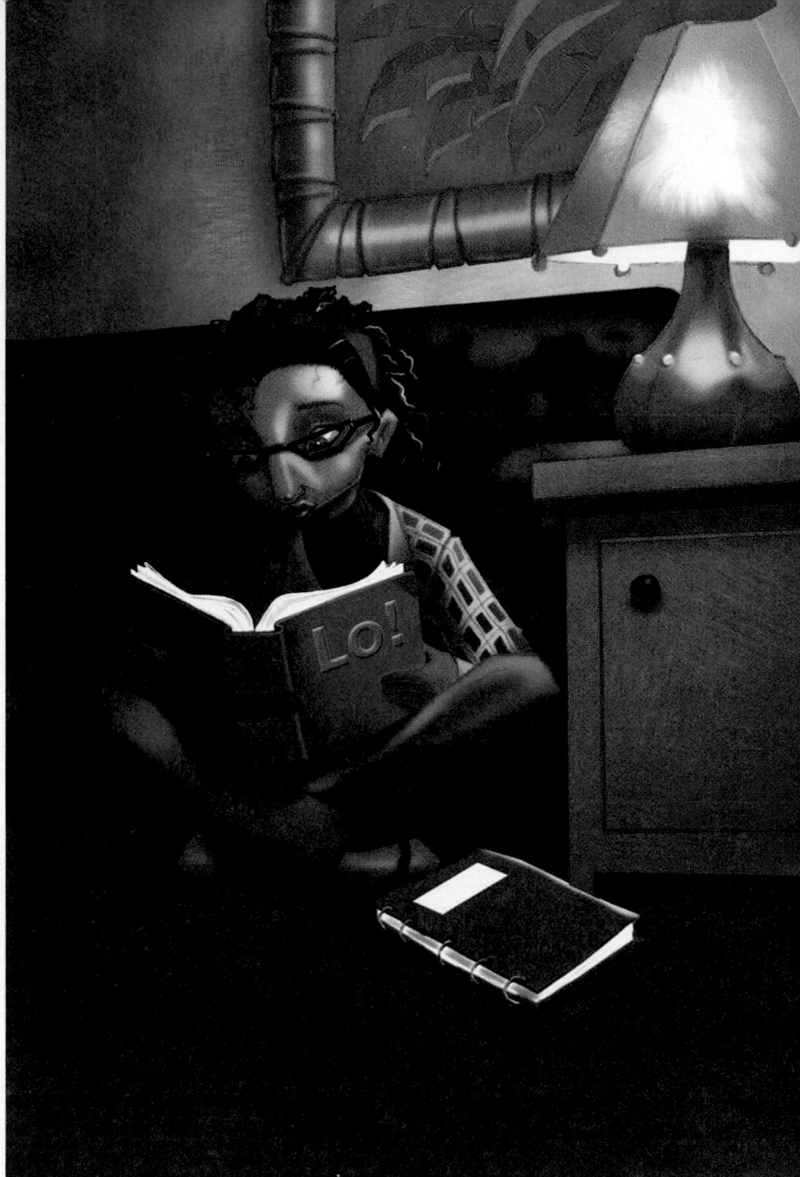

That night, flipping around in *Lo!*, Petra was more and more amazed. She had never seen a book like this. It was, first of all, peppered with quotes from journals and newspapers around the world—there was the *London Times*, the *Quebec Daily Mercury*, the *New Zealand Times*, the *Woodbury Daily Times*, the *New York American*, *The Gentleman's Magazine*, the *Ceylon Observer* . . . the list went on and on.

There were hundreds of stories of bizarre happenings, many of them similar. Venomous snakes dropped into backyards in Oxfordshire, England; red and brown worms fell with snowflakes in Sweden; bushels of periwinkles fell from the sky on Cromer Gardens Road, outside Worcester, England; luminous, floating lights traveled slowly over open land in North Carolina and in Norfolk, England. Wild animals turned up where they shouldn't have. People disappeared and then were found far away, disoriented and confused. There were crashes and explosions that no one could explain.

Fort had apparently spent twenty-seven years going through old newspapers in libraries. He had copied out thousands of articles about unexplained goings-on. . . .

Rereading each sentence in pieces, she began to get a grip on what Fort was saying: Depending on how you looked at things, your world could change completely. His thought was that most people bent over backward to fit everything that happened to them into something they could understand. In other words, people sometimes twisted what was actually in front of them to fit what they thought should

---

bizarre, very unusual and strange
venomous, poisonous
periwinkles, small ocean creatures that live in shells
goings-on, activities or events that are strange or interesting
get a grip on, understand
bent over backward, did as much as possible

be there, never even realizing they were doing it. People liked to see what they were supposed to see, and find what they were supposed to find. It was quite an idea. . . .

Why wasn't more time in school spent studying things that were unknown or not understood instead of things that had already been discovered and explained? Ms. Hussey always asked for their ideas. Wouldn't it be great to go digging for weird facts like Charles Fort did? To try to piece together a meaning behind events that didn't seem to fit?

And why wasn't this book a piece of art? She grabbed her notebook and began to write:

This object is hard on the outside and bendable on the inside. It is the color of an unripe raspberry, and it weighs about as much as a pair of blue jeans. It smells like a closet in an old house, and it is an ancient shape. It holds things that are hard to believe. There are living creatures falling like rain and objects that float by themselves. People vanish and reappear.

It is made of ***substances*** *that once grew, that once bent in the wind and felt the night air. It is older than trips to the moon or computers or stereo systems or television. Our grandparents might have seen it new when they were young.*

There was a woman's name in faded brown ink inside the cover. Petra wondered who else had loved this book and why it had ended up outside Powell's. Why had it been thrown away?

She would never lose it. Not ever.

---

substances, materials

LITERARY CHECK

What ***character traits*** *do Petra and Ms. Hussey share?*

ABOUT THE AUTHOR

Blue Balliett, like Ms. Hussey, loves mysteries and unexplained happenings. She was a teacher in Hyde Park, Chicago, for ten years. Many of the ideas and characters in *Chasing Vermeer* come from her experiences as a teacher and mother. Balliett spends a lot of time in museums, too. One of the goals of *Chasing Vermeer* and its sequel, *The Wright 3*, is to encourage students to solve mysteries, love art, and think for themselves. *Chasing Vermeer* was on the children's bestseller list and won the 2004 Chicago Tribune Prize for Young Adult Fiction.

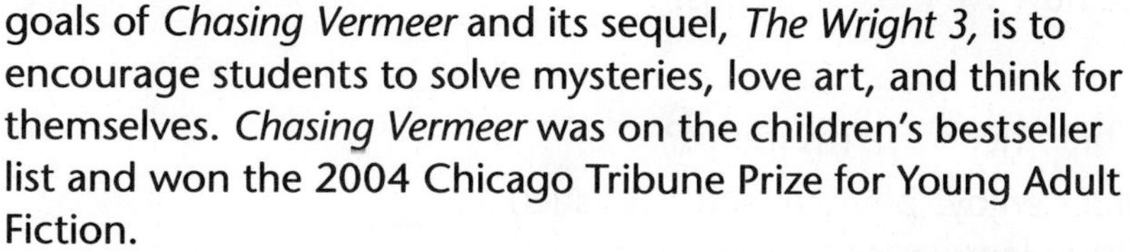

BEFORE YOU GO ON

1. How does Petra feel as she reads *Lo!*?
2. Who wrote *Lo!* and where did the information in it come from?

On Your Own

Do you think that some of the mysterious events described in *Lo!* could actually have happened? Explain.

READING 1

Review and Practice

READER'S THEATER

Act out the following scene between Petra and Calder.

Calder: Did you find something to bring in for Ms. Hussey's assignment?

Petra: Yes, I did, but it was hard. At first, I couldn't find anything that seemed like art.

Calder: Me, too. What did you end up choosing?

Petra: I found a cool old book published in 1931 called *Lo!*

Calder: Where did you find it?

Petra: Well, this man was leaving Powell's bookstore. I saw him look around in a mysterious way, and then he dropped the book in the giveaway box.

Calder: That's strange! What's the book about?

Petra: The author, Charles Fort, spent years going through newspapers and finding things that were hard to explain.

Calder: Like what?

Petra: Like snakes and periwinkles falling from the sky!

Calder: Wow! I want to see this book.

Speaking TIP

Speak naturally and with feeling.

COMPREHENSION

Right There

1. Where is Ms. Hussey's classroom?
2. What does Ms. Hussey ask the class to find?

Think and Search

3. Who are the three main characters? Briefly describe each one.
4. What is Fort's theory about how we look at things?

Author and You

5. Which of Petra's traits will help her solve mysteries?
6. Why do you think that Calder enjoys physical activities such as making stamps and using sign language?

On Your Own

7. In your opinion, what character traits make the individuals in a novel seem like real people even though they are not?
8. Think about what Petra says about school. Should more time be spent studying things that are unknown or not understood instead of things that have already been discovered and explained? Why?

DISCUSSION

Listening TIP

Listen carefully to other classmates' ideas. Compare them to your own.

Discuss in pairs or small groups.

1. Ms. Hussey tells the class: "Picasso said that art is a lie, but a lie that tells the truth." Picasso was a famous twentieth-century artist. What did he mean by this statement? How can art lie and tell the truth at the same time?
2. What objects in Petra's home does she consider when she is looking for a work of art? Choose one, and explain why Petra doesn't select it.
3. The book *Lo!* tells of strange events. What is the strangest event you have ever heard about? What made this event so strange?

Q Can all mysteries be solved? Ms. Hussey's students have a chance to explore many unsolved mysteries. Would you enjoy being in Ms. Hussey's class? Why or why not?

RESPONSE TO LITERATURE

Imagine that you are in Ms. Hussey's class. Find an object in your home that you think is a work of art. In your notebook, explain why you think the object is art. Then write a paragraph-long description of the object. Use Petra's description of *Lo!* as a model. Include details the way Petra did. For example, you might write about the object's color, texture, shape, and size. Share your description with a classmate.

This vase by Picasso is in the shape of a dove. Do you think it's a work of art? Why? ▶

Grammar and Writing

GRAMMAR, USAGE, AND MECHANICS

Distinguishing Parts of Speech

Studying parts of speech will help you with your writing. A complete sentence must contain a subject and a verb. The subject can be a noun, pronoun, or noun phrase that performs, or does, the action. The verb is the action word in a sentence or a word that describes a fact or state.

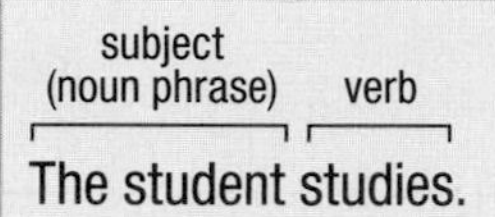

Many sentences also contain an object—the noun, pronoun, or noun phrase that receives the action of a verb. Other parts of speech include *prepositions* and *adjectives*.

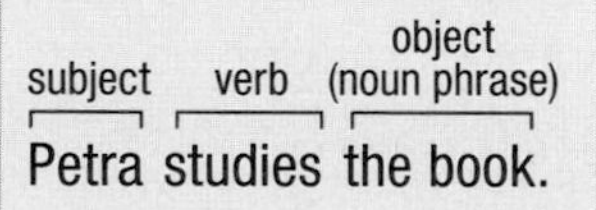

Objects often follow a preposition. Prepositions show location and time, such as *at*, *on*, and *in*. A preposition plus an object is called a *prepositional phrase*. An adjective describes a noun, pronoun, or noun phrase. It usually comes before the noun it modifies, or describes.

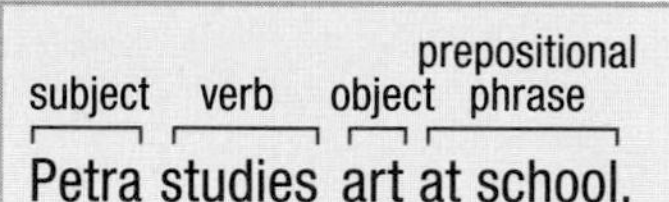

Practice

Copy the sentences below into your notebook. Work with a partner. Label the parts of speech in each sentence, as in the example.

subject *verb* *prepositional phrase*

1. The classroom was in a tall building.
2. They invented a sign language.
3. She tucked the book under her arm.
4. Venomous snakes dropped into backyards.

WRITING A DESCRIPTIVE PARAGRAPH

Describe a Character

Physical traits	Character traits

Before you write a descriptive essay, you need to learn some of the skills writers use to describe people, places, and things. On this page, you'll learn how to describe a character. You'll use a graphic organizer like the one at the right to help you write a descriptive paragraph.

When writers describe a character, they usually include both physical traits and character traits. To describe a character's physical traits, you use words to create a picture of how the character looks. For example, you might describe the character's height, clothing, and hair color. Writers also describe a character's traits. To do this, you show how the character speaks, acts, and thinks.

Here is a model of a descriptive paragraph about Ms. Hussey. Notice the different traits the writer includes. Also, notice the way the writer *shows* you what Ms. Hussey is like, instead of just *telling* you.

Andrew C. Dubin

Ms. Hussey

Ms. Hussey is a sixth-grade teacher. She has a long ponytail and wears three earrings in each ear. The middle school she teaches at is located on the University of Chicago campus, in the Hyde Park neighborhood of Chicago. Ms. Hussey is a different kind of teacher. She wants her students to work on projects that make them think instead of just reading books. Ms. Hussey is fascinating to her students. She is honest and unpredictable. She once even admitted that she didn't know what she was doing, but seemed excited about that. Her students like the way she listens carefully to their ideas and doesn't care if their answers are right or wrong. To Petra and Calder, she is a perfect teacher.

WORD CHOICE:

☑ I chose my words carefully to create a clear description of a character.

ORGANIZATION:

☑ I put physical details and character traits in a logical order.

CONVENTIONS:

☑ I put adjectives in the right place.

Practice

Write a paragraph describing Petra. Use words to "paint a picture" of her physical traits and her character traits. Copy the T-chart above into your notebook. List your ideas on the chart. Decide on a logical order for presenting your ideas. Be sure to use parts of speech correctly.

READING 2

Prepare to Read

What You Will Learn

Reading

- Vocabulary building: *Context, dictionary skills, word study*
- Reading strategy: *Use visuals 1*
- Text type: *Informational text (math/science)*

Grammar, Usage, and Mechanics
Making comparisons: *-er than* and *as . . . as*

Writing
Describe an object

THE BIG QUESTION

Can all mysteries be solved? Have you ever seen any interesting and unusual patterns in nature? Look at the photograph below of the head of a sunflower. Study it closely. What shapes and patterns do you see? Describe them in your notebook. Now look at the following series of numbers. Can you guess the next number in the series? Can you figure out what the numbers have to do with the sunflower? Don't worry if you can't. This number puzzle will be solved when you read the next selection.

1, 1, 2, 3, 5, 8, 13

The spirals at the center of this sunflower are an example of a mysterious pattern. ▶

BUILD BACKGROUND

People who study numbers are called mathematicians. Many great mathematicians have studied objects in nature in order to develop mathematical ideas. ***G Is for Googol*** is an informational text about an Italian mathematician named Fibonacci. He discovered a mysterious number pattern through his study of nature. This pattern is called the Fibonacci sequence. It appears in many living things, such as flowers, plants, and snail shells. In fact, the sunflower you just wrote about contains the Fibonacci sequence.

▲ Fibonacci discovered an intriguing pattern in nature.

VOCABULARY

Learn Key Words

Read these sentences. Use the context to figure out the meaning of the **red** words. Use a dictionary to check your answers. Then write each word and its meaning in your notebook.

1. The **architecture** of our city is very varied. All the buildings have different styles and designs.
2. I didn't notice the **gradual** growth of the oak tree outside. It occurred very slowly.
3. The pattern of numbers continued to **infinity**. It never ended.
4. Sometimes we use Roman **numerals** to write numbers: IV (4), X (10), III (3).
5. You can see **spirals** in the head of a sunflower. Some of these curves go clockwise, and some go counterclockwise.
6. The steps are very **steep**. Each one is over a foot high.

Key Words

architecture
gradual
infinity
numerals
spirals
steep

Practice

Write the sentences in your notebook. Choose a key word to complete each sentence. Then take turns reading the sentences aloud with a partner.

1. In class, we use Roman ______ when we make an outline.
   a. spirals b. numerals
2. Many patterns end, while others go on and on to ______.
   a. infinity b. architecture
3. Seashells form ______, not straight lines.
   a. spirals b. numerals
4. A ______ increase occurs bit by bit, and not all at once.
   a. gradual b. steep
5. Because the trail was so ______, it was hard to climb.
   a. gradual b. steep
6. People who study ______ learn all about buildings.
   a. infinity b. architecture

▲ Many clocks and watches still use Roman numerals.

Learn Academic Words

Study the **red** words and their meanings. You will find these words useful when talking and writing about informational texts. Write each word and its meaning in your notebook. After you read the excerpt from *G Is for Googol,* try to use these words to respond to the text.

Academic Words

constant
illustrate
sequence
unique

constant = happening regularly or all the time	➡	Light travels at a **constant** speed of 299,792,458 meters (186,282 mi.) per second.
illustrate = explain or make something clear by giving examples	➡	Photographs of plants help to **illustrate** patterns in nature.
sequence = a series of related events, actions, or numbers that have a particular order	➡	Fibonacci discovered a **sequence** of numbers with a regular pattern: 1, 1, 2, 3, 5, 8, and so on.
unique = the only one of its type	➡	Each tiger has a **unique** pattern of stripes on its coat. No two tigers have exactly the same markings.

◀ Each tiger's coat is unique.

Practice

Write the sentences in your notebook. Choose a **red** word from the box above to complete each sentence. Then take turns reading the sentences aloud with a partner.

1. Each person has ______ physical traits and character traits.
2. The ______ crying of the baby kept the family awake all night.
3. Each morning I go through the same ______ of steps.
4. The student drew a picture to ______ the shape of a snail.

Word Study: Spelling Words with *ai, ay, ee,* and *oa*

Learning to identify sound-spelling patterns will help you read and spell words correctly. Vowel digraphs, or vowel teams, are two letters that work as a team to stand for one vowel sound. For example, in the word *pail,* the digraph *ai* stands for one sound: the /ā/ sound. In English, the digraphs *ai, ay, ee,* or *oa* often stand for a long vowel sound. The first letter in these digraphs usually tells you what the long vowel sound will be. Look at the chart below. Take turns reading the words aloud with a partner. Notice the digraphs in each word and the vowel sounds they stand for.

/ā/ spelled *ai*	/ā/ spelled *ay*	/ē/ spelled *ee*	/ō/ spelled *oa*
p**ai**nter	s**ay**	s**ee**d	**oa**k
sn**ai**l	tr**ay**	kn**ee**	fl**oa**t
aim	spr**ay**	f**ee**l	s**oa**p

Practice

Work with a partner. Copy the chart above into your notebook. Say a word from the chart, and ask your partner to spell it aloud. Then have your partner say the next word. Continue until you can spell all of the words correctly. Now work with your partner to spell these words: *toad, always, steeply, pairs, coast, maintains, okay, needles.* Add them to the chart under the correct headings.

READING STRATEGY USE VISUALS 1

Using visuals helps you understand the text better. Visuals include art, photographs, diagrams (labeled pictures), and charts. Many informational texts include visuals. To use visuals, follow these steps:

- Look at the visual. Ask yourself, "What does the visual show? How does it help me understand the reading?"
- Read any titles, headings, labels, or captions carefully.

As you read *G Is for Googol,* pay close attention to the visuals. Think about how they help you understand the text.

READING 2

INFORMATIONAL TEXT

MATH / SCIENCE

Set a purpose for reading What mysterious number pattern occurs in pinecones, flowers, and seashells? Read to find out who Fibonacci was and what he discovered about nature.

from

G Is for Googol

David M. Schwartz

Did you know that a googol is a 1 followed by 100 zeros? G Is for Googol *is a math alphabet book that explains many unusual mathematical words and facts. Read two sections from this amazing book. Both are about a mysterious number sequence.*

F Is for Fibonacci

In the 1200s, an Italian mathematician named Leonardo of Pisa wrote a book about numbers. He signed his name *Fibonacci* (pronounced fib-o-NOTCH-ee).

In his book, Fibonacci said that the people of Europe should stop using Roman numerals. He wanted everyone to switch to the numerals used in the Arabic world. Instead of writing LXXVIII, they could write 78. Isn't 78 easier to write than LXXVIII? Well, Fibonacci thought so, and because of him, we use Arabic numerals today.

Fibonacci's book also included story problems. One was about rabbits: How many pairs of rabbits will there be each month if you start with one pair of newborn rabbits, and that pair produces a pair of babies every month? The rabbits start producing babies when they are two months old, and their babies also have their first babies when they become two months old.

producing, having

1 1 2 3 5 8 13 21 34 55 89

Here's one way to look at it:

After How Long?	How Many Rabbits?
Starting point	1 pair
After 1 month	1 pair
After 2 months	2 pairs
After 3 months	3 pairs
After 4 months	5 pairs
After 5 months	8 pairs
After 6 months	13 pairs
After 7 months	21 pairs
After 8 months	34 pairs
After 9 months	55 pairs
After 10 months	89 pairs
After 11 months	144 pairs

Let's look at the answers another way:

1	1	2	3	5	8	13	21	34	55	89	144

These are the first 12 numbers in the famous *Fibonacci sequence* of numbers.

See if you can figure out what's so special about the Fibonacci sequence. After the first two numbers, how can the others be made? Think about it before you read on.

Whenever you add one number to the next, you get the following number in the sequence. Try it. Add 2 and 3. What do you get? Now add 5 and 8. Got it? Okay, now what number comes after 144 in the Fibonacci sequence?

Fibonacci numbers are interesting, but what's *amazing* about them is how often they appear. You can find Fibonacci numbers in art, architecture, music, poetry, and nature. Read **N is for Nature.** Get ready to be amazed.

figure out, think about a problem or situation until you find the answer or understand what has happened

▼ **Within eleven months one pair of rabbits and their offspring will produce 144 pairs of rabbits.**

BEFORE YOU GO ON

1. Where and when did Fibonacci live?
2. What number comes after 144 in the Fibonacci sequence?

On Your Own
Where do you think Fibonacci numbers will show up in nature? Use the visuals on pages 24–25 to make predictions about the text.

N Is for Nature

There are numbers in *nature*. Lots.

Do you remember the Fibonacci sequence of numbers? Here are the first twelve numbers of the Fibonacci sequence:

1	1	2	3	5	8	13	21	34	55	89	144

Fibonacci discovered this number sequence, but he did not invent it. Nature invented it. If each page of this book stated one way that Fibonacci numbers appear in nature, we'd need a book so heavy you couldn't lift it. Here are just a few.

The number of **petals** in a flower is usually a Fibonacci number. Some flowers, like daisies, don't have true petals, but petal-like parts called *florets*. Florets come in Fibonacci numbers, too.

---

petals, the brightly colored parts of a flower

Pine needles come in groups, or *bundles*. The bundles almost always have 1, 2, 3, or 5 needles. Do these numbers look familiar?

But pine needles aren't nearly as interesting as pinecones. Find a pinecone. The hard little knobby parts are called *bracts*. (Make sure your pinecone is in good condition, with no missing bracts.) Turn the cone so you're looking at its base. Can you see how the bracts make spirals? There are clockwise spirals, and there are counterclockwise spirals. Follow one spiral as it winds all the way around the cone to the pointy end. Dab a little paint on each bract in that spiral. Now dab a different color on a spiral going in the other direction. You'll see that one spiral winds gradually, and the other one winds more steeply. How many of each type are there? Count them. Remember, it's not the number of bracts that you're counting; it's the number of spirals.

The petal-like parts of a daisy come in Fibonacci numbers. ▶

If you count the clockwise or counterclockwise spirals on the bottom of a pinecone, you will get a Fibonacci number. ▼

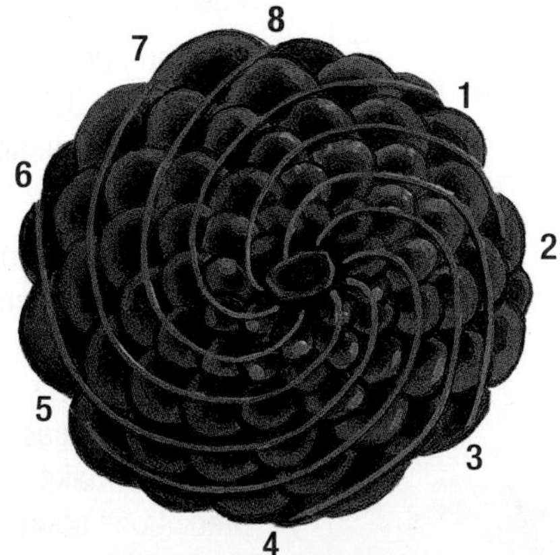

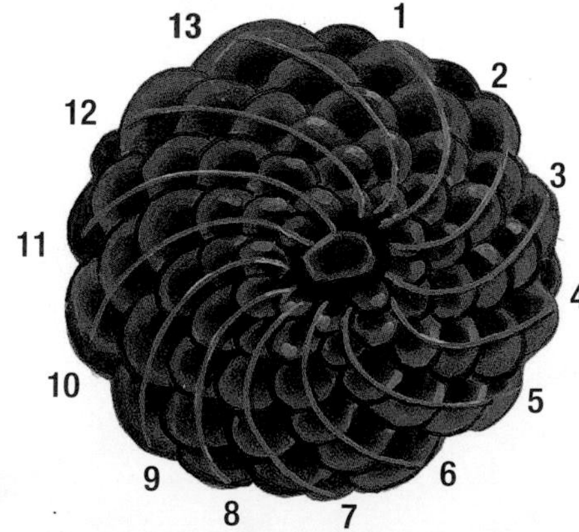

Some pinecones have 3 gradual spirals and 5 steep spirals. Some have 5 gradual and 8 steep. Or 8 and 13. Or 13 and 21. A pinecone's spirals come in Fibonacci numbers. In fact, Fibonacci numbers are sometimes called "pinecone numbers."

Fibonacci numbers could also be called "sunflower numbers," "artichoke numbers," or "pineapple numbers" because you will find the numbers in spirals formed by a sunflower's seeds, an artichoke's leaves, and a pineapple's scales (the diamond-shaped markings on the outside).

Fibonacci strikes again!

No one really understands why Fibonacci numbers show up so much in nature. It's a mystery!

Here's another way that Fibonacci numbers are found in nature: They make a spiral that maintains a constant proportion all the way to infinity. To find that spiral, take a rectangle that has "Fibonacci" proportions, say 3" x 5", then repeat that same proportioned rectangle, smaller and smaller . . .

---

maintains, continues in the same way

proportion, the amount of something compared to something else

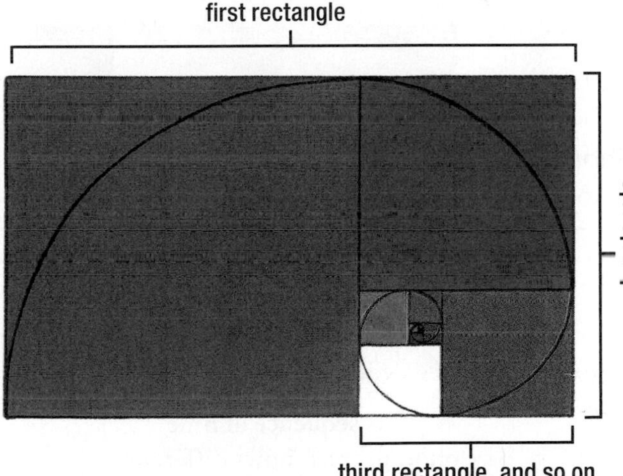

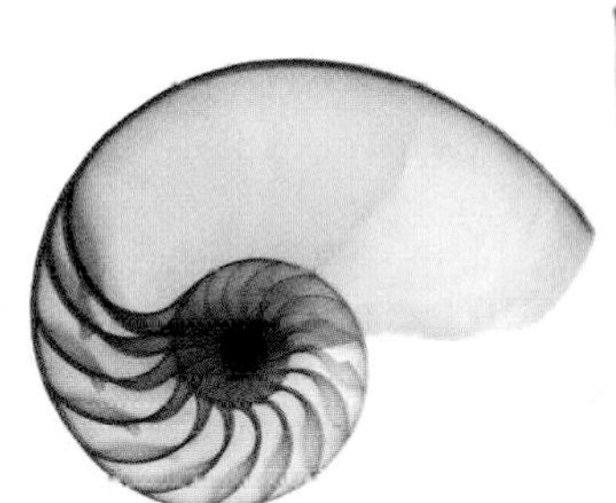

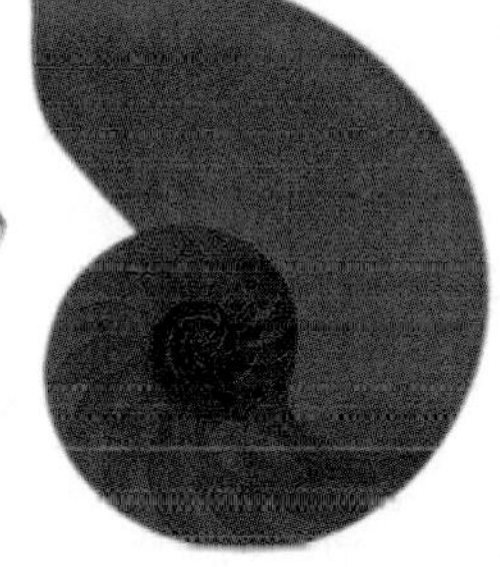

▲ These seashells have spirals that follow the Fibonacci sequence.

BEFORE YOU GO ON

1. Which part of a pinecone comes in Fibonacci numbers?
2. Where do Fibonacci numbers show up in a sunflower, an artichoke, and a pineapple?

On Your Own
Do you think that scientists will ever be able to explain why Fibonacci numbers show up throughout nature? Explain.

ABOUT THE AUTHOR

David M. Schwartz enjoys all things mathematical. In addition to *G Is for Googol*, he has written other award-winning books, including *How Much Is a Million?* and *If You Made a Million*. Each year, Schwartz visits more than fifty schools and conferences to spread his enthusiasm about numbers. He is also fascinated by the stars in the night sky, birds in the rain forest, and other natural wonders.

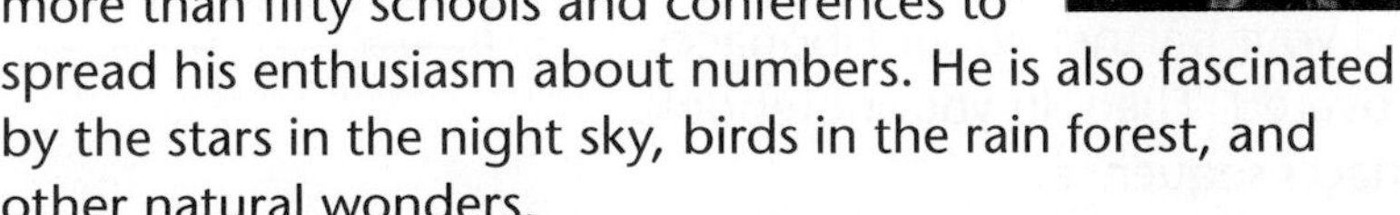

READING 2 Review and Practice

COMPREHENSION

Right There

1. Which type of numerals did Fibonacci want people to use?
2. What are the first twelve numbers in the Fibonacci sequence?

Think and Search

3. What is so special about the Fibonacci sequence?
4. How do the numbers of spirals on the bottom of a pinecone illustrate the Fibonacci sequence?

Author and You

5. Why does the author say that Fibonacci did not invent the Fibonacci sequence?
6. How did the author use visuals to explain the Fibonacci sequence? Did this help you understand the author's ideas? Why?

On Your Own

7. Think about nature. Have you ever noticed an interesting pattern on an animal or in a plant, flower, or body of water? Describe the pattern and why it attracted your attention.
8. Think about what you have learned in your math classes. What is something you find interesting about numbers or number patterns? Why?

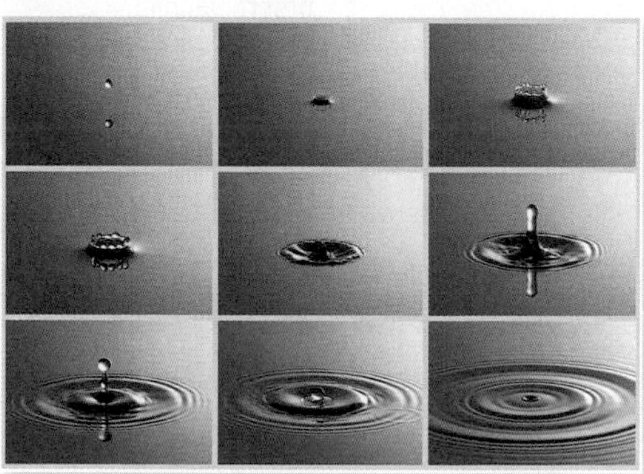

▲ This sequence of nine photographs shows different kinds of water patterns.

IN YOUR OWN WORDS

Work with a partner. Imagine that you are teaching a younger student about Fibonacci and his discovery. Tell your partner five important facts that you learned in the reading. You may want to use actual objects or visuals, such as diagrams and photographs, to help explain some of the facts. Take turns telling your partner about Fibonacci and the number sequence he discovered. Then, in your notebook, describe one example of the Fibonacci sequence.

Use words that help your partner visualize and understand facts about Fibonacci and the Fibonacci sequence.

DISCUSSION

Discuss in pairs or small groups.

1. How do daisies, seashells, and rabbits illustrate the Fibonacci sequence?
2. Fibonacci made life easier by having people use Arabic numerals rather than Roman numerals. What would happen if we suddenly had to use Roman numerals again? How would our lives change?

Q **Can all mysteries be solved?** What is mysterious about the Fibonacci sequence? Does knowing about the Fibonacci sequence help you understand other mysteries in nature? Explain.

Listening TIP

If you don't understand something a classmate says, wait until the next speaker has finished and then ask your question.

READ FOR FLUENCY

It is often easier to read a text if you understand the difficult words and phrases. Work with a partner. Choose a paragraph from the reading. Identify the words and phrases you do not know or have trouble pronouncing. Look up the difficult words in a dictionary.

Take turns pronouncing the words and phrases with your partner. If necessary, ask your teacher to model the correct pronunciation. Then take turns reading the paragraph aloud. Give each other feedback on your reading.

EXTENSION

Fibonacci was a famous mathematician. Many other people made important contributions to mathematics. Go to the library or do research on the Internet to find information about another famous mathematician, for example, Archimedes, Descartes, Pascal, or Pythagoras. Then write a brief report on the mathematician. Explain why the person is important. Tell what you learned about math from your research. Use this chart to organize your research:

Who?	
Where?	
When?	
What?	
Why?	

Grammar and Writing

GRAMMAR, USAGE, AND MECHANICS

Making Comparisons: *-er than* and *as . . . as*

Certain kinds of words are useful when you want to describe how two things are the same or different. An adjective is a word that describes a noun. Comparative adjectives compare two things.

For most one-syllable adjectives, you add *-r* or *-er* to form a comparative adjective. For two-syllable adjectives ending in *y*, you change *y* to *i* and add *-er*. The word *than* usually follows a comparative. Study the chart. Notice the spelling changes that occur in comparatives.

small (+ *-er*)	This rectangle is small**er than** the others.
large (+ *-r*)	Sunflowers are large**r than** daisies.
big (double the last letter + *-er*)	A bear is big**ger than** a cat.
easy (change *y* to *i* + *-er*)	Isn't 78 eas**ier** to write **than** LXXVIII?

Another way to compare two things is to use the expression *as . . . as*. Use *as . . . as* to show that the two things being compared are equal. Use *not as . . . as* to show that the two things being compared are not equal.

The oak tree is **as tall as** our house. Pine needles are **not as interesting as** pinecones.

Practice

Copy the sentences below into your notebook. Complete each sentence by forming the comparative adjective of the word in parentheses.

1. Cats are ______ than rabbits when they have babies. (old)
2. Arabic numerals aren't as ______ as Roman numerals. (difficult)
3. A book about Fibonacci numbers would be ______ than this textbook. (heavy)
4. The number 144 is ______ than the number 89. (large)
5. The Fibonacci sequence is as ______ today as it was in the 1200s. (mysterious)

WRITING A DESCRIPTIVE PARAGRAPH

Describe an Object

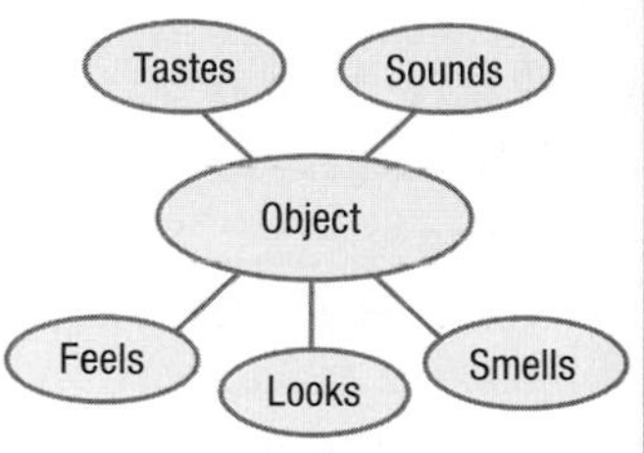

You have already described a person's traits. Now you will describe an object using a graphic organizer like the one at the right. When writers describe something, they often use words that appeal to the five senses: sight, hearing, touch, taste, and smell. Using words that appeal to the senses, or sensory details, makes writing come alive.

Here is a model of a descriptive paragraph about a pineapple. Notice the sensory details the writer includes to illustrate what the object looks, sounds, feels, tastes, and smells like.

Wendy Willner

The Pineapple

The pineapple is dark, hard, and elongated in shape. Its stiff dark-green leaves stand silently on the table. The pineapple seems as if it wants to tell you something, but it doesn't want to tell you too much. When you pick the fruit up, the coarse skin scratches your hands. The scales form three sets of spirals. A set of five spirals goes gradually up to the right. A set of eight spirals goes more steeply down to the left, and a set of thirteen spirals goes very steeply up to the right. These are Fibonacci numbers. When you slice the pineapple open, it is as bright and yellow as the sun at noon. Put a slice in your mouth, and it tastes sweet and juicy. The fresh-cut pineapple fills any room with a refreshing smell. When you eat it with your hands (you shouldn't but I do), it feels as if you are touching liquid gold.

Practice

Write a paragraph describing a fruit or vegetable. Use a sensory-details web like the one above to gather and organize details. Include at least one detail for each sense: sight, hearing, touch, taste, and smell. If the feel or scent of the object reminds you of something else, use comparatives and other expressions to compare.

Writing Checklist

VOICE:

☑ I included many sensory details so that my reader can feel what I felt.

IDEAS AND CONTENT:

☑ I used details and comparisons to make my description fun to read.

READING 3 Prepare to Read

What You Will Learn

Reading

- Vocabulary building: *Context, dictionary skills, word study*
- Reading strategy: *Preview*
- Text type: *Informational text (social studies)*

Grammar, Usage, and Mechanics

Passive voice

Writing

Describe a place

THE BIG QUESTION

Can all mysteries be solved? You are going to read about a series of real-life mysteries. The first concerns the Egyptian pyramids. Work with a partner to explore everything you know about pyramids. What do they look like? Where, when, and how were they built? In your notebook, record what you already know.

Now look at the picture below. Read the facts about the Great Pyramid at Giza in Egypt. Discuss the picture and facts with your partner.

The pyramid is as tall as a forty-story building. It took 20,000 workers twenty years to build it.

It is made up of more than 2 million blocks of stone. Each block weighs about 2,200 kilograms (5,000 lb.).

The bottom of the pyramid is as big as eight football fields.

Workers used a knotted string as a measurement tool.

Workers used logs and ramps.

BUILD BACKGROUND

"Fact or Fiction?" explores mysterious places, creatures, and events from the past. First, this nonfiction article focuses on the pyramids of Egypt, one of the most puzzling of mysteries. Then it goes on to explore other historical puzzles: *What happened to the people of Machu Picchu? Is there really a curse on King Tutankhamen's tomb? What mysterious creatures live in the depths of the sea? Is there a monster in a lake in Scotland?* As you read, think about how you would try to solve one of these mysteries.

VOCABULARY

Learn Key Words

Read these sentences. Use the context to figure out the meaning of the **red** words. Use a dictionary to check your answers. Then write each word and its meaning in your notebook.

1. The **archaeologist** tried to understand the past by digging through the ruins of old buildings.
2. To understand the mysterious ruins, scientists used **clues** from the soil, statues, and ancient scrolls.
3. A mysterious **creature** lived in the forest. People believed it was part human and part horse.
4. The first English colony in America **disappeared** mysteriously. One day, all the people were gone.
5. The unicorn is a **fantasy**. It is an unreal animal that lives only in the imagination.
6. A church, a temple, and a mosque are three kinds of **sacred** buildings.

Key Words

archaeologist
clues
creature
disappeared
fantasy
sacred

▲ The unicorn was a popular fantasy during the middle ages.

Practice

Work with a partner to answer these questions. Try to include the **red** word in your answer. Write the sentences in your notebook.

1. What does an **archaeologist** do?
2. What **clues** would the police use to track a bank robber?
3. Which **creature** scares you the most? Why?
4. Why do you think dinosaurs **disappeared** millions of years ago?
5. Why do people sometimes like **fantasy** better than reality?
6. What is something that is **sacred** to you or someone you know?

Learn Academic Words

Study the **red** words and their meanings. You will find these words useful when talking and writing about informational texts. Write each word and its meaning in your notebook. After you read "Fact or Fiction?" try to use these words to respond to the text.

Academic Words

accurate
create
evidence
survive

accurate = correct or exact	➡	Archaeologists must collect **accurate** information when they try to solve mysteries from the past.
create = make something exist	➡	The scientist wanted to **create** a model pyramid to see how it was made.
evidence = facts, objects, or signs that make you believe that something exists or is true	➡	The scientist looked for **evidence** to prove when the building had been constructed.
survive = continue to live or exist	➡	No one knows why the animals did not **survive** after the storm; all of them died.

Practice

Work with a partner to answer these questions. Try to include the **red** word in your answer. Write the answers in your notebook.

1. Where could you find **accurate** information about ancient Egypt?
2. How could you **create** a model of a pyramid? What materials would you use to make the model?
3. What types of **evidence** might archaeologists use to figure out why a group of people suddenly died out or vanished?
4. What kinds of things do human beings need in order to **survive**?

▲ Although the Inca people died out, they left behind evidence of what their culture was like. One example is this counting necklace.

Word Study: Same Sound, Different Spellings

In English, sometimes the same sound can be spelled in different ways. The only way to figure out the correct spelling is to check the word in a dictionary and memorize it. When you read "Fact or Fiction?" you will come across the words *calend**ar**, togeth**er**, calculat**or***. Say each word aloud with a partner. What sound do you hear in the final syllable of each word? Notice that the final sound /ər/ is the same, though the spellings are different.

The sound /ər/ can be spelled in different ways when it comes at the end of a word in an unstressed syllable. Study the chart for more examples.

ar	er	or
sug**ar**	feath**er**	auth**or**
cell**ar**	Decemb**er**	mirr**or**
regul**ar**	pitch**er**	neighb**or**

Practice

Work with a partner. Copy the chart above into your notebook. Say a word from the chart, and ask your partner to spell it aloud. Then have your partner say the next word. Continue until you can spell all of these words correctly. Then work with your partner to spell the following words: *beggar, cracker, doctor, dollar, hammer,* and *tractor.* Add them to the chart under the correct headings.

Reading Strategy PREVIEW

Previewing a text helps you understand the content more quickly. When you preview a text, you prepare yourself for the information you are about to learn. To preview, follow these steps:

- Read the title and headings (section titles).
- Try to turn the headings into questions.
- Look at the visuals and read the captions or labels.
- Think about what you already know about the subject.

Before you read "Fact or Fiction?" look at the title, headings, visuals, and captions. Think about what you already know about these subjects. What more would you like to know?

Set a purpose for reading Preview the text. What kinds of mysteries do you think the text will present? Read to find out why some mysteries are so hard to solve.

Fact or Fiction?

Path to the Stars?

About 4,500 years ago, the pharaoh Cheops and his son and grandson built the three Pyramids of Giza in Egypt. These pyramids were tombs, or places to bury the dead. For thousands of years, people didn't understand why these three pyramids were grouped together.

Then Belgian engineer Robert Bauval noticed that the shape of the three pyramids was the same as part of a group of stars in the sky called Orion's Belt. The whole group of stars—Orion—was sacred to the Egyptians. When Cheops died, he was buried in the Great Pyramid of Giza. The Egyptians made a shaft—or hole—in this pyramid. The shaft led from Cheops's tomb to the sky and the three stars of Orion's Belt. Scientists believe that the Egyptians built this shaft so that Cheops could fly from the pyramid to Orion. There, he would become a god.

---

pharaoh, ancient Egyptian ruler
engineer, person who plans how to build machines, roads, and so on

▲ The three stars in Orion's belt

▲ The three Pyramids of Giza from high above

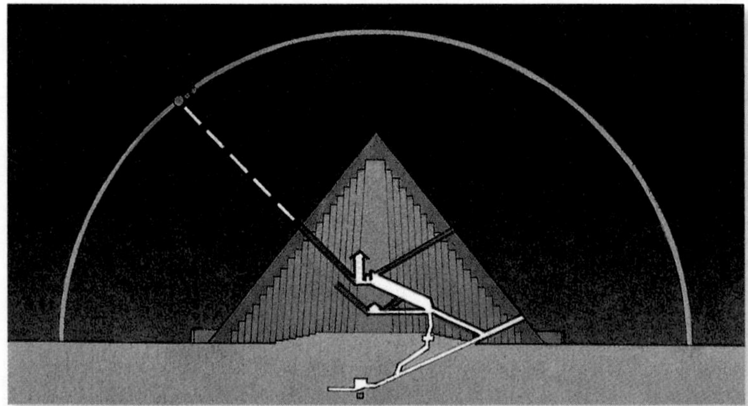

▲ This diagram shows the shaft in the pyramid.

The Secret of the Great Sphinx

A huge statue with the head of a man and the body of a lion stands in Giza, Egypt. Known as the Great Sphinx, it seems to defend the pyramids behind it. Like the pyramids, the Sphinx is made from limestone, which is very common in Egypt. The exact age of the Sphinx remains one of the world's great mysteries. For thousands of years, wind and sand have eroded this enormous sculpture. Some archaeologists believe that water also damaged the Sphinx many centuries ago. Was the Sphinx once buried at the bottom of the sea? No one knows for sure.

▲ **The Sphinx has the head of a man and the body of a lion.**

Mysterious Cities

Some ancient cities were abandoned and no one knows why. One of these cities is Machu Picchu, located about 2,440 meters (8,000 ft.) high in the Andes Mountains of Peru. The Inca built Machu Picchu from about 1460 to 1470 C.E. They lived in parts of South America, including what is now Peru. They used stone blocks to make most of the buildings. The blocks fit together perfectly.

In the early 1500s, everyone left the city. No one knows why. Perhaps people died or left because of smallpox, a deadly disease that was brought to the Americas by European explorers and colonists. Machu Picchu was forgotten for hundreds of years. Then, in 1911, the American explorer Hiram Bingham rediscovered it. Today, tourists from all over the world visit this unique city.

---

statue, shape of a person or animal made of stone, metal, or wood
limestone, a type of rock that contains calcium, often used to make buildings
eroded, slowly destroyed
centuries, periods of 100 years
abandoned, left completely behind and not used anymore
colonists, people who settle in a new country or area

▼ **The abandoned city of Machu Picchu**

BEFORE YOU GO ON

- Why do scientists think that the Egyptians made a shaft in the Great Pyramid?
- What has happened to the Sphinx over time?

On Your Own
Why do you think people might leave a city forever?

▲ Some stones at Stonehenge came from 480 kilometers (300 mi.) away. How people moved them is a mystery.

Stonehenge

Stonehenge is a mysterious monument of huge stones in England. Ancient peoples built Stonehenge about 5,000 years ago. No one really knows who these people were or why they built this strange circle of rocks.

Some people believe that Stonehenge was a temple to the sun. Other people believe that Stonehenge was a great stone calendar or calculator. They think that the stones were arranged to measure the sun's movements. For example, the stones may have been used to measure the summer and winter solstices—the longest and shortest days of the year. Perhaps Stonehenge was created to mark the rise of the sun and moon throughout the centuries. How will we ever know for sure?

Island of Giants

Easter Island is a tiny island in the Pacific Ocean, 3,620 kilometers (2,250 mi.) off the coast of Chile. It was named by Dutch explorers who arrived there on Easter Sunday, 1722. The island is covered with nearly 900 large statues, called "moai." Scientists believe the statues are the gods of the ancient people of Easter Island—the Rapa Nui people. But no one knows for sure. Another mystery is how the Rapa Nui people moved the heavy stones as far as 23 kilometers (14 mi.).

Archaeologists have found wooden tablets with the ancient language of the Rapa Nui people on them. No one knows how to read this language today. So the history of the Rapa Nui people is still a puzzle. Only the great stone statues remain to watch over the island.

▲ The Moai have an average height of 4 meters (13 ft.).

---

monument, something that is built to help people to remember an important person or event

temple, holy building

calculator, instrument used to figure out mathematical problems

Easter Sunday, a special Sunday in March or April when Christians remember Christ's death and his return to life

Curse of the Pharaoh

Tutankhamen was a pharaoh in ancient Egypt from 1333 to 1324 B.C.E. When he died, Tutankhamen was buried in a tomb with gold and other treasures.

In 1922, a group led by British archaeologists Howard Carter and Lord Carnarvon opened the tomb of Tutankhamen. They found many treasures, including a beautiful gold mask. Some people believed that a message carved in the tomb wall said, "Death will slay with his wings whoever disturbs the peace of the pharaoh." Lord Carnarvon died soon after opening the tomb. According to one story, Carnarvon's dog died at the same time at his home in England. Then, five months after Carnarvon died, his younger brother died suddenly.

According to one report, six of the twenty-six people at the opening of Tutankhamen's tomb died within ten years. However, many other people who were there when the tomb was opened lived to be very old. Was there really a curse? What do you think?

▲ Tutankhamen's mask

---

message, piece of information that is communicated in words or signals
slay, kill
curse, wish that something bad would happen to someone

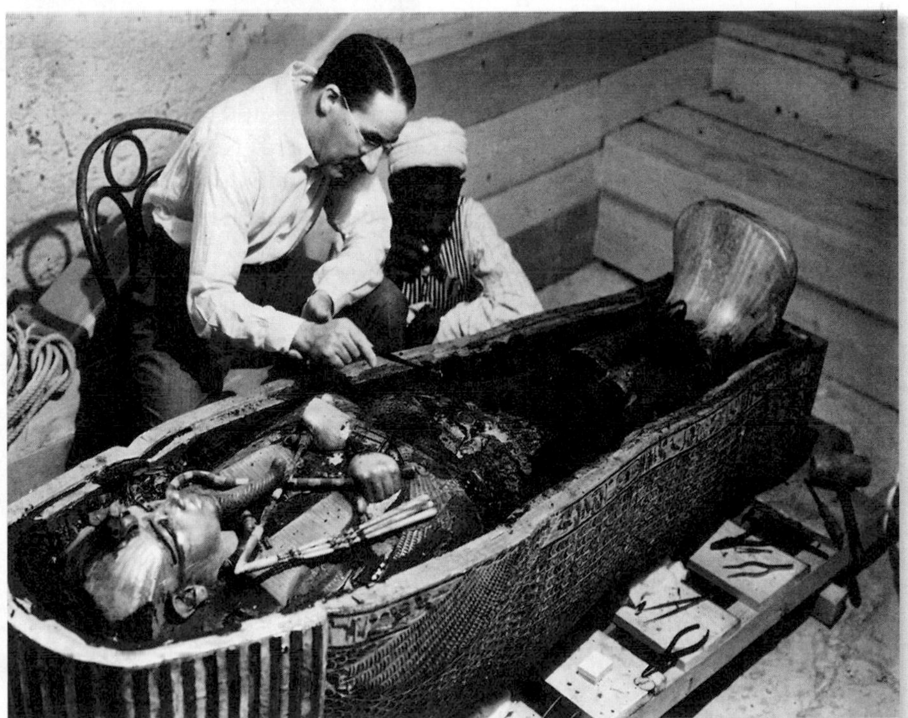

◀ Howard Carter and Tutankhamen's mummy

BEFORE YOU GO ON

1. What is mysterious about Stonehenge and Easter Island?
2. What is the "curse of the pharaoh"?

On Your Own
How do you think Howard Carter and Lord Carnarvon felt when they opened the tomb of Tutankhamen? Would you have liked to be there? Why or why not?

Terrifying Tentacles

Scientists say that we know more about Mars than we do about the mysteries at the bottom of the ocean. For instance, little is known about giant octopuses and squid. These sea creatures are usually only about 60 to 90 centimeters (2–3 ft.) long. However, there have been reports of giant octopuses and squid with tentacles long enough to pull a ship underwater. In 1753, a man in Norway described seeing a huge sea monster "full of arms." The man said that the monster looked big enough to crush a large ship. More recently, giant squid have been discovered with tentacles 10 meters (33 ft.) long. Imagine eating calamari rings the size of truck tires!

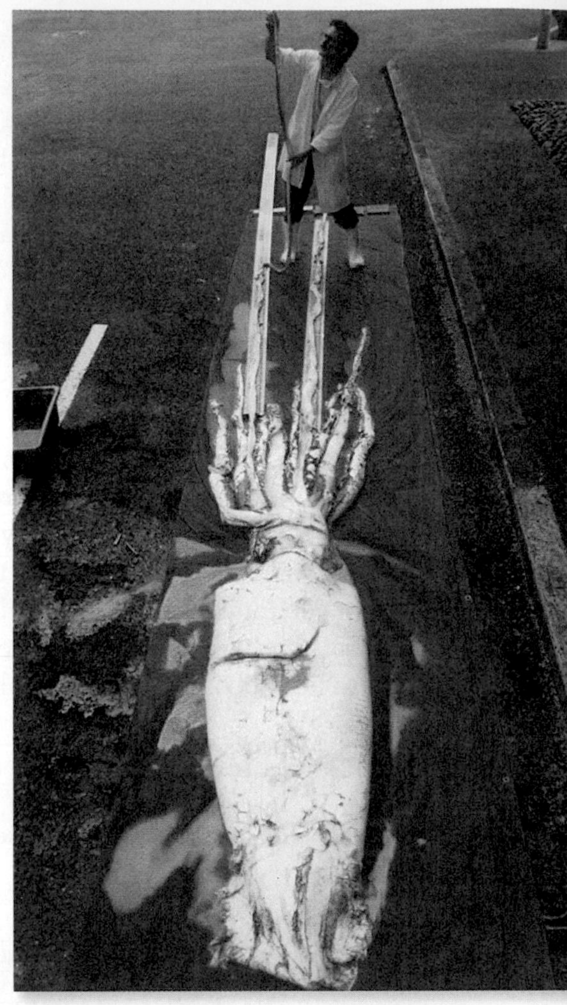

▲ **A giant squid caught in the deep ocean off New Zealand. Giant squid live about 550 meters (1,800 ft.) beneath the sea.**

Scary Monsters

Most people believe that dinosaurs disappeared millions of years ago. However, a few dinosaurs may have survived. The famous Loch Ness monster may be a living dinosaur-like reptile called a plesiosaur.

People first reported seeing the Loch Ness monster in April 1933 when a new road was built on the north shore of Loch Ness, a lake in Scotland. A man and woman saw a huge creature with two black humps swimming across the lake. Then two more people saw a strange animal crossing the road with a sheep in its mouth. There is now a Loch Ness Investigation Bureau, but most scientists believe that the Loch Ness monster is a creature of fantasy.

---

tentacles, long, thin arm-like parts
calamari rings, sliced squid, often served fried or in a salad
reptile, type of animal, such as a snake or lizard, whose blood changes temperature according to the temperature around it
humps, raised parts on the back of an animal

This famous photograph of the Loch Ness monster is not authentic. The photographer tied a plastic head to a toy submarine. ▶

Bigfoot and the Yeti

In various parts of the world, people have told stories about seeing large ape-like creatures. Different cultures give the creature different names. In the United States, for example, this creature is called Bigfoot or Sasquatch. In Tibet, it is called the yeti.

The first reports of Bigfoot date back to 1811. At that time, a man reported seeing footprints 36 centimeters (14 in.) long. In 1924, another man claimed that Bigfoot had kidnapped him. Each year many people in the United States claim to see Bigfoot. They often report seeing the creature in the forests of the Northwest.

Reports of a huge creature frightened the first European travelers in Tibet. (In Tibet, the word *yeti* means "man-like creature.") In 1951, a Mount Everest explorer found giant footprints in the snow.

Do creatures like the yeti and Bigfoot really exist, or are they figments of the imagination? Bernard Heuvelmans (1916–2001), a famous zoologist, believed that the world is full of creatures still unknown to science. What do you think?

◀ Bigfoot (above) and the Yeti (below) look like giant apes. ▼

---

various, different
figments of the imagination, things imagined to be real that do not exist
zoologist, scientist who studies animals

BEFORE YOU GO ON

1. Do most scientists believe that the Loch Ness monster is real or a fantasy?
2. In the United States, where is Bigfoot usually seen?

On Your Own
Do you believe that mysterious animals like the yeti or the Loch Ness monster exist? What is your opinion?

READING 3

Review and Practice

COMPREHENSION

Right There

1. Who built the three Pyramids of Giza?
2. What did archaeologists find on Easter Island?

Think and Search

3. In what ways are the pyramids and the Sphinx different?
4. How are the mysteries of Machu Picchu and Easter Island similar?

Author and You

5. Do you think that the author believes in the Loch Ness monster or Bigfoot? Explain.
6. How do you think the author feels about the mysteries described in "Fact or Fiction?" Give examples that reveal the author's feelings about four of the subjects.

On Your Own

7. Would you like to be part of the Loch Ness Investigation Bureau? Why?
8. Do you believe that there are still many creatures unknown to science? Why or why not?

The dragon shown in this tile is a creature of fantasy. Or is it? ▶

IN YOUR OWN WORDS

Work with a partner. Imagine that you are telling a younger student about "Fact or Fiction?" First make a list of the key topics and main ideas in the article. You may want to use the headings in the article as a guide. Then take turns explaining the information you remember from the article. Try to use some of these words: *pharaoh, engineer, centuries, eroded, survive, disappeared, sacred, temple, clues, statues, archaeologists, message, unique, accurate, evidence, humps, creature,* and *fantasy.*

Speaking TIP

Write your important ideas on note cards. Write just a few words in big letters on each card. Use the cards to help you remember your main ideas.

DISCUSSION

Discuss in pairs or small groups.

1. What might have caused the people of Machu Picchu to disappear?
2. Which place described in "Fact or Fiction?" would you most like to visit? Explain.

Q **Can all mysteries be solved?** Which of the mysteries in the selection do you predict will be solved first? Explain.

Listening TIP

Be quiet and pay attention while others are speaking. Open your eyes and ears.

READ FOR FLUENCY

Reading with feeling helps make what you read more interesting. Work with a partner. Choose a paragraph from the reading. Read the paragraph to yourselves. Ask each other how you felt after reading the paragraph. Did you feel happy or sad?

Take turns reading the paragraph aloud to each other with a tone of voice that represents how you felt when you read it the first time. Give each other feedback.

EXTENSION

Workbook Page 19

Archaeologists and scientists examine information and data to learn more about mysteries. Imagine that you are an archaeologist. Go to the library or do research on the Internet to find more information about one of the mysteries from "Fact or Fiction?" Then present the new information to the class.

Grammar and Writing

GRAMMAR, USAGE, AND MECHANICS

Passive Voice

When you read, you will see text in both the active voice and the passive voice. The active voice is used when the focus is on who or what does the action, also called the performer. The passive voice is used when the focus is on the receiver of the action. Form the passive voice with a form of the verb *be* + the past participle. A *by*-phrase identifies the performer.

Active Voice	Passive Voice
The pharaoh **built** the Pyramids of Giza. [focus is on the pharaoh]	The Pyramids of Giza **were built** by the pharaoh. [focus is on the Pyramids of Giza]
The Inca **abandoned** Machu Picchu. [focus is on the Inca]	Machu Picchu **was abandoned** by the Inca. [focus is on Machu Picchu]
Dutch explorers **discovered** Easter Island. [focus is on the Dutch explorers]	Easter Island **was discovered** by Dutch explorers. [focus is on Easter Island]
A huge creature **frightened** the travelers in Tibet. [focus is on a huge creature]	The travelers in Tibet **were frightened** by a huge creature. [focus is on the travelers in Tibet]

Practice

Rewrite the sentences below in your notebook, changing each from the active to the passive voice. The first one has been done for you. Discuss each answer with a partner. Does the sentence sound better in the active or passive voice? Why?

1. The Egyptians built the pyramids.
   The pyramids were built by the Egyptians.
2. Explorers discovered nearly 900 statues.
3. Many people reported sightings of the Loch Ness monster.
4. Last year, thousands of tourists visited Machu Picchu.
5. The ancient Egyptians respected the dead.
6. Ancient peoples arranged the stones.

WRITING A DESCRIPTIVE PARAGRAPH

Describe a Place

Top
Middle
Bottom

You described a character and an object. Now you will describe a place, using a graphic organizer like the one on the right.

First, gather sensory details to show readers the physical qualities and mood of the place. Next, put the details in a logical order. One way to arrange the details is to put them in spatial order. This means arranging details from *near to far, left to right, large to small,* or some other spatial way. Pretend to be a movie camera. Use signal words to guide your reader's "eye" from one part of the place to another. Use words such as *close up, in the distance, to the right, above,* and *below.*

Here is a model of a descriptive paragraph that describes a pyramid at Chichén Itzá, Mexico. Notice how the writer uses spatial order to guide your eye from one part of this place to another.

Angelina Xing

Chichén Itzá

The ruins of Chichén Itzá are located on the Yucatan Peninsula of Mexico. As you approach the site, the tallest pyramid, Kukulkan, looks intimidating. It is seventy-nine feet high. When you get closer, you can see the ninety-one original steps that you must climb to get to the top. Before climbing, you can enter an inner temple through a narrow passageway on the north side of the pyramid. Inside is a statue of a scarlet jaguar with eyes made of jade that glow green. Then you can go outside and climb up to the top for a spectacular view of the surrounding ruins. When there is an equinox, crowds of people gather below to see a serpent crawling down the pyramid, an illusion created by the shadow of the sun.

Practice

Write a paragraph that describes a mysterious place. Use a sensory details web like the one on page 29 to gather details. Then use a spatial-order chart to arrange the details. Use the passive voice if you focus on the place as a receiver of an action, for example: *The house was torn down a long time ago.*

WORD CHOICE:

☑ I included details to guide readers from one part of the place to another.

ORGANIZATION:

☑ I put my ideas and details in spatial order.

READING 4

Prepare to Read

What You Will Learn

Reading

- Vocabulary building: *Literary terms, word study, dictionary skills*
- Reading strategy: *Draw conclusions*
- Text type: *Literature (short stories)*

Grammar, Usage, and Mechanics

Subject-verb agreement with indefinite pronouns

Writing

Describe an event

THE BIG QUESTION

Can all mysteries be solved? A detective is someone who solves mysteries for a living. A detective's most important tool is his or her brain. That's because detectives are problem solvers. But what other tools do they use? Work with a partner. How do detectives solve crimes? In your opinion, what is the most important tool they use? Share what you know with the class.

BUILD BACKGROUND

Teenage Detectives contains two short stories about two young detectives who are cousins. Their names are Max and Nina. These characters are fictional, or make-believe, but they act like real detectives. They use realistic tools and clues to solve mysteries.

People read mystery stories like these because they enjoy trying to figure out the mystery. Mystery stories are often called "whodunit" stories. *Whodunit* is a made-up word. Look at it carefully. It really says, "Who done it?" It means, "Who did the crime?" Readers want to find out who committed the crime. How did the detectives solve the mystery? What clues did they use? Read *Teenage Detectives* to discover "whodunit"!

▲ Tools detectives use to find fingerprints

VOCABULARY

Learn Literary Words

Writers often use words in new and exciting ways. The authors of *Teenage Detectives* use **idioms** and **puns** to make their stories funny and interesting to read. Idioms are expressions that have a meaning that is different from the meanings of the individual words that make them up.

In one of the mystery stories in *Teenage Detectives*, the writer says that a character "mopped his brow." The word *brow* means a person's forehead, the part of the head immediately above the eyes. The character didn't really wipe his forehead with a mop. The writer uses this idiom to create a picture.

Like many writers, the authors of *Teenage Detectives* also make jokes with words. To do this, they use a literary tool called a pun. Puns can be formed in two ways. First, a writer can make a pun by using a word that has two meanings. Second, a writer can make a pun by using words that have the same sound but different meanings.

Here's an example of a pun from one of the stories in *Teenage Detectives*. It's the last line of the first story: "'I had *concrete* evidence,' Nina answered." The pun is on the word *concrete*. The word has two meanings. As a noun, *concrete* refers to the material used to make sidewalks. As an adjective, *concrete* means "real." As you read *Teenage Detectives*, look for puns.

Literary Words

idioms
puns

▲ **What does the idiom "a fork in the road" mean?**

Practice

Take turns reading these idioms and puns with a partner. Identify what each idiom means. Explain the humor in the puns.

Idioms
Bees in her bonnet
Flew off the handle
It's a whole new ballgame

Puns
What did the triangle say to the circle? You're so pointless.
The baker stopped making donuts after he got tired of the hole thing.
When a clock is hungry, it goes back for seconds.

Learn Academic Words

Study the **red** words and their meanings. You will find these words useful when talking and writing about literature. Write each word and its meaning in your notebook. After you read *Teenage Detectives*, try to use these words to respond to the text.

Academic Words

aware
intelligent
motive
pursue

aware = realizing that something is true, exists, or is happening	➡	Detectives are **aware** of how criminals act, and they know which clues will help them solve a case.
intelligent = having a high ability to learn, understand, and think about things	➡	Detectives are **intelligent**, which makes them good problem-solvers.
motive = the reason that makes someone do something, especially when this reason is kept hidden	➡	The man's **motive** for stealing was that he didn't have any money for food.
pursue = chase or follow someone or something to catch him, her, or it	➡	The detective had to **pursue** the criminal from one city to another in order to catch him.

Practice

Workbook Page 23

Work with a partner to answer these questions. Try to include the **red** word in your answer. Write the answers in your notebook.

1. How do you become **aware** of world events?
2. Why do archaeologists and detectives both have to be **intelligent**?
3. What **motive** could a criminal have for committing a murder?
4. Is it easier for the police to **pursue** a suspect by car or on foot? Why?

▲ What motive might this man have for hiding in the shadows?

Word Study: Compound Nouns

A compound noun is made up of more than one word. Some are written as one word, as in *airplane* or *courthouse*. Some are written as two words, as in *bubble bath*. Some are written with hyphens between the words, as in *sister-in-law*. Study the examples in the chart below.

One Word	With a Hyphen (-)	Two Words
footprints	take-off	tree house
shortcut	mix-up	boarding pass

New compound nouns are formed in English all the time. Knowing how to divide compound words into their parts helps you spell them and understand what they mean. If you are not sure how to spell a compound noun, check a dictionary. If the compound noun you are looking for is not in a large dictionary, it is spelled as two words.

Practice

Work with a partner. Write two headings in your notebook: *Nouns* and *Compound Nouns*. Copy these words into the Nouns column: *fire*, sun, *eye*, *news*. See how many compound words you can form using these nouns (for example, *firefly*, *sunshine*, *eyelash*, *newspaper*). Write them in the Compound Noun column.

Reading Strategy: DRAW CONCLUSIONS

Drawing conclusions helps you figure out the meanings of clues and events in a text. Good readers are like detectives. They put together the clues until they can draw a conclusion. To draw a conclusion, follow these steps:

- Read until you come to a passage that is hard to understand.
- Ask yourself, "What do I think the author means?"
- Look for clues in the text, and think about what you already know from similar situations that you have read about or experienced.
- Add the clues and what you know together, in order to draw a conclusion about what is happening in the text.

Read the first part of "The Case of the Defaced Sidewalk" on pages 48–49. Stop before you come to the heading "How did Nina figure it out?" Draw a conclusion. Finish reading the story. Was your conclusion correct?

READING 4

LITERATURE

SHORT STORIES

Set a purpose for reading How do Max and Nina solve two detective cases? Look for the types of detective tools they use.

Teenage Detectives

The Case of the Defaced Sidewalk

Carol Farley

Teenage cousins Max and Nina love solving crimes in their town, Harborville. In these short stories, they solve two different cases. See if you notice the same clues the detectives do.

One Saturday morning, Nina saw the three musketeers in the mall. Jenny, Brittany, and Mitzi called themselves the three musketeers because they were always together.

"I've been shopping for sandals," Jenny told Nina. "But I have such a wide foot nothing seems to fit. We've been looking everywhere."

"And it's been slow going," Mitzi added. "On account of Brittany's—"

"I know," Nina said, looking at Brittany. "I heard you sprained your ankle in gym yesterday. Does it still hurt a lot?"

"It's okay as long as I move really slowly," Brittany told her. "We're going to get ice cream at the Just Desserts Shop now. Want to join us?"

"Better not. Max is meeting me at home. See you later."

Nina was taking a shortcut through Harborville's city park when she saw Mr. Hansen kneeling beside a new sidewalk. The city maintenance man frowned as she drew closer.

LITERARY CHECK

What does the ***idiom*** *"taking a shortcut" mean? Use your own words to define it.*

---

three musketeers, characters from the novel *The Three Musketeers* about a group of adventurous young soldiers
sandals, open shoes worn in warm weather
slow going, not happening quickly
sprained, hurt but didn't break
maintenance man, man who fixes and cleans things

"Somebody jumped right in the middle here while the cement was still wet," he said, pointing at two narrow footprints embedded in the concrete. "Now I'll have to rip out this section and redo it. I sure can't leave the sidewalk looking like this!"

"Any idea of who did it?" Nina asked.

"A kid over there on the slide said that three girls named Brittany, Mitzi, and Jenny were the only ones near here. But he doesn't know which one ruined my sidewalk."

"I know who did it," Nina declared.

How did Nina figure it out?

The footprints were narrow. Jenny has wide feet. Brittany couldn't have jumped because of her sprained ankle. So Mitzi had to be the guilty one.

"You were able to walk into a quick solution for this case," Max told Nina later. "I sure am glad that I'm on your side."

"I had concrete evidence," Nina answered.

BEFORE YOU GO ON

1 What happened to Brittany in gym class?

2 Why is Mr. Hansen frowning?

On Your Own What conclusion did you draw about the three girls and "whodunit"?

The Case of the Disappearing Signs

Hy Conrad

Nina was eating cold pizza for lunch at Max's house one hot July day. Max's mom, Mrs. Decker, a real-estate agent, came in looking warm and weary.

"I'm so disgusted," she said. "Remember that old house over on Norton Drive that I listed? I put a FOR SALE sign up in the yard early this morning. I just drove by now and it's gone. This is the third sign this month that has disappeared."

"Why would anyone steal a realtor's signs?" Nina asked. "What would anybody do with them?"

"Who knows?" Mrs. Decker poured herself a glass of lemonade. "Probably some kids with nothing better to do. I suppose they could use the signs to build something. They were the wooden ones."

Max nudged Nina. "Want to bike over and see what we can find out?"

"Not much there to see," his mother told him. "Only two houses on that whole street. An old lady—Mrs. Stearns—lives in the house next to the empty one."

"Maybe she saw something," Nina said. "Let's go ask."

Half an hour later, the two were biking toward the end of Norton Drive. A pick-up truck was parked in front of the empty house. A man was standing on the sidewalk looking in all directions.

---

real-estate agent, person who sells houses
disgusted, upset or angry
listed, advertised; put on a list of items for sale
realtor's signs, signs that advertise that a house is for sale
nudged, pushed someone in a gentle way, using your elbow
pick-up truck, vehicle with an open part at the back, used for carrying things

"Do you kids know anything about this place?" he asked. "I'm from out of town, and my nephew, Paul, has been checking houses for me this past month. He thought I might like the one at the end of Norton Drive, so he let me borrow his truck to drive over here. But I don't know if this is the house he meant. There aren't any signs."

"This house is for sale," Max told him. "My mom is the real-estate agent."

"Great! Then can you tell me her name and company? I'd like to ask about this property. Paul tells me that houses in this part of town sell fast. He says this one has been on the market for quite some time. I'm glad I got here before it was sold! I just couldn't get over here any sooner."

As soon as Max gave him the information, the man drove off.

Nina stared after the truck. "Know what? His nephew, Paul, might have taken the signs. Maybe he didn't want people to see that the house was for sale until his uncle had a chance to look at it. You can put lots of things in the back of a truck."

Max nodded. "Let's ask Mrs. Stearns if she saw anything this morning."

Mrs. Stearns came to the door as soon as they knocked. She was gray-haired, but she stood straight and tall. "Oh, I think I know who might have taken those signs," she told them. "Freddie Swanson. He lives a block away, and he's always up to mischief."

---

on the market, for sale
mischief, bad behavior, especially by children

BEFORE YOU GO ON

1. Who does Mrs. Decker think stole the signs?
2. Why does Nina think that Paul might have stolen the signs?

On Your Own
What motive do you think someone might have for stealing a FOR SALE sign?

She held the door open as she talked, and Nina peeked inside. She liked the cozy living room. The sofa and chairs were velvet-covered antiques. Lace doilies covered the end tables. A large painting hung over the intricately carved fireplace mantel, and a cheerful fire crackled below.

"I know Freddie," Max said. "And I know where he lives. Let's go see him."

Freddie was putting a lawn mower in the garage when they reached his house. He mopped his brow as he talked to them. "Why would I take a dumb old sign?" he asked. "Besides, I've been out here doing yard work all morning."

---

antiques, very old, valuable objects
doilies, small circular mats or napkins
crackled, made popping sounds

Nina stared past him at the garage. Her parents could hardly get their car in her garage at home because of all the stuff in it, but this one was practically bare. Then she noticed a crudely built tree house in the yard. The boards were gray and weather-beaten.

She and Max talked as they biked back to his house. Mrs. Decker was washing the lunch dishes when they ran into the house.

"We think we know who took the signs," Nina told her.

How did Nina and Max figure it out?

There was no evidence to show that Paul had used his truck to transport the signs. The boards in Freddie's tree house were too old and worn to have been made with the signs. Mrs. Stearns had a fire in her fireplace on a hot July day. She didn't want neighbors moving in next door, so she took the signs and burned them in her fireplace so nobody would know the house was for sale.

"That fire was a hot tip," Nina said later as she joined Max and Mrs. Decker for a cold drink of lemonade.

LITERARY CHECK

In this story, why is the phrase "a hot tip" a ***pun****?*

---

practically bare, nearly empty
crudely built, not carefully made
transport, move or carry goods or people from one place to another
a hot tip, a good clue

ABOUT THE AUTHORS

Carol Farley has always loved mysteries. Her first book, *Mystery of the Fog Man,* came from an idea she had in the sixth grade. She has written many books for children, including *The Case of the Vanishing Villain* and *The Case of the Lost Look-Alike.*

Hy Conrad has written ten books of short mysteries, including *Whodunit Crime Mysteries* and *Historical Whodunits.* His books have been translated into over a dozen languages. He has developed board games for major toy companies and is a writer and producer of the television series *Monk.*

BEFORE YOU GO ON

1. What does Nina like about Mrs. Stearns's house?
2. What does Nina notice about Freddie's garage and backyard?

On Your Own
Do you think that fictional mysteries like these two short stories are easier or harder to solve than real-life mysteries? Explain.

READING 4

Review and Practice

READER'S THEATER

Act out the following scene between Max and Nina.

Nina: Which of our cases did you like the best?

Max: Well, I really enjoyed solving the case of the missing signs. It was fun because the clues were difficult to find. This made the mystery more exciting for me. What about your favorite case?

Nina: I liked that case a lot, too. I like how we figured out that it wasn't Freddie. I wouldn't have wanted him to get the blame for something he didn't do.

Max: Being a detective is a lot of fun, especially when we have a chance to help people.

Nina: I enjoyed figuring out who stepped in the cement. This time, we got to protect property rather than people.

Max: That's true. Now people who visit the city park will have a smooth sidewalk to walk on. Being detectives lets us help people in so many ways.

Speaking TIP

Use gestures to help express your character's thoughts and feelings.

COMPREHENSION

Right There

1. Who jumped in the wet concrete?
2. Who stole the FOR SALE signs?

Think and Search

3. What clues did Nina use to solve "The Case of the Defaced Sidewalk"?
4. What motive did Mrs. Stearns have for her actions?

Author and You

5. Why does the author present three possible suspects for each crime? Why do mystery writers make readers suspect more than one character?
6. How can you tell that the authors of *Teenage Detectives* have a sense of humor?

On Your Own

7. Would you like to pursue a career as a detective when you grow up? Why or why not?
8. Some people enjoy puns, while other people think they are silly. What is your opinion of puns? Do you find them funny? Explain.

DISCUSSION

Do not interrupt your classmates when they are speaking. Save your questions until the speaker is finished.

Discuss in pairs or small groups.

1. Do you think Mitzi should have to fix the sidewalk? Why?
2. Can you think of a better way that Mrs. Stearns could have prevented people from moving in next door to her?
3. Mrs. Stearns does not want neighbors. A poet once said: "Good fences make good neighbors." He did not think neighbors should be too friendly. Explain what makes someone a good neighbor. Should neighbors be friendly or not?

Q **Can all mysteries be solved?** Were serious crimes committed in these stories? What is the difference between a minor crime and a serious one? Give examples of each.

RESPONSE TO LITERATURE

Max and Nina solved two mysteries. They used clues and what they already knew. Take one of these stories and change a few of the clues so that the outcome is different. You may want to use a chart like the one below:

Story title:	
Original Clue 1:	New Clue 1:
Original Clue 2:	New Clue 2:
Original Clue 3:	New Clue 3:
Original outcome:	New outcome:

When you are done writing, share your story with a partner. Don't read the ending! See if your partner can figure out the new ending.

Grammar and Writing

GRAMMAR, USAGE, AND MECHANICS

Subject-Verb Agreement with Indefinite Pronouns

Indefinite pronouns are words that don't name a specific person, place, or thing. In the mystery stories you just read, the authors use indefinite pronouns to make generalizations or to refer to a previously used noun.

Generalization:
Why would **anyone** steal a realtor's sign? [non-specific person]

Previously used noun:
Brittany, Mitzi, and Jenny were the only **ones** near here. But he doesn't know which **one** ruined my sidewalk. [*ones* refers to Brittany, Mitzi, AND Jenny; *one* refers to Brittany, Mitzi, OR Jenny]

An indefinite pronoun must agree with the verb in the sentence. An indefinite pronoun is either singular (one person or thing) or plural (more than one person or thing). If the indefinite pronoun is singular, the verb must be singular; if it is plural, the verb must be plural.

Singular			
anybody	somebody	everybody	nobody
anyone	someone	everyone	no one
anything	something	everything	nothing
each	one		

Plural
both
few
many
ones

Practice

Copy the sentences into your notebook. Work with a partner. Circle the verb in each sentence that agrees with the indefinite pronoun.

1. Each (thinks / think) Freddie stole the signs.
2. Everything in the story (is / are) interesting.
3. Someone (was / were) guilty of stepping in the cement.
4. Both (loves / love) solving mysteries.
5. Which ones (uses / use) clues to solve mysteries?
6. No one (was / were) in the house.

WRITING A DESCRIPTIVE PARAGRAPH

Describe an Event

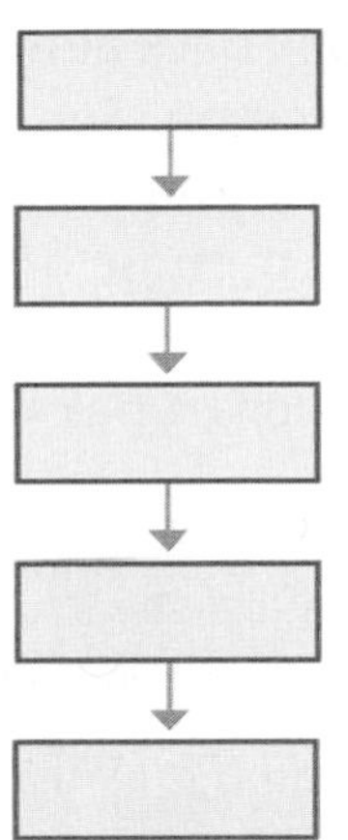

On this page, you will describe a mysterious event using a graphic organizer like the one at the right. Think about the four readings in Unit 1. How did each writer describe puzzling events? Write three headings in your notebook: *Event, People, Place.* Jot down ideas and details under the headings.

One of the simplest ways to organize a description of an event is to put the ideas and details in chronological, or time, order. This means putting the events in the order in which they occurred, from first to last. Use words that help your reader follow each step in the sequence of what happened. These words include *first, second, last, next, then, finally, today,* and *yesterday.*

Here is a model of a descriptive paragraph about a mysterious event. Notice that the writer puts her details in chronological order and includes a pun.

Anna Espínola

The Case of the Missing Hoop

I'm a good detective, but even I had trouble with one case. I bought my sister Sue a striped hula hoop for her birthday this year. First, I hid it in a shopping bag under a pile of old clothes in the closet. Then I decided not to tell anybody because I wanted it to be a big surprise. When Sue's big day came, Mom asked Sue to take some old clothes to our local thrift shop. Finally, I had a chance to wrap the gift, but the hoop had vanished. I looked everywhere but couldn't find it. A week later, I solved the mystery. I was passing the thrift store and saw the hoop in the window for $5. When Sue had dropped off the clothes, she had given away the hoop, too, without knowing it. I bought the hoop again, and gave it to her. Boy did I have to jump through hoops for my sister this year.

VOICE:

☑ My paragraph describes an event in a unique way; it is humorous and includes puns and idioms.

ORGANIZATION:

☑ My paragraph presents details in a clear chronological order.

Practice

Write a descriptive paragraph about a made-up event that puzzled you. Try to include some humor, puns, and idioms. Use a sequence-of-events chart to organize your ideas and details. Check your subject-verb agreement.

Link the Readings

Critical Thinking

Look back at the readings in this unit. Think about what they have in common. They all tell about mysteries. Yet they do not all have the same purpose. The purpose of one reading might be to inform, while the purpose of another might be to entertain or persuade. In addition, the content of each reading relates to mysteries differently. Now copy the chart below into your notebook and complete it.

Title of Reading	Purpose	Big Question Link
From *Chasing Vermeer*		
From *G Is for Googol*	to inform	
"Fact or Fiction?"		
Teenage Detectives		The characters solve mysteries.

Discussion

Discuss in pairs or small groups.

- How is the excerpt from *Chasing Vermeer* different from the excerpt from *G Is for Googol*? How do both readings concern mysteries?

Q **Can all mysteries be solved?** What conclusion can you draw about mysteries in nature, based on what you read in "Fact or Fiction?" and *G Is for Googol*? How are these mysteries the same as fictional mysteries such as the ones in *Teenage Detectives*? How are they different?

Fluency Check

Work with a partner. Choose a paragraph from one of the readings. Take turns reading it for one minute. Count the total number of words you read. Practice saying the words you had trouble reading. Take turns reading the paragraph three more times. Did you read more words each time? Copy the chart below into your notebook and record your speeds.

	1st Speed	2nd Speed	3rd Speed	4th Speed
Words Per Minute				

Projects

Work in pairs or small groups. Choose one of these projects.

1 Create a skit based on *Teenage Detectives*. Choose one of the stories and perform it as a play for the class. You may wish to include simple costumes and music, too.

2 Create a scale model of one of the real-life places described in "Fact or Fiction?" For example, you might construct a model of the Great Pyramid at Giza, Stonehenge, or Machu Picchu. Start by establishing your scale (for example, 1 centimeter equals 5 meters or 1 inch equals 10 feet). Then choose a building material and create your model. Write a description of the mystery on an index card to put with the model.

3 What do you think happens in the next chapter of *Chasing Vermeer*? Tell a classmate what you think will happen in the next chapter. Then read the book to see if your prediction is correct.

4 Draw a picture of something from nature that shows the Fibonacci sequence. You may choose a sunflower or pinecone, for instance. Explain the number sequence to your classmates.

Further Reading

To find out more about the theme of this unit, choose from these reading suggestions.

Stranger than Fiction Urban Myths, Phil Healey and Rick Glanvill
This Penguin Reader® is full of strange, funny, and sometimes unbelievable myths.

The Wright 3, Blue Balliett
In this sequel to *Chasing Vermeer*, Petra, Calder, and a new member of the detective team join forces to save Frank Lloyd Wright's Robie House.

From the Mixed-Up Files of Mrs. Basil E. Frankweiler,
E.L. Konigsburg
Hiding in New York's Museum of Metropolitan Art, a sister and brother spot a beautiful angel statue. Could it be a work by Michelangelo? Mrs. Frankweiler, the statue's previous owner, holds the key to the mystery.

Put It All Together

LISTENING & SPEAKING WORKSHOP

Description Guessing Game

You will describe an object or place and let your classmates guess what it is.

1 THINK ABOUT IT In this unit, you've learned about all kinds of solved and unsolved mysteries. You've also learned how to write descriptions. Now you are going to play a guessing game in which you will describe an object or place related to a crime. Your classmates will act as detectives and try to guess what your object or place is.

In small groups, discuss some of the objects and places discussed in the unit readings. Think of other objects and places that might be related to a crime. Write down your ideas.

Work on your own to make a list of objects and places you could describe in this guessing game. Choose one, and don't tell anyone what it is.

2 GATHER AND ORGANIZE INFORMATION Brainstorm details about the object or place you have chosen. Organize them in a sensory details web.

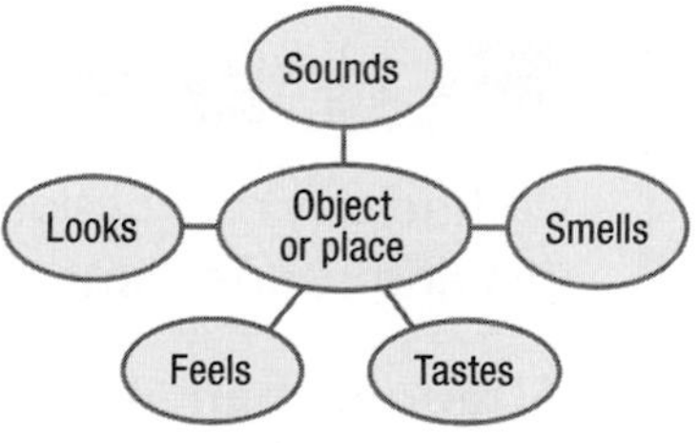

Research Go to the library, look at pictures, or use the Internet to get more information about your object or place. Add the new details to your web.

Order Your Notes Think about how you will describe your object or place to the class. Which details will you include? Write them on separate note cards. Do you want to begin with the most important detail and end with the least important one? Do you want to use spatial order, such as top to bottom or left to right? Select the method of organization that works best with your topic. Put your note cards in that order.

Use Visuals Find or draw a picture of your object or place. You will show it to the class after someone guesses your object or place. Do not show it to anyone now!

▲ Alfred Hitchcock was famous for making mysterious movies.

3 PRACTICE AND PRESENT

Use your note cards as an outline, but practice describing your object or place without reading them. Ask a friend or family member to listen to your presentation, or tape-record yourself and listen to the tape. Find the places where you need more work. Keep practicing until you can present your description smoothly and confidently. Try to include enough details so that the audience can guess your object or place, but not so many that you give away the answer too easily. Remember not to let anyone see your visual.

Deliver Your Description Speak loudly enough so that everyone can hear you. Look at people as you speak. Emphasize key details with your voice and gestures. When you're finished, invite students to guess your topic. After someone guesses correctly, or if no one guesses correctly, show your picture of the object or place.

Speaking TIPS

Be sure you are speaking slowly and clearly. Ask your listeners for feedback. Can they understand all of your words?

Try to stay relaxed and have fun as you give your description. Remember, this is a game!

Listening TIPS

Listen for clues to the speaker's topic. Try to figure out right away if the topic is an object or a place. Then you can get more specific.

Write down key details as you listen. Think about how they relate to objects and places you know.

4 EVALUATE THE PRESENTATION

A good way to improve your skills as a speaker and listener is by evaluating each presentation you give and hear. Use this checklist to help you judge your presentation and the presentations of your classmates.

- ☑ Did the description include lots of sensory details?
- ☑ Could you picture the object or place that was being described?
- ☑ Could you hear and understand what the speaker was saying?
- ☑ Did the speaker seem to be having fun?
- ☑ What suggestions do you have for improving the presentation?

WRITING WORKSHOP

Descriptive Essay

In this workshop you will write a descriptive essay. An essay is a group of paragraphs that develops a specific idea. Most essays include an introduction, two or more body paragraphs, and a conclusion. In a descriptive essay, the writer describes a person, place, thing, event, or experience. Sensory details help create a vivid picture of the topic in readers' minds. Information is presented in an order that makes sense: chronological order, spatial order, or order of importance.

Your assignment for this workshop is to write a five-paragraph descriptive essay about a mysterious and memorable scene that amazed you.

1 PREWRITE Brainstorm possible topics for your essay in your notebook. Choose a topic that is full of sensory details. You might want to describe a spectacular dinosaur exhibit or the best July 4th fireworks display you ever experienced. Or you might want to describe an amusement park or a wax museum.

List and Organize Ideas and Details After you choose a topic, use a graphic organizer such as a sensory details chart or a word web to develop your essay. A student named Talia wrote about what she saw during a visit to Carlsbad Caverns, New Mexico. She used a word web to gather her ideas and details.

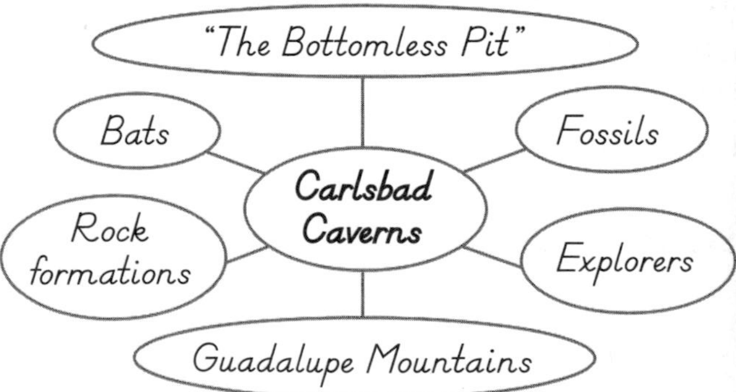

Carlsbad Caverns ▼

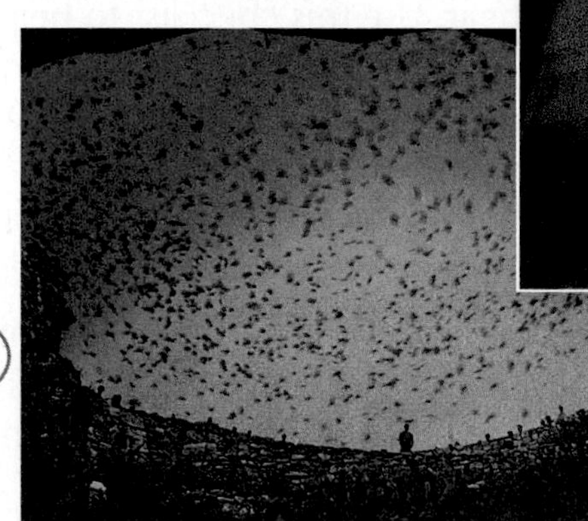

2 DRAFT Use the model on page 65 and your graphic organizer to help you write a first draft. Remember to include an introductory paragraph, three body paragraphs, and a concluding paragraph.

3 **REVISE** Read over your draft. As you do so, ask yourself the questions in the writing checklist. Use the questions to help you revise your essay.

SIX TRAITS OF WRITING CHECKLIST

- ✔ **IDEAS:** Does my essay describe a memorable and mysterious scene?
- ✔ **ORGANIZATION:** Are my ideas presented in an order that makes sense?
- ✔ **VOICE:** Does my writing express who I am?
- ✔ **WORD CHOICE:** Do I include vivid sensory details?
- ✔ **SENTENCE FLUENCY:** Do my sentences flow smoothly?
- ✔ **CONVENTIONS:** Does my writing follow the rules of grammar, usage, and mechanics?

Here are the changes Talia plans to make when she revises her first draft:

Carlsbad Caverns

Imagine ~~you are~~ taking an elevator down into another world—a world where there are stalagmites sticking up in front of you and stalactites hanging from above. [Inside this place,] ~~It's~~ it's ~~more~~ cold[er] and damp[er] than the world you just left. Bats ~~fly~~ [swoop] all around and, if you look hard enough, you might even find the fossil of an ancient sea snail. These are examples of what a traveler might discover on a trip into Carlsbad Caverns.

Although you can find different rock formations in all caves, the ones in Carlsbad Caverns are particularly special. People have given very funny-sounding names to these different formations, because the rocks sometimes look like everyday objects. "Cave Popcorn,"

"Limestone Curtain," and "Bent Straw," are just a few of the oddly shaped rocks in these caves.

All the different "rooms" of the caves also have unique names, like "Mystery Room, "Chocolate High," and "Ballroom Bedroom." The Bottomless Pit got its name when early explorers tossed stones down the hole to see how deep it was. Since the explorers ~~They~~ never heard a sound, they figured the pit didn't have a bottom. Later exploration proved that the pit was only 140 feet deep, but the soft dirt at the bottom muffled the sound of the falling rocks.

Nowadays, lots of bats live in Carlsbad caverns. In addition to rock formations, there are living things and traces of other living things found in the caves The presence of ocean fossils reveals that around 250 million years ago the area was a coastline that eventually turned into a limestone layer of rock. In fact, there are sixteen species of bats, but most are Mexican Free-tailed bats.

Carlsbad Caverns are located in the Guadalupe Mountains in Southeast New Mexico. If you are ever in that area, you will definitely want to check out Carlsbad Caverns. They are as mysterious and memorable as a strange land in an amazing dream.

4 EDIT AND PROOFREAD

Copy your revised essay onto a clean sheet of paper. Read it again. Correct any errors in grammar, word usage, mechanics, and spelling. Here are the additional changes Talia plans to make when she prepares her final draft.

Talia Marcus

Carlsbad Caverns

Imagine taking an elevator down into another world—a world where there are stalagmites sticking up in front of you and stalactites hanging from above. Inside this place, it's colder and damper than the world you just left. Bats swoop all around and, if you look hard enough, you might even find the fossil of an ancient sea snail. These are examples of what a traveler might discover on a trip into Carlsbad Caverns.

Although you can find different rock formations in all caves, the ones in Carlsbad Caverns are particularly special. People have given very funny-sounding names to these different formations, because the rocks sometimes look like everyday objects. "Cave Popcorn," "Limestone Curtain," and "Bent Straw," are just a few of the oddly shaped rocks in these caves.

All the different "rooms" of the caves also have unique names, like "Mystery Room," "Chocolate High," and "Ballroom Bedroom." The Bottomless Pit got its name when early explorers tossed stones down the hole to see how deep it was. Since the explorers never heard a sound, they figured the pit didn't have a bottom. Later exploration proved that the pit was only 140 feet deep, but the soft dirt at the bottom muffled the sound of the falling rocks.

In addition to rock formations, there are living things and traces of other living things found in the caves. The presence of ocean fossils reveals that around 250 million years ago the area was a coastline that eventually turned into a limestone layer of rock. Nowadays, lots of bats live in Carlsbad caverns. In fact, there are sixteen species of bats, but most are Mexican Free-tailed bats.

Carlsbad Caverns are located in the Guadalupe Mountains in Southeast New Mexico. If you are ever in that area, you will definitely want to check out Carlsbad Caverns. They are as mysterious and memorable as a strange land in an amazing dream.

5 PUBLISH Prepare your final draft. Share your essay with your teacher and classmates.

Learn about Art with the

Smithsonian American Art Museum

Solving the PUZZLE of Letters and NUMBERS

Most of us have seen movies in which someone must figure out a code. Sometimes the character has to find a treasure. Other times he or she might have to use the code to save a friend. Often the code uses letters. We can recognize the letters but not the words they spell. They make no sense until we figure out the pattern of the code.

Some American artists even hide coded messages or stories in their work. They like to use them because the codes add a little mystery and fun!

Mike Wilkins, *Preamble* (1987)

When you look at them one by one, none of the license plates in Mike Wilkins's *Preamble* makes much sense. The trick is to read the license plates from left to right, starting in the top left corner. By the end of the first line, you realize that Wilkins is composing the preamble to the United States Constitution. The letters on the first two license plates, WE TH and P PUL, stand for the words "We the People . . . " LIBBER is part of the word "Liberty."

The plates are listed in alphabetical order by state, with Alabama first and Wyoming last. Wilkins put the license plates against a large square background.

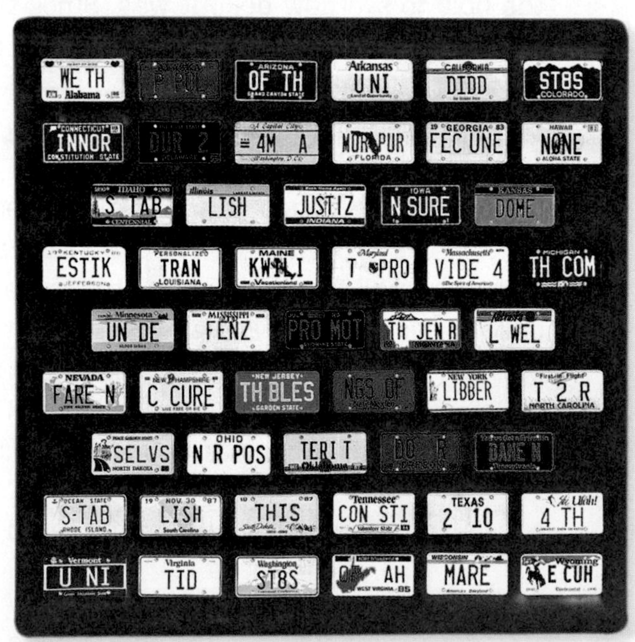

▲ Mike Wilkins, *Preamble*, 1987, metal, 96 x 96 in., Smithsonian American Art Museum

The background brings all the license plates together into one work of art. It also highlights the differences in color between the plates.

It took a year for Wilkins to get license plates from all fifty states and the District of Columbia. He had to figure out word and number combinations that worked together to form the preamble. Each state has different laws about the number of letters and numbers that could be used on a plate. Eventually, Wilkins put this rebus (a puzzle that uses letters and numbers) together. This artwork celebrates the way the fifty states and the capital work together to form the United States.

▲ Robert Indiana, *Five*, 1984, wood beam, 69⅛ x 26¾ x 18½ in., Smithsonian American Art Museum

Robert Indiana, *Five* (1984)

The artist Robert Indiana based *Five* on a poem called "The Great Figure," which is about a fire truck. He used objects that people had thrown away, like an old wood beam from a house. He also used a wooden dowel (the pole running through the beam) and two metal wheels to make the sculpture. At the top of the beam, he painted a small number 5 and a larger 5 over a red five-point star. They all come together to form one image.

Indiana's color choices seem bright when seen against the dull wood beam. He liked to use letters and numbers to make the printed portions of his work look as though they were part of a commercial sign. The red letter *L* on the very top adds to the idea that there is some mystery or story going on that we must figure out. In the same way that we would read a road sign, we must study how all of the various shapes and colors work with each other to create a "story" or message.

As a boy, Indiana spent a lot of time on the highway. He loved the way road signs play with numbers, letters, and bright colors to capture people's attention. Think about some of the signs you see every day on streets and highways: STOP, 55 MPH, YIELD.

The best codes and rebuses force you to use old images in new ways. They celebrate the mystery and beauty of shapes and the way those shapes work together when placed in unexpected patterns.

Apply What You Learned

1. How do both Mike Wilkins and Robert Indiana use codes in their artworks?
2. In what way are both of these artworks related to cars and other kinds of vehicles?

Big Question
How would you make artwork with a mystery or puzzle? Would you want viewers to be able to solve the mystery or puzzle? Why?

Workbook
Pages 31–32

UNIT 2

How does growing up change us?

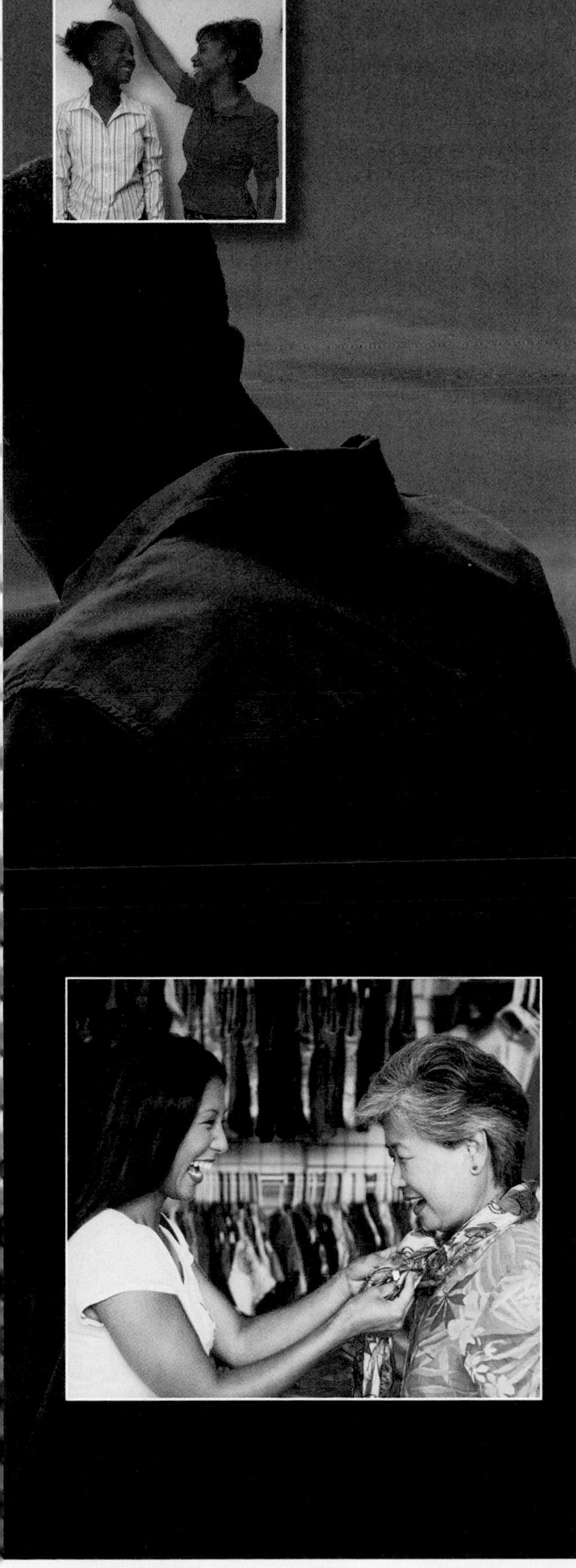

This unit is about what happens to people, plants, and animals as they grow and change. You will read about growing up in three ancient cultures and fun facts about plant and animal growth. You will read novel excerpts and a folk tale about conflicts within families and lessons family members teach one another. As you explore growing up, you will grow as a reader and practice the academic and literary language you need to use in school.

READING 1: Social Studies Article

- "Ancient Kids"

READING 2: Novel Excerpt

- From *Becoming Naomi León* by Pam Muñoz Ryan

READING 3: Novel Excerpt

- From *Later, Gator* by Laurence Yep

READING 4: Science Article and Folk Tale

- "Amazing Growth Facts"
- "The Old Grandfather and His Little Grandson" by Leo Tolstoy

Listening and Speaking

At the end of this unit, you will perform a skit about ancient kids.

Writing

In this unit you will practice **narrative writing**. This type of writing tells a story. After each reading you will learn a skill to help you write a narrative paragraph. At the end of this unit, you will write an essay-length fictional narrative.

QuickWrite

In your notebook, write several sentences about your first day in school. Who was your teacher? What happened?

Visit *LongmanKeystone.com*

READING 1 Prepare to Read

What You Will Learn

Reading

- Vocabulary building: *Context, dictionary skills, word study*
- Reading strategy: *Compare and contrast*
- Text type: *Informational text (social studies)*

Grammar, Usage, and Mechanics

Showing contrast: transitions and coordinating conjunctions

Writing

Write a friendly letter

THE BIG QUESTION

How does growing up change us? What is daily life like for children growing up today? How do children get an education? What sports do they play and watch? What games and toys do they like to play with? Which animals do they keep as pets? Work with a partner. Copy these headings: *Education*, *Sports*, *Games*, and *Pets* into your notebook. List your ideas under each heading. Then share what you know with the class.

BUILD BACKGROUND

"Ancient Kids" describes children's lives thousands of years ago in three different cultures. It tells about growing up among the ancient Greeks, Romans, and Maya. Ancient Greece was a great civilization from around 2000 to 146 B.C.E. The Greeks created the first democracy, or government by the people. They left behind beautiful architecture, sculptures, and vase paintings. They also wrote works of literature and philosophy that are still read today.

Rome became powerful after Greece (and remained so up to 476 C.E.). The Romans made important contributions in the areas of building, medicine, and government. They built more than 80 million meters (50,000 mi.) of roads. Many are still used to this day. They also had a government with three branches.

The ancient Maya established a great civilization in southern Mexico and Central America from 1000 B.C.E. to 1550 C.E. They made accurate studies of the stars, planets, sun, and moon. They had their own calendar, mathematical system, and form of writing. They built remarkable stone temples that are still standing.

Knucklebones was a popular ancient game, played with five small objects made from ankle joints of small animals. ▶

VOCABULARY

Learn Key Words

Read these sentences. Use the context to figure out the meaning of the **red** words. Use a dictionary to check your answers. Then write each word and its meaning in your notebook.

1. Studying **ancient** cultures, or cultures from thousands of years ago, helps us learn about ourselves.
2. At a wedding **ceremony**, people celebrate a marriage.
3. The girl learned what was expected of her and became a good **citizen**.
4. Long ago, boys and girls did not get the same type of **education**. They learned different things.
5. In the past, women did not have many **rights**. They could not vote or own property.
6. People long ago had **rituals**, including specific songs and dances, to celebrate important events.

Key Words

ancient
ceremony
citizen
education
rights
rituals

Practice

Work with a partner to answer these questions. Try to include the **red** word in your answer. Write the sentences in your notebook.

1. What are three objects that we use today that **ancient** people didn't have?
2. What would you expect to happen at a graduation **ceremony**?
3. What are some rules a **citizen** has to follow in the United States?
4. Which subjects are important to your **education** at school?
5. What **rights** do you think are most important? Why?
6. What **rituals** does your family perform to celebrate a birthday?

This ancient Greek vase shows a ceremony honoring an important man. ▶

Learn Academic Words

Study the **red** words and their meanings. You will find these words useful when talking and writing about informational texts. Write each word and its meaning in your notebook. After you read "Ancient Kids," try to use these words to respond to the text.

Academic Words
- classical
- cultural
- feature
- philosophy

classical = belonging to the culture of ancient Greece or ancient Rome	➡	**Classical** plays from thousands of years ago are still performed in large, outdoor theaters in Greece and Rome.
cultural = relating to a particular society and its way of life	➡	Creating art, music, and literature are **cultural** activities.
feature = quality, element, or characteristic of something that seems important, interesting, or typical	➡	A special **feature** of Maya culture is its system of writing.
philosophy = the study of what it means to exist, what good and evil are, what knowledge is, or how people should live	➡	People still read ancient Greek **philosophy** today. They learn how people thought and what they valued.

Practice

Work with a partner to answer these questions. Try to include the **red** word in your answer. Write the sentences in your notebook.

1. Where might you look to see **classical** art from long ago?
2. What part of American **cultural** life do you know most about? Do you know about music, art, or literature?
3. What is a unique **feature** of your school? What makes it different from other schools?
4. Why do you think people study **philosophy**?

Classical plays were performed in theaters like this one. ▼

Socrates taught philosophy in ancient Greece. ▶

Word Study: Spelling Words with Long Vowel Sound /ē/

In English, the long vowel sound /ē/ can be spelled in many different ways. For example, when you read "Ancient Kids," you will read the words in the first row of the chart below. Say each word with a partner. Notice the /ē/ sound and its spelling. Study the rest of the chart for more examples.

e	ee	ea	ie	y	ey
evil	Gr**ee**ce	wr**ea**ths	marr**ie**d	bab**y**	journ**ey**
h**e**	fr**ee**	tr**ea**t	f**ie**lds	lad**y**	hon**ey**
r**e**do	wh**ee**ls	l**ea**ve	bur**ie**d	ceremon**y**	mon**ey**

Practice

Work with a partner. Copy the chart above into your notebook. Say a word from the chart, and ask your partner to spell it aloud. Then have your partner say the next word. Continue until you can spell all of these words correctly. Now spell the words in the box below and add them to the chart under the correct headings. Circle the letters that stand for /ē/.

bead	families	philosophy	studied	valley
even	geese	response	treat	vary

READING STRATEGY COMPARE AND CONTRAST

Comparing and contrasting helps you to understand what you read more clearly. When you compare, you see how things are similar. When you contrast, you see how things are different. To compare and contrast, follow these steps:

- Look for words the author uses to show that things are similar, such as *alike, also, too, in the same way,* and *likewise.*
- Look for words the author uses to show that things are different, such as *one main difference, but, however, yet, unlike,* and *opposite.*
- Use a graphic organizer to list your comparisons and contrasts.

As you read "Ancient Kids," compare and contrast the Greek, Roman, and Maya cultures.

READING 1

INFORMATIONAL TEXT

SOCIAL STUDIES

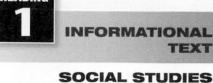

Set a purpose for reading Compare and contrast what it was like growing up among the ancient Greeks, Romans, and Maya. How did each culture treat children differently? What is different about growing up today?

ANCIENT KIDS

Growing Up in Ancient Greece

ANCIENT GREECE

2000 B.C.E. 146 B.C.E. 0 2000 C.E.

When a baby was born in ancient Greece, the father performed a ritual. He did a dance, holding the newborn baby. For boy babies, the family decorated the house with wreaths of olives. For girl babies, the family decorated the house with wreaths made of wool.

There were many differences in the lives of boys and girls as they grew up. One main difference was that girls did not go to school and boys did. Some girls learned to play musical instruments.

Mostly, girls helped their mothers with chores in the house or in the fields. They didn't leave their houses very often. Sometimes they went to festivals or funerals. They also visited neighbors.

Girls stayed home with their parents until they got married. Girls' fathers usually decided whom the girls would marry.

▲ Some girls learned to read and write at home.

---

decorated, made it look more attractive by adding things to it
wreaths, circles made from flowers, plants, or leaves
instruments, objects used for making music
chores, small jobs

Boys stayed home until they were six or seven years old. They helped grow crops in the fields, and they learned to sail boats and to fish.

When boys were about seven years old, they started their formal education. They went to school and learned reading, writing, and mathematics. They had to memorize everything because there were no school books! They memorized the poetry of Homer, a famous poet. They also learned to play a musical instrument, such as the lyre.

At school, boys learned about the arts and war. They also learned how to be good citizens. At the age of eighteen, boys went to military school for two years.

Children played with many toys, such as rattles, clay animals, pull-toys on four wheels, yo-yos, and terra-cotta dolls. Children also had pets, such as birds, dogs, goats, tortoises, and mice.

▲ **A student and his teacher working together**

---

crops, wheat, corn, fruit, and so on, that a farmer grows
formal education, education in a subject or skill that you get in school rather than by practical experience
lyre, ancient instrument, similar to a guitar
military school, school where students learn to fight in wars
terra-cotta, baked red clay
tortoises, land animals that move very slowly, with a hard shell covering their bodies

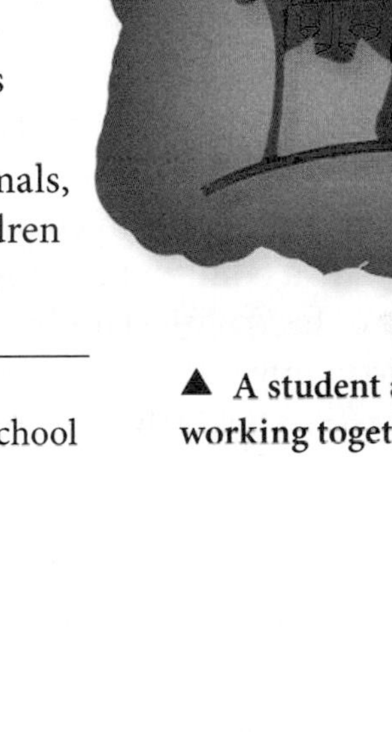

◀ **People placed these clay figures in the graves of children to keep them company in the afterlife.**

BEFORE YOU GO ON

1. How were boys' lives different from girls' lives in ancient Greece?
2. What toys did children play with?

On Your Own
Did your family have any special ceremonies when you were born? Describe them.

Growing Up in Ancient Rome

ANCIENT ROME

753 B.C.E. — 0 — 476 C.E. — 2000 C.E.

ANCIENT GREECE

2000 B.C.E. — 146 B.C.E. — 0 — 2000 C.E.

When a Roman baby was born, a relative put the baby at the feet of the father. The father picked up the baby to accept it into the family. The baby was named nine days after birth.

The oldest man in a family—the father, the grandfather, or an uncle—was the "head of the family." However, women were also important to family life. They managed the house and household finances. In the early years of ancient Rome, women did not have many rights. In later years, they had more rights. They were allowed to own land and to have some types of jobs. They could manage some businesses, but they were still not allowed to hold jobs in the government or to become lawyers or teachers.

Girls and boys wore a special locket, called a *bulla*, around their necks. The bulla protected them from evil. A girl wore the bulla until her wedding day. A boy wore the bulla until he became a citizen. A boy became a citizen at age sixteen or seventeen. The family had a big celebration on this day.

Some Greeks lived in southern Italy and Sicily. The ancient Greeks had a cultural influence on the Romans. Greek teachers introduced the Romans to the Greek gods and goddesses and to Greek literature and philosophy.

▲ **Roman children dressed like their parents. They wore long shirts called tunics.**

Marble heads of a ▼ Roman girl and boy

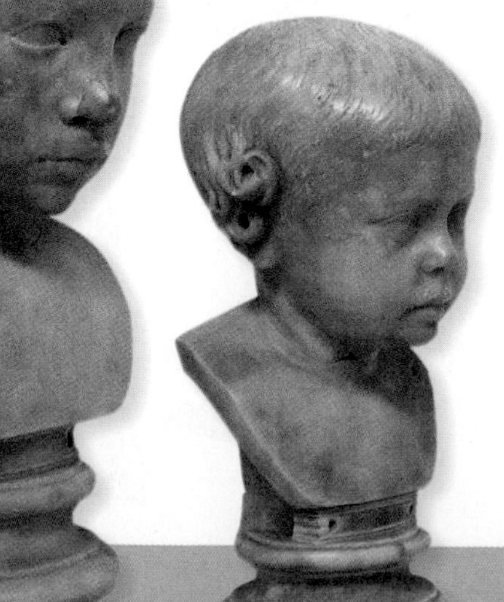

---

head of the family, person who is in charge of the family
managed, controlled or directed
finances, money matters
locket, piece of jewelry like a small round box in which you put a picture of someone
influence, effect

▲ Glass and clay marbles

School was not free. Most children in ancient Rome were not from rich families. They were poor. In poor families, parents taught their children at home. Many poor children did not learn to read or write.

Rich families sent their children to school at age seven to learn basic subjects. Girls did not continue in school after they learned the basic subjects. They stayed at home, where their mothers taught them how to be good wives and mothers.

Boys from rich families continued their education in formal schools or with **tutors**. They became lawyers or worked in government.

What did children do after school? They played with friends, pets, or toys. Toys included balls, hobbyhorses, kites, **models** of people and animals, hoops, **stilts**, marbles, and knucklebones. War games were popular with boys. Girls played with dolls. They also played board games, tic-tac-toe, and ball games.

What kind of pets did children play with in ancient Rome? Dogs were the favorite pets. Roman children also kept birds—pigeons, ducks, **quail**, and geese—as pets. Some children even had pet monkeys.

---

tutors, teachers of one student or a small group of students
models, small copies
stilts, a pair of poles to stand on, used for walking high above the ground
quail, small fat birds that are hunted and shot for food and sport

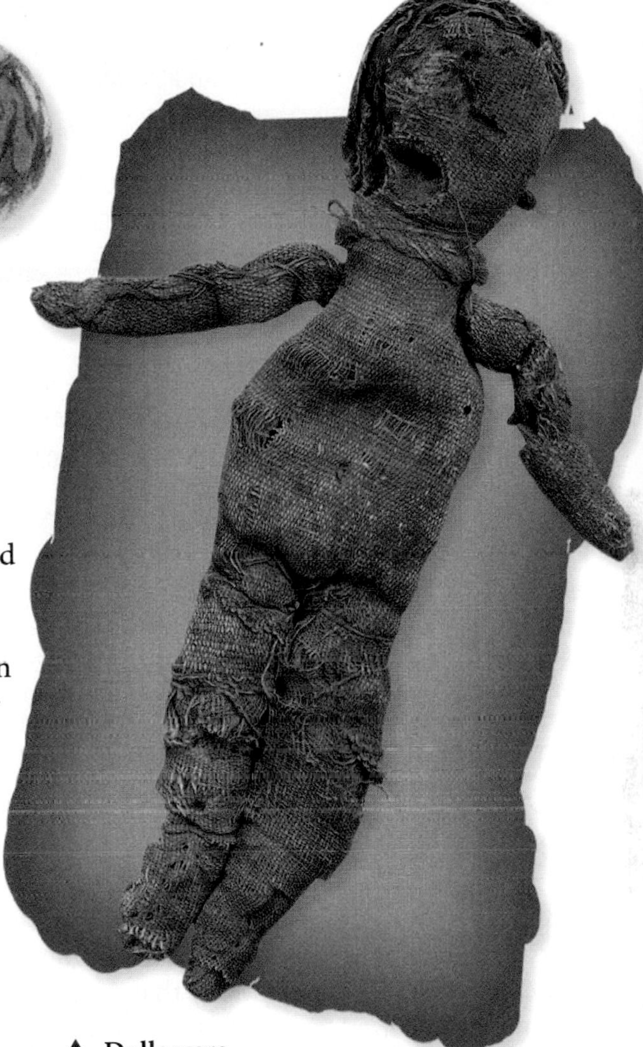

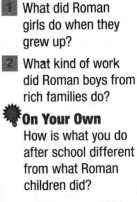

▲ Dolls were popular toys.

BEFORE YOU GO ON

1. What did Roman girls do when they grew up?
2. What kind of work did Roman boys from rich families do?

On Your Own
How is what you do after school different from what Roman children did?

Growing Up in the Ancient Maya Culture

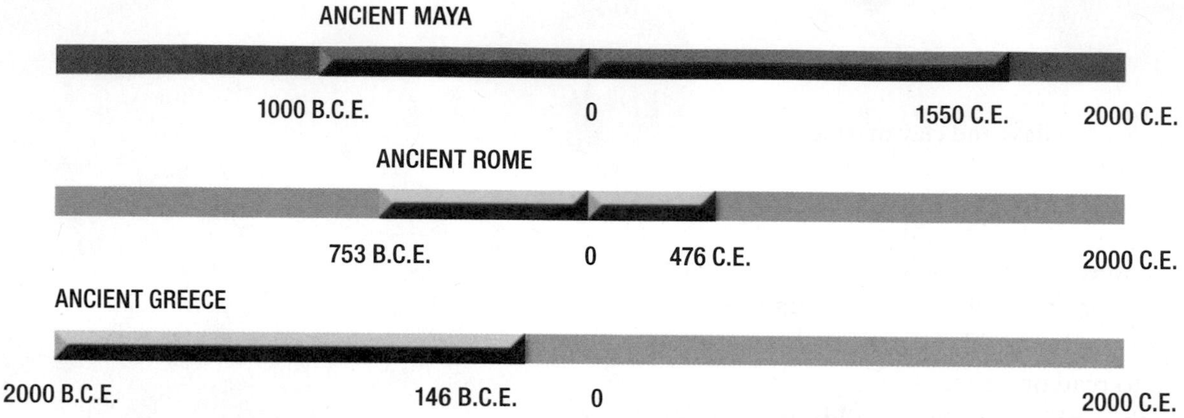

The Maya lived throughout parts of southern Mexico and Central America, including Belize and Guatemala. They built large cities and created extraordinary art and architecture. You can visit the ruins of some ancient Maya cities, such as Chichén Itzá in Mexico's Yucatan region.

In Maya culture, the father was the head of the family. Maya men worked hard to support their families, and they paid taxes to the government. Women in Maya society cooked, made cloth, sewed clothing, and took care of the children.

When a boy was about five years old, the Maya tied a small white bead to the top of his head. When a girl was about five, the Maya tied a red shell around her waist. When boys and girls were twelve or thirteen years old, the village had a big ceremony that marked the end of childhood. During the ceremony, a priest cut the beads from the boys' heads. Mothers removed the red shells from the girls' waists. After the ceremony, boys and girls could get married. Young men painted themselves black until they were married.

Maya boys and girls, unlike Roman children, did not have to pay to go to school. They learned from their parents, too. Girls learned

All women did some weaving and spinning. They made things for their families and to sell. ▼

---

ruins, parts of buildings that are left after other parts have been destroyed
taxes, money that must be given

◀ This Maya vase shows a jaguar.

▲ A toy dog on wheels

how to weave and cook. Boys learned to hunt and fish. Children also learned how to grow crops, such as corn. At age seventeen, boys joined the army to learn about war and fighting.

Children played games and they played with toys. Some of their toys had wheels. Surprisingly, the Maya did not use wheels in their work or transportation. However, toys, such as animal pull-toys, had wheels.

Animals were important in everyday life and religion. The Maya used animals in their art. They decorated various items with pictures of foxes, owls, jaguars, hummingbirds, eagles, and other animals. The Maya sometimes ate dogs, but they mainly used dogs for hunting. The Maya thought that dogs could guide people on the journey to the afterlife. This is why they buried dogs with their owners.

---

jaguars, large wild cats with black spots
guide, show the way to
afterlife, life that some people believe you have after death

BEFORE YOU GO ON

1. What are three modern-day countries where the ancient Maya lived?
2. Why did Maya boys and girls have a special ceremony when they turned twelve or thirteen?

On Your Own
What would you have enjoyed about growing up among the Maya?

READING 1 Review and Practice

COMPREHENSION

Right There

1. What pets did the children of ancient Greece have?
2. What did Greek teachers introduce to the Romans?

Think and Search

3. Who taught ancient Maya girls how to weave and cook?
4. What did both six-year-old girls and boys in ancient Greece do?

Author and You

5. Why do you think grown-ups in all three cultures had toys for their children?
6. What do you think was the most important feature of education in ancient Rome?

On Your Own

7. Do you think that cultural activities are as important today as they were in ancient times? Why?
8. What do you think makes a person well educated? What do you think people should learn in school?

IN YOUR OWN WORDS

Summarize the reading. Use the topics and vocabulary below to tell a partner about growing up among the Greeks, Romans, and Maya.

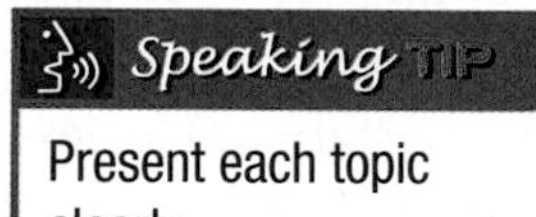

Present each topic clearly.

Ancient Greeks	Ancient Romans	Ancient Maya
The Birth of a Baby	The Birth of a Baby	Life for Men and Women
Education for Boys	Women's Rights	Ceremonies
Education for Girls	Education for Boys	Education for Boys
Learning to Play Music	Education for Girls	Education for Girls
Toys	Toys	Toys
Pets	Pets	Animals

DISCUSSION

Discuss in pairs or small groups.

1. What are some examples of ceremonies in "Ancient Kids"? What ceremonies are important to family life today?
2. Which ancient society would you have wanted to grow up in—the Greek, Roman, or Maya culture? Why?
3. Why do you think education is important for children?

Q **How does growing up change us?** Compare and contrast what it was like growing up in ancient cultures to growing up today. What is different for kids today? What is similar?

Listening TIP

Respect each speaker. Listen politely, even if you disagree with the speaker's ideas.

READ FOR FLUENCY

When we read aloud to communicate meaning, we group words into phrases, pause or slow down to make important points, and emphasize important words. Pause for a short time when you reach a comma and for a longer time when you reach a period. Pay attention to rising and falling intonation at the end of sentences.

Work with a partner. Choose a paragraph from the reading. Discuss which words seem important for communicating meaning. Practice pronouncing difficult words. Give each other feedback.

EXTENSION

In "Ancient Kids" you learned about growing up long ago. Choose any one of the three cultures you read about. Think about what features of the culture you would like to research. For example, you could read more about ancient Greek games like knucklebones or find out about an ancient Maya ballgame called pok-a-tok. Select a cultural feature to research. Then use encyclopedias, books, and the Internet to find the information. Share the information with your classmates.

▲ The ancient Maya played pok-a-tok on large ball courts.

Grammar and Writing

GRAMMAR, USAGE, AND MECHANICS

Showing Contrast: Transitions and Coordinating Conjunctions

When you want to contrast two things in your writing, transitions and coordinating conjunctions can help you. Certain transitions and coordinating conjunctions point out differences.

Study the charts and explanations below. Notice that transitions begin the sentences, but coordinating conjunctions join two sentences. Use a comma (,) after a transition and before a coordinating conjunction.

Transitions	Coordinating Conjunctions
The oldest man was the "head of the family." **However,** women were also important to family life.	The Maya sometimes ate some dogs, **but** they used most dogs for hunting.
The Maya did not use wheels in their work or transportation. **On the other hand,** toys, such as animal pull-toys, had wheels.	Women could manage some businesses, **yet** they were still not allowed to hold jobs in the government.

Practice

Work with a partner. Copy the sentence starters in Column A into your notebook. Find the contrasting idea in Column B that best completes each sentence. Finish writing each sentence in your notebook.

Column A	Column B
1. The father was the head of the family, yet	they were also eaten.
2. Animals were kept as pets. However,	they still had time for fun.
3. Children worked hard in school, but	women had some rights.
4. A girl learned to weave and cook, but	Greek girls did not.
5. Greek boys went to school. However,	a boy learned to hunt and fish.

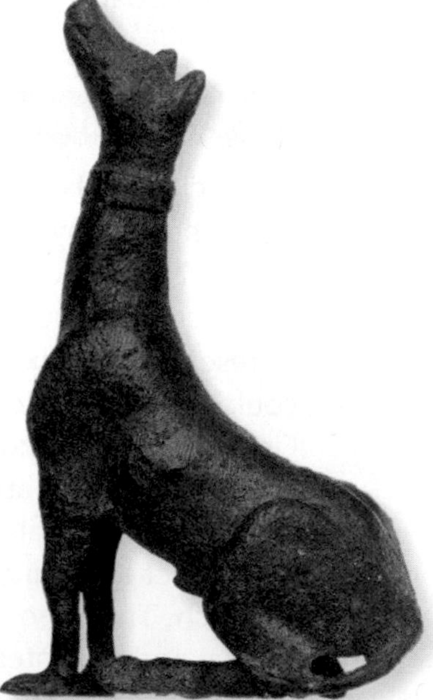

▲ A statue of a Roman guard dog

WRITING A NARRATIVE PARAGRAPH

Write a Friendly Letter

On this page, you'll write a narrative paragraph in the form of a friendly letter. You'll use a graphic organizer like the one at the right to help you put your narrative paragraph into a letter format.

A narrative is a real or make-believe story that describes characters and events. When writers tell stories, they include ideas, memories, and sensory details to make the story interesting. Sometimes people tell a memorable story in a friendly letter. A friendly letter has five parts: the date, the greeting (or salutation), the body, the closing, and the signature.

Here is a model of a friendly letter written by a student named Tyler Welsh. Notice how the writer tells his grandfather a sequence of events in time order.

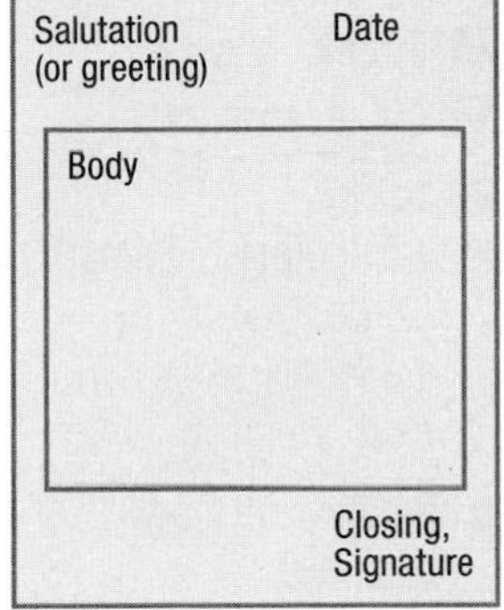

July 23, 2009

Dear Grandpa,

Did I ever tell you how being in my school play helped me overcome stage fright? I was only six years old, and I didn't really enjoy performing in front of others. All week, my class and I practiced hard, but I couldn't get over my fear. Then, on the night of the play, I was so nervous! When I walked on stage, I had the urge to run away. The heat from the stage lighting was almost unbearable. During the performance, I felt as if the eyes of everyone in the audience were glaring at me. Yet I performed well, even though I was really nervous. Afterwards, I felt an amazing sense of accomplishment. Since you saw the play, I wanted to share my memory of that night with you.

Love,

Tyler

Practice

Write a friendly letter to an older family member. Tell a story about an event that occurred when you were younger. Use the "parts of a letter" organizer to put your story into the correct format. Tell your story in time order. Use transitions and coordinating conjunctions if you want to contrast two things.

Writing Checklist

WORD CHOICE:

☑ I included vivid sensory details and memories in my narrative.

ORGANIZATION:

☑ I put my narrative in time order.

READING 2 Prepare to Read

What You Will Learn

Reading

- Vocabulary building: *Literary terms, dictionary skills, word study*
- Reading strategy: *Visualize*
- Text type: *Literature (novel excerpt)*

Grammar, Usage, and Mechanics
Non-action verbs

Writing
Write about a character and setting

THE BIG QUESTION

How does growing up change us? What kinds of families do children grow up in? Some grow up in large families, with two parents, a grandparent, and many children. Others grow up in small families, with one parent and one or two children. Sometimes children are raised by their grandparents, aunts, or uncles.

Work with a partner. Talk about the kinds of families you know about from your own experience and from stories in books and on TV. In your notebook, draw a picture of a family from a TV show or a book. Label the members of the family using words such as *mother, father, sister, brother, aunt, uncle, grandmother, grandfather, stepmother, or stepfather.* Discuss how our families influence who we become.

BUILD BACKGROUND

Becoming Naomi León is a realistic novel—a fictional narrative about events that could happen in everyday life. The main character, Naomi Soledad León Outlaw, lives in Lemon Tree, California—in a whale-like trailer called Baby Beluga. She and her younger brother, Owen, have been well cared for by Gram, their great-grandmother, ever since their mother left them seven years ago. Despite Gram's loving care, Naomi often feels unhappy. To cheer herself up, she writes lists and carves beautiful objects out of soap. In the novel excerpt, you will read about Naomi's reunion with her father in Oaxaca, Mexico.

Oaxaca is a city in southern Mexico. The people there hold a radish-carving festival every year in which they make many lovely sculptures out of radishes. After reading the novel excerpt, you may want to try carving, too. A how-to piece called "Soap Carving" will tell you how.

A radish carving ▶

VOCABULARY

Learn Literary Words

In fiction, you can learn a lot about a character by paying attention to what the character says. **Dialogue** is the exact words spoken by two or more characters. Writers use dialogue to reveal what the characters in a story are like. Often, dialogue makes the characters seem like real people.

Read the examples of dialogue below. They are from *Becoming Naomi León*. Notice that each bit of dialogue begins and ends with quotation marks ("__").

Literary Words
dialogue
setting

"I will go with you," said Santiago, and they headed towards the garden.
"Do not be sad," he whispered.

Another important part of a story is the **setting**—the time and place where the narrative occurs. Identifying the setting will help you better understand what is happening in a story. Sometimes writers state the setting directly. In other cases, you must use clues to figure out where the narrative takes place. Clues might include details about the type of clothing, houses, land, weather, time of day, and transportation.

Practice

Work with a partner. Take turns reading each setting aloud. First, identify the time—past, present, or future—of the setting. Then identify the place.

Type of Literature	Setting
Mystery story	Joe walked down a dark road on the edge of town. It was raining hard and flashes of lightning lit up the deserted house at the end of the street. Joe heard a clock strike midnight and a dog howl in the distance. He took out his cell phone, but the battery was dead.
Science fiction novel	In the year 3050, a strange yellow aircraft landed on Earth. Two huge insect-like creatures stepped out. They waved their many legs in the air but did not speak.
Historical novel	In the 1850s, I met a woman who ran a big cattle ranch in Texas. She used to ride into town on a palomino pony, wearing a big leather hat and a long cotton skirt.

Learn Academic Words

Study the **red** words and their meanings. You will find these words useful when talking and writing about literature and informational texts. Write each word and its meaning in your notebook. After you read the excerpt from *Becoming Naomi León,* try to use these words to respond to the text.

Academic Words

assist
bond
conflict
process

assist = help someone do something	➡	Grandparents sometimes **assist** parents with child care.
bond = a feeling or interest that unites two or more people or groups	➡	Children usually feel a strong **bond** with their parents.
conflict = disagreement	➡	The two friends solved their **conflict** by discussing their disagreement openly.
process = a series of actions that someone does in order to achieve a particular result	➡	There are many steps in the **process** of writing a story.

Practice

Write the sentences in your notebook. Choose a **red** word from the box above to complete each sentence. Then take turns reading the sentences aloud with a partner.

1. We want this _______ between the two countries to be settled right away. Otherwise, the two countries may go to war.
2. Brothers and sisters often have a close _______. They feel attached to each other.
3. My friend from Oaxaca explained the steps involved in the _______ of carving radishes.
4. I often _______ my aunt when she is caring for her son. I help her make his lunch.

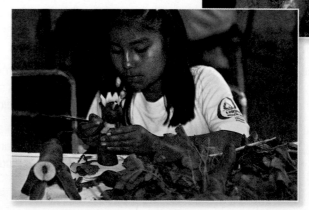

A young girl in the process of carving radishes ▶

Word Study: Suffixes *-ness*, *-tion*, and *-ation*

A suffix is a letter or a group of letters placed at the end of a base word. A suffix can change a word's part of speech and its meaning. Sometimes when a suffix that begins with a vowel is added to a base word that ends in a vowel, the last letter is dropped from the base word. Study the examples in the chart below. The letter *e* in the verb *admire* is dropped before adding the suffix *-ation*.

Word	Suffix	New Word
fierce (adjective)	-ness	fierceness (noun)
admire (verb)	-ation	admiration (noun)
consider (verb)	-ation	consideration (noun)

Practice

Copy the chart below into your notebook. Work with a partner. Add the suffix to the end of the word to create a new word. Check the dictionary to make sure that you have written the word correctly. Write the word in the chart.

Word	Suffix	New Word
good (adjective)	-ness	(noun)
imagine (verb)	-ation	(noun)
transport (verb)	-ation	(noun)

Reading Strategy VISUALIZE

Visualizing helps you understand what the author wants you to see. When you visualize, you make pictures in your mind. To visualize what you are reading, follow these steps:

- Read the text, such as these sentences from *Becoming Naomi León:*

  Tied to the branches with transparent fishing line, the carved wooden animals appeared suspended. When a warm breeze tickled the dragons, reptiles, birds, and lions, they twirled and swayed.
- Now, close your eyes and visualize what you read. What do you see?
- As you read, look for descriptive words the author uses.

As you read the excerpt from *Becoming Naomi León*, ask yourself, "What words help me create a picture of what things look like and what is happening?"

READING 2

LITERATURE

NOVEL

Set a purpose for reading Naomi is reunited with her father in Oaxaca after many years. How does the experience change her?

from

Becoming Naomi León

Pam Muñoz Ryan

Life changes when eleven-year-old Naomi's mother, Skyla, comes back and tries to obtain custody of Naomi. Gram and the children flee in their trailer, Baby Beluga, to Oaxaca in search of the children's father, hoping that he will make Gram the children's legal guardian. They arrive just in time for Oaxaca's radish-carving festival. Naomi finally finds her father and discovers that he loves carving, too.

LITERARY CHECK

Describe the ***setting*** *at the beginning of the excerpt.*

On Christmas morning Owen and I stood in the yard and looked up. I had to pinch myself to make sure I was not dreaming. A jungle of painted beasts floated beneath the jacaranda tree, the leaves and purple flowers like a canopy above them. Tied to the branches with transparent fishing line, the carved wooden animals appeared suspended. When a warm breeze tickled the dragons, reptiles, birds, and lions, they twirled and swayed.

Owen and I lay down on the ground and watched them. A few minutes later Santiago came out from behind the trailer, where he had been waiting. He lay down next to us and we watched the spectacle to the music of Owen's raspy laughter.

Later in the afternoon I sat outside, carving with Santiago. He was an expert on wood and had brought some of the special copal branches from the trees in the mountains. I loved watching him carve.

He held up a curved branch. "Each piece has a personality. Sometimes you can look at the wood and see exactly what it might be. The promise

---

custody of, the right to legally care for
jacaranda, type of tropical American tree with purple flowers
canopy, cover attached above a bed or seat, used as decoration or as a shelter
transparent, clear and easy to see through
spectacle, public scene or show that is very impressive
raspy, rough sounding

reveals itself early. Other times you must let your imagination dictate what you will find. How do you see your soap today? It is a dog, right?"

I nodded. I had been working on it for several days. "This end will be the tail. And here"—I pointed to the bottom corner—"will be one of its legs, running."

Santiago nodded.

Almost done, I pulled my knife across the soap but dug a little too deep and a large piece crumbled to the ground. With one slip of the knife, I had accidentally carved off the running leg.

I gasped.

"No, do not be sad," said Santiago. "There is still some magic left inside. Let us say that the missing leg is *simbólico* of a tragedy or something the dog has lost. Or that its destiny was to be a dog with three legs." He picked up my carving, and with a few strokes of the knife smoothed the ragged piece into a perfect three-legged dog. "You must carve so that what is inside can become what it is meant to be. When you are finished, the magic will show itself for what it really is."

---

dictate, influence or control
simbólico, Spanish for "symbolic"; standing for a particular event, process, or situation
tragedy, event that is extremely sad, especially one that involves death

BEFORE YOU GO ON

1. How do Owen and Naomi spend Christmas morning?
2. What is Naomi carving out of her bar of soap?

On Your Own
Have you ever created something and in the process allowed your imagination to "dictate what you find"? Describe the experience.

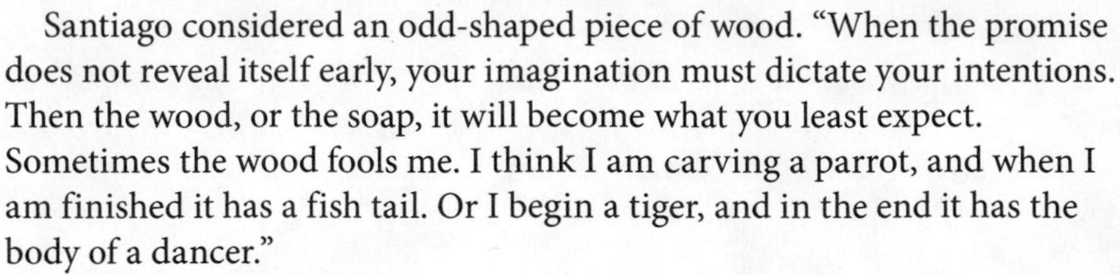

Santiago considered an odd-shaped piece of wood. "When the promise does not reveal itself early, your imagination must dictate your intentions. Then the wood, or the soap, it will become what you least expect. Sometimes the wood fools me. I think I am carving a parrot, and when I am finished it has a fish tail. Or I begin a tiger, and in the end it has the body of a dancer."

Literary Check
How does the ***dialogue*** *reveal Santiago's feelings about carving?*

With the small machete, he scraped at the layers of the bark that had built up over time, exposing the innards of what used to be a tree branch and revealing the unprotected heart meat. He traded the machete for a knife and chaffed at the wood with quick strokes. Soon he handed me a rough figure.

I held it up in the air. I could see that is was a lion's body with a human's head, maybe that of a girl.

As I turned it around, admiring it, Gram came out of the house and slowly sat down in one of the chairs. She stared at her folded hands and cleared her throat. "I just checked in with [our neighbor] Mrs. Maloney [in Lemon Tree]. The mediator, a young woman, showed up at Avocado Acres yesterday to interview her. Imagine showing up on Christmas Eve! The woman asked Mrs. Maloney where we were because she needs to talk to all of us by Friday, January third. Mrs. Maloney told her we'd return from our family vacation in time for the interview, which is what I had told her to say if anybody asked. That's in nine days, and what with four or five days' driving ahead of us . . . I'm sorry, Naomi, but we should leave the day after tomorrow."

---

machete, knife with a broad, heavy blade, used as a cutting tool
innards, inside parts
mediator, person who tries to help two groups to stop arguing and make an agreement

I took a deep breath and looked around the yard. "Can't we just stay here?" I asked, my hands suddenly quivering. "You like it here. You said so yourself." I heard Owen's and Rubén's giggles coming from the garden. "Owen loves it and we could . . . we could go to school here. We're learning Spanish real good. Or . . . or we could go to Puerto Escondido and live in the little house and help sell the carvings. . . . I could learn to paint them, like Aunt Teresa . . . and . . ."

Santiago pulled me from my chair to his side on a small wooden bench. He put his arm around me.

"Naomi, I would love for you to come to my house, but right now your life is in California. I have written the letter for the judge. I told the truth about your mother and that my wishes are for you and Owen to live with María [Gram]. I told that I want to be a part of your life and see you . . . maybe in the summer for vacations if that is all right with you and Owen. More, if it is possible."

My lips trembled. I stared at the ground.

"I did not fight for you when you were little," said Santiago. "It is something for which I am sorry. I should not have believed your mother when she said I would never be able to see you. If I had been stronger, maybe things could have been different, but maybe they would not have been so different. . . . How will we ever know?"

I looked at him. "But why can't you come with us?"

"For that to happen," he said, "I would have to prepare. Much would need to be done. Sell my house. My boat. Much of my money comes from my carvings, which are sold only in Oaxaca. My work, it is here."

"But what if the judge—"

"Naomi," said Gram, "we are not going to consider the worst that could happen. Thinking that way does not help self-prophecies."

Since we'd found Santiago, Gram was wearing her fierceness again. At least on the outside.

"I guess I better tell Owen," said Gram.

"I will go with you," said Santiago, and they headed toward the garden.

Alone, beneath the jacaranda, I stared at the three-legged dog and the lion girl in my lap.

We rode home to Lemon Tree silently. The truck and Baby Beluga seemed to drag along the highway. We traveled with less than we had brought. . . . So why did we seem to plod along? Did the weight of our memories slow us down?

---

quivering, shaking slightly because of nervousness or worry
Puerto Escondido, Spanish for "Hidden Port," a port city in the state of Oaxaca, Mexico
trembled, shook because of fear
self-prophecies, predictions about yourself that could come true

LITERARY CHECK

*What does the **dialogue** between Gram and Naomi show about Gram's character?*

BEFORE YOU GO ON

1. What does Santiago carve out of the tree branch?
2. Where does Santiago sell his carvings?

On Your Own
How would you feel if you were Naomi? Would you want to stay in Oaxaca? Why?

For hundreds of kilometers, I held the lion girl and thought about all that I wanted to tell [my friend] Blanca, especially about my father.

On our last days in Oaxaca, Owen and I had gone everywhere with Santiago: to visit Aunt Teresa, to *el zócalo*, to *el Mercado* for pineapple-coconut ice cream. And to admire the statue of Soledad in *la basilica*.

I would never forget that day. The statue with the long robe, a crown of gold, the sparkling stained-glass windows. Our footsteps echoing on the floor. Holding Santiago's hand and listening to his adoration.

"*Our Lady of Solitude* is loved by sailors and fisherman," he said. "She protects us at sea: when our boats are rocking in a storm, when it is foggy and we cannot see the way, when we need to get home and our motor fails us. Then we ask for her assistance. She is part of Oaxaca. And since you have her name and have been here to see the wonder of this city, Oaxaca is part of you."

The morning we left, Santiago came early to help load the last of the luggage. He cut down all the animals hanging from the jacaranda and gave them to Owen and me.

It was a long good-bye . . . the kind of good-bye where everyone hugged and kissed every single person, then stood around talking and looking at each other, then all of a sudden started hugging and kissing everyone again, crying a little each time.

When we were finally ready to climb into the truck, Santiago hugged me and said, "Be brave, Naomi León."

I nodded, but when he took me in his arms one more time and rocked me back and forth, I didn't pretend to be brave.

"Do not be sad," he whispered. "We have found each other. I will write. You will write. We have much for which to be thankful and everything will be the way it was meant to be. You will see. I promise. I promise. Now you must promise."

"I promise." . . .

Oaxaca had long disappeared from our view. I opened my notebook to make a list of all that I hoped to remember, but I closed it. My pen seemed too heavy to lift.

---

el zócalo, a public square/town square
el Mercado, the market
la basilica, the church

Soap Carving

Here's how you can learn to carve soap like Naomi.

What you will need:

- Newspapers or a tray or a bowl (something to catch the soap shavings)
- Scissors
- Craft sticks
- Tracing paper (optional)
- A bar (or bars) of pure and natural soap that will need to be aired overnight (see steps 2 and 3 below)
- Pencil or ballpoint pen
- Sheet of paper

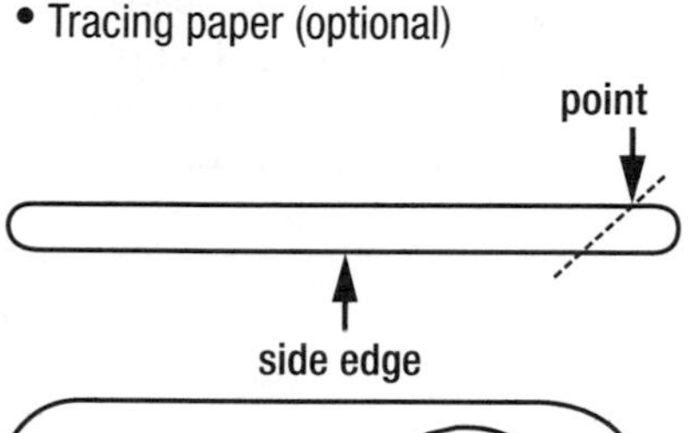

1. Using your scissors, cut off the tip of your craft stick at an angle, creating a point.
2. Unwrap the soap. Using the long edge of a craft stick, scrape the logo from each side of the bar so that you will have a flat surface.
3. Let the soap air out overnight.
4. Draw or trace a design (or create your own) onto a piece of paper such as the ones on the left. Remember, the design should be no larger than your bar of soap. Or you can carve without a pattern and create your own abstract design.
5. Place the piece of paper with the design against the broad, flat side of the soap. Using a ballpoint pen or a pencil, trace the outline of the design, pressing hard so it will leave an impression on your soap.
6. Following the basic rectangular shape of the soap, block out your design. Using the side edge of the angled craft stick, cut away the soap you don't need in thin layers. (Note: Cutting away too much at once will likely cause your soap to crumble apart.)
7. Once the basic angles have been established, start rounding your form. Keep turning your piece, working evenly and from all angles.

ABOUT THE AUTHOR

Pam Muñoz Ryan grew up in California's San Joaquin Valley. Her grandparents and many of her aunts and uncles lived nearby. The stories her family told had a big influence on her as she was growing up. Ryan loved reading as a child and became a bilingual teacher before she began writing her own stories for children. Some of her other well-known novels include *Riding Freedom* and *Esperanza Rising,* both of which have won many literary awards. Ryan still lives in southern California with her husband and four teenage children.

BEFORE YOU GO ON

1. Where do Owen and Naomi go on their last days in Oaxaca?
2. What does Santiago give to Owen and Naomi before they leave?

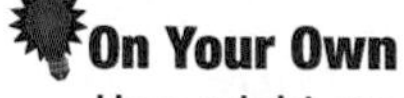

On Your Own
How might creating something in writing, carving, or some other artistic form make an unhappy person feel better?

READING 2

Review and Practice

READER'S THEATER

Act out the following scene between Naomi and her father.

Santiago: Let me teach you how to carve. Be careful with the tools.

Naomi: I'll try, but the soap gets slippery in my hands.

Santiago: Start by drawing the design you want on the soap. Choose something simple, like a dog or cat.

Naomi: I'll draw a dog. There . . . that looks good. Now I'm ready to start carving. First, I'll carve the outside pieces. This will be the dog's shape.

Santiago: Wonderful, Naomi! Now, be very careful when you start carving the legs. They're more difficult to carve because they are so thin.

Naomi: Oh, no! Look what I've done. I cut off the running leg!

Santiago: Don't worry. We'll make a different kind of dog, one that has lost something. Look now. Isn't this three-legged dog even more lovely?

Naomi: Yes, it's not the dog I planned, but it is beautiful.

Speaking TIP

Face your partner when you are speaking to him or her. Speak clearly and loudly so that your audience can hear you.

COMPREHENSION

Workbook Page 44

Right There

1. What does Mrs. Maloney tell the mediator about the Leóns?
2. What wishes does Santiago express in his letter to the judge?

Think and Search

3. What are several reasons why Naomi wants to stay in Oaxaca?
4. Why would it be hard for Santiago to go to California?

Author and You

5. Why does Naomi say, "My pen seemed too heavy to lift"?
6. Will Naomi be allowed to stay with Gram? Predict what will happen.

On Your Own

7. With what person in your life do you have a strong bond? Why?
8. Have you ever loved a place so much that you felt that it was "part of you"? Describe the place and your feelings about it.

DISCUSSION

Discuss in pairs or small groups.

1. In your opinion, should Naomi and Owen live with Santiago, Gram, or Skyla? Give reasons for your answer.
2. Imagine that you could travel anywhere in the United States or Mexico. Where would you go and why?

Q How does growing up change us? What sorts of feelings did Naomi have when she had to say good-bye to her father? Why do you think that she felt the way she did? How do you think that kind of experience affects a person her age?

Listening TIP

If you don't understand an answer, ask the person to repeat or explain his or her answer.

RESPONSE TO LITERATURE

Think about what you have learned about Oaxaca from *Becoming Naomi León*. Jot down words and phrases that the author uses to describe the setting. Based on what you have learned, write a short travel brochure in which you tell people why Oaxaca would be a nice place to visit. Describe three features of Oaxaca that would attract tourists. Use descriptive words that will make people want to travel there. You may want to find several photographs or make some drawings for your brochure. Share your completed travel brochure with a classmate.

◀ The streets of Oaxaca City

Grammar and Writing

GRAMMAR, USAGE, AND MECHANICS

Non-action Verbs

Use non-action verbs to describe conditions or situations. Non-action verbs are mostly used only in the simple present, past, or future. Non-action verbs express mental states (*want, need, know*), emotional states (*like, love, prefer*), possession (*have, own, belong*), senses (*taste, smell, feel, see, hear*), and other states of being (*seem, sound, look like*). Notice that all the examples below are in the simple present, past, or future.

> Skyla **wants** to obtain legal custody of Naomi.
> The woman **needs** to talk to all of us by Friday, January third.
> You **like** it here.
> We **have** much for which to be thankful. You **will see**.
> My pen **seemed** too heavy to lift.

Practice

Copy the sentences below into your notebook. Complete each sentence with the correct form of a non-action verb from the box. The first one has been done for you.

feel	have	hear	look like	love	want

1. Naomi discovers her father ___loves___ carving, too.
2. Santiago _______ many carved wooden animals hanging in his tree.
3. Naomi _______ the raspy sound of her brother giggling.
4. Santiago _______ to carve a parrot, but in the end it _______ a fish.
5. Naomi _______ sad that she can't be with her father.

WRITING A NARRATIVE PARAGRAPH

Write about a Character and Setting

On this page, you will write a narrative about a made-up character in a realistic setting. You'll use a graphic organizer like the one at the right to gather details about the character and setting.

When you write a narrative about a character in a particular setting, you include character and physical traits and sensory details. To describe the character, you tell how the character looks, acts, and thinks. To describe the setting, you tell about the time and place.

Character (Who)
Setting (Where and When)

Here is a model of a paragraph that describes a character in a realistic place during the present. Notice the words the writer uses to tell you what the character and setting are like and how the character and setting are connected.

Talia Marcus

At Camp

I will never forget the day I met Laura at Camp Hillcrest. It was Laura's first day at sleep-away camp, but I had been going there for three years and loved Hillcrest. It's located on a beautiful hill near a huge lake and has great activities. I had just arrived when I noticed her. She's a very tall girl with very short hair, and she was standing all by herself. She seemed shy, so I talked to her and tried to make her feel comfortable. I discovered we both play tennis! For a while, Laura seemed fine. Then, at bedtime, she suddenly felt homesick and wanted to see her parents. She looked distraught! I told her that everyone feels this way at first, and if she gave Hillcrest a try, she would really like it. After that, Laura calmed down and went to sleep. She ended up loving camp, just like I knew she would.

Practice

Write a narrative paragraph about a made-up character in a realistic setting. Start your paragraph with this sentence: *I will never forget the day I met (character's name) in (real place).* Use a character/setting chart to gather details for your paragraph. Put your details in an order that makes sense. Use non-action verbs to describe the situation and the character's appearance and feelings.

IDEAS:

☑ I created a clear picture of a character in a particular place.

CONVENTIONS:

☑ I checked my grammar, spelling, and punctuation.

READING 3

Prepare to Read

What You Will Learn

Reading

- Vocabulary building: *Literary terms, word study*
- Reading strategy: *Recognize sequence*
- Text type: *Literature (novel excerpt)*

Grammar, Usage, and Mechanics
Making comparisons

Writing
Write a story from another point of view

THE BIG QUESTION

How does growing up change us? Why do pets often play an important role in our lives when we're growing up? What kind of a pet would you like to have? Would you choose a common pet such as a dog, cat, or bird? Or would you prefer a less common pet like a pig, rabbit, or snake?

Work with a partner. Talk about what kind of pets you like and what kind you do not like. Then share your ideas with the class. Explain why you prefer a certain kind of pet.

▲ Dogs are popular pets with children and adults.

BUILD BACKGROUND

Later, Gator is a realistic and funny novel about two brothers who are very different from each other. The older brother, Teddy, is jealous of his younger brother, Bobby.

Jealousy is a strong feeling that can sometimes make people (and characters) say mean things or act badly. As children grow up, they often have feelings of jealousy. Sometimes a younger child is jealous of an older child because he or she can do more things. Sometimes an older child is jealous of a younger child because he or she gets more attention. In *Later, Gator,* jealousy plays a big part in what happens between Teddy and his brother.

VOCABULARY

Learn Literary Words

Literary Words
- plot
- point of view
- narrator

Plot is what happens in a story. Most plots include a problem, the events that lead to solving the problem, and the solution to the problem. Usually, plots move forward in time. They have a beginning, middle, and end.

Point of view is the position from which a story is told. Some stories are told from the point of view of one of the characters. The character tells the events as if they are happening to him or her. This is called *first-person point of view.* The person telling the story uses the pronouns *I, me, my,* and *we.* Other stories are told from the *third-person point of view.* The **narrator**, or person telling the story, uses the pronouns *she, he,* and *they.* The narrator can be one of the characters in the story, or just someone telling the story from the outside. Read the examples below and notice the pronouns.

> **First-person point of view:** I was so excited when my older sister bought me a blue parakeet for my birthday.
>
> **Third-person point of view:** Gerry was overjoyed when he received a blue parakeet from his sister on his sixth birthday.

Practice

Work with a partner. Reread the chapter from *Becoming Naomi León* on pages 88–92. Then answer the questions below in your notebook:

1. What is the plot of the story? Describe the problem, events that lead to a solution, and the solution.
2. Is the story told from the first-person point of view or the third-person point of view? How can you tell?
3. How would the story have been different if it had been told from Santiago's point of view?

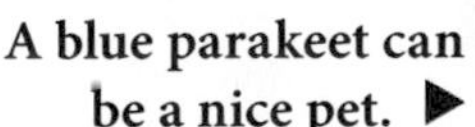

A blue parakeet can be a nice pet. ▶

Learn Academic Words

Study the **red** words and their meanings. You will find these words useful when talking and writing about literature. Write each word and its meaning in your notebook. After you read the excerpt from *Later, Gator,* try to use these words to respond to the text.

Academic Words
affect
author
effect
perspective

affect = do something that produces a change in someone or something; influence	➡	Jealousy can **affect** the way people act. Sometimes, it can change how two people feel about each another.
author = someone who writes a book, story, article, or play	➡	Laurence Yep is the **author** of *Later, Gator.* He is the writer of this novel.
effect = a result, or a reaction to something or someone	➡	Owning a pet can have a good **effect** on a person. It gives people a sense of responsibility and companionship.
perspective = a way of thinking about something that is influenced by the type of person you are or what you do	➡	From my **perspective**, dogs are better pets than cats because they are more friendly and loyal. However, my sister has the opposite point of view.

Hint: People often confuse the words *affect* and *effect*. Use the verb *affect* to talk about making changes, and use the noun *effect* to talk about the results of changes. Remember, *effect* is almost always a noun that means "result."

Practice

Work with a partner to answer these questions. Try to include the **red** word in your answer. Write the sentences in your notebook.

1. How does a lack of sleep **affect** you?
2. Who is your favorite **author**? Why?
3. What **effect** would a new pet have on your family?
4 What is your **perspective** on having a snake as a pet?

How would having a pet iguana affect your day-to-day life? ▶

Word Study: Animal Verbs and Idioms

Writers often use colorful verbs and idioms to make their writing more lively. Some of the most vivid English verbs and idioms involve animals and animal comparisons. Read the sentences and definitions below. Think about why these words and phrases have these meanings.

Jody always tries **to weasel out of** doing her chores.
[*To weasel out of* means "to avoid."]

It bugs me when you yell in my ear.
[*To bug* means "to annoy someone."]

Why don't you **hold your horses**? We'll be there soon.
[*To hold your horses* means "to be patient."]

I'm completely soaked. It's **raining cats and dogs** outside.
[*To rain cats and dogs* means "to rain very heavily."]

Practice

Work with a partner to write a sentence of your own for each of the animal verbs and idioms above.

Reading Strategy RECOGNIZE SEQUENCE

Recognizing sequence will help you understand what you read. Knowing the sequence, or order, of events in a story helps you to understand the plot. To recognize sequence, follow these steps:

- As you read, look for words that show sequence, such as *first, second, then, next, last,* and *after.*
- Look for dates, days of the week, and times, such as *morning, next Thursday, yesterday, in 2010.*

As you read the excerpt from *Later, Gator,* identify the sequence of events. Ask yourself, "What happens at the beginning, in the middle, and at the end of the story?"

READING 3

LITERATURE

NOVEL

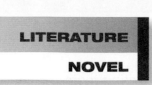

Set a purpose for reading How might jealousy change the relationship between two brothers as they grow up? Read to find out how jealousy affects the characters and plot of this story.

from

Later, Gator

Laurence Yep

In this story, Teddy, the narrator, is jealous of his younger brother, Bobby, because everyone likes him. When their mother asks Teddy to buy Bobby a birthday present, Teddy plans to buy him something that he hopes will scare Bobby.

The alligator was Mother's fault. She told me to buy something special. Mother, as usual, blames me. She says that I've got more imagination than brains.

That's not my little brother's problem. Last Christmas I gave him a pair of socks. Bobby was too dumb to understand the insult. Instead of getting mad, he said to me, "They're neat-o and just what I wanted."

Yeah, sure, I thought to myself.

Bobby had to put on his new socks right away and wriggle his toes at me. "They're very warm and comfortable. Thank you," he said.

Do you see what I mean? Bobby is a walking Hallmark card.

blames me, says I did something bad
imagination, ability to form pictures or ideas in the mind
neat-o, great (slang)
wriggle, turn or twist with small, quick movements

Mother had understood, though. So this year, on Friday, the week before Bobby's eighth birthday, she took me aside. "Why can't you get along with your little brother? What has he ever done to you?"

"Nothing," I confessed. That was the trouble. What kind of little brother doesn't bug his big brother? Bobby was not normal.

Mother clicked her tongue. "Everybody else likes your brother. He's so sweet."

"Bobby's a regular mint chocolate bar, all right," I said, and thought to myself, And I am a raisin cookie.

"Then why haven't you ever bought him something special?" Mother demanded. She would make a good prosecutor.

"You always said it's the spirit that counts," I grumbled.

Mother frowned. "Only a mean person buys a cheap pair of white cotton socks."

"He liked the baseball."

Mother folded her hands in front of her. "Which you then used and lost."

"The Christmas before I got him comic books," I pointed out.

"Which he couldn't read."

"I read them to him," I said. Mother just looked at me until I admitted, "Sometimes."

"You treat him like he's an enemy. Don't you love your brother?" Mother asked.

"Of course I do," I lied. (But really, how can I love a little angel who makes me feel mean and selfish and bad?)

"Then show your love," Mother said. "Get something Bobby wants."

I tried to weasel out of it. "I can't afford the official Willie Mays baseball glove."

"No, I mean something he wants even more. I've talked it over with your father, and he's agreed that Bobby is now old enough to have a pet," Mother said.

She went to a cabinet and took out a big paper bag. From the bag, she slid out a kidney-shaped plastic tray. A wall of transparent plastic some three inches high ran around the edge of the tray. Part of the bottom rose up into an island in the center. A plastic palm tree grew from the island's middle.

---

get along with, have a friendly relationship with
prosecutor, lawyer who asks questions in court
spirit, thought or attitude
Willie Mays, a famous baseball player
kidney-shaped, having a wide, curved shape
island, land surrounded by water

Literary Check

*Who is the **narrator** of this selection?*

BEFORE YOU GO ON

1. Why does Teddy have trouble loving his younger brother?
2. What does Mother want Teddy to do for Bobby?

On Your Own
What are the advantages of growing up with brothers and sisters? What are the advantages of being an only child?

"I got the idea when he was watching a nature show on TV. He likes animals," Mother said. "He always wants to go to the zoo or the Academy of Sciences." The academy was in Golden Gate Park and had an aquarium, a hall with stuffed animals, and a reptile section.

It wasn't fair, I told myself. I figured he watched educational shows to please our parents and to make me look bad. I'll take the **Three Stooges** over a nature show anytime.

"Then I saw an ad in the newspaper," Mother said, "and I bought this. It's a turtle home. You go down to the department store. They've got turtles on sale. You can buy him a pet."

Feeling **miserable** but caught, I promised.

For the rest of the week, I put it off. There was no fun in giving Bobby something he wanted. Instead, I just hung around the apartment and **moped**.

On the morning of his birthday, he was up bright and early and jumping around, pretending to catch fly balls over the shoulder like Willie Mays. He had made so much noise that I had got up early, too, even though it was Saturday.

Mother served his favorite breakfast. We each had a scrambled egg with rice and slices of Chinese sausage. The problem was that Mother served it every morning. It was typical of Bobby to play up to Mother that way. I would have asked for scrambled eggs, bacon, and toast.

When Father asked Bobby what he wanted to do on his birthday, Bobby **volunteered** to help him in the fish shop. Any normal kid would have asked for money for a movie—for him and for his older brother. Boy, he really **drove me crazy**.

After Father and Bobby left for work, Mother stood over me. "Well, did you buy Bobby's pet?" she asked.

I **squirmed** on my chair. "I didn't want to get it too soon. If Bobby found it, it would ruin the surprise."

"I thought so." Mother handed me a folded-up piece of paper. "I cut out the ad from the newspaper so you would know where to go. After you wash the dishes, go down and buy Bobby's pet."

"That's Bobby's chore today," I whined.

Three Stooges, popular TV comedy, starring three comedians
miserable, very unhappy
moped, felt sad
volunteered, offered
drove me crazy, made me angry
squirmed, turned and twisted

LITERARY CHECK

Is this narrative told from the first-person ***point of view*** *or the third-person point of view? How can you tell?*

BEFORE YOU GO ON

1. Why does Mother think Bobby likes animals?
2. Why doesn't Teddy want to buy Bobby a turtle?

On Your Own
What do you like to do on your birthday?

"It's his birthday," Mother said. "I have to buy tonight's dinner. When I come home, I want to find that turtle waiting for me. You can leave it in our bedroom until we give out the presents." She wasn't going to leave me any way to escape. "If you need money, go down to the garbage cans. I saw lots of empty soda bottles."

After Mother left, I heaved a big sigh. Going into the kitchen, I turned on the radio for music and began washing the dishes.

As I was finishing up, I saw the newspaper ad on the table. It was for a department store in the Stonestown mall, where Mother worked. It would take me most of the morning to get out there.

Above the address was a big drawing of a boy and girl gazing happily at a turtle. It was grinning back from a plastic bowl like the one Mother had bought. In big type, the ad announced the turtles were on sale for fifty cents. Then I saw the small print: BABY ALLIGATORS ON SALE. And like an omen, the radio began playing a funny song from the past. "See you later, alligator," the radio sang. "After a while, crocodile."

If there had been a light bulb over my head, it would have suddenly shone as bright as the sun. Carefully I reviewed Mother's words. As far as I could remember, she had said to buy Bobby a pet. I chuckled. Poor Mother. She thought she had trapped me, but she had given me a loophole.

Literary Check

*What is the **plot** of the story so far?*

---

escape, get away from something
gazing, staring
type, printed letters
omen, sign that something will happen
loophole, way to escape

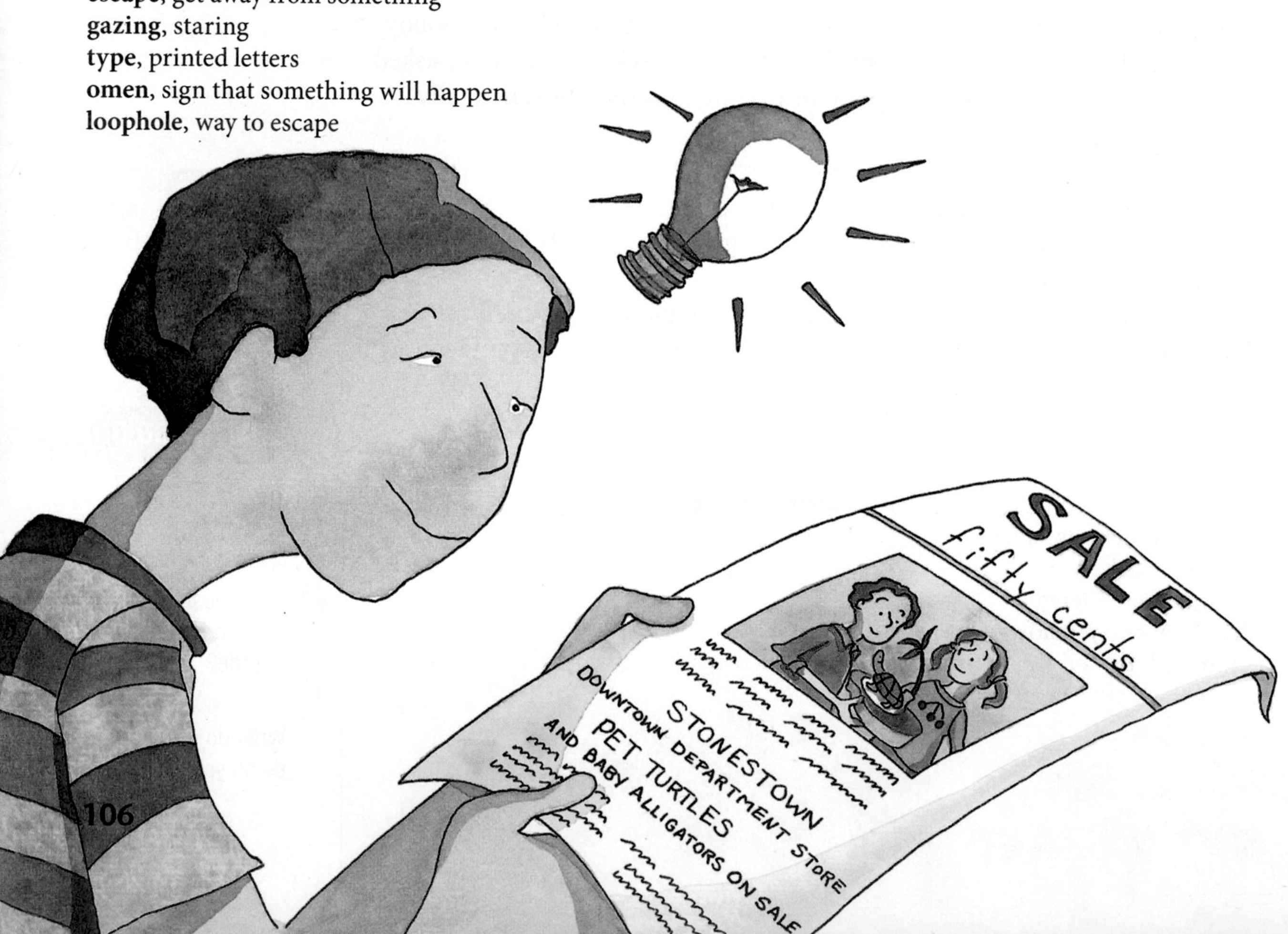

A plan began to build in my mind. First, though, I called up the department store having the sale. When I got the operator, I asked her, "I'd like to buy my brother something special from your pet department. If he doesn't like it, can I return it?"

"You can return anything within seventy-two hours after the sale." She added, "But the pet has to be alive."

"It won't be here long enough to die," I laughed, and hung up. I imagined what would happen tonight when Bobby opened his present. He would probably run shrieking from the room.

In my mind, I played out many marvelous scenes, ranging from a horrified Bobby to an outraged one. In any case, I would have to return it and get my money back. At the same time Mother would learn her lesson too.

It was the perfect gift. I could keep my promise to Mother because it would be nature stuff as well as something special. I could keep my promise to myself because it would be weird enough.

---

operator, person who answers phone calls
shrieking, screaming
marvelous, good; wonderful
horrified, very upset
outraged, extremely angry

LITERARY CHECK

Why would this narrative have been very different if the story had been told from Bobby's ***point of view?***

ABOUT THE AUTHOR

Laurence Yep has written many award-winning books for children and adults, including the Newbery Honor Books *Dragonwings* and *Dragon's Gate*. He was born in 1948, in California. He wrote his first stories for a science-fiction magazine when he was in high school. When he was growing up, Yep really did buy his little brother an alligator as a pet!

BEFORE YOU GO ON

1. What does Teddy think Bobby will do when he opens the present?
2. Does Teddy have a good imagination? Explain.

On Your Own
When you were Bobby's age, would you have liked to get an alligator as a birthday present? Why or why not?

READING 3 Review and Practice

READER'S THEATER

Act out this scene between Teddy and his mother.

Teddy: It's not fair, Mom! Why do I have to buy my little brother a birthday present? He gets presents from you and Dad.

Mother: Teddy, stop whining. You should *want* to buy your brother a present. Bobby's your brother. Don't you love him?

Teddy: I do, but we don't get along. You know that, Mom.

Mother: Why can't you get along? He's nice to you.

Teddy: Mom! He's so good that he makes me look bad. Everyone likes him better than they like me.

Mother: You don't have any reason to be jealous of Bobby, dear. Your father and I love you both the same.

Teddy: Okay, Mom. I'll get him a pet at the pet store tomorrow.

Mother: Thank you, Teddy. I'm sure Bobby will be very pleased.

Speaking TIP

Use realistic voices and facial expressions so that your audience can visualize the characters and their feelings.

COMPREHENSION

Right There

1. What gift did Teddy buy his little brother Bobby for Christmas?
2. What is on sale at the department store?

Think and Search

3. What effect does Teddy's Christmas gift have on Bobby?
4. Why does Mother tell Teddy what to buy Bobby for his birthday?

Author and You

5. From whose point of view is this story told? How can you tell?
6. How does Teddy's jealousy of Bobby affect his actions?

On Your Own

7. "Sibling rivalry" is a term used to describe the competition between brothers and sisters. What do you think causes sibling rivalry? What are some ways to avoid it?
8. When were you jealous of someone? Describe the experience.

DISCUSSION

Discuss in pairs or small groups.

1. Why do you think Teddy called the pet store to make sure that he can return pets? What does this tell you about Teddy?
2. What do you predict will happen when Teddy brings home the alligator? What will Bobby do? What will Teddy's parents do?
3. Do you think that wild animals such as alligators should be sold as pets? Why or why not?

Q How does growing up change us? Imagine that you have a younger brother who gets all the attention. What things might you do so that you could get some positive attention?

Listening TIP

Take notes as you discuss the questions about the story and growing up. This will help you remember what you and your classmates said.

RESPONSE TO LITERATURE

Teddy is very jealous of his younger brother Bobby. Imagine that twenty years have passed. Teddy and Bobby have grown up. How do they get along now? Are they close friends? Is Teddy still jealous of Bobby? Is Bobby still as popular and nice? Imagine that you are the boys' mother. Write a journal entry in which you describe how the boys get along with each other now. Use the chart below to help you begin.

Then		Now
Teddy was jealous of Bobby.	➡	
Bobby was popular.	➡	
Bobby did not know that Teddy was jealous of him.	➡	

When you are finished writing, share your journal entry with a partner. See whether your partner agrees with your description of the boys' relationship in the future.

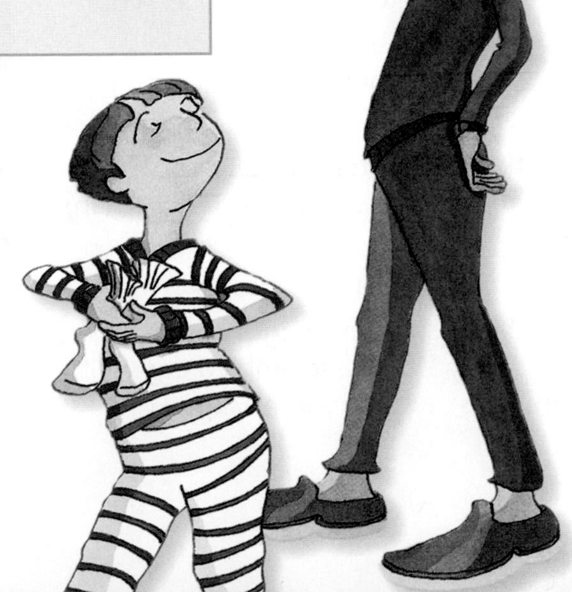

Grammar and Writing

GRAMMAR, USAGE, AND MECHANICS

Making Comparisons

Making comparisons can help you write clear descriptions and lively narratives. You can use a comparative adjective + *than* to compare two people, places, or things. For most one-syllable adjectives, add *-r* or *-er* to form a comparative. For two-syllable adjectives that end in *y*, change the *y* to *i* and add *-er*. For adjectives that are two syllables or more, use *more . . . than* or *less . . . than*. When you want to point out that two people, places, or things are equal or unequal, use *as . . . as* or *not as . . . as*.

Comparatives with *-er + than:*
Bobby is **sweeter than** Teddy. My dog is **heavier than** your dog.
Comparatives with *more . . . than* and *less . . . than:*
Teddy is **more imaginative than** Bobby. Teddy is **less helpful than** Bobby.
Comparatives with *as . . . as* and *not as . . . as:*
Tony is **as tall as** his mother. The moon is **not as bright as** it was a week ago.

Practice

Work with a partner. Copy the sentences below into your notebook. Decide which choice best completes each sentence. Write the answers in your notebook.

1. Bobby is ______ old ______ Teddy. (not as . . . as / as . . . as)
2. Teddy thinks alligators are ______ scary ______ turtles. (as . . . as / more . . . than)
3. Bobby ______ jealous ______ Teddy. (more . . .than / not as . . . as)
4. Teddy thinks scrambled eggs with rice is ______ tasty ______ scrambled eggs with bacon. (less . . . than / as . . . as)

WRITING A NARRATIVE PARAGRAPH

Write a Story from Another Point of View

You have written two narratives. Now you will write a known story from another character's perspective. You'll use a graphic organizer to contrast different characters' points of view.

Have you ever noticed how a story can change depending on who is telling it? Each character in a story acts and thinks in a unique way. One character may see an event or object from one perspective, but another character may have a completely different point of view.

Here is a model of a familiar story (*Later, Gator*) from the mother's point of view. The writer used a T-chart to contrast the original narrator's and the new narrator's perspectives. Notice how the mother's point of view is different from Teddy's.

Teddy's POV	Mother's POV

Koji Mori

That Teddy!

I can't believe what Teddy has done this time! He's very imaginative, but he's full of mischief and loves to torment his brother. He's jealous of Bobby, my younger son, who is certainly a calmer, easier child than Teddy. Anyway, I suppose I should have known better when I told Teddy to buy Bobby something special for his birthday. I even made a suggestion! I thought a little turtle would be a wonderful gift, since Bobby is just old enough to care for a pet. I should have guessed that Teddy would outsmart me. As it turns out, he saw a newspaper ad for a different kind of reptile. When I came home from work, I found a baby alligator in the turtle bowl! I shrieked, which is what Teddy probably hoped that Bobby would do. Of course, I made Teddy take the alligator back. I have to admit, though, I had to laugh!

Practice

Write a paragraph telling a familiar story from another character's point of view. Use a T-chart to contrast the perspectives of the original narrator and the new one. Use the pronouns *I*, *me*, *my*, *we*, and *us* to tell the story from the first-person point of view. To compare and contrast characters and events, use comparatives.

Writing Checklist

VOICE:

☑ I used a new voice that reflects the new narrator's point of view.

CONVENTIONS:

☑ I used the pronouns *I*, *me*, *my*, *we*, and *us* to tell the story from a charcter's point of view.

READING 4 Prepare to Read

What You Will Learn

Reading

- Vocabulary building: *Context, dictionary skills, word study*
- Reading strategy: *Use visuals 2*
- Text type: *Informational text (science article); Literature (folk tale)*

Grammar, Usage, and Mechanics
Simple past: regular and irregular verbs

Writing
Write a personal narrative

THE BIG QUESTION

How does growing up change us? How is growing up different for plants and animals than it is for human beings? Some plants and animals are very small when they are fully grown. Others are very big. Which animals are very small even when they are completely grown? What are the largest animals you can name? What are the tallest plants you can name? Share what you know with the class.

BUILD BACKGROUND

"Amazing Growth Facts" and **"The Old Grandfather and His Little Grandson"** are two very different kinds of texts. The first is a science article about physical growth. It presents interesting facts about how living things grow in size. The second text is a folk tale about another kind of growth. It is a narrative about a young child who teaches his parents a lesson. The child's actions help the parents grow as human beings.

Folk tales are old stories that are passed down over the years. They are often told to children to teach them lessons. Some folk tales warn children to stay away from danger. Others teach children to be kind to others.

▲ Giant Sequoias are the tallest trees in the world.

Giraffes are 1.83 meters (6 ft.) tall when they are born, but they grow to be 5.49 meters (18 ft.) tall. ▶

VOCABULARY

Learn Key Words

Read these sentences. Use the context to figure out the meaning of the **red** words. Use a dictionary to check your answers. Then write each word and its meaning in your notebook.

1. At birth, the **average** baby weighs about 3.5 kilograms (7 or 8 lbs.).
2. We use a **conversion** chart to change numbers from one system of measurement to another. For example, we can change centimeters to inches, meters to feet, or kilograms to pounds.
3. The building's **height** is 30 meters (around 100 ft.) from the bottom to the top.
4. The anaconda is the longest snake in the world. It can grow to more than 10.5 meters (close to 35 ft.) in **length**.
5. A baby has a very fast **rate** of growth. It can grow almost 18 centimeters (about 7 in.) in one year!
6. We measure **weight** to figure out how heavy someone or something is.

Key Words

average
conversion
height
length
rate
weight

Practice

Work with a partner to answer these questions. Try to include the **red** word in your answer. Write the sentences in your notebook.

1. How do you figure out the **average** of a series of ten numbers?
2. When might you need to use a **conversion** chart?
3. What tools could you use to measure someone's **height**?
4. How does the **length** of your hand compare to the length of your feet?
5. Why do you think that babies grow at such a fast **rate**?
6. What can people do to lower their **weight**?

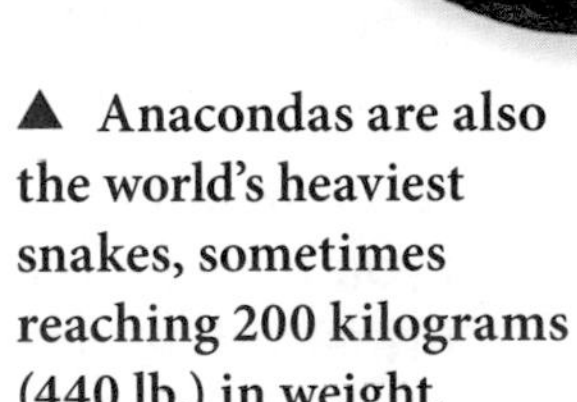

▲ Anacondas are also the world's heaviest snakes, sometimes reaching 200 kilograms (440 lb.) in weight.

Learn Academic Words

Study the **red** words and their meanings. You will find these words useful when talking and writing about informational texts and literature. Write each word and its meaning in your notebook. After you read "Amazing Growth Facts" and "The Old Grandfather and His Little Grandson," try to use these words to respond to the text.

Academic Words

benefit
category
enormous
percent

benefit = something that gives you an advantage, that helps you, or that has a good effect	➡	Growing fast is a great **benefit** to animals. It helps them live on their own sooner.
category = group of people or things that have related characteristcs	➡	Bears and deer belong to the **category** of warm-blooded animals. Snakes and lizards belong to a different group.
enormous = extremely large in size or amount	➡	The elephant is **enormous**! It is a huge animal.
percent = equal to a particular amount in every hundred	➡	About 75 **percent** of the eggs hatched. The rest of the eggs did not hatch.

Practice

Work with a partner to answer these questions. Try to include the **red** word in your answer. Write the sentences in your notebook.

1. What is a **benefit** of living in your city or town?
2. What **category** would you use to group cars, trucks, boats, and trains?
3. What are some of the most **enormous** animals you have seen in pictures or at a nature preserve?
4. Why do students feel good when they get 100 **percent** on a test?

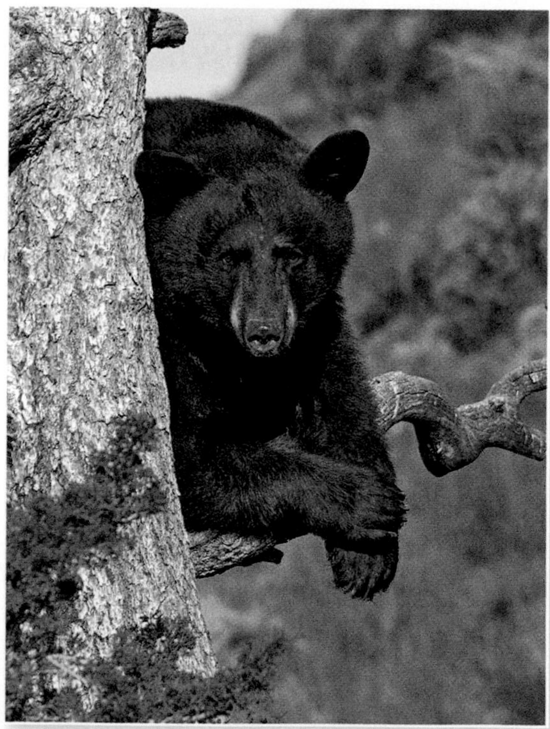

▲ Bears are in the category of warm-blooded animals.

Word Study: Spelling Words with Long Vowel Sound /ō/

Learning to identify sound-spelling patterns will help you read and spell words correctly. The long vowel sound /ō/ can be spelled in many ways. Four common spellings are *o* as in *cold*, *o_e* as in *bone*, *oa* as in roast, and *ow* as in *snow*. Look at the chart below. Take turns reading the words aloud with a partner. Notice the sound-spelling patterns for /ō/.

/ō/ spelled *o*	/ō/ spelled *o_e*	/ō/ spelled *oa*	/ō/ spelled *ow*
scold	stone	toast	grown
so	close	loaf	slow
kilo	stove	coast	below

Practice

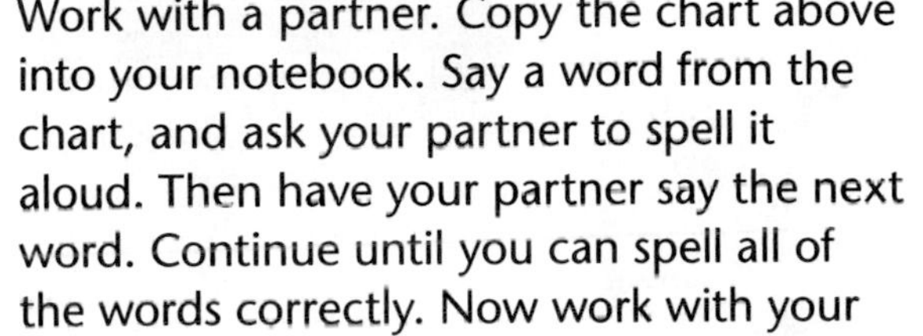

Work with a partner. Copy the chart above into your notebook. Say a word from the chart, and ask your partner to spell it aloud. Then have your partner say the next word. Continue until you can spell all of the words correctly. Now work with your partner to spell these words: *jumbo, soap, tone, bowl, home, gold, show, oak*. Add them to the chart under the correct headings.

Reading Strategy USE VISUALS 2

Using visuals helps you understand what you are reading. Visuals include photographs, art, diagrams, charts, and maps. Informational texts often have visuals. Sometimes visuals give you information that is not in the text. To use visuals, follow these steps:

- Look at the visual. Ask yourself, "What does it show? How does it help me understand what I am reading?"
- Read the titles, headings, labels, or captions carefully.
- Think about how the visual helps you understand what is in the text. Does the visual give you extra information? In what way?

As you read "Amazing Growth Facts," pay close attention to the visuals. What do they show? How do they help you understand the text better?

READING 4

INFORMATIONAL TEXT

SCIENCE

Set a purpose for reading How do different plants and animals grow? As you read the article, think about how all living things change when they grow up.

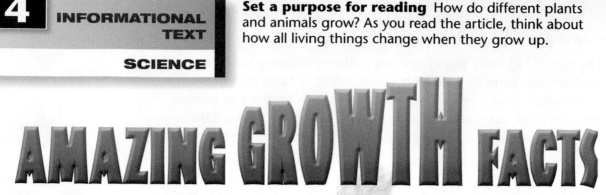

AMAZING GROWTH FACTS

It is one of the wonders of nature that all living things increase in size. Think about how a tiny acorn can grow into an enormous oak tree. Growth occurs at different rates. Sometimes growth is very fast. Other times it is very slow.

The average newborn baby is 50 centimeters long and weighs 3.4 kilograms. When the baby grows up and becomes an adult, he or she increases on average to 3.4 times that length and 21 times that weight. Girls and boys are about the same height and weight until early adulthood. Then boys usually grow taller and weigh more than girls.

Bamboo can grow 90 centimeters in one day—the height of an average three-year-old child. Pacific giant kelp (a kind of seaweed) can grow as much as 45 centimeters in one day.

An ant can lift more than 100 times its weight. One hundred times the weight of a 64-kilogram person would be the same weight as three cars!

A baby kangaroo is the size and weight of a paper clip (1 gram). An adult kangaroo is 30,000 times heavier (30 kilograms). If a human grew at this rate, a 3.4-kilogram baby would weigh 102,000 kilograms as an adult—that's as much as

▲ If we were as strong as ants, we could lift three cars!

---

increase, become bigger

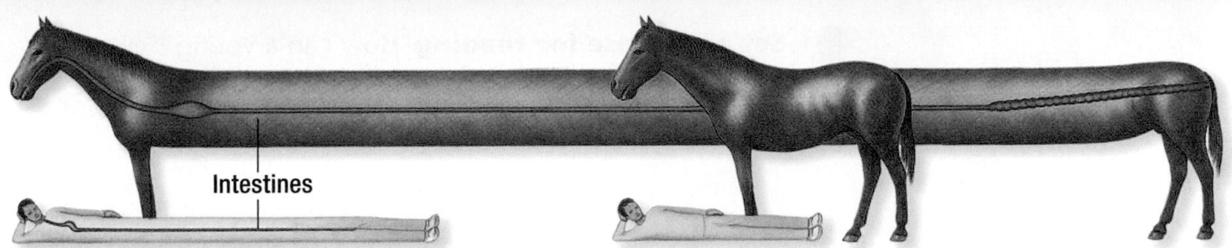

a large whale! An average man weighs about 80 kilograms.

The egg of a golden eagle and the egg of a Nile crocodile are both 8 centimeters long. But look how much bigger the crocodile grows!

A 26-centimeter baby crocodile can grow into a 5-meter adult crocodile. If humans grew at the same rate as Nile crocodiles, a 50-centimeter baby would grow into a 9.5-meter adult—more than 5 times as tall as the average person!

Clams are among the longest living and slowest growing of all creatures. A deep-sea clam takes 100 years to grow 8 millimeters. That's as big as your fingernail!

In the average human life of 70 years, a heart pumps enough blood around the body to fill the fuel tanks of 700 jumbo jets. The food that we eat in our lifetime is equal in weight to the weight of six elephants! A horse's intestines are about 27 meters long. A human's intestines are about 7.5 meters long. Luckily, the intestines are curled up inside the body. Otherwise, people and horses would look very strange!

---

jumbo jets, very large airplanes
intestines, tubes that take food from the stomach out of the body

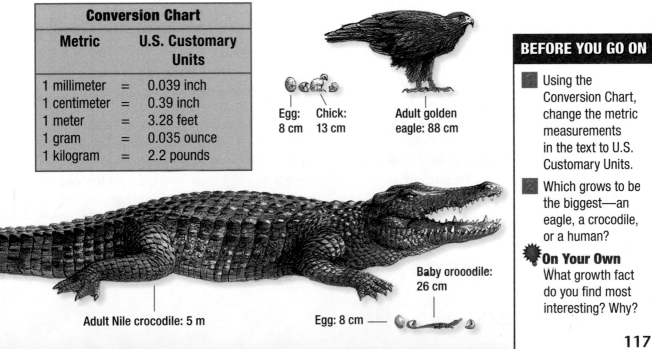

Conversion Chart		
Metric		**U.S. Customary Units**
1 millimeter	=	0.039 inch
1 centimeter	=	0.39 inch
1 meter	=	3.28 feet
1 gram	=	0.035 ounce
1 kilogram	=	2.2 pounds

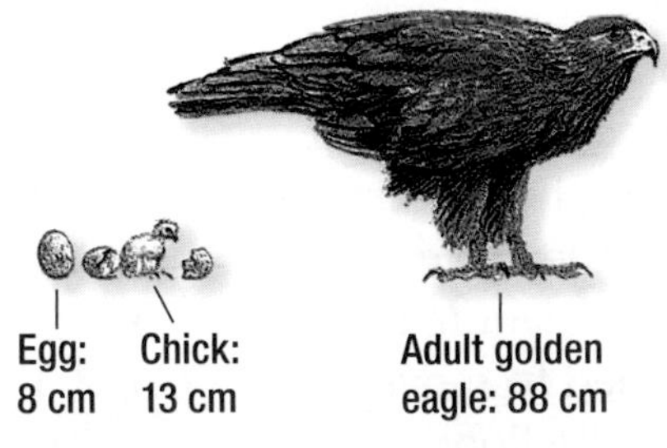

BEFORE YOU GO ON

1. Using the Conversion Chart, change the metric measurements in the text to U.S. Customary Units.
2. Which grows to be the biggest—an eagle, a crocodile, or a human?

On Your Own
What growth fact do you find most interesting? Why?

LITERATURE

FOLK TALE

Set a purpose for reading How can a young boy help his parents grow up? As you read this folk tale, think about how Misha's actions help his parents grow and change.

The Old Grandfather and His Little Grandson

An adapted folk tale by Leo Tolstoy

The grandfather had become very old. His legs would not carry him. His eyes could not see and his ears could not hear. He had no teeth. Sometimes when he ate, bits of food dropped out of his mouth. His son and his son's wife no longer let him eat with them at the table. He had to eat his meals in the corner near the stove.

One day they gave the grandfather his food in a bowl. He tried to move the bowl closer. It fell to the floor and broke. His daughter-in-law scolded him. She told him that he spoiled everything in the house and broke their dishes. She said that from now on, he would get his food in a wooden dish.

The old man sighed and said nothing.

A few days later, the old man's son and his wife were in their hut, resting. They watched their little boy playing on the floor. He was making something out of small pieces of wood. His father said, "What are you making, Misha?"

The little grandson said, "I'm making a wooden bucket. When you and Mama get old, I'll feed you out of this wooden dish."

The young man and his wife looked at each other. Tears filled their eyes. They were ashamed they had treated the old grandfather so badly. From that day on, they let the old man eat at the table with them, and they took better care of him.

---

scolded, spoke angrily to
spoiled, ruined

ashamed, embarrassed or guilty

ABOUT THE AUTHOR

Leo Tolstoy was born in 1828 in Russia. A writer, dramatist, and philosopher, he is considered by many to be the founder of realistic fiction. Tolstoy is most famous for his novel *War and Peace*. Many literary critics consider this book to be one of the greatest books ever written.

BEFORE YOU GO ON

1. Why do the man and his wife make the grandfather eat his meals in the corner?
2. Why does Misha's bowl make his parents feel ashamed?

On Your Own
How can children benefit from living with their grandparents?

READING 4

Review and Practice

COMPREHENSION

Right There

1. According to the article, how long does it take a clam to grow 8 millimeters?
2. In the folk tale, what object does Misha make for his parents?

Think and Search

3. Based on "Amazing Growth Facts," what category would you use to group bamboo and Pacific giant kelp together?
4. In the folk tale, why are the man and his wife angry with the grandfather?

Author and You

5. In what ways is "Amazing Growth Facts" both informative and entertaining?
6. What lesson does Misha teach his parents?

On Your Own

7. What advantages do enormous animals have?
8. What can children learn from their parents? What can parents learn from their children?

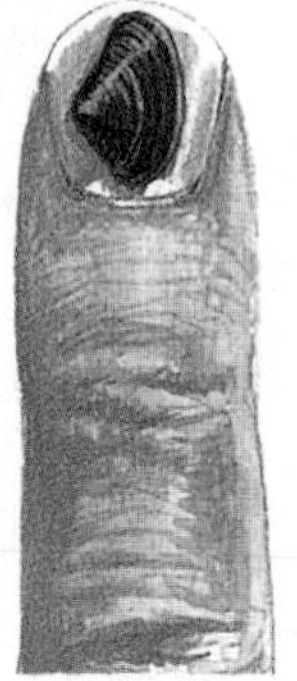

▲ **How does this artwork help you visualize the size of a slow-growing clam?**

IN YOUR OWN WORDS

Summarize each of the readings. Copy the following chart into your notebook. Use it to help you organize your summaries. Then share your summaries with a partner.

"Amazing Growth Facts"	"The Old Grandfather and His Little Grandson"
Fact 1:	Beginning:
Fact 2:	Middle:
Fact 3:	End:
Overall summary:	Overall plot summary:

Speaking TIP

Use notes and pictures to help you remember important facts.

DISCUSSION

Discuss in pairs or small groups.

1. Why do you think the two readings were paired? How are they similar? How are they different?
2. What other information would you like to learn about growth? Give at least two examples.
3. Are you more interested in very large animals or very small ones? Why?

Q **How does growing up change us?** What do you think your life will be like sixty-five years from now? Describe what you think you will be like. Will you want to be with people your own age, with younger people, or both? Why?

Listening TIP

Do not interrupt your classmates when they are speaking. Save your questions until a speaker is finished.

READ FOR FLUENCY

Reading with feeling helps make what you read more interesting. Work with a partner. Choose a paragraph from the folk tale. Read the paragraph to yourselves. Ask each other how you felt after reading the paragraph. Did you feel happy or sad?

Take turns reading the paragraph aloud to each other with a tone of voice that represents how you felt when you read it the first time. Give each other feedback.

EXTENSION

"Amazing Growth Facts" presents interesting information about how certain living things grow. Learn more about the growth of other plants and animals. Use encyclopedias, reference books, and the Internet. Share your findings with your classmates.

▲ You can track your growth by measuring yourself against a wall every few months.

Grammar and Writing

GRAMMAR, USAGE, AND MECHANICS

Simple Past: Regular and Irregular Verbs

Use the simple past to talk about actions that began and ended in the past. Form the simple past of regular verbs by adding *-d* or *-ed* to the base form of the verb. If the verb ends in *y*, change the *y* to *i* and add *-ed*. Sometimes you must double the consonant and then add *-ed*. Study the examples.

Base Form	Simple Past
watch	They watch**ed** their little boy playing on the floor.
drop	Bits of food drop**ped** out of his mouth.
try	He tr**ied** to move the bowl closer.

Many common verbs are irregular and must be memorized.

Base Form	Simple Past
have	He **had** a grandson.
give	One day they **gave** the grandfather his food in a bowl.
say	The old man sighed and **said** nothing.
be	The old man's son and his wife **were** in their hut.
let	They **let** the old man eat at the table with them.

Practice

Work with a partner. Copy the sentences below into your notebook. Complete the sentences with the simple past of the verbs in parentheses. Use a dictionary if necessary.

1. When I ______ (be) six, my two front teeth ______ (be) missing.
2. My mother ______ (let) me eat lots of custard and ice cream.
3. My brother or sister ______ (watch) me every day after school until my parents came home from work.
4. They ______ (say) they didn't mind baby-sitting.
5. The school bus ______ (drop) me off about a block from our house.
6. Sometimes my sister ______ (give) me help with my homework.

WRITING A NARRATIVE PARAGRAPH

Write a Personal Narrative

You have written three narratives and explored plot, setting, character, and point of view. Now you will write a personal narrative about something that occurred when you were growing up. You'll use a graphic organizer like the one at the right to put the events in your narrative in chronological order.

Beginning → Middle → End

When you write a personal narrative, you create and develop a situation, including what happened at the beginning, during the middle, and at the end. You use concrete details to describe the setting and people involved. You also try to explain why the experience or situation was memorable.

Here is a model of a personal narrative about a boy's relationship with his grandfather. Notice how the writer has put the events in time order and has explained why the events were worth writing about.

Brandon Saiz

My Abuelo

One day I went to my abuelo's house to visit. My abuelo said, "Do you want to help me learn how to use the computer?" He is kind and has helped me with many things, so I was happy that I could help him this time. We sat down in the kitchen, where he had set up the computer on the counter. He said, "Show me how to turn on the Internet." I automatically clicked the browser because that is what I do on my computer at home. I could see Abuelo was pleased because his eyes opened wider as he studied the screen through his reading glasses. Then he asked me if I could find the Spanish newspaper for him on the Internet, which I did. Finally, I showed him how to turn off the computer. He liked that. Abuelo is now able to show other people how to use the Internet.

VOICE:

☑ I told the narrative from my point of view.

IDEAS:

☑ I used concrete details to describe the events, people, and setting.

Practice

Write a personal narrative about some aspect of growing up. You might want to write about a game you played with an adult or about a lesson you taught or learned. Use a sequence-of-events chart to put your narrative in chronological order. Remember to use regular and irregular verbs in the simple past correctly.

Link the Readings

Critical Thinking

Look back at the readings in this unit. Think about what they have in common. They all tell about growing up. Yet they do not all have the same purpose. The purpose of one reading might be to inform, while the purpose of another might be to entertain or persuade. In addition, the content of each reading relates to growing up differently. Now copy the chart below into your notebook and complete it.

Title of Reading	Purpose	Big Question Link
"Ancient Kids"		
From *Becoming Naomi León*		
From *Later, Gator*	to entertain	tells about brothers growing up
"Amazing Growth Facts," "The Old Grandfather and His Little Grandson"		

Discussion

Discuss in pairs or small groups.

- What similarities can you see between *Becoming Naomi León* and "The Old Grandfather and His Little Grandson"?
- **How does growing up change us?** What conclusions can you draw about growing up, based on what you learned in each of the readings?

Fluency Check

Work with a partner. Choose a paragraph from one of the readings. Take turns reading it for one minute. Count the total number of words you read. Practice saying the words you had trouble reading. Take turns reading the paragraph three more times. Did you read more words each time? Copy the chart below into your notebook and record your speeds.

	1st Speed	2nd Speed	3rd Speed	4th Speed
Words Per Minute				

Projects

1 What do you think happens at the end of *Becoming Naomi León*? Write a paragraph that predicts what will happen. Then read the book to see if your prediction is correct.

2 Make a thank-you card that Bobby might send to Teddy to thank him for the alligator. Include a drawing of the alligator, as well as a note about how Bobby feels about the gift.

3 Make a soap carving. Follow the directions in "Soap Carving" on page 93. You may want to make an animal, as Naomi does. Or you can make something else. Write a title for the figure on an index card to put with it. Have your classmates place their carved figures next to yours to make a class art display.

4 Share a folk tale with your class. You can retell "The Old Grandfather and His Little Grandson" in your own words. Or you can choose another folk tale to share.

Further Reading

To find out more about the theme of this unit, choose from these reading suggestions.

Rip Van Winkle and the Legend of Sleepy Hollow,
Washington Irving
This Penguin Reader® includes adaptations of Irving's two beloved classics.

The Barefoot Book of Heroic Children, Rebecca Hazel
This book presents inspiring stories of some of the most amazing young people in history.

Just Juice, Karen Hesse
A family in Appalachia faces many challenges and, together, overcomes them.

Put It All Together

LISTENING & SPEAKING WORKSHOP

Skit

You will write and perform a skit about growing up in ancient times.

1 **THINK ABOUT IT** Work in small groups. Choose one of the ancient cultures you read about in "Ancient Kids": Greek, Roman, or Maya. Talk about growing up in that time and place. Focus on topics such as school, families, ceremonies, gifts, toys, and foods. Also, discuss how girls and boys were treated and how brothers and sisters might have felt about each other. Do you think that ancient kids felt jealous, the way Teddy did in *Later, Gator*? Think of a situation in your ancient culture that you could present as a skit, or short play. Write down your ideas.

2 **GATHER AND ORGANIZE INFORMATION** Work with your group to plan your skit. Include a character for each group member.

Research Go to the library or use the Internet to gather more information about your ancient culture. Take notes on what you find. Discuss which information you can use to create a clear picture of your ancient culture.

Order Your Notes Write these headings in your notebook: *Characters, Setting, Plot*. Make notes under each heading. For example, under *Plot*, list the main events you will include in your skit.

Prepare a Script Use your notes to write a script for your skit. The dialogue should look like this:

Jason: I don't want to go to school today. I want to stay home and play with my new yo-yo.

Jacinda: You should be grateful that you can go to school! Girls like me have to stay home all the time.

Jason: That sounds like fun.

Jacinda: Well, you're wrong! I hardly ever have time to play. Mother keeps me busy doing chores all day.

Include important details about the setting, props, and action:

Jason stops playing with his yo-yo and frowns. Then he starts to get ready for school.

Use Visuals Make or find the costumes and props you need for your skit.

3 PRACTICE AND PRESENT

As a group, practice your skit until you can perform it without looking at the script. If possible, ask a friend or family member to serve as *prompter* while you practice. (A prompter watches the skit and follows along in the script. If someone forgets what to say or do, the prompter quietly reminds him or her.) Practice using your props and wearing your costumes.

Perform Your Skit Speak loudly enough so that everyone in the class can hear you. Say each word carefully so that it is clear. Be sure to face the audience as you speak, even if your body is pointing in another direction. Pay attention to the other actors, and be ready when it's your turn to speak or move!

4 EVALUATE THE PRESENTATION

A good way to improve your speaking and listening skills is to evaluate your own performance and the performances of your classmates. When you evaluate yourself, you think about what you did well and what you can do better. Use this checklist to help you judge your group's skit and the skits of your classmates.

- ☑ Could you understand the plot?
- ☑ Did the skit show what it was like to grow up in an ancient time?
- ☑ Were the costumes and props helpful and appropriate?
- ☑ Could you hear and understand the actors' words?
- ☑ What suggestions do you have for improving the skit?

Speaking TIPS

Speak naturally and with feeling.

Use gestures and facial expressions to help convey your character's actions and emotions to the audience.

Listening TIPS

Listen carefully to the other actors so that you know when to say your lines. Learn your *cues*—words or actions that signal when it is your turn to speak.

When you watch a skit, look for actions and gestures to help you understand what people are saying.

WRITING WORKSHOP

Fictional Narrative

You've learned how to write a variety of narrative paragraphs. Now, you'll use your skills to write a longer fictional narrative. A fictional narrative is a make-believe story. Two important features of a fictional narrative include the setting, or the time and place of events, and the characters. The characters can be people or animals. Another important feature of a fictional narrative is the plot. The plot is the series of events in a story. These events usually take place in chronological order and build to a climax, or high point. Most plots focus on a problem or conflict that is resolved by the story's end. The point of view, or the perspective from which a story is told, helps shape readers' understanding of what happens. Dialogue also helps show what the characters think and feel.

Your assignment for this workshop is to write a fictional narrative about jealousy between two friends or family members.

1 PREWRITE Brainstorm some ideas for your story in your notebook. What sort of characters would be jealous of each other? Why would the jealousy occur? What effect would it have on the characters' relationship? What would be the story's climax, or high point? How would the story end?

Develop and Organize Ideas Use one or more graphic organizers to develop your story. For example, you might use a T-chart to list the traits of your two characters or a sensory details web to develop a setting. A student named Wendy decided to write about a brother who is jealous of his sister. She used this story chart to organize her ideas:

CHARACTERS Who?	SETTING Where?	PROBLEM What is the conflict?	SOLUTION What is the resolution?
Max Joni their parents	their home	Joni gets all the family's attention. Max is jealous.	Max tells about volunteering. Parents are proud of him.

2 DRAFT Use your graphic organizer and the model on page 131 to help you write a first draft. Remember to tell events in chronological order. Include dialogue to help show what your characters are thinking and feeling.

3 REVISE Read over your draft. As you do so, ask yourself the questions in the writing checklist. Use the questions to help you revise your fictional narrative.

SIX TRAITS OF WRITING CHECKLIST

- ✔ **IDEAS:** Is my plot focused on jealousy between two characters?
- ✔ **ORGANIZATION:** Does my story have a beginning, middle, and end?
- ✔ **VOICE:** Does my story have a clear point of view?
- ✔ **WORD CHOICE:** Do I include realistic dialogue?
- ✔ **SENTENCE FLUENCY:** Do my sentences vary in length and type?
- ✔ **CONVENTIONS:** Does my writing follow the rules of grammar, usage, and mechanics?

Here are the changes Wendy plans to make when she revises her first draft:

Max Learns a Lesson

For a long time, ^ I thought my sister was better than I was at everything. I ~~worked so hard~~ ^struggled for a B average. ^Yet Joni ~~got~~ ^just breezed through with an A in every class My parents weren't upset with my grades; they just paid a lot more attention to Joni. My sister also is a ~~good~~ ^terrific athlete.

Last month, ^ I helped rebuild homes damaged by a flood in a nearby community. I ~~liked~~ ^was excited about making a difference in other people's lives. ^On the other hand, Every afternoon, the only thing Joni and my parents talked about was Joni!

One night, ^as we were having dinner I got sick and tired of the world revolving around her. Doesn't anybody ever want to hear about me? ^" I demanded. " I'm working with a family whose house was really messed up by the flood."

My parents looked ~~at me.~~ surprised "Of course we want to hear about you," my father said. "You don't always seem to want to tell us anything. Usually, when we ask, you just shrug." I had to admit to myself that was true.

"I knew the school asked you to volunteer," my mother said slowly. "But I wasn't sure exactly what you were doing." So I ~~telled~~ told them about working hard to repair soggy floors and repaint water-stained walls.

Just then, joni spoke up. I figured she was about to say something even more wonderful~~er~~ about herself, but instead ~~S~~she said, "Max, did you tell Mom and Dad you made the debate team." I was stu*n*ned she cared!

Since then, I try to ~~talk~~ share more about my interests and activities. My parents congratulated me on volunteering and making the team. I'm no longer jealous of Joni because my parents seem~~ed~~ just as proud of me. They know that we are each special in our own way.

4 EDIT AND PROOFREAD

Copy your revised story onto a clean sheet of paper. Read it again. Correct any errors in grammar, word usage, mechanics, and spelling. Here are the additional changes Wendy plans to make when she prepares her final draft.

Wendy Willner

Max Learns a Lesson

For a long time, I thought my sister was better than I was at everything. I struggled for a B average. Yet Joni just breezed through with an A in every class My parents weren't upset with my grades; they just paid a lot more attention to Joni. My sister also is a terrific athlete.

Last month, I helped rebuild homes damaged by a flood in a nearby community. I was excited about making a difference in other people's lives. On the other hand, every afternoon, the only thing Joni and my parents talked about was Joni!

One night as we were having dinner, I got sick and tired of the world revolving around her. Doesn't anybody ever want to hear about me?" I demanded. "I'm working with a family whose house was really messed up by the flood."

My parents looked surprised. "Of course we want to hear about you," my father said. "You don't always seem to want to tell us anything. Usually, when we ask, you just shrug." I had to admit to myself that was true.

"I knew the school asked you to volunteer," my mother said slowly. "But I wasn't sure exactly what you were doing." So I told them about working hard to repair soggy floors and repaint water-stained walls.

Just then, joni spoke up. I figured she was about to say something even more wonderful about herself, but instead she said, "Max, did you tell Mom and Dad you made the debate team." I was stunned she cared!

My parents congratulated me on volunteering and making the team. Since then, I try to share more about my interests and activities. I'm no longer jealous of Joni because my parents seem just as proud of me. They know that we are each special in our own way.

5 PUBLISH Prepare your final draft. Share your fictional narrative with your teacher and classmates.

Learn about Art with the
Smithsonian American Art Museum

Capturing Childhood

Artists have used many methods to try to capture how people grow up. Many use photographs and paintings. Sometimes families hand these images down over the years, from generation to generation. The clothes and the favorite toys in the images may change over time. Usually, though, there's something familiar in the parade of family faces.

Albert Bisbee, *Child on a Rocking Horse* (about 1855)

This little girl with curly hair stares out at you. She looks a bit uncertain about sitting on the rocking horse. Albert Bisbee, who took a lot of family portraits, once said that he liked to photograph children as soon as they sat on the horse. If he missed his early chance, he felt it got more difficult with each passing minute because the child would get restless.

It took a lot more time to create a photograph in 1855 than it does today. The child had to sit very still. This was because Bisbee used an early photographic process called a daguerreotype. The image was printed directly on a sheet of silver-plated copper. If someone moved even a little bit, the photograph would be blurry.

Photographs were expensive over 150 years ago. Many families had only one or two pictures taken of their children as they grew up. Most of them wanted their child's photograph to be taken on a toy horse. The rocking horse was a very popular toy in nineteenth-century America. The little girl's face in this photograph shows how serious it was to have your picture taken. She wears a checkered dress trimmed with lace. She also wears fancy shoes. She is all dressed up for this important event.

▲ **Albert Bisbee, *Child on a Rocking Horse*, about 1855, daguerreotype, 4¼ x 4½ in., Smithsonian American Art Museum**

William Holbrook Beard, *The Lost Balloon* (1882)

The balloon off in the distance in William Holbrook Beard's painting *The Lost Balloon* is not a toy. It is a hot-air balloon floating beneath the clouds. A group of nine children and a dog are on the edge of a great ledge, watching the balloon as it moves through the sunlight.

An enormous rock face, which rises to their right, is partly hidden by stormy clouds. The children stand very close to the rim of a sharp drop-off in the landscape. Oddly, there are no adults with them. Perhaps Beard was trying to capture the quickly changing nature of childhood. In the painting, he seems to be saying that childhood is like the lovely balloon hanging on the edge of a storm. The children certainly seem very small against the wilderness.

Both of these artists captured an instant in childhood that's temporary, but somehow timeless. Each of us must move on from being ten or twelve or fourteen and face the next stage in life.

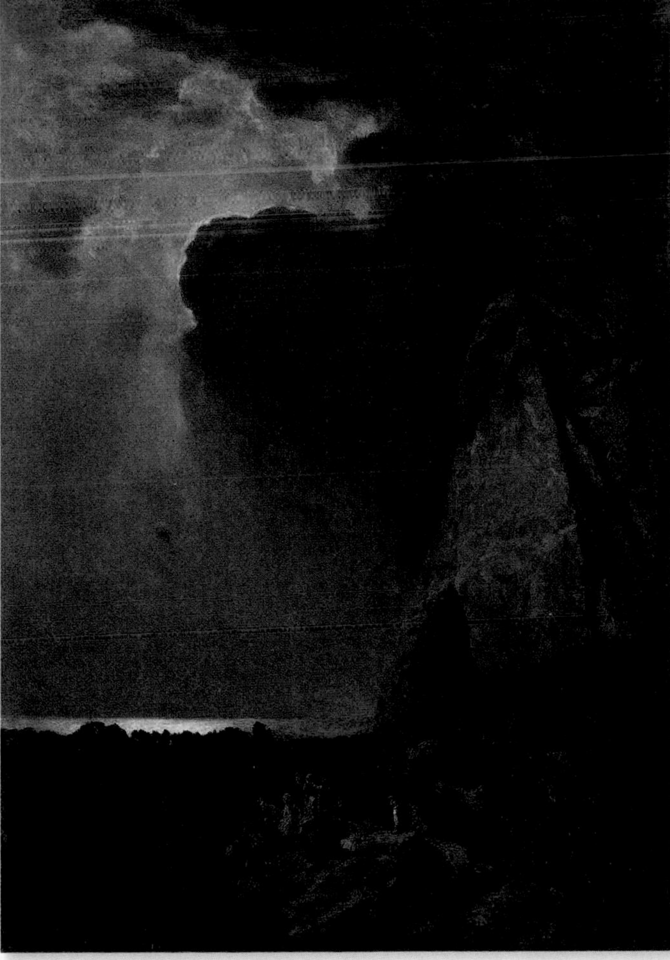

◀ **William Holbrook Beard, *The Lost Balloon*, 1882, oil, 47¾ x 33¾ in., Smithsonian American Art Museum**

Apply What You Learned

1. In what way does each of these artworks capture a moment in childhood?
2. Which medium do you feel is better at capturing the feelings of childhood—photography or painting? Explain.

Big Question
Why do you think that many artworks are about childhood and change?

Workbook Pages 63–64

UNIT 3

THE BIG QUESTION

How does helping others help us all?

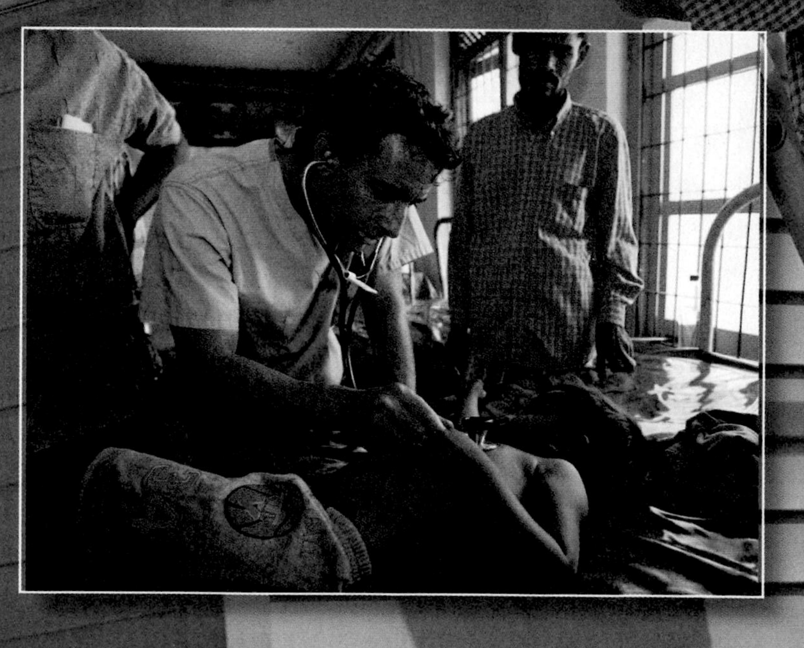

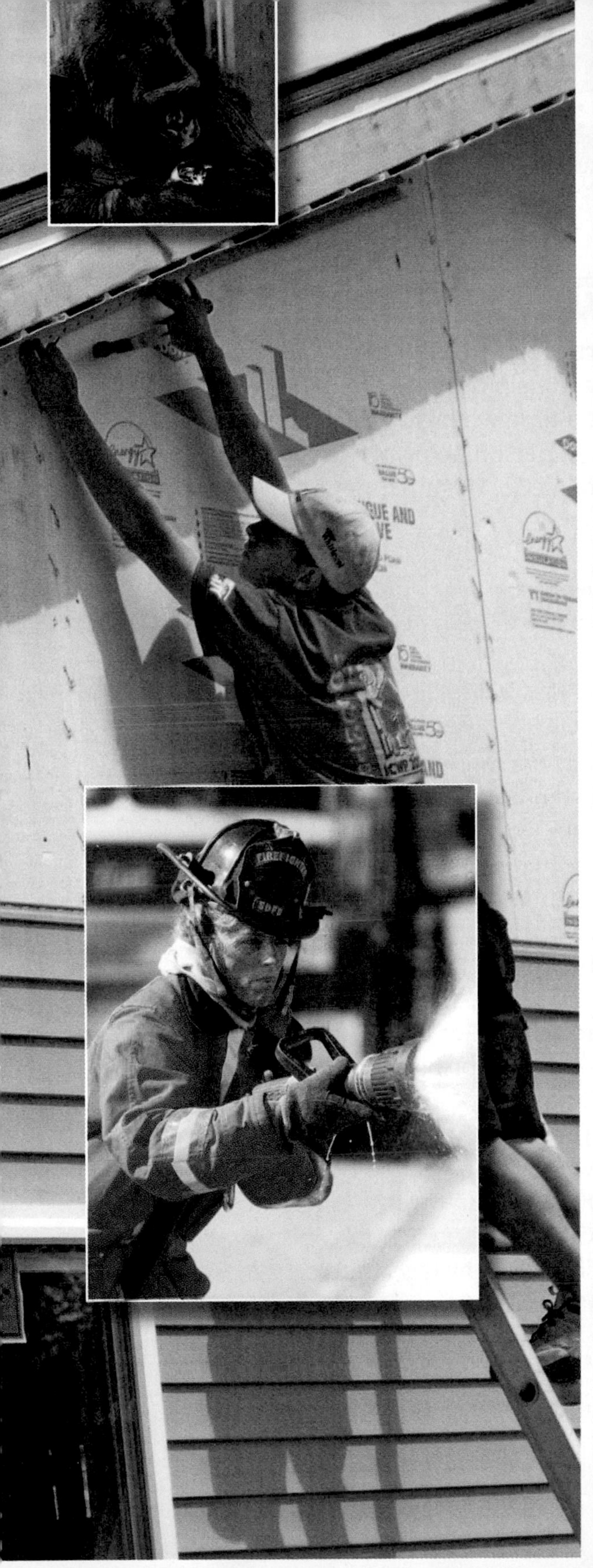

Visit *LongmanKeystone.com*

This unit is about living creatures helping one another. You'll read about an Apache boy who receives help from a farm family and biographies about people who devoted their lives to helping others. You'll read a girl's diary entries that ask for peace in her war-torn country, and you'll read about a baby hippo that receives help from an unlikely fellow creature. As you read, you'll practice the academic and literary language you need to use in school.

READING 1: Novel Excerpt

- From *Run Away Home* by Patricia C. McKissack

READING 2: Social Studies Article

- "Extraordinary People: Serving Others"

READING 3: Diary Excerpt

- From *Zlata's Diary* by Zlata Filipović

READING 4: Science Article

- "Friendship and Cooperation in the Animal Kingdom"

Listening and Speaking

At the end of this unit, you'll present a **TV talk show** about a person you admire.

Writing

In this unit, you will practice **persuasive writing**. This type of writing tries to get the reader to do something or agree with a viewpoint. After each reading, you will learn a skill to help you write a persuasive paragraph. At the end of the unit, you will write a persuasive speech.

QuickWrite

In your notebook, write several persuasive sentences about why it is important for friends to help one another.

READING 1

Prepare to Read

What You Will Learn

Reading

- Vocabulary building: *Literary terms, word study*
- Reading strategy: *Make inferences*
- Text type: *Literature (novel excerpt)*

Grammar, Usage, and Mechanics

Simple and compound sentences

Writing

Write a book review

THE BIG QUESTION

How does helping others help us all? Everyone needs help sometimes. Sometimes we need help because of a big problem or a small problem. Think about a time when you needed help. What was the situation? How did that person help you? Think about a time when you helped someone else. What happened? How did you feel? Discuss with a partner.

BUILD BACKGROUND

Run Away Home takes place on a farm in Alabama in 1888. Novels that take place in a real time and place in the past are called historical fiction. In *Run Away Home,* the main characters are an African-American farm family and an Apache boy. The main characters and plot are imaginary, but certain people and events mentioned in the novel are real.

In 1888, many Apaches were forced to move onto reservations in Alabama. A reservation is land set aside for Native Americans by the U.S. government. Living conditions on the reservations were poor, and many Native Americans became sick.

Some Native American children were sent from reservations to schools far away. At school, they had to stop speaking their native languages and speak only English. They had to eat, dress, and act like whites. The Apache boy in *Run Away Home* doesn't want to be sent to the Carlisle Indian School. This was a real school for Native Americans in Carlisle, Pennsylvania, near Harrisburg.

▲ An 1880 class photo from the Carlisle Indian School

VOCABULARY

Learn Literary Words

Literary Words
- dialect
- mood
- suspense

To make stories realistic, writers sometimes use **dialect** when they write dialogue. Dialect is the way people speak in a specific region. For example, in the southern part of the United States, people use different expressions and may say words differently from the way people do in other parts of the country. Read the examples of dialect. How are these examples of dialect different from the English you are asked to use in school?

> I **might can't** save him. (I may not be able to save him.)
> He's **fixin'** to leave. (He's getting ready to leave.)

Usually, writers create a **mood**, or feeling, in a narrative. For example, they might create a funny, sad, hopeful, or tense mood. One mood that many writers create is a feeling of **suspense**, or uncertainty about what will happen. Suspense keeps readers interested and makes them want to read on to find out what will happen. Read the example below. What mood does the writer create?

> It was a dark moonless night outside the cabin. My father and I were alone for the weekend and were about to go to bed. Suddenly, we heard the sound of heavy footsteps coming closer. We stayed very still and listened. The footsteps sounded like a steady heartbeat getting louder and louder. I shivered.

Practice

Work with a partner. Take turns reading the examples of dialect from *Run Away Home.* Discuss how the dialect might be different from the English you hear at school.

> "What are you thinkin' 'bout, Georgianne? How could you bring trouble to our front door like this? Mr. Wratten was just here lookin' for this boy, and here we got him in our house, takin' care of him."
> "Aine it enough 'round here to do, besides taking on a sick boy, somebody we don't even-now know. What business is it of ours?"

Now read these sentences aloud in the English you hear at school. There might be many ways to say the same sentence.

Learn Academic Words

Study the **red** words and their meanings. You will find these words useful when talking and writing about literature. Write each word and its meaning in your notebook. After you read the excerpt from *Run Away Home*, try to use these words to respond to the text.

Academic Words

appropriate
communicate
period
precise

appropriate = suitable for a particular time, situation, or purpose	➡	It is **appropriate** to say "thank you" when someone helps you.
communicate = express your thoughts and feelings so that others understand them	➡	Some people **communicate** their ideas by writing fiction.
period = a particular length of time in history or in a person's life	➡	Some novels take place during a specific **period** in history. For example, historical fiction might be set in the nineteenth century.
precise = exact and correct in every detail	➡	Directions must be **precise** so that students know exactly what to do.

Practice

Work with a partner to answer these questions. Try to include the **red** word in your answer. Write the sentences in your notebook.

1. What is **appropriate** to say to someone after he or she has helped you?
2. What might you do to **communicate** that you need help?
3. Which **period** in history do you like to read about? Why?
4. Why is it important for travelers to get **precise** directions?

Apache "burden baskets" were used to carry loads during the 1800s—a period of great change for the Apache people. ▶

Word Study: Uses of the Apostrophe

A contraction is a word that is made up of two words that have been shortened into one. An apostrophe is a mark of punctuation that shows where letters have been left out in contractions. Read the examples below.

Two Words	Contraction
is not	isn't
do not	don't

▲ The sun is shining. There isn't a cloud in the sky.

An apostrophe is also used in dialect to show that letters are missing. Read the examples below. What letters does the apostrophe replace in each example of dialect?

Word	Dialect
thinking	thinkin'
children	chil'en or chill'un

Practice

Workbook Page 67

Write these contractions and examples of dialect in your notebook: *I'll, he'd, shouldn't, 'cause, 'round, 'til.* Work with a partner to identify the letter or letters each apostrophe replaces. Then rewrite the words by replacing apostrophes with the letters that are missing.

Reading Strategy MAKE INFERENCES

Making inferences helps you figure out information that authors do not state directly. When you make inferences, you are figuring out what the author means. To make inferences, follow the steps in this example:

- Read the sentence: *By then, the boy was shaking with chills.*
- Think about your own experiences. Ask yourself: "What are chills? How do I feel when I shake with chills?"
- Use the information in the text and your own experiences to make an inference. You can infer (or make the inference) that the boy is probably shaking with chills because he is sick.

As you read the excerpt from *Run Away Home*, make inferences. Think about what the author means but does not say directly.

Workbook Page 68

READING 1

LITERATURE

NOVEL

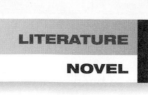

Set a purpose for reading Does it take courage to help someone who is very ill? Read to find out what happens to the sick boy that Sarah and her mother find in their barn. Who is he, and why does he need their help?

from

Run Away Home

Patricia C. McKissack

It is 1888 in Alabama when eleven-year-old Sarah Crossman sees an Apache boy escape from a train taking him to a reservation. Later Sarah and her mother find the boy dying of swamp fever in their barn.

When we pulled the shirt over Sky's head, Mama sucked in her breath and clicked her teeth. I covered my mouth to keep from screaming. He was covered with what looked like hundreds and hundreds of mosquito bites. He had scratched them and they had formed sores.

"Swamp fever," Mama whispered. By then, the boy was shaking with chills. We covered him with quilts, and wrapped his hands with strips of cloth so he couldn't scratch and **infect** himself more.

---

infect, spread disease throughout

"Boil water for sassafras tea," Mama snapped an order. "We've got to drive the impurities out of his body."

Mama began humming, the way she did when she was deep thinking, worried, or unsure. "I need quinine," she said. "Run get yo' daddy."

Turning around, I ran right into Mr. Wratten, who looked larger than life, framing the doorway. "I have some quinine in my saddlebag," he said. Right away, I guessed Mr. Wratten had not gone back to Mount Vernon, but had hung around, suspecting maybe that Sky was hiding out at our place, or we were hiding him. He'd probably seen us carry Sky into the house and come to get him. Seeing how sick Sky was, Mr. Wratten's face softened with concern. "Looks bad," he said. "If I try to take him back to Mount Vernon, he'll never make it."

"Leave him here, then." I said, knowing I was speaking out of place, getting deeper and deeper into trouble with Mama. But I couldn't help myself. I went right on talking. "Mama knows Indian ways; she can help him."

Mr. Wratten looked to Mama for her consent. Sky coughed and moaned. She mopped his forehead with a cool cloth. "I might can't save him," she said. "But I can try."

Mr. Wratten studied on the idea, shifting his weight from foot to foot. "So many Apaches died in Florida," he said, looking beyond Mama to some place in his past. "They're a mountain people, used to dry, cool weather." He mumbled something about the damp climate that seemed to sap the life right out of the Apaches. He was talking more to himself than us.

"Can the boy speak English?" Mama asked. "That might make things a whole lot easier later on."

"Sky speaks Apache and Spanish," he answered. "But he can manage English better than most. He learned it mostly by listening and from a few nuns who used to come several times a week to teach those who were interested. Sky is interested in everything."

Literary Check

*What is the **mood** of the story at this point? Do you feel any **suspense**? Why?*

---

impurities, poisons, or unclean substances that cause sickness
quinine, a drug used for treating fevers
larger than life, important and exciting
suspecting, thinking that
consent, permission
sap, drain

BEFORE YOU GO ON

1. Why does Mama ask Sarah to boil sassafras tea for Sky?
2. Why did many Apaches die in Florida?

On Your Own
Have you or someone close to you ever nursed someone who was very sick? What was it like?

Mr. Wratten sighed deeply. "Sky will be better off here for the time being," he said. "I guess I'll just say I couldn't find him."

I felt relieved. "If he doesn't make it," he added, "wire me that *the quilt is torn*. If he makes it, wire me that *the quilt is ready*, and I'll come get him. Don't let Sky know I've been here or he'll run again." Mama agreed.

Following Mr. Wratten out to his horse to get the quinine, I asked, "Why did Sky run?"

"Sky is the first Apache who has run away. I don't think he wants to go to Carlisle School for Indians up in Pennsylvania. And I can't say as I blame him. Most Apaches who go there come back home in a coffin. As many of them die of homesickness as they do from diseases."

I had many more questions, but it was not the time to ask. Mr. Wratten was gone by the time Papa came in from the fields for noontime meal.

When Papa didn't smell anything cooking and saw who we had made the sickroom for, he commenced to fussing. "What are you thinkin' 'bout, Georgianne? How could you bring trouble to our front door like this? Mr. Wratten was just here lookin' for this boy, and here we got him in our house, takin' care of him."

"He's sick and needs our help," Mama said. "And besides," she added, "Mr. Wratten knows he's here and asked me to care for him 'til he gets better."

"Aine it enough 'round here to do, besides taking on a sick boy, somebody we don't even-now know. What business is it of ours?"

Mama had started a pot to boil some rice. But she stopped and raised the wooden spoon as if she planned to use it as a weapon. "Lee Andy, you the one always talkin' 'bout how you s'posed to love yo' neighbor as yo'self. What meaning is in them words?" Mama asked.

Right away, Papa fled to the barn. Within the half hour he came back, Bible story in hand.

"I'm reminded here of the parable of the Good Samaritan who took care of a stranger he found 'side the road. It is right that we should take care of this poor soul who is in need. I've made up my mind, now. So, don't try to talk me out of it."

"Yes, you're right, Lee Andy," Mama said.

I turned away so Papa wouldn't see me smiling as I spooned hot tea into Sky's mouth.

Literary Check

*How do the examples of **dialect** on this page help to communicate what Mama and Papa are like?*

---

for the time being, for now
homesickness, feelings of sadness when away from home
diseases, illnesses
commenced to, began
business, personal responsibility or task

Getting Sky through the night took a powerful lot of doctoring. I sat by his bedside, hoping some and praying some, always helping Mama by fetching and carrying whatever was needed. Sky tossed and turned, and yelled out in his feverish sleep, calling Geronimo's name, and mumbling words in Apache. "Fight," I whispered to him. "Fight to stay alive. Don't give up."

Mama burned herbs and called upon her grandmother for guidance. And then she rattled her bag of bones over his body and sang a song her father had taught her. . . .

All through the night I rubbed Sky's arms and legs with a soothing paste Mama'd made from dried roots. . . .

Sky's fever broke early the next morning, shortly before the southbound rumbled through Quincy. But he wasn't out of the woods yet—far from it. On the third day, his breathing settled into a steady rhythm as his body stayed cool. "He'll make it," said Mama, giving her head a quick nod, the way she did when she felt triumphant. Strengthened by her success, Mama stopped humming and sang a happy tune while preparing breakfast.

But I was bone tired because I hadn't slept more than a few hours in days. Now that it looked like Sky would live, I yawned and stretched and dragged into the kitchen. "Put a little life in your step," Mama said in a lively way. "You're too young to know what tired is."

Geronimo, a famous Apache chief who fought to protect his people's lands
guidance, help and advice
out of the woods, out of trouble
triumphant, victorious
bone tired, extremely tired

BEFORE YOU GO ON

1. What does Mama say to convince Papa to help Sky?
2. Why is Sarah bone tired?

On Your Own
What does it mean "to love yo' neighbor as yo'self"? Is this a good saying? Why?

Yes I do, I wanted to say, but dared not be that sassy. I was forever getting my legs switched for talking back, talking out of turn, or just plain talking too much. When I'm all grown up, I thought, I'm going to say what's on my mind. But that was a ways off. As far as I knew I was still on the wrong side of Mama, even though she hadn't mentioned anything to Papa about my part in Sky's escape. I decided it was best not to rile her. So I kept my mouth shut and took joy in knowing we would not have to wire Mr. Wratten that *the quilt is torn.*

Buster met me at the door, yelping all kinds of questions. I explained everything to him, putting in all the details about how we'd saved Sky's life. He listened, head cocked to one side as if he understood everything I was saying. "Buster, I'm so glad I've got you to talk to," I said. "You're a good dog, no matter what Papa thinks."

The smells of Mama's kitchen must have awakened Sky. He was sitting bolt straight in the bed, looking wild-eyed and frightened when I brought a plate of food to him. He asked something in Apache. When I shook my head to show I didn't understand, he switched to English. "Where is this place?" he asked, trying to get up, but he was too weak.

Putting my hand on his shoulder, I smiled, saying, "Here, lie back down, before you . . . "

Sky pulled away and his first words to me were, "I don't know you!" He snapped at me in very clear English, "I don't know you." This time, I snatched my hands away like I'd touched a sleeping alligator by accident. He tried to sit up, but once more he flopped back down on his pallet.

"I was just trying to help," I said, feeling put out. The past few days, I'd imagined a lot of things about Sky, but I never expected him to be an Un-person. In my way of thinking, an Un-person was one who was unkind, ungrateful, unpleasant, unfair, unanything.

The patient wasn't any nicer to Mama. When she tried to get him to eat, he shoved it away. "No pig meat," he said, looking down in disgust.

---

rile, anger or upset
put out, hurt or unfairly treated
patient, person getting medical care

Maybe the fever had addled his brain, I thought.

"Eat a few grits, then," Mama insisted. "You need to build up your strength again. You're still sick."

"I am not sick!" he scoffed. Sky would have nothing to do with us. He pulled the sheet up to his chin, and refused everything we offered him. By then I was close to tossing the food on his head. Just then Papa came in.

Papa introduced everybody by name, including himself. "This is my family." Sky shook his head, never taking his eyes off Mama, who stood at the foot of the bed. "Son, you're 'mongst the living this morning, 'cause of the Good Lord working through my wife and daughter." Sky seemed to be hanging on every word Papa said. "Now, let's get this understanding," Papa went on. "As long as you're in this house, you'll treat them with respect or I'm gon' know why. Clear?"

It took me back when Sky's whole attitude changed in a hurry—I mean, right now. He commenced to eating, shoving down three helpings of grits, eggs, and biscuits—but he still wouldn't touch the pork.

He was still an Un-person, I decided—ungrateful! But I remembered one of Papa's favorite sayings. "Tote the load of another person 'fore you pass judgment." So I put myself in Sky's shoes. He had awakened in a strange man's house and bed with that man's family attending to him in a very personal way. Maybe he wasn't being rude, but waiting until he had been welcomed by the head of the household—Papa. Somehow Sky had gotten a welcome in Papa's words—the permission he needed to feel comfortable with us. I may have been all wrong, but my reason made good sense to me.

LITERARY CHECK

*Why do you think the author has Papa speak in **dialect**? How does his way of speaking reveal his character?*

---

addled his brain, confused him
grits, crushed dried corn that is cooked and eaten for breakfast
hanging on every word, listening closely to every word
tote, carry
put myself in Sky's shoes, put myself in his place
attending to, taking care of
personal, private

ABOUT THE AUTHOR

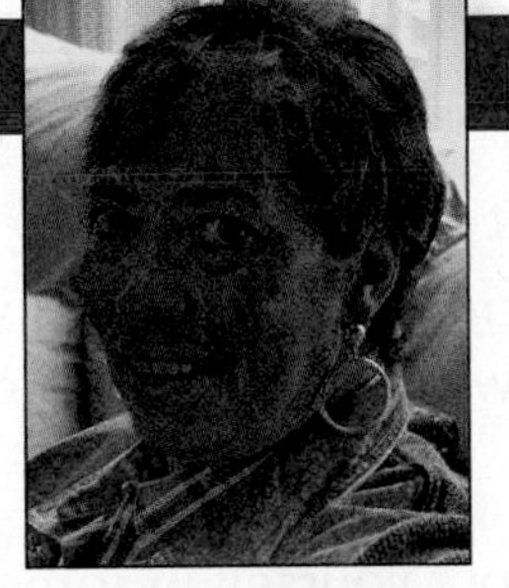

Patricia C. McKissack based *Run Away Home* in part on a family story her great-uncle told about her great-great-great-great-grandfather, who was a Native American. She has written numerous award-winning novels and nonfiction books. McKissack sometimes writes biographies and nonfiction books with her husband, and she has also written one book, *Black Diamond: The Story of the Negro Baseball Leagues*, with her son.

BEFORE YOU GO ON

1. Why does Sarah snatch her hands away as if she had touched an alligator?
2. What does Sarah mean when she calls Sky an Un-person?

On Your Own
What do you think of the Crossmans? What kind of people are they?

READING 1

Review and Practice

READER'S THEATER

Act out this scene between Sarah and her mother.

Sarah: Mama, how sick is Sky? All those sores look pretty bad.

Mama: He is very sick, Sarah. He has a bad disease. Sky might die.

Sarah: Oh, no! Can you cure him, Mama? How can you help him?

Mama: I am going to give him a medicine called quinine. It will help lower his fever. If we can get his fever down, he will probably recover. I will wash him with cool water, too.

Sarah: What can I do to help you? Should I get some water?

Mama: Get your father. I need his help, too. Then boil some water for sassafras tea. Sky will need to drink a lot of this tea in order to get the poisons out of his body.

Sarah: Okay, Mama. I really hope that Sky gets better.

Mama: Hurry up now, and get your Papa.

Speaking TIP

Try to use your voice to communicate your character's traits. For example, Mama would speak in a strong, grown-up way, but Sarah would sound less sure of herself.

COMPREHENSION

Right There

1. What illness does Sky have?
2. What message is Mama to send if Sky lives?

Think and Search

3. During what time period does this novel take place?
4. What are some things that Mama does to help Sky get well?

Author and You

5. Why do you think that Sky only listens to Papa?
6. How does the writer create suspense? At what point in the selection did you know that Sky would get better?

On Your Own

7. Does it help to try to put yourself in someone else's shoes? Why?
8. When have you or someone close to you felt homesick?

▲ This advertisement shows how quinine was once used to treat fevers.

DISCUSSION

Discuss in pairs or small groups.

1. How does Mama get Papa to do what she wants? Explain.
2. Papa says, "Tote the load of another person 'fore you pass judgment." What does he mean by this?
3. How do you think Sky knew that he would not like the Carlisle Indian School? What inferences can you make about Sky's character and feelings?

Q **How does helping others help us all?** How do the Crossmans feel when Sky gets better? Do they feel better about themselves for helping him? Why?

Listening TIP

Ask questions if you want more information. If you don't understand what someone is saying, ask the person to repeat or explain his or her answer.

RESPONSE TO LITERATURE

Imagine that you are in Sky's shoes. Why did you run away? How do you feel about having Mama and Sarah take care of you? Write a journal entry in which you communicate your experiences and feelings. Describe the following:

- Why I ran away
- What happened to me
- How I feel about being sick
- How I feel about being cared for by a girl and her mother

When you are done writing, share your journal entry with a partner. Discuss which details in the selection helped you write your journal entry.

Geronimo, the Apache chief who fought to protect Apache lands from settlers ▶

Grammar and Writing

GRAMMAR, USAGE, AND MECHANICS

Simple and Compound Sentences

Remember that a sentence is a group of words that expresses a complete thought. A simple sentence has a subject and a verb. Read the example of a simple sentence from *Run Away Home.*

subject	verb
Mr. Wratten	sighed.

Good writers include sentences of varying lengths in their writing. When you want to combine two simple sentences, use a coordinating conjunction, such as *and, but,* or *or.* This will make your writing flow better. Two simple sentences joined by a coordinating conjunction form a compound sentence. When joining two simple sentences, you usually place a comma before the coordinating conjunction. Read these examples.

> He had scratched them**, and** they had formed sores.
> I had more questions**, but** it was not the time to ask.

Practice

Work with a partner. Copy the pairs of simple sentences below into your notebook. Then combine each pair into a compound sentence, using a coordinating conjunction, such as *and, but,* or *or.* Write the compound sentences.

1. Sky could die.
   He could get better.
2. Mama stopped humming nervously.
   She started whistling a happy tune.
3. I may be wrong about Sky.
   My reason made sense to me.

WRITING A PERSUASIVE PARAGRAPH

Write a Book Review

On this page, you'll use a graphic organizer like the one at the right to help you write a book review. When you write a review, you state your opinion of the book and tell whether it is worth reading or not. In either case, you give reasons for your point of view and support them with convincing examples. Providing one or more reasons and presenting them simply and logically makes the review persuasive. Begin by stating your opinion. Then give reasons and provide examples from the book. End your review with a persuasive conclusion. For example, you might recommend the book to others.

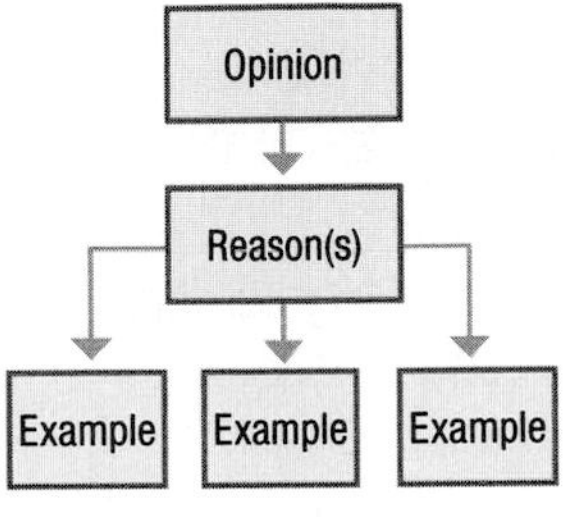

Here is a model book review of *Run Away Home*. Notice how the writer gives her opinion and a recommendation, and supports her opinion and recommendation with reasons and examples.

Danielle Christian

Run Away Home

Run Away Home is the most exciting book I've read in a long time, and I think that many students would feel the same way. It is the story of a runaway Apache boy who is helped by an African-American farm family in Alabama in 1888. One reason why I liked the book is that it is full of suspense. When the Crossmans find Sky dying of swamp fever, I was in suspense until I knew whether Sky would live or die. I had to keep reading until I found out. I also liked the book because I identify with the main characters. I liked all of the characters, but I identify most with Sarah. She is brave, kind, and rebellious. I would choose someone like Sarah for my friend. In addition, I enjoyed the book because it was about people who care for others. Each of the Crossmans helped to protect Sky. I recommend Run Away Home to anyone who likes suspense, real-life characters, or stories about helping others.

IDEAS:

☑ I included my opinion, reasons that support it, and a recommendation.

SENTENCE FLUENCY:

☑ I used both simple and compound sentences.

Practice

Review a book or story that you like very much. Use an opinion and reasons chart to list your ideas. Include both simple and compound sentences in your review.

READING 2

Prepare to Read

What You Will Learn

Reading

- Vocabulary building: *Context, dictionary skills, word study*
- Reading strategy: *Identify problems and solutions*
- Text type: *Informational text (social studies)*

Grammar, Usage, and Mechanics
Prepositions of time: *in, on,* and *at*

Writing
Use a question-and-answer format

THE BIG QUESTION

How does helping others help us all? Heroes are people whom we admire and respect because they've helped others. Sometimes people do heroic things because of their work. Firefighters, teachers, doctors, men and women who serve in the military—they can all be heroes. Who are your heroes? How are, or were, they heroic? How do, or did, they help others?

BUILD BACKGROUND

"Extraordinary People: Serving Others" is a series of short biographies of heroic figures from around the world. Many readers will be inspired by the stories of these remarkable people and how they helped change the world. All of these heroic figures are greatly admired for their bravery, strength, and willingness to help others.

Two of the people you will read about also had to face their own physical challenges. Helen Keller became blind and deaf as a young child. Franklin Delano Roosevelt lost the ability to walk when he was thirty-nine years old. Both of these extraordinary people worked hard to conquer their physical challenges. Heroes always face challenges, but they don't give up.

▲ President Roosevelt had to wear leg braces to help him walk.

◀ Anne Sullivan (right) helped Helen Keller (left) learn how to communicate.

VOCABULARY

Learn Key Words

Read these sentences. Use the context to figure out the meaning of the **red** words. Use a dictionary to check your answers. Then write each word and its meaning in your notebook.

1. Sometimes leaders are **assassinated**. Kings, presidents, and other important people have been killed by surprise attack.
2. The doctor had **extraordinary** abilities. She saved the lives of three children whose injuries were thought to be beyond hope.
3. The **founders** of this school wanted to establish a place of learning for students with special needs.
4. The people showed **resistance** to the law by voting against it.
5. The **superintendent** of our group makes all the rules and is in charge.
6. You show **tolerance** by respecting other people's ideas.

Key Words

assassinated
extraordinary
founders
resistance
superintendent
tolerance

Practice

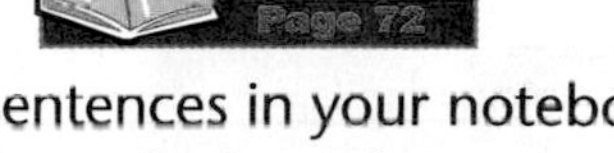

Write the sentences in your notebook. Choose a **red** word from the box above to complete each sentence. Then take turns reading the sentences aloud with a partner.

1. At first there was much ______ to the new idea, but everyone finally came to accept it.
2. ______ helps people live peacefully because it encourages people to respect one another's ideas.
3. In the 1960s, three important U.S. leaders—John F. Kennedy, Martin Luther King Jr., and Robert F. Kennedy—were all ______ by gunmen.
4. The doctor was one of the three ______ of the hospital in 1938.
5. Tiger Woods is an ______ golfer. He has amazing abilities.
6. The ______ hired all the nurses and was in charge of running the hospital.

▲ Senator Robert F. Kennedy attends the funeral of assassinated civil rights leader Dr. Martin Luther King Jr.

Learn Academic Words

Study the **red** words and their meanings. You will find these words useful when talking and writing about informational texts. Write each word and its meaning in your notebook. After you read "Extraordinary People: Serving Others," try to use these words to respond to the text.

Academic Words

achieve
alter
impact
role

achieve = succeed in doing or getting something as a result of your actions	➡	Some people **achieve** success by getting important things done.
alter = change in some way	➡	Many people want to **alter** the health-care system in the United States.
impact = the effect that something or someone has on someone or something	➡	Doctors have a big **impact** on the health and well-being of their patients.
role = the position, job, or function someone or something has in a particular situation or activity	➡	Nurses play an important **role** in a hospital. They help doctors, and they help sick people get well.

Practice

Work with a partner to complete these statements. Try to include the **red** word in your answer. Write the sentences in your notebook.

1. By the time I am a grown-up, I would like to **achieve** . . .
2. When it rains, I **alter** my plans by . . .
3. I think my close friends have an **impact** on my life because . . .
4. First-grade teachers play an important **role** in a child's life because . . .

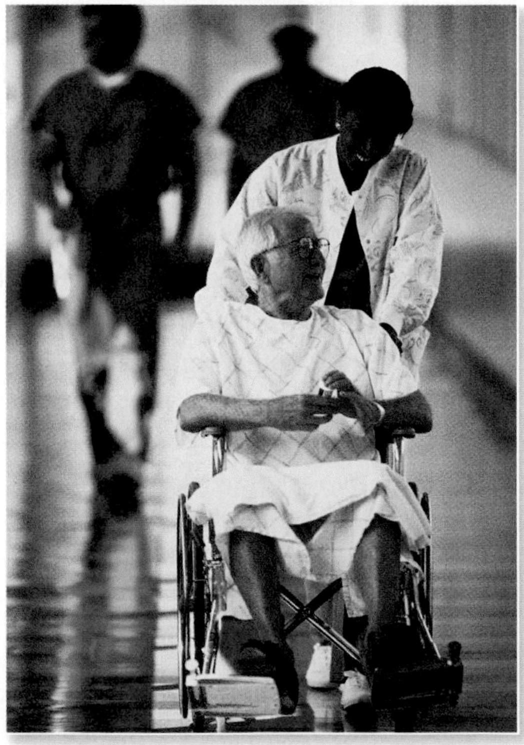

▲ This nurse plays an important role in caring for senior citizens.

Word Study: Spelling Words with Silent *gh*

In English, the letters *gh* are often, but not always, silent. Study the words in the chart. You will read some of these words in "Extraordinary People: Serving Others." Notice that in these words, the letters *gh* are silent.

brought	daughter	fought	night	rights	sight

Practice

Say a word from the chart, and ask your partner to spell it aloud. Then have your partner say the next word. Continue until you can spell all of the words correctly. Now think of three more words that contain the silent letters *gh*. Say the words one by one. Ask your partner to spell each word.

READING STRATEGY IDENTIFY PROBLEMS AND SOLUTIONS

Identifying problems and solutions helps you understand a text better. Many texts include a problem that a person, group, or character has to solve (or find a solution to). To identify problems and solutions, ask yourself:

- What problem or problems does the person or group have?
- How does the person or group solve or try to solve the problem?

In "Extraordinary People: Serving Others," heroes face problems and find solutions. As you read the biographies, think about each problem and its possible solutions. Read to find out how the problem was solved.

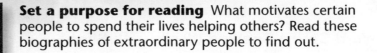

Set a purpose for reading What motivates certain people to spend their lives helping others? Read these biographies of extraordinary people to find out.

Extraordinary People: Serving Others

In different places and at different times, people have achieved extraordinary things. In the short biographies that follow, you will read about people from different times in history who helped others in many ways. You will also read about a group of people who continue to do extraordinary things in troubled parts of the world today.

Benito Juárez

Benito Juárez (1806–1872) is a national hero in Mexico. He was the son of poor Zapotec Indian farmers in the state of Oaxaca, Mexico. At age thirteen he couldn't read, write, or speak Spanish. He trained to become a priest, but later he decided to become a lawyer. As a young man, he became interested in social justice, especially the rights of native peoples. He was very popular among the native Indian population. In 1847, he was elected governor of Oaxaca.

In 1861, Juárez became the first Zapotec Indian president of Mexico. He improved education. For the first time, it was possible for every child to go to school. He stopped the French from colonizing Mexico. His many reforms made Mexico a fairer, more modern society.

▲ **Benito Juárez fought for the rights of all people in Mexico.**

---

social justice, fairness for all people
colonizing, controlling a country and sending your own people to live there
reforms, changes that improve a system

Florence Nightingale

Florence Nightingale (1820–1910) came from a wealthy English family. Against her parents' wishes, she became a nurse.

In 1853, she became superintendent of a hospital for women in London. In 1854, Britain, France, and Turkey fought against Russia in the Crimean War. Nightingale volunteered to go to Turkey to help. She took thirty-eight nurses with her. They helped many wounded soldiers recover. Nightingale often visited the soldiers at night, carrying a lamp. Soldiers called her "the lady with the lamp."

When Nightingale returned to England, she started a school for nurses. The school still exists today.

▲ **Florence Nightingale worked for many long hours to help the sick and dying men.**

Mohandas Gandhi

Mohandas Gandhi (1869–1948) was born in the coastal city of Porbandar, in the western part of India. At that time, India was a British colony. Gandhi went to England in 1888 and studied law. He returned to India and worked as a lawyer in Bombay (Mumbai).

In 1893, Gandhi traveled to South Africa. The government of South Africa had a system of racial separation, called apartheid. A group of white South Africans attacked Gandhi and beat him. After this experience, he encouraged people to practice passive resistance against the South African authorities and apartheid.

After he returned to India in 1915, Gandhi became a leader in India's struggle for independence. He became the international symbol of nonviolent protest. He believed in religious tolerance. In 1947, Britain finally ended its 190-year rule in India. Then, in 1948, Gandhi was assassinated by someone who didn't agree with his beliefs.

Gandhi inspired nonviolent movements elsewhere. In the United States, Dr. Martin Luther King Jr. used passive resistance when he became leader of the civil rights movement in the 1950s and 1960s.

---

wealthy, very rich
apartheid, a system in which different races in a country are separated
inspired, caused; influenced people to express interest in

▲ **Gandhi was imprisoned many times for his beliefs.**

BEFORE YOU GO ON

1. What role did Florence Nightingale play during the Crimean War?
2. What system was Mohandas Gandhi trying to change through passive resistance?

On Your Own
Why do you think Benito Juárez wanted to stop the French from colonizing Mexico?

Franklin Delano Roosevelt

Franklin Delano Roosevelt (1882–1945) was elected as the thirty-second president of the United States in 1932. During the 1930s, the country was experiencing deep **economic** troubles. This period in American history is called the Great Depression. Banks shut down, workers lost their jobs, and farms failed. Roosevelt declared that Americans had "nothing to fear but fear itself." He put into place a series of new government programs that brought hope to the American people. Many people returned to work.

Roosevelt soon faced another challenge. The Second World War in Europe and the Pacific began in 1939. Great Britain, France, Russia, and other countries (the Allies) fought against Germany and Japan. In 1941, the Japanese bombed Pearl Harbor in Hawaii. Roosevelt asked for and received a declaration of war on Japan, and the United States entered the war. The United States and the Allies fought many brave battles and eventually won the war in 1945.

▲ **President Roosevelt overcame polio to lead the United States through two of its most difficult times: the Great Depression and World War II.**

Roosevelt faced personal challenges as well. He came down with **polio** at the age of thirty-nine, and lost the use of his legs. However, Roosevelt did not allow his physical condition to prevent him from contributing to society. Roosevelt is now considered by many historians to be one of the greatest U.S. presidents.

Helen Keller

Helen Keller (1880–1968) was nineteen months old when she became sick with a fever. The sickness left her without sight or hearing. Because she was so young when this happened, it was hard for her to learn to communicate. Because she could not see, she was unable to use sign language—the language of hearing-**impaired** people. She also couldn't "read lips," as many hearing-impaired people do. Although these challenges made young Helen very **frustrated**, she was also extremely intelligent. With the help of a skilled teacher, named Anne Sullivan, she learned that everything had a name and that these names were words. Because of the help of others and her own determination, she was eventually able to learn different ways to communicate. For instance, she learned to "hear" and understand speech by touching a speaker's lips and throat.

▲ **Helen Keller was the first sight- and hearing-impaired person to graduate from college.**

---

economic, relating to business, industry, and managing money
polio, an infectious disease of the nerves in the spine that can cause paralysis
impaired, damaged, or less strong, or less good
frustrated, upset because you can't do something

Keller gave lectures (with her teacher's help) and wrote a number of books. Her public talks and her writings inspired countless people with hearing, sight, and other physical problems. She inspired others to not give up in the face of adversity. Keller also toured the world. She raised funds for programs to help people with impaired hearing and sight. To this day, Helen Keller remains a figure of inspiration.

Doctors Without Borders

Doctors Without Borders is an international organization whose members believe that every person in every country has the right to medical care. It helps victims of war, disease, and natural disasters. A small group of French doctors started Doctors Without Borders (Médecins Sans Frontières) in 1971. Each year, thousands of volunteer doctors, nurses, and administrators from countries all over the world provide medical aid to people in more than seventy countries. They provide health care, perform surgery, organize nutrition and sanitation programs, train local medical staff, and provide mental health care.

Doctors Without Borders works with the United Nations, governments, and the media to tell the world about their patients' suffering and concerns. For example, Doctors Without Borders volunteers told the media about the atrocities they saw in Chechnya, Angola, and Kosovo.

Doctors Without Borders won the Nobel Peace Prize in 1999. Accepting the award, one of the organization's founders, Bernard Kouchner, said, "I'm deeply moved, and I'm thinking of all the people who died without aid, of all those who died waiting for someone to knock on their door."

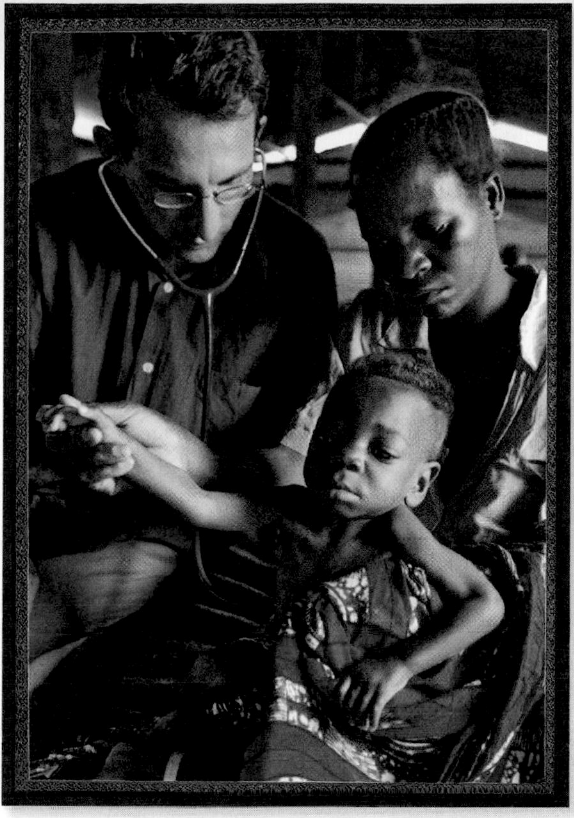

▲ **A doctor helps a child in Angola, where many children die of starvation or disease.**

---

adversity, difficulties or problems
borders, official lines that separate two countries
administrators, people who manage businesses or organizations
nutrition, food for good health and growth
sanitation, hygiene; cleanliness
atrocities, extremely violent actions

BEFORE YOU GO ON

1. How did Franklin Delano Roosevelt help pull the United States out of the Depression?
2. Why did Helen Keller have trouble communicating?

On Your Own
Would you like to work for Doctors Without Borders? Why or why not?

READING 2

Review and Practice

COMPREHENSION

Right There

1. What happened to Benito Juárez in 1861?
2. Franklin Delano Roosevelt was president during which war?

Think and Search

3. Why was Helen Keller's childhood so difficult?
4. What North American leader believed in passive resistance?

Author and You

5. Why do you think the author chose to write about Florence Nightingale?
6. Who do you think had the most lasting impact on others? Why?

On Your Own

7. Why is it important for all children to get an education?
8. Describe someone you think is extraordinary. Why is that person special?

IN YOUR OWN WORDS

Imagine that you are telling a small group of friends about "Extraordinary People: Serving Others." Tell your friends about each person or organization in the text. Use the chart to help you summarize the history of each person or organization. Then share your summaries with a classmate. See how they compare.

Speaking TIPS

Make eye contact with your classmates.

Talk to your audience, not your chart.

Famous People	Summary
Benito Juárez	
Florence Nightingale	
Mohandas Gandhi	
Franklin Delano Roosevelt	
Helen Keller	
Doctors Without Borders	

DISCUSSION

Discuss in pairs or small groups.

1. In what ways did Helen Keller's teacher, Anne Sullivan, help her?
2. How are Benito Juárez and Mohandas Gandhi similar? How are they different?
3. What kind of qualities do you think members of Doctors Without Borders have in common?

Q How does helping others help us all? In what ways did Mohandas Gandhi, Helen Keller, and Doctors Without Borders make the world better for all of us?

Listening TIP

When listening to your classmates, listen for examples they use to illustrate their ideas. Think about how these ideas are similar to or different from your own.

READ FOR FLUENCY

When we read aloud to communicate meaning, we group words into phrases, pause or slow down to make important points, and emphasize important words. Pause for a short time when you reach a comma and for a longer time when you reach a period. Pay attention to rising and falling intonation at the end of sentences.

Work with a partner. Choose a paragraph from the reading. Discuss which words seem important for communicating meaning. Practice pronouncing difficult words. Take turns reading the paragraph aloud and give each other feedback.

▲ Helen Keller had to rely on her sense of touch and smell.

EXTENSION

Workbook Page 76

Learn more about the people and organization described in "Extraordinary People: Helping Others." Choose any two subjects described in the text. Use encyclopedias, reference books, and reliable websites to do research. Then share your findings with a classmate.

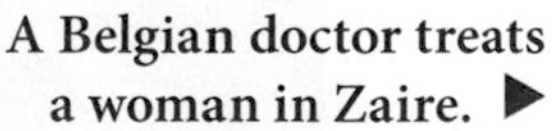

A Belgian doctor treats a woman in Zaire. ▶

Grammar and Writing

GRAMMAR, USAGE, AND MECHANICS

Prepositions of Time: *in, on,* and *at*

Biographies refer to specific moments in time. The prepositions *in, on,* and *at* can be used to show a point in time. Use *in* for months, years, centuries, and seasons. Use *on* for days and exact dates, and use *at* for times of day. Read these examples.

In 1893, Mohandas Gandhi traveled to South Africa.
On Friday, Helen Keller started to study with her teacher.
During the day and **at** night, Florence Nightingale took care of her patients.

Study the chart below. It shows how prepositions of time are used.

in	on	at
October 2009 a month the summer the morning	October 7 Friday Friday morning a winter day my birthday	twelve o'clock noon midnight dawn sunset

Note: The preposition *in* is used with *in the morning, in the afternoon*, and *in the evening,* but the preposition *at* is used with *at night.*

Practice

Work with a partner. Write the sentences in your notebook. Use the correct preposition for each sentence.

1. ______ 1861, Benito Juárez became president.
2. Congress declared war ______ December 8, 1941.
3. Florence Nightingale visited the patients ______ the morning.
4. ______ December 17, the doctors accepted the award.
5. Gandhi met with the government of South Africa ______ five o'clock.
6. The doctor received a call for help ______ night.

The sky at night ▼

WRITING A PERSUASIVE PARAGRAPH

Use a Question-and-Answer Format

On this page, you'll write a persuasive paragraph that asks and answers a specific question. Your paragraph will justify, or give reasons why, someone is extraordinary and admirable. You'll use a graphic organizer like the one at the right to structure your paragraph.

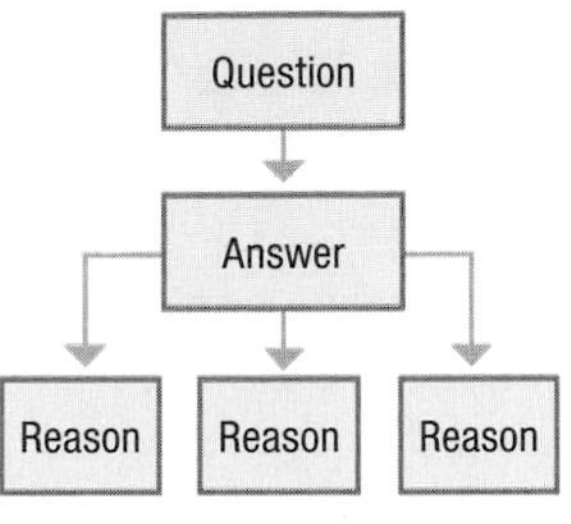

Asking and answering a question is one way to focus and organize a paragraph. First, you pose a question. Then you not only give an answer, but you explain your answer by giving facts, details, and examples to support it. The support you give should convince readers to agree with your point of view.

Here is a model of a paragraph that uses a question-and-answer format. Notice how the writer asks a question first, then follows with a persuasive answer that is supported by facts, details, and examples.

Tamar Honig

Mohandas Gandhi

What extraordinary things did Gandhi do that set him apart from other people of his time? He developed peaceful, nonviolent methods of protest in the face of violence and injustice, and he was an inspiration to millions of people around the world. While in South Africa, he encouraged people to practice passive resistance against apartheid. In India, he played a major role in the country's struggle for independence by organizing nonviolent demonstrations. Lastly, Gandhi inspired others, including leaders of the U.S. civil rights movement to use nonviolent methods of protest. Tragically, this peaceful man was assassinated on January 30, 1948.

Practice

Choose someone who you think is truly extraordinary. Then write a persuasive paragraph that answers the question, What extraordinary things did this person do? Use a question-and-answer chart like the one above to organize your ideas. Include at least three reasons for your opinion. Justify each reason with facts, details, or examples. Use prepositions of time if this will make your explanation clearer.

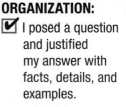

Writing Checklist

ORGANIZATION:

☑ I posed a question and justified my answer with facts, details, and examples.

CONVENTIONS:

☑ I used prepositions of time correctly.

READING 3

Prepare to Read

What You Will Learn

Reading

- Vocabulary building: *Literary terms, word study, dictionary skills*
- Reading strategy: *Distinguish fact from opinion*
- Text type: *Literature (diary excerpt)*

Grammar, Usage, and Mechanics
Placement of adjectives

Writing
Write a diary entry

THE BIG QUESTION

How does helping others help us all? Have you ever kept or wanted to keep a diary? People who keep a diary write about their experiences, observations, and feelings. How could keeping a diary help someone get through a difficult time? What can others learn from that diary if they read it? Discuss with a partner.

BUILD BACKGROUND

Zlata Filipović, an eleven-year-old Bosnian girl, wrote ***Zlata's Diary*** in 1992, during the Bosnian War. Zlata lived in Sarajevo, the capital of Bosnia and Herzegovina, where some of the worst fighting occurred. She used her diary to write about her daily experiences during the war.

Look at the map. It shows the borders of the former Yugoslavia in 1991, just before the Bosnian War. It also shows the six republics that once had been part of the Yugoslav Federation: Bosnia and Herzegovina, Croatia, Macedonia, Montenegro, Slovenia, and Serbia. During the 1980s and 1990s, long-standing national and ethnic conflicts caused war among citizens of Yugoslavia. Before the war, Bosnia and Herzegovina had been a republic within Yugoslavia. As a result of the war, Bosnia and Herzegovina and other republics within Yugoslavia broke away and declared their independence. During this time, much blood was shed.

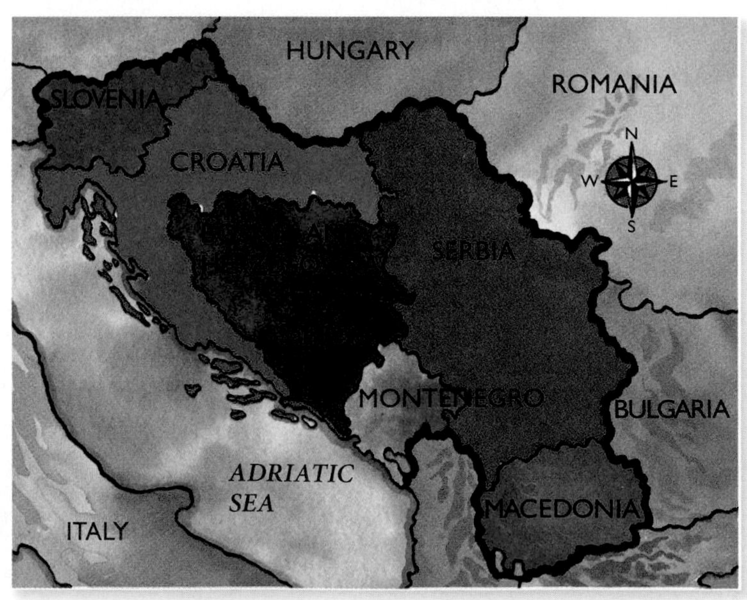

▲ The six republics of the former Yugoslav Federation

VOCABULARY

Learn Literary Words

People often use words in ways that do not match the literal, or basic, dictionary definitions of the words. For example, when we say that someone is *driving us crazy*, we do not mean this literally. We are trying to express a feeling of frustration.

A group of words that is used in a different way from the usual meanings of the words is called a **figure of speech**. Here are some examples.

Literary Words
figure of speech
hyperbole

> The girl **jumped out of her skin** when she heard a blast.
> The man's **head was spinning** after hearing all the bad news.

The girl can't really jump out of her skin. This figure of speech means that the girl was very frightened. Likewise, the man's head does not go around and around. This is another way of saying that the man was confused and upset.

A figure of speech that uses exaggeration, or overstatement, is called **hyperbole**. Many everyday expressions are examples of hyperbole. For example, when we are hungry, we say: *I could eat a horse.*

Writers use hyperbole to create an effect, emphasize something, or express a feeling. Here are two examples of hyperbole. What do these figures of speech mean to you?

> Her laughter was **like a meteor shower** brightening up the dark room.
> It would **take a thousand years** to figure out what happened.

Practice

Take turns reading these everyday figures of speech with a partner. Rephrase each one in your own words.

1. I've told you **a million times** to be more careful.
2. Her love for her parents was **deeper than the ocean**.
3. During the war, she and her friends didn't know what would happen. They were all **in the same boat**.

In your notebook, list several other everyday examples of hyperbole. Then try to create two exaggerated statements of your own.

Learn Academic Words

Study the **red** words and their meanings. You will find these words useful when talking and writing about literature. Write each word and its meaning in your notebook. After you read this excerpt from *Zlata's Diary,* try to use these words to respond to the text.

Academic Words

consist
establish
method
stress

consist = are made up of or contain particular things or people	➡	Diaries **consist** of a writer's feelings and observations. They are made up of daily entries.
establish = create; organize	➡	Concerned people in our community want to **establish** a neighborhood cleanup project.
method = a planned way of doing something	➡	The girl had her own **method** of keeping her house safe during bombings. Many of the neighbors liked her way of doing this.
stress = continuous feelings of worry caused by difficulties in your life	➡	People in wars are under a lot of **stress**. They feel great anxiety and worry.

Practice

Work with a partner to answer these questions. Try to include the **red** word in your answer. Write the sentences in your notebook.

1. In your opinion, what does a perfect graduation party **consist** of? What things or people would it include?
2. How can countries **establish** peace after a war? What can be done to make people put down their weapons and live peacefully together?
3. What is your **method** of getting to school in the morning? What is your way of getting there on time?
4. How do you deal with **stress**? What do you do to relax?

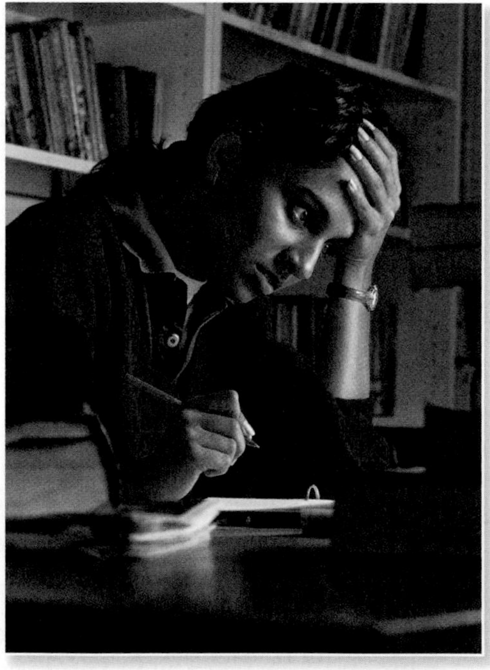

▲ It is important to take breaks from your work if you are under a lot of stress.

Word Study: Synonyms and Antonyms

Use context clues to figure out the meanings of unfamiliar words. Look for definitions, synonyms, and antonyms. Synonyms are words with the same or nearly the same meanings. Antonyms are words with the opposite or nearly the opposite meanings. Read the examples. Clues to the meanings of the boldfaced words are underlined.

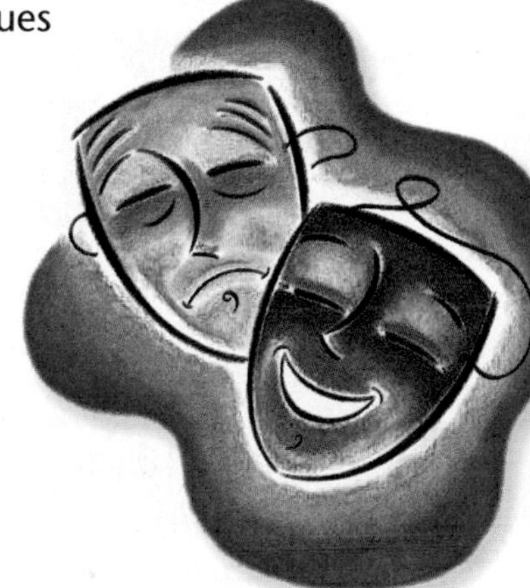

▲ *Tragedy* is the antonym of *comedy*.

The war made people go **berserk**, or act crazy. (synonym clue)
I was filled with sadness. He felt a similar **sorrow.** (synonym clue)
This war is madness. We have lost our **sanity**. (antonym clue)

Practice

Copy the sentences into your notebook. Work with a partner to figure out the meanings of the boldfaced words. Circle words or phrases that are clues to meaning. Then write your own definition of each boldfaced term. Check your definitions in a dictionary.

1. We saw the worst **massacre**, or killing of many helpless people.
2. During the war, we never lost hope. We never gave in to **despair**.
3. People who were welcomed before are now being **expelled**.
4. The warring groups need to talk and come to an agreement. When will they begin to **negotiate** a settlement?

Reading Strategy | DISTINGUISH FACT FROM OPINION

Distinguishing a fact from an opinion will help you evaluate what you read. A fact is something that can be proven through evidence. An opinion is what someone believes or thinks. Opinions express a point of view, but aren't necessarily wrong. They just can't be proven. To distinguish facts from opinions, follow these steps:

- Read the text. Then ask yourself: "Can I check this information in a reliable source?" If you can, it's probably a fact.
- Look for words that signal opinions, such as *I think* and *to me*.
- Ask yourself: "Is this what someone thinks or believes? Can it be proven?" If it cannot be proven, it's probably an opinion.

As you read *Zlata's Diary*, distinguish between the facts and opinions.

READING 3

LITERATURE

DIARY

Set a purpose for reading How does Zlata use her diary to help herself and others? Read this important account of the Bosnian War to find out.

from ZLATA'S DIARY

Zlata Filipović

When Zlata Filipović wrote her diary, which she calls "Mimmy," she was eleven years old and living in Sarajevo. The people of Sarajevo, including Zlata's family and friends, were caught in the middle of a war.

▲ Zlata Filipović

Saturday, May 23, 1992

Dear Mimmy,

I'm not writing to you about me anymore. I'm writing to you about war, death, injuries, shells, sadness and sorrow. Almost all my friends have left. Even if they were here, who knows whether we'd be able to see one another. The phones aren't working, we couldn't even talk to one another. Vanja and Andrej have gone to join Srdjan in Dubrovnik. The war has stopped there. They're lucky. I was so unhappy because of that war in Dubrovnik. I never dreamed it would move to Sarajevo. . . .

I now spend all my time with Bojana and Maja. They're my best friends now. Bojana is a year-and-a-half older than me, she's finished seventh grade and we have a lot in common. Maja is in her last year of school. She's much older than I am, but she's wonderful. I'm lucky to have them, otherwise I'd be all alone among the grown-ups.

---

shells, bombs
grown-ups, adults

On the news they reported the death of Silva Rizvanbegović, a doctor at the Emergency Clinic, who's Mommy's friend. She was in an ambulance. They were driving a wounded man to get him help. Lots of people Mommy and Daddy know have been killed. Oh, God, what is happening here???

Love, Zlata

Tuesday, May 26, 1992

Dear Mimmy,

I keep thinking about Mirna; May 13 was her birthday. I would love to see her so much. I keep asking Mommy and Daddy to take me to her. She left Mojmilo with her mother and father to go to her grandparents' place. Their apartment was shelled and they had to leave it.

There's no shooting, the past few days have been quiet. I asked Daddy to take me to Mirna's because I made her a little birthday present. I miss her. I wish I could see her.

I was such a nag that Daddy decided to take me to her. We went there, but the downstairs door was locked. We couldn't call out to them and I came home feeling disappointed. The present is waiting for her, so am I. I suppose we'll see each other.

Love, Zlata

Emergency Clinic, place to go for emergency medical attention

nag, person who asks for something again and again

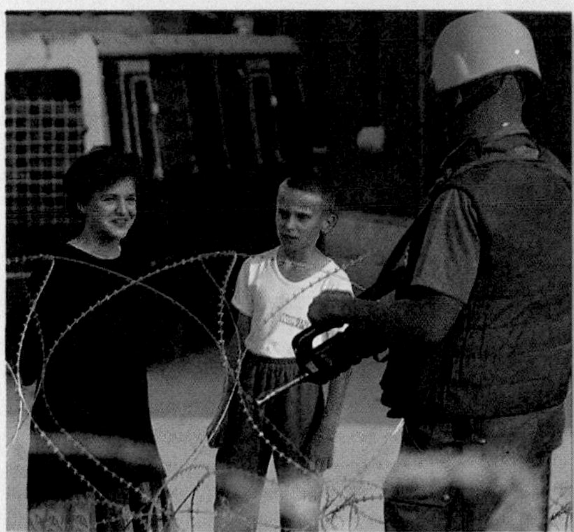

United Nations peacekeepers arrive. ▶

BEFORE YOU GO ON

1. What fact do you learn about Silva Rizvanbegović?
2. Why is Zlata disappointed when she goes to visit Mirna?

On Your Own
How do you think you would feel if you were living in Sarajevo in 1992?

Wednesday, May 27, 1992

Dear Mimmy,

SLAUGHTER! MASSACRE! HORROR! CRIME! BLOOD! SCREAMS! TEARS! DESPAIR!

That's what Vaso Miskin Street looks like today. Two shells exploded in the street and one in the market. Mommy was nearby at the time. She ran to Grandma and Granddad's. Daddy and I were beside ourselves because she hadn't come home. I saw some of it on TV but still can't believe what I actually saw. It's unbelievable. I've got a lump in my throat and a knot in my tummy. HORRIBLE! They're taking the wounded to the hospital. It's a madhouse. We kept going to the window hoping to see Mommy, but she wasn't back. They released a list of the dead and wounded. Daddy and I were tearing our hair out. We didn't know what had happened to her. Was she alive? At 4:00 Daddy decided to go and check the hospital. He got dressed, and I got ready to go to the Bobars', so as not to stay home alone. I looked out the window one more time and . . . I SAW MOMMY RUNNING ACROSS THE BRIDGE. As she came into the house she started shaking and crying. Through her tears she told us how she had seen dismembered bodies. All the neighbors came because they had been afraid for her. Thank God, Mommy is with us. Thank God.

A HORRIBLE DAY. UNFORGETTABLE. HORRIBLE! HORRIBLE!

Your Zlata

LITERARY CHECK

*What **figures of speech** does Zlata use to express her feelings of fear and horror?*

▲ **An injured woman is taken to the hospital.**

---

beside ourselves, very worried
I've got a lump in my throat, I feel like crying
knot in my tummy, bad feeling about something
madhouse, place where everyone seems crazy
tearing our hair out, feeling very worried
dismembered bodies, bodies with missing arms or legs

Thursday, October 1, 1992

Dear Mimmy,

Spring has been and gone, summer has been and gone, and now it's autumn. October has started. And the war is still on. The days are getting shorter and colder. Soon we'll move the stove upstairs to the apartment. But how will we keep warm? God, is anyone thinking of us here in Sarajevo? Are we going to start winter without electricity, water or gas, and with a war going on?

▲ **Cooking is quite an achievement without electricity.**

The "kids" are negotiating. Will they finally negotiate something? Are they thinking about us when they negotiate, or are they just trying to outwit each other, and leave us to our fate?

Daddy has been checking the attic and cellar for wood. It looks to me as though part of the furniture is going to wind up in the stove if this keeps up until winter. It seems that nobody is thinking of us, that this madness is going to go on and on. We have no choice, we have to rely on ourselves, to take care of ourselves and find a way to fight off the oncoming winter.

Mommy came home from work in a state of shock today. Two of her colleagues came from Grbavica. It really is true that people are being expelled from there. There's no sign of Mommy's and Nedo's relatives or of Lalo. Nedo is going berserk.

Your Zlata

---

the "kids," Zlata's slang for the politicians
outwit, be more clever than; trick
wind up, end up; finally be
colleagues, fellow workers

BEFORE YOU GO ON

1. How do Zlata and her father feel after the massacre on Vaso Miskin Street? Why?
2. What is the "madness" that Zlata refers to?

On Your Own
What would you do if you were in Zlata's family?

Monday, December 28, 1992

Dear Mimmy,

I've been walking my feet off these past few days.

I'm at home today. I had my first piano lesson. My teacher and I kissed and hugged, we hadn't seen each other since March. Then we moved on to Czerny, Bach, Mozart, and Chopin, to the étude, the invention, the sonata and the "piece." It's not going to be easy. But I'm not going to school now and I'll give it my all. It makes me happy. Mimmy, I'm now in my fifth year of music.

LITERARY CHECK

*What does the **figure of speech** "I'll give it my all" mean?*

You know, Mimmy, we've had no water or electricity for ages. When I go out and when there's no shooting it's as if the war were over, but this business with the electricity and water, this darkness, this winter, the shortage of wood and food, brings me back to earth and then I realize that the war is still on. Why? Why on earth don't those "kids" come to some agreement? They really are playing games. And it's us they're playing with.

▲ **Zlata expresses her concern about her family in her diary.**

As I sit writing to you, my dear Mimmy, I look over at Mommy and Daddy. They are reading. They lift their eyes from the page and think about something. What are they thinking about? About the book they are reading or are they trying to put together the scattered pieces of this war puzzle? I think it must be the latter. Somehow they look even sadder to me in the light of the oil lamp (we have no more wax candles, so we make our own oil lamps). I look at Daddy. He really has lost a lot of weight. The scales say 25 kilos, but looking at him I think it must be more. I think

---

walking my feet off, walking a lot
Czerny, Bach, Mozart, and Chopin, composers who wrote piano music
for ages, for a long time
shortage, lack
back to earth, back to reality
scattered, spread out
latter, the second of two things or people

▲ Sarejevo

even his glasses are too big for him. Mommy has lost weight too. She's shrunk somehow, the war has given her **wrinkles**. God, what is this war doing to my parents? They don't look like my old Mommy and Daddy anymore. Will this ever stop? Will our suffering stop so that my parents can be what they used to be—cheerful, smiling, nice-looking?

This stupid war is destroying my childhood, it's destroying my parents' lives. WHY? STOP THE WAR! PEACE! I NEED PEACE!

I'm going to play a game of cards with them!

Love from your Zlata

LITERARY CHECK

*Why do you think that Zlata uses **hyperbole** to describe how her parents look?*

---

wrinkles, lines on the face or skin that people get as they age

ABOUT THE AUTHOR

Zlata Filipović escaped to Paris in December 1993, where she began to study at the International School. Her diary has been translated into more than twenty languages. With the money from her book, Zlata helped to start a charity for victims of the Bosnian War. Zlata was awarded the Special Child of Courage Award. She is also co-editor of *Stolen Voices: Young People's Diaries from World War I to Iraq*.

BEFORE YOU GO ON

1. What has Zlata begun studying again?
2. Why is Zlata worried about her parents?

On Your Own
How can a diary like Zlata's help people today?

READING 3

Review and Practice

READER'S THEATER

Act out this scene between Zlata and her mother.

Zlata: MOMMY! I am so glad to see you! When the shells exploded in the market and you did not come home, I was so so worried. Are you okay?

Mother: Yes, Zlata, dear. I'm all right. When I heard the explosion, I ran to Grandma and Granddad's home. I am safe and not harmed, but I saw the most terrible things.

Zlata: What happened? What did you see?

Mother: I saw people lying wounded on the ground. Some had lost limbs. It was the most horrible thing I have ever seen. I couldn't stop crying and shaking!

Zlata: Mommy, how awful. Why is this happening in Sarajevo?

Mother: I don't know, but this war must stop. We need peace in our country. We have been torn apart by fighting for too long.

Speaking TIP

Use your voice to express the emotions Zlata and her mother are feeling.

▲ The historic Stari Most bridge in Bosnia was nearly destroyed during the war in 1993.

COMPREHENSION

Right There

1. Zlata says that she does not write about herself anymore. What does she write about now?
2. What happened on Vaso Miskin Street?

Think and Search

3. How have Zlata's parents changed since the war began?
4. What is Zlata's method for coping with the stress of war?

Author and You

5. How does Zlata think life in Sarajevo has changed since the war started?
6. What does Zlata think about the "kids'" ability to establish peace?

▲ After being rebuilt to look as it did originally, the bridge was reopened in July 2004.

On Your Own

7. Do you think that a diary could influence people to be more tolerant and less likely to go to war? Explain.
8. If you kept a diary, would you want it to be published and read by others? Or would you want it to be only for yourself? Explain.

DISCUSSION

Discuss in pairs or small groups.

1. What do you predict will happen to Zlata and her family when the war finally ends?
2. How is Zlata's diary a clear account of the Bosnian War? How is it not? Discuss some of the facts Zlata presents about the war. Then discuss some of her opinions.
3. Do you think people who live in a country that is at war feel helpless? Why or why not?

How does helping others help us all? What are some other difficult experiences that a person might go through? What can a person do to help him or herself and others get through these events?

Listening TIP

When you listen to your classmates debate an issue, take notes. This will help you evaluate other people's points of view.

Zlata writes at her desk, as the sound of guns echoes from the hills. ▶

RESPONSE TO LITERATURE

Reread the excerpt from *Zlata's Diary*. In your notebook, write the dates of the five days she writes about. Then write something important that happened to Zlata on each of these days. Compare what you write in pairs or small groups.

Grammar and Writing

GRAMMAR, USAGE, AND MECHANICS

Placement of Adjectives

Zlata uses many adjectives to describe her feelings and observations about the war around her. Using well-chosen adjectives helps to make writing precise. It also helps writers persuade readers to agree with their point of view.

An adjective describes a noun. It can appear before the noun it describes or after a linking verb. Linking verbs describe states of being. They include such verbs as *get, become, seem, appear, feel, taste, sound, smell,* and *look,* and forms of *be*. Study the examples below.

Adjective + Noun	Linking Verb + Adjective
They were driving a **wounded man** to get him help. I'm now in my **fifth year** of music. This **stupid war** is destroying my childhood.	I **am lucky** to have them. I **felt disappointed**. The days **are shorter** and **colder**. My parents **were cheerful**, **smiling**, **nice-looking**.

Practice

Write these sentences in your notebook. Choose one adjective from the box below to complete each sentence.

eager	eleventh	humorous	troubled	violent

1. On my ______ birthday, my parents gave me a diary.
2. I was ______ to begin recording my thoughts and feelings.
3. I wrote ______ entries about funny events in my life.
4. Then a ______ tornado struck our house, and our lives changed.
5. I was ______ by the changes that occurred, so I wrote about them.

▲ A teenager writes in his diary.

WRITING A PERSUASIVE PARAGRAPH

Write a Diary Entry

On this page, you'll write a persuasive paragraph in the form of a diary entry. You'll present *both* sides of an issue before stating your opinion. You'll use a graphic organizer like the one at the right to organize your argument, or position.

ISSUE	
For	Against
Facts Opinions	Facts Opinions

Many people who keep diaries describe the world around them. They also examine their feelings and ideas about issues and express their opinions. Look back at Zlata's entries. Notice the format she uses. She dates each entry and addresses it to "Mimmy."

Here is a model of a diary entry. Notice how the writer, Talia Marcus, presents both sides of an issue that she feels strongly about. Then she states an opinion. Notice the adjectives she uses to persuade.

August 20, 2009

Dear Diary,

It is clear after reading Zlata's Diary and "Extraordinary People" that violence and war have a negative effect on people's lives. Zlata wrote her diary during the war in Sarajevo. She could rarely leave her house because of the violence. Her family was scared and didn't have electricity, water, or gas. In war, innocent people, like Zlata and her family, suffer. Gandhi understood the senselessness of violence and showed how passive resistance was a better way to solve problems. In my opinion, it is much smarter to follow Gandhi's example. The people who fought in Sarajevo couldn't come to an agreement and resorted to violence. They thought the only way to respond to violence was with more violence. However, violence hurts everybody. Peaceful protest sends a powerful message and is less likely to harm others.

Writing Checklist

VOICE:

☑ I used strong words and phrases that expressed my argument clearly.

WORD CHOICE:

☑ I used adjectives to persuade.

Practice

Write a diary entry about an important issue. Use a T-chart to list facts and opinions about both sides of the issue. Then write a diary entry that examines both sides and comes to a conclusion. Use figurative expressions and adjectives to help bring your feelings across. Place your adjectives before nouns and after linking verbs.

READING 4

Prepare to Read

What You Will Learn

Reading

- Vocabulary building: *Context, dictionary skills, word study*
- Reading strategy: *Identify main idea and details*
- Text type: *Informational text (science)*

Grammar, Usage, and Mechanics
Prepositions of location

Writing
Write a critical evaluation

THE BIG QUESTION

How does helping others help us all? What do you know about animal friendships? Which animals help each other? Are they usually in the same family group, such as monkeys and gorillas? Are they in packs or herds, such as wolves or horses?

Work with a partner to see what you know about animal friendship and cooperation. In your notebook, make a T-chart with two headings: *Kind of Animal* and *How They Act Together.* Complete the chart with the facts you know. Then share what you know with the class.

BUILD BACKGROUND

"Friendship and Cooperation in the Animal Kingdom" is a science article. It describes how certain animals rely on one another, often in unusual ways.

Symbiosis means "living together." When two living things help each other, we say that they have a *symbiotic relationship.* One example of a symbiotic relationship is that between the tickbird and the rhinoceros. The tickbird picks insects called ticks off the rhino. Both animals are helped by this relationship. The tickbird gets food and protection (other animals don't attack the tickbird because it is sitting on the rhino!), and the rhino is not bothered by ticks.

Animals can be friends, too. Like people, animals can enjoy one another's company. Perhaps you have a cat and a dog. They may fight a lot—or they may be best friends.

▲ The rhino and the tickbird have a symbiotic relationship.

VOCABULARY

Learn Key Words

Read these sentences. Use the context to figure out the meaning of the **red** words. Use a dictionary to check your answers. Then write each word and its meaning in your notebook.

1. Lions have an **arrangement**. The females hunt in a group. The males eat first.
2. Some animals, such as buffalo, **cooperate** with one another. They work together to help the whole herd.
3. A strong wind can do a lot of **damage** to trees. It can tear off branches and blow the trees down.
4. The blue whale is a **gigantic** mammal—the biggest in the world.
5. An **intruder** broke into the herd of zebras. The unwelcome creature was a hungry lion.
6. After the earthquake, a **tsunami** crashed into the shore. This series of huge waves destroyed many houses and trees.

Key Words

arrangement
cooperate
damage
gigantic
intruder
tsunami

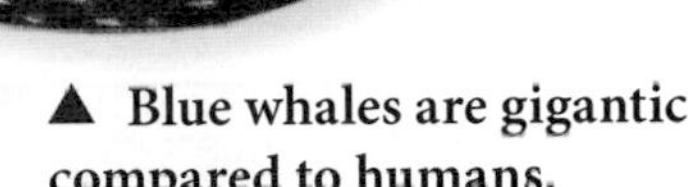

▲ Blue whales are gigantic compared to humans.

Practice

Write the sentences in your notebook. Choose a **red** word from the box above to complete each sentence. Then take turns reading the sentences aloud with a partner.

1. A hippo is a _______ animal. Even a baby hippo weighs 272 kilograms (or 600 lb.).
2. A _______ looks like a huge wall of water. It is often caused by an earthquake.
3. Sometimes my three cats _______. They work together to chase mice.
4. I made an _______ with my best friend to take care of my pets while I'm away.
5. The storm caused a lot of _______. The town was destroyed.
6. The _______ broke into the nature preserve at night. He knew he wasn't supposed to be there, but he loved watching the seals.

Learn Academic Words

Study the **red** words and their meanings. You will find these words useful when talking and writing about informational texts. Write each word and its meaning in your notebook. After you read "Friendship and Cooperation in the Animal Kingdom," try to use these words to respond to the text.

Academic Words

attitude
comment
concept
rely on

attitude = the opinions and feelings that you usually have about someone or something	➡	After she fell off her horse, she developed a negative **attitude** about horses.
comment = a stated opinion made about someone or something	➡	The speaker made a short **comment** about the hippo. Then he went on to speak about birds.
concept = an idea of how something is or how something should be done	➡	We learned the **concept** of animal cooperation. It was fun to know that they helped each other.
rely on = trust or depend on someone or something	➡	Some animals **rely on** one another for safety.

Practice

Write the sentences in your notebook. Choose a **red** word from the box above to complete each sentence. Then take turns reading the sentences aloud with a partner.

1. The boy began to understand the _______ of two animals working together. He listened as the scientist talked about how it happens.
2. The cub will _______ his mother for care. The cub needs her to help find food.
3. The girl's _______ toward crocodiles changed when she saw the movie about them.
4. The vet made an important _______ about pets and their need for attention. The pet owner listened to his opinion.

▲ Crocodiles in Long Xuyen, Vietnam

Word Study: Greek and Latin Roots

English has borrowed many words from other languages. Many English words come from ancient Greek or Latin word parts, called roots. For example, the word *disaster* contains a Greek root (*aster*), meaning "star." In ancient times, people who suffered disasters were thought to be living under a "bad star." Study the chart below. Notice the relationships between the roots, their meanings, and the English words that contain them.

▲ The aster is a star-shaped flower.

Root	Meaning	Origin	English Words
anima	breath, life, spirit	Latin	animal animation
aster/astro	star	Greek	aster astrology
bios	life	Greek	biology symbiosis

Practice

Work with a partner. Use a large dictionary to look up each of the English words in the chart above. Discuss how the meaning of each Greek or Latin root is related to the meaning of each English word.

READING STRATEGY IDENTIFY MAIN IDEA AND DETAILS

Identifying the main idea and details in a reading helps you see the key points the author is making. The main idea is the most important idea about a topic. Details are small pieces of information that support the main idea. To identify the main idea and details, follow these steps.

- Look at the title. Ask yourself: "What is the topic of this text?"
- As you read each paragraph, identify the author's main idea about the topic. Sometimes the author will state the main idea in a sentence. Other times you will have to put the main idea into your own words.
- As you read, look for examples, facts, dates, and sentences that tell more about the main idea. These are the supporting details.

As you read "Friendship and Cooperation in the Animal Kingdom," identify the main idea of each paragraph and of the whole article. Then find details that support the author's main idea about the topic.

READING 4

INFORMATIONAL TEXT

SCIENCE

Set a purpose for reading Can animals really cooperate and form friendships? As you read, think about the friendships animals develop. Why do you think animals help each other?

Friendship and Cooperation in the Animal Kingdom

You know that people help other people, but do animals help other animals? It's a "dog-eat-dog" world out there, isn't it? Not always! It's true that animals often fight. However, at other times, they help each other out.

Life in the wild can be very difficult for animals. It is not easy for them to find food and water and stay safe. Animals struggle every day to survive.

That's why animals of the same species, or group, such as lions or blue jays, sometimes cooperate. By helping one another, they help their group survive.

Some animals become partners with other kinds of animals. The two types of animals depend on each other for survival. This is called symbiosis, and animals who depend on each other are said to be in a symbiotic relationship. Sometimes the two animals would die without each other. Other times, they might be able to live, but they would not be as healthy.

One example of symbiosis is the relationship between the plover and the crocodile. The plover is a small wading bird. It helps pick clean the Nile crocodile's body and even its teeth. The crocodile will open its jaws and let the bird enter its mouth safely. Amazingly, the crocodile will not snap its jaws shut. Instead, it patiently allows the plover to eat the small, harmful animals on the crocodile's teeth. The crocodile gets its teeth cleaned, and the plover gets an easy meal!

"dog-eat-dog," very competitive

◀ **A Nile crocodile keeps its jaws open while a plover is in its mouth.**

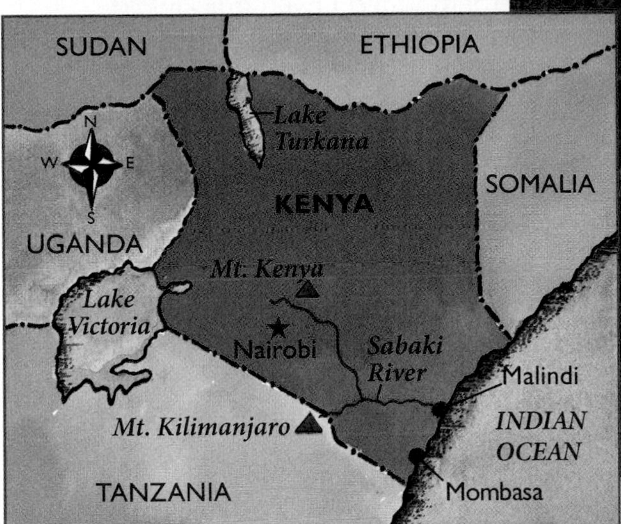

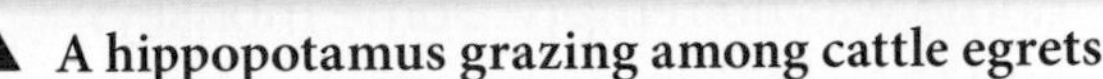

▲ A hippopotamus grazing among cattle egrets

Symbiosis is a working relationship. Many animal species have worked out this arrangement with other animal species. Sometimes, however, animals simply become friends with other animals. There may not be an obvious reason. Perhaps they just like the companionship.

Animals can find friends in the strangest places. For an example, take Owen, a baby hippopotamus. It is hard to believe, but Owen actually became best friends with a 318-kilogram (700-lb.) tortoise named Mzee (mm-ZAY).

Owen, the hippo, lived in the country of Kenya on the east coast of Africa. He was just one year old, and he already weighed 272 kilograms (600 lb.). He lived happily with his mother in a group of about twenty hippos. They grazed on the grass along the Sabaki River near the small village of Malindi.

On December 26, 2004, a disaster struck. There was a huge earthquake under the ocean floor near Indonesia. This caused a gigantic tsunami. The tsunami wiped out towns and villages throughout Asia. Around 230,000 people died. By the time the tsunami reached the east coast of Africa, the waves had lost a great deal of power. However, they still caused flooding and widespread damage. Owen had been swimming in the river with his mother when the tsunami hit. The enormous waves separated Owen from his mother and swept him out to sea.

The next day, the people of Malindi saw the struggling baby hippo, without its mother, stranded on a coral reef. It was Owen. He was tired and frightened. Owen could not reach the shore on his own. It took hours for the villagers to rescue Owen from the coral reef.

coral reef, line of hard material formed by the skeletons of small ocean creatures that live in warm water

BEFORE YOU GO ON

1. What is the main idea of the second paragraph on page 180?
2. How do plovers help Nile crocodiles?

On Your Own
What do you think the villagers will do to help Owen?

But what should they do with a 272-kilogram (600-lb.) baby hippo? The people could not return him to the wild. Owen had not yet learned to take care of himself. Another hippo group would not accept him. Other hippos would think Owen was an intruder and probably attack him.

Luckily for Owen, there was an animal shelter nearby named Haller Park. The workers prepared a perfect home for Owen. It had a pond, a mud hole, tall trees, and lots of grass. This seemed perfect for a hippo, but Owen's new home was not empty. Some monkeys and the 318-kilogram tortoise Mzee already lived in Haller Park.

It took hours for the people of Malindi to load Owen into a pickup truck. Owen was very angry, and he was also very frightened. He had lost his mother and his friends. He did not know where he was or where he was going.

When Owen arrived at Haller Park, he quickly left the pickup truck and ran right to Mzee. The workers looked in amazement when Owen quickly hid behind the giant tortoise. This is exactly the way a baby hippo would hide behind its mother if it felt the need for protection.

Mzee was shocked and surprised. He had originally come from Aldabra Island. This is part of the country of Seychelles in the Indian Ocean. Sailors had probably taken Mzee from his home to be used for food. He must have escaped from the ship, maybe during a shipwreck, and come ashore somewhere on the eastern coast of Africa. That was a long time before, because Mzee was about 130 years old. (Some giant tortoises live to be 200 years old!)

Mzee must have seen a lot in his long life. Like most giant tortoises, he was not very friendly. He preferred to be left alone. So, at first, Mzee tried to crawl away from Owen. However, as you know, tortoises cannot move very quickly. Owen just watched where Mzee went and then followed him around. For some reason, Mzee began to like his new companion.

◀ Owen following Mzee

▲ **Owen and Mzee nuzzling**

Over the next few days, the two giant animals became good friends. Then they became great friends. In fact, Owen and Mzee soon refused to be separated. They would spend all their time together, eating, swimming, sleeping, and playing. Mzee would stretch out his neck and Owen would **tickle** it. At night, the two huge animals would cuddle up next to each other. Mzee and Owen even developed their own way of "talking" with each other.

It is a bit of a mystery why Owen and Mzee became such good friends. After all, Owen is a mammal and Mzee is a reptile. Perhaps Mzee's coloring and round shape reminded Owen of his mother. Maybe Owen looked like another tortoise to Mzee. For whatever reason, they surprised scientists with the strength of their friendship.

Mzee's name means "wise man" in Swahili (one of the main languages of Kenya). It turned out that Mzee's name was well chosen. When Owen the hippo needed a friend, Mzee was there for him. Owen suffered a tremendous loss, but he never gave up. He kept trying and now has a happy life.

tickle, touch a person or animal lightly, often in order to make him or her laugh

BEFORE YOU GO ON

1. Why is Owen upset when the people of Malindi put him into the truck?
2. What does Mzee's name mean in Swahili?

On Your Own
What do you think about the friendship between Owen and Mzee?

READING 4

Review and Practice

COMPREHENSION

Workbook Page 90

▲ Some dogs and cats get along well together.

Right There

1. Why can't Owen be returned to the wild?
2. Where was Owen born?

Think and Search

3. How does Mzee's attitude toward Owen change?
4. How is symbiosis similar to friendship? How is it different?

Author and You

5. What helps the writer infer that Mzee and Owen have become great friends?
6. What main idea, or overall concept, does "Friendship and Cooperation in the Animal Kingdom" present?

On Your Own

7. Why do you think the author says, "It's a 'dog-eat-dog' world out there"? What do you think the author means?
8. What examples can you think of in which animals help people survive?

IN YOUR OWN WORDS

Imagine that you are telling a classmate about "Friendship and Cooperation in the Animal Kingdom." Use a chart like the one below to help you organize your ideas. Then share your summary with a classmate.

Main Idea about Symbiosis	Main Idea about Friendship
Definition of *symbiosis*:	Definition of *friendship*:
Examples:	Examples:

Speaking TIP

Write your main ideas on note cards. Put just a few words in big letters on each card. Use the cards to help you remember your main ideas.

DISCUSSION

Discuss in pairs or small groups.

1. Which do you think is more common in the animal kingdom—symbiosis or friendship? Why?
2. Owen and Mzee live in Haller Park, an animal shelter. Do you think animals should live in shelters and nature preserves? Or should they be allowed to live in the wild? Explain.

Q **How does helping others help us all?** You have thought about how animals can help people. Now describe some specific examples in which people can help animals.

Listening TIP

Respect each speaker. Listen politely, even if you disagree with the speaker's ideas.

READ FOR FLUENCY

Reading with feeling helps make what you read more interesting. Work with a partner. Choose a paragraph from the reading. Read the paragraph. Ask each other how you felt after reading the paragraph. Did you feel happy or sad?

Take turns reading the paragraph aloud to each other with a tone of voice that represents how you felt when you read it the first time. Give each other feedback.

EXTENSION

In "Friendship and Cooperation in the Animal Kingdom," you learned about different kinds of animals. Learn more about one of the animals described in the article. Use encyclopedias, reference books, and reliable websites. Copy the chart below into your notebook. Use it to organize the information you find. Add more columns if necessary. Share your findings with the class.

Animal	Habitat (where the animal lives)	Size	Life Span	Foods

Grammar and Writing

GRAMMAR, USAGE, AND MECHANICS

Prepositions of Location

Remember that a preposition is a word that shows location or time. Using the correct preposition in your persuasive writing helps you be specific when giving information.

Here are some common prepositions of location: *above, across, behind, below, beside, between, in, near, on, outside,* and *under.* Read the example sentences below. Notice the prepositions.

There was a huge earthquake **under** the ocean floor **near** Indonesia.
Owen quickly hid **behind** the giant tortoise.
The hippo cuddled up **beside** the tortoise.
The plover picked clean the area **between** the crocodile's teeth.
Owen, the hippo, lived **in** the country of Kenya **on** the east coast of Africa.

Practice

Choose five prepositions from the example sentences above. Write a sentence in your notebook using each preposition. Compare your sentences with a partner's.

▲ Koko the gorilla holds a visiting kitty in her arms.

WRITING A PERSUASIVE PARAGRAPH

Write a Critical Evaluation

On this page, you'll write a critical evaluation of a person or issue, using an outline. When you evaluate a topic critically, you examine it against a set of standards. You then make a judgment about whether the person or thing meets those standards. Imagine that you are writing a critical evaluation of someone who is running for class president. You might use the outline below.

I. Class presidents must have certain traits.
  A. leadership ability (standard)
  B. good communication skills (standard)

II. Joe is a good candidate in my judgment.
  A. examples of his leadership ability
  B. examples that prove he can communicate well

Here is a model of a critical evaluation. Notice how the writer presents the topic and a set of standards to judge it against.

I. Main idea
(introduce standards)
A.
B.
II. Main idea
(judge topic)
A.
B.

Tyler Welsh

The Perfect Student

Good students need to have certain traits. They must be smart. They also must be dedicated, proud, confident, and willing to share what they know. Many students possess one or two of these traits, but very few possess them all. Michaela, a classmate who sits next to me, is an exception. She is very smart. She reads everything, from science to historical fiction. She studies hard and does well in school. Michaela takes pride in her work. She has a relaxed and friendly attitude in class. When she gives an oral report, she speaks clearly and with confidence. In addition, she is very willing to help others. This year, she helped me when I was having trouble in one of my classes. To me, Michaela is the perfect example of a good student.

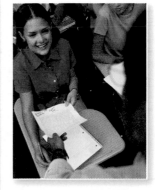

ORGANIZATION:

☑ I introduced the topic and explained my critical standards.

CONVENTIONS:

☑ I checked my writing for errors in grammar and spelling.

Practice

Write a critical evaluation of a person or issue. Use an outline to organize your ideas. First, present your standards for judging the topic. Then make a judgment supported by examples. Use prepositions of location to help clarify your ideas.

Link the Readings

Critical Thinking

Look back at the readings in this unit. Think about what they have in common. They all tell about helping others. Yet they do not all have the same purpose. The purpose of one reading might be to inform, while the purpose of another might be to entertain or persuade. In addition, the content of each reading relates to helping others differently. Now copy the chart below into your notebook and complete it.

Title of Reading	Purpose	Big Question Link
From *Run Away Home*		
"Extraordinary People: Serving Others"		
From *Zlata's Diary*	to persuade	
"Friendship and Cooperation in the Animal Kingdom"		discusses how animals help each other

Discussion

Discuss in pairs or small groups.

- How does the purpose of *Run Away Home* differ from the purpose of "Friendship and Cooperation in the Animal Kingdom"?
- **How does helping others help us all?** Compare and contrast the readings in this unit. In your opinion, which reading best expresses the importance of helping others? Why? Based on the readings, do you think it's more important to help others or to help yourself? Explain.

Fluency Check

Work with a partner. Choose a paragraph from one of the readings. Take turns reading it for one minute. Count the total number of words you read. Practice saying the words you had trouble reading. Take turns reading the paragraph three more times. Did you read more words each time? Copy the chart below into your notebook and record your speeds.

	1st Speed	2nd Speed	3rd Speed	4th Speed
Words Per Minute				

Projects

Work in pairs or small groups. Choose one of these projects.

1 Work in small groups to think of some ways in which people help others. You might research a recycling project or volunteers who take food to homebound people.

2 What do you think happens at the end of *Run Away Home*? Write a summary of what you think will happen at the end. Then read the entire book to see if your prediction is correct.

3 Think about a time when you helped a friend. Write a diary entry about what you did and how you felt about the experience.

4 Look for a documentary about Kenya's wildlife in your library. View it with your class.

5 Prepare an oral report about Sarajevo today. The war has ended, but has the country been rebuilt? Look for visuals to use in your presentation. Be sure to use reliable sources for your report.

Further Reading

To find out more about the theme of this unit, choose from these reading suggestions.

Gandhi, Jane Rollason
This Penguin Reader® biography describes the life of Mohandas Gandhi, whose message of peaceful resistance changed the world.

Anne Frank: The Diary of a Young Girl, Anne Frank
To escape Nazi persecution in Holland, Anne Frank and her family hid for two years in a secret warehouse annex. There, Anne wrote her extraordinary diary.

Free At Last, The Story of Martin Luther King Jr., Angela Bull
Civil rights leader Martin Luther King Jr. dreamed of an America where people would be judged by "the content of their character, not the color of their skin."

Put It All Together

LISTENING & SPEAKING WORKSHOP

TV Talk Show

With a group, you will present a TV talk show about a person you admire for his or her efforts to help others. One person will be the talk show host, and another will be the special guest. The remaining group members will play other guests who give their perspectives on the person's life or work.

1 THINK ABOUT IT In a group, discuss the selection "Extraordinary People: Serving Others." Then talk about what it would be like to host one of those amazing people on your own TV talk show. Discuss how you would introduce the person and what questions you would ask him or her.

Work together to develop a list of other people, living or dead, who have done a lot to help others. For example:

- Eleanor Roosevelt
- Bono
- Jonas Salk

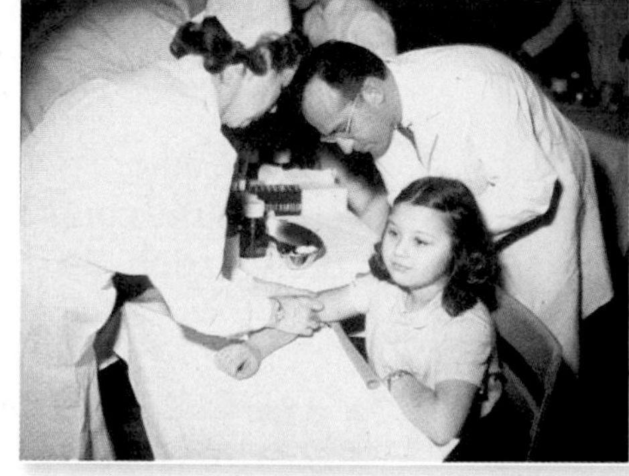

Jonas Salk, developer of the polio vaccine ▶

2 GATHER AND ORGANIZE INFORMATION With your group, choose a person from your list. Write down what you already know and what you want to find out about the person. Decide who will play the talk show host and the special guest. Then decide what parts the other group members will play (for example, a coworker or someone the person helped).

Research Go to the library or use the Internet to gather information about your person's efforts to help others. Look for facts, details, and examples that show why the person is great and why the audience should admire him or her. Take notes on what you find.

Order Your Notes Use your notes to make an outline for your TV show. Choose which information the host will include in the introduction and what questions he or she will ask each guest. Decide the order in which the guests will appear, and create a list of main points for each one to discuss.

Use Visuals Think about how you should dress for the show. Wear a simple costume, or bring an appropriate prop to help express your role. You may also wish to display a photo of the person your show is about.

3 PRACTICE AND PRESENT

As a group, practice your TV talk show. Keep your outline handy for reference, but try to speak naturally, without reading. Place your chairs at an angle so that the host and guests can see each other and the audience. Be careful not to turn your face away from the audience when you speak. Keep practicing until you can present your show confidently, with smooth transitions between speakers.

Deliver Your TV Talk Show TV talk shows are informal and relaxed. Try to create that atmosphere during your presentation. Saying things you didn't rehearse ("ad-libbing") can help. Speak loudly enough so that everyone in the class can hear you. Use natural hand and body movements, too. For example, lean forward and reach out when you are making an important point.

4 EVALUATE THE PRESENTATION

You can improve your skills as a speaker and a listener by evaluating each presentation you give and hear. Use this checklist to help you judge your group's TV talk show and the talk shows of other groups.

- ☑ Did the group clearly show how this person has helped others and why he or she is admirable?
- ☑ Did the host give a persuasive introduction?
- ☑ Did the guests provide interesting examples and opinions?
- ☑ Did you understand each speaker's relationship to the special guest?
- ☑ Could you hear and understand the speakers easily?
- ☑ What suggestions do you have for improving the talk show?

Speaking TIPS

Ask a friend or classmate to listen and give feedback as your group practices. Or tape-record your rehearsal, if possible. Listen to the tape together, and find the places where you can improve your presentation.

Use specific details to present your facts. Use persuasive words to give your opinions.

Listening TIPS

As you listen, think about what you already know about this person. Has the presentation changed your feelings about him or her?

When you participate in a talk show, listen carefully. If you don't understand a question or answer, ask the host or guest to repeat or explain it.

WRITING WORKSHOP

Persuasive Speech

You have written four persuasive paragraphs. Now you will use your skills to write a persuasive speech. In a persuasive speech, you try to convince listeners to agree with your opinion on an issue. A good persuasive speech begins with a paragraph that introduces the issue. This paragraph presents both sides of the argument and then gives the writer's own opinion. Body paragraphs support the writer's position with carefully organized reasons, facts, and examples. Most persuasive speeches conclude with a paragraph that restates the writer's opinion in a new and memorable way. Speechwriters often use strong and persuasive words to appeal to listeners' emotions.

You will write a five-paragraph speech that tries to persuade listeners to agree with your opinion on an issue you care about.

1 PREWRITE Brainstorm possible topics for your speech. You might focus on the theme of helping others. For example, is there something you believe your school should do to help the community? Is there a leader who in your opinion deserves extra praise for helping humanity? Do you want your friends to volunteer for a specific cause? Choose a topic. Then think about how you can persuade listeners to agree with your opinion on the issue.

List and Organize Ideas and Details Use a graphic organizer to gather your ideas and information. A student named Tyler decided to write a persuasive speech about a man he admired—former president Franklin D. Roosevelt. Here is the opinion-and-reason chart Tyler prepared.

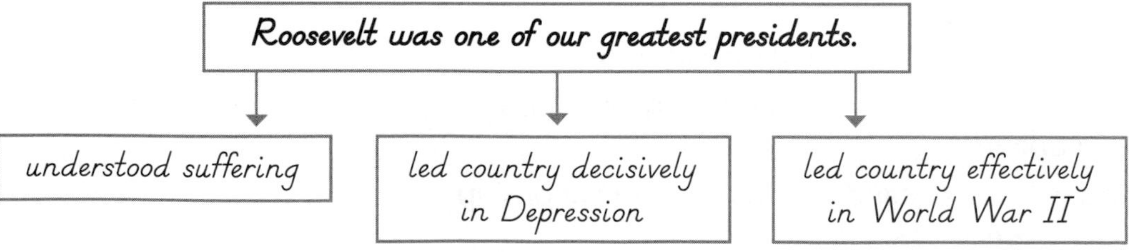

2 DRAFT Use the model on page 195 and your graphic organizer to help you write your first draft. Remember to state your opinion clearly in your first paragraph and to restate your opinion in your conclusion.

3 **REVISE** Read over your draft. As you do so, ask yourself the questions in the writing checklist. Use the questions to help you revise your speech.

SIX TRAITS OF WRITING CHECKLIST

- ☑ **IDEAS:** Do I present both sides of the issue?
- ☑ **ORGANIZATION:** Do I support my opinion with persuasive reasons, facts, and examples?
- ☑ **VOICE:** Does my writing show my feelings about the issue?
- ☑ **WORD CHOICE:** Do I use vivid words that will appeal to listeners?
- ☑ **SENTENCE FLUENCY:** Do my sentences flow well when read aloud?
- ☑ **CONVENTIONS:** Does my writing follow the rules of grammar, usage, and mechanics?

Here are the changes Tyler plans to make when he revises his first draft:

A Great President

Franklin Delano Roosevelt, the 32nd President of the United States, is known for overcoming hardships. He became president at a time of world and national crisis ~~on~~ in 1933. Some people believe Roosevelt created even more problems by increasing the government's powers~~.~~, but I believe he used the government's powers in exciting new ways to help people. In my opinion, Roosevelt was one of the greatest presidents in U.S. history.

Roosevelt himself understood human suffering, in part because he had experienced tragedy. He was born on January 30 1882, in Hyde Park, New York. ~~On~~ In 1921, at age 39, he was diagnosed with polio. The disease left him partially paralyzed. He felt despair at first~~.~~, but ~~T~~then he fought with all his strength to regain use of his legs. Although he never was able to walk again without assistance he went on to a brilliant political career.

Elected president during the Great Depression, Roosevelt was a leader decisive and passionate who wanted to get the country back on its feet. His administration also worked to create jobs for the unemployed to assist struggling farmers, to feed the hungry, and to provide for the elderly. During his presidency, laws were passed to regulate the stock market. Roosevelt cared about everyone!

Roosevelt was equally effective during wartime. In World War II, he showed tremendous leadership in preparing the way for an Allied victory. In addition, he thought about the future of peace~~.~~ and ~~H~~he supported the idea of a global peacekeeping organization. Today, that organization is called the United Nations.

At age 63, Roosevelt died suddenly during his fourth term in office. His death caused sorrow ~~to~~ across the country. Roosevelt was a great president. He inspired hope, introduced important social programs, and led the nation brilliantly during wartime. Without his decisiveness and passion, the United states would not be the country it is today.

4 EDIT AND PROOFREAD

Copy your revised speech onto a clean sheet of paper. Read it again. Correct any errors in grammar, word usage, mechanics, and spelling. Here are the additional changes Tyler plans to make when he prepares his final draft.

Tyler Welsh

A Great President

Franklin Delano Roosevelt, the 32nd President of the United States, is known for overcoming hardships. He became president at a time of world and national crisis in 1933. Some people believe Roosevelt created even more problems by increasing the government's powers, but I believe he used the government's powers in exciting new ways to help people In my opinion, Roosevelt was one of the greatest presidents in U.S. history.

Roosevelt himself understood human suffering, in part because he had experienced tragedy. He was born on January 30 1882, in Hyde Park, New York. In 1921, at age 39, he was diagnosed with polio. The disease left him partially paralyzed. He felt despair at first, but then he fought with all his strength to regain use of his legs. Although he never was able to walk again without assistance he went on to a brilliant political career.

Elected president during the Great Depression, Roosevelt was a decisive and passionate leader who wanted to get the country back on its feet. During his presidency, laws were passed to regulate the stock market. His administration also worked to create jobs for the unemployed to assist struggling farmers, to feed the hungry, and to provide for the elderly. Roosevelt cared about everyone!

Roosevelt was equally effective during wartime. In World War II, he showed tremendous leadership in preparing the way for an Allied victory. In addition, he thought about the future of peace, and he supported the idea of a global peacekeeping organization. Today, that organization is called the United Nations.

At age 63, Roosevelt died suddenly during his fourth term in office. His death caused sorrow across the country. Roosevelt was a great president, He inspired hope, introduced important social programs, and led the nation brilliantly during wartime. Without his decisiveness and passion, the United states would not be the country it is today.

5 PUBLISH Prepare your final draft. Share your speech with your teacher and classmates.

Learn about Art with the Smithsonian American Art Museum

Respect

Sometimes the best way to help someone else is to listen. When you are silent and just listen, you show that you care and respect the person you are listening to. Caring about someone and respecting that person are all important pieces of a larger feeling we call love. Many American artists try to show this emotion in their work.

Jesse Treviño, *Mis Hermanos* (1976)

In this painting, Mexican-born Jesse Treviño uses a large canvas to capture the daily life of Mexican Americans in San Antonio, Texas, the city where he lives. The title of the painting, *Mis Hermanos,* is Spanish for "My Brothers." But the title refers to both members of the Mexican-American community, as well as Treviño's actual family. The sunlight shines across the shirts of his six brothers and the artist himself (center, in striped shirt). The sunlight brings the men together like a strong emotion. Treviño shows the men standing or sitting in different positions against a fence. He captures the crinkles in their shirts and the liquid in the glasses that several of them hold in their hands. Treviño uses a painting style that creates an image almost as realistic as a photograph.

Treviño showed great promise as an artist when he was a young man. Then he lost his right arm when he served as a soldier in the Vietnam War. When he returned to the

▲ **Jesse Treviño, *Mis Hermanos*, 1976, acrylic, 48 x 70 in., Smithsonian American Art Museum**

United States, he had to teach himself to paint all over again with his left hand. His family and friends helped him as he recovered from his war injury. In *Mis Hermanos*, Treviño captures the respect and support the brothers give each other. Notice the hand of the brother in the back row resting on Treviño's shoulder. Each of the men touches another in some fashion, which adds to the warmth of the portrait.

▲ **Jacob Lawrence, *"Men exist for the sake of one another . . . ,"* 1958, oil, 20¾ x 16¾ in., Smithsonian American Art Museum**

Jacob Lawrence, *"Men exist for the sake of one another . . ."* (1958)

In *"Men exist for the sake of one another . . . ,"* an adult sits among four children. The man, though very large, bends gently toward the children. He holds a small tree that still has its roots. This means that the tree can be replanted. The older children, two girls, look sad and in need of comfort. The blue background mirrors their unhappy mood. But the child in the center smiles up at the man. The man's long fingers seem to touch her face, and her hand touches his leg. The warmth they show each other also envelops the smallest child, who looks up at the adult with a happy expression. Flowers bloom at their feet.

Jacob Lawrence had a difficult childhood. His father left when Lawrence was young, and his mother moved many times to find work. Lawrence lived in foster care—where another family takes you in until your own family can support you again. Fortunately, like the girls in this painting, Lawrence got support from adults in his community who cared for him.

Lawrence and other artists were hired by a company to create paintings that matched quotations from famous works in Western literature. Lawrence based his painting on a quotation from the Roman emperor Marcus Aurelius Antoninus. The emperor's statement (the title of Lawrence's painting) tells people that they should respect one another.

Respecting others strengthens our sense of community and the quality of our own lives. Both of these artists' works celebrate this give and take.

Apply What You Learned

1. In what ways are these two paintings similar? How are they different?
2. Why do you think that Jacob Lawrence showed a tree that could be replanted in his painting? What do you think this tree stands for?

Big Question

In what ways are helping people and having respect for them related?

Workbook Pages 95–96

UNIT 4

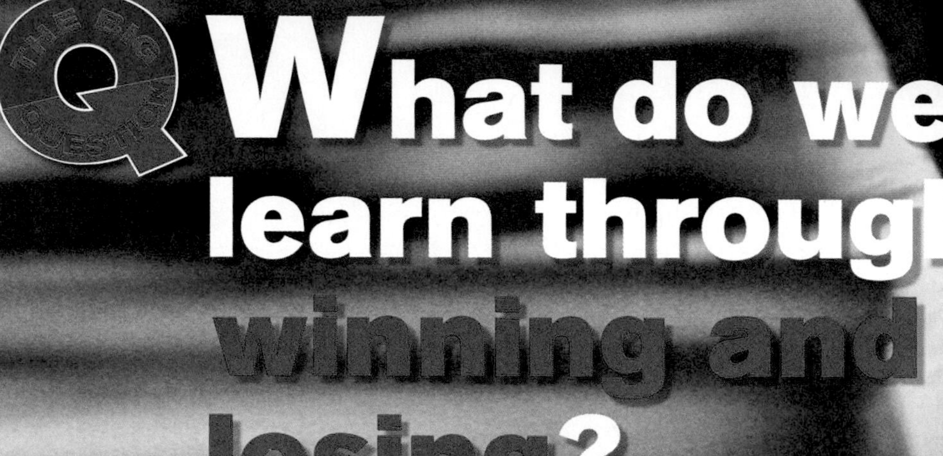

THE BIG QUESTION

What do we learn through winning and losing?

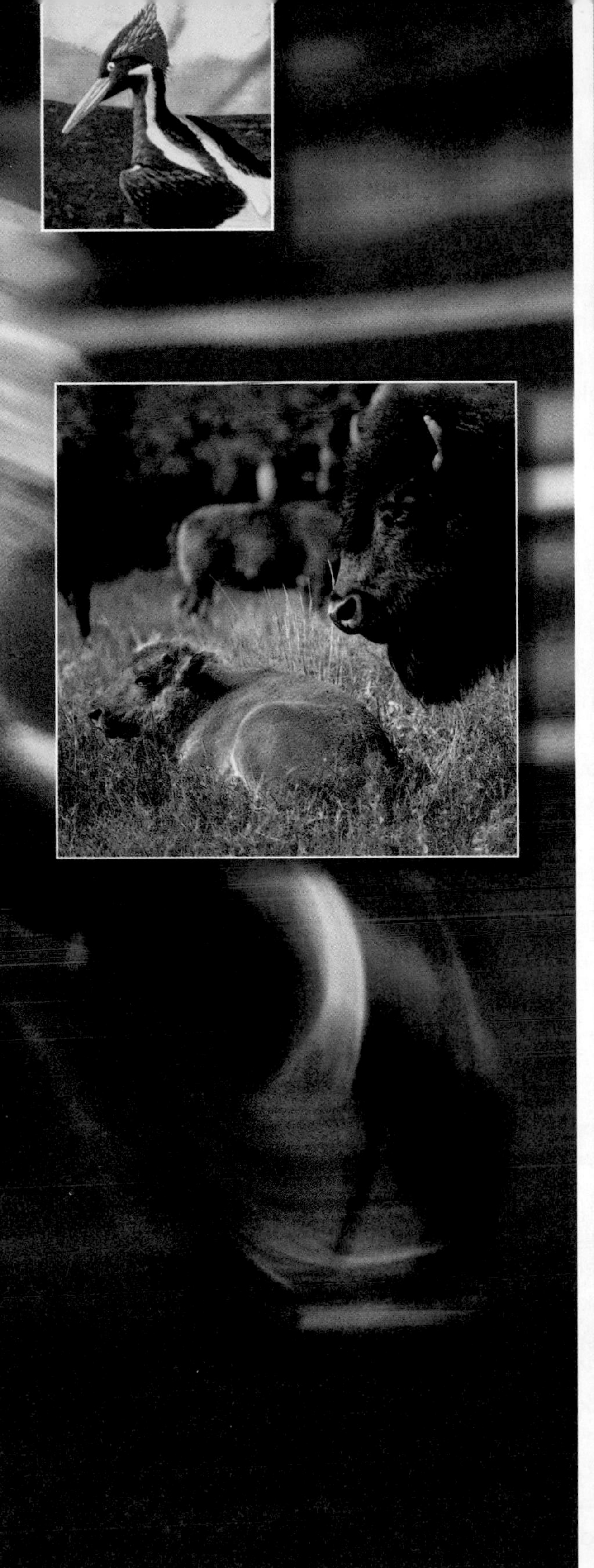

Visit LongmanKeystone.com

This unit is about winning and losing. You'll read about winning a soccer game and winning a race. You'll read about different kinds of loss. You'll learn about sportsmanship and how "it's not whether you win or lose, it's how you play the game." As you read, you'll practice the academic and literary language you need to use in school.

READING 1: **Social Studies Article**

- "Soccer: The World Sport" by Jane Schwartz

READING 2: **Poetry**

- "Casey at the Bat" by Ernest Lawrence Thayer
- "Swift Things Are Beautiful" by Elizabeth Coatsworth
- "Buffalo Dusk" by Carl Sandburg

READING 3: **Fable and Myth**

- "The Hare and the Tortoise" by Aesop
- "Orpheus and Eurydice"

READING 4: **Science Articles**

- "Going, Going, Gone?"
- "Ivory-Billed Woodpeckers Make Noise" by Jill Egan

Listening and Speaking

At the end of this unit, you'll present a **TV sports report** as if you were a newscaster.

Writing

In this unit you will practice **expository writing**, or writing that explains a topic. You'll write an expository paragraph after each reading and an expository essay at the end of the unit.

QuickWrite

Write several sentences about a time when you lost a contest, game, or object.

READING 1

Prepare to Read

What You Will Learn

Reading

- Vocabulary building: *Context, dictionary skills, word study*
- Reading strategy: *Ask questions*
- Text type: *Informational text (social studies)*

Grammar, Usage, and Mechanics

Present perfect

Writing

Write a newspaper article

THE BIG QUESTION

What do we learn through winning and losing? Why do people admire someone who wins a game, a sports match, an election, or some other type of contest? Winners use their skills to do something better than anyone else. Of course, no one wins all the time. Winning and losing are both part of competing. Giving it your all and achieving your personal best are just as important.

Work with a partner. Look at the events listed below. How do you win each activity? Look up any information you need to know to complete the chart. When you are finished, share your ideas with the class.

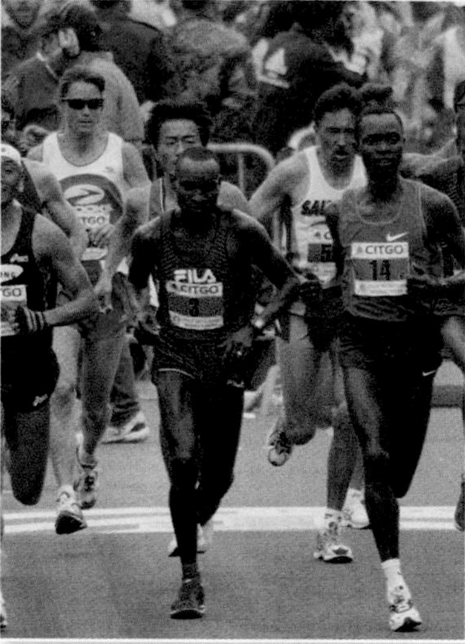

▲ Marathon runners

Activity	How to Win
Spelling bee	Spell each word correctly.
Game of chess	
Soccer game	
Marathon race	

BUILD BACKGROUND

"Soccer: The World Sport" is a nonfiction article that gives facts about the world's most popular sport. According to one survey, over 240 million people play soccer regularly. Two people from different parts of the world, who speak different languages, might have nothing in common except for soccer. Soccer is a common interest that almost the whole world shares.

The article explains how soccer is played and traces the history of the game. Soccer has been around longer than any other sport. Historians have found evidence that the game was played in China, Japan, Greece, and Italy as long as 2,000 years ago. Today, soccer is more popular than ever and is still being spread to countries throughout the world.

VOCABULARY

Learn Key Words

Read these sentences. Use the context to figure out the meaning of the **red** words. Use a dictionary to check your answers. Then write each word and its meaning in your notebook.

1. Each team has many fine **athletes**. These players are good at sports.
2. The coach marked the field's **boundaries** with chalk. The players can't kick the ball outside of these lines.
3. **Professional** players get paid for being on a team. It is their job.
4. The players have many **responsibilities**. There are many things that they must do.
5. Players **sacrifice** things in order to have time to practice. They give up TV, or school clubs, or time with friends.
6. You can tell the teams apart by the color of their **uniforms**. Each team wears a different outfit.

Key Words

athletes
boundaries
professional
responsibilities
sacrifice
uniforms

Practice

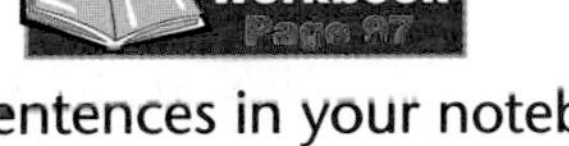

Write the sentences in your notebook. Choose a **red** word from the box above to complete each sentence. Then take turns reading the sentences aloud with a partner.

1. There are many _______ baseball players. They are paid to play ball.
2. The team's new _______ are blue and white. They have the players' names and numbers on the back.
3. The sports team has five new _______ who all play soccer well.
4. Players often must _______ sleeping late on weekend mornings.
5. Luisa has many _______ as the team captain. There are many things she must do.
6. The _______ of the playing field are clearly marked.

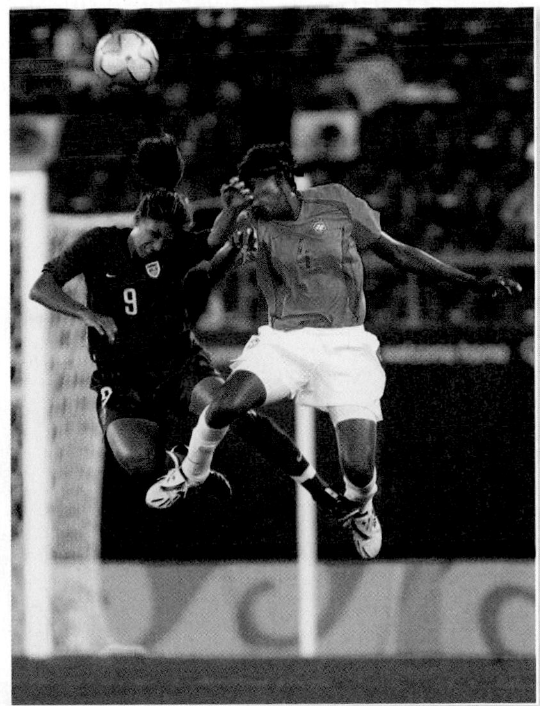

▲ Professional soccer player Mia Hamm goes for the ball at the Olympics, 2004.

Learn Academic Words

Study the **red** words and their meanings. You will find these words useful when talking and writing about informational texts. Write each word and its meaning in your notebook. After you read "Soccer: The World Sport," try to use these words to respond to the text.

Academic Words

element
focus
positive
require

element = one part of a plan, system, piece of writing, and so on	➡	Teamwork is an important **element** in baseball, soccer, and football.
focus = give all your attention to a particular person or thing	➡	Baseball players must **focus** on the ball at all times.
positive = good or useful	➡	Team sports can have a **positive** effect. Players learn to help one another.
require = need something	➡	The team will **require** new uniforms. Their old ones are torn.

Practice

Work with a partner to answer these questions. Try to include the **red** word in your answer. Write the sentences in your notebook.

1. What is the most important **element** that makes a team successful?
2. What do you **focus** on when you watch a baseball game?
3. Why is playing sports a **positive** experience?
4. What items do tennis players **require**?

Soccer players must focus on the ball. ▶

Word Study: Multiple-Meaning Words

Many English words have more than one meaning. You must figure out which meaning fits the particular context. First, look at the context in which you found the word. Are there any clues to meaning in the words and sentences surrounding the word? See which meaning makes most sense in the sentence. Also, identify the word's part of speech. It may be an important clue to the correct meaning. If you still need help, look up the word in a dictionary. Read all the meanings for the word. Select the one that makes most sense in the sentence.

Sentence	Part of Speech	Word and Meaning
In the northeast, each **season** has different weather.	Noun	**season**: one of the four main periods in the year: winter, spring, summer, or fall
We **season** the sauce to make it spicy.	Verb	**season**: add salt, pepper, and other spices to food in order to make it taste better

Practice

Work with a partner to explore the different meanings of these words: *boom, field, goal, matches,* and *meet*. Start by looking up each word in a dictionary. Then use each word in two sentences to show two of the word's meanings. Write the sentences in your notebook.

Reading Strategy ASK QUESTIONS

Asking questions makes you a better reader because you get more information from the text. The five questions you should ask are: *Who? Where? When? What? Why?* These questions are sometimes called the 5Ws. They focus on people, places, time, events, and reasons. To ask questions, follow these steps:

- Read a paragraph. Stop and ask yourself one of the five questions.
- Now try to answer the question from what you've learned in the text.
- Read on and see if your answer is correct. Then ask more questions.

As you read "Soccer: The World Sport," ask yourself all of the five questions. Make a note of the answers.

READING 1

INFORMATIONAL TEXT

SOCIAL STUDIES

Set a purpose for reading Why do soccer players work so hard to win the game, and why do crowds love this sport so much? Read this article to find out.

Soccer: The World Sport

Jane Schwartz

Americans call the game *soccer*. The British, and almost everyone else in the world, call it *football*. Under either name, soccer has become the most popular sport in the world. It is played almost everywhere. More than 200 countries have national professional teams. Every four years, more people watch the final game of the World Cup tournament on TV than any other sporting event. In 2006, the TV audience was 1.3 billion viewers. Compare that to the Superbowl—the most-watched sports program in the United States. American football, however, is not a major sport in any other country—only 95 million people watched it.

The Simplest Sport

Soccer is often called "the simplest sport." That's probably one reason for its wide appeal. It requires very little equipment. You don't use bats, racquets, clubs, paddles, or sticks. You don't wear gloves, mitts, helmets, or goggles. You don't need skis, sleds, anything that floats, or anything with an engine in it. All you need is a round ball and some space. Even the youngest kids in the poorest parts of the world can usually put together those two things.

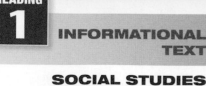

▲ Young people enjoy a game of soccer in Egypt.

---

tournament, sports competition
equipment, things needed for a particular activity
goggles, special glasses that protect the eyes

The rules of the game are also simple. Two teams of eleven players each try to get the ball into the other team's goal. You can kick the ball or use your head to move it. No one except the goalkeeper (or "goalie") is allowed to touch the ball with hands or arms. This is what makes soccer unique among sports. Think about it. Even in everyday life, what actions do you perform *without* using your hands? The answer is: none or almost none. It's certainly true in sports. You are always using your hands in sports. You *hit*, *shoot*, *pass*, and *carry*. You *serve*, dunk, rebound, and *throw*. Even in the simple childhood game of "tag," you have to *tag* the other players to get them out!

There is an old saying: "Necessity is the mother of invention." This means that if people need something, they will find a way to invent it. The rules of soccer took away the use of the players' hands. This

goal, area in which you try to put the ball to win a point
goalkeeper, player on a team who tries to stop the ball before it goes into the goal
dunk, jump up and slam the ball from above into the basket in a game of basketball
rebound, catch a basketball after a player has tried but failed to get a point
necessity, being in need

▲ A goalkeeper stops the ball from entering the goal.

forced soccer players to "invent" new ways to use their feet. Soccer players don't just *pass* the ball with their feet. They *protect* it, *block* it, and *steal* it from their opponents. Their footwork is so fast and so skillful that sometimes it's hard to follow without replaying the action in slow motion. In addition, players often dazzle audiences with leaping kicks that are as awesome as the flying dunks of professional basketball players.

dazzle, amaze with an inspiring display

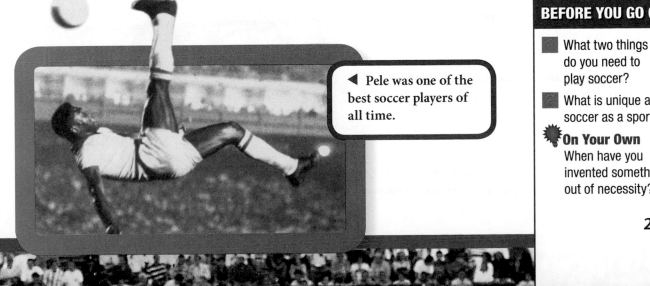

◀ Pele was one of the best soccer players of all time.

BEFORE YOU GO ON

1. What two things do you need to play soccer?
2. What is unique about soccer as a sport?

On Your Own
When have you invented something out of necessity?

A Little History

No one knows exactly where or when soccer began. Written records from 2,000 years ago in China describe games in which a ball was kicked into a goal. Other records have been found in Japan, Greece, and Italy.

The modern game of soccer was developed from the eighth to the nineteenth century in England. In 1863, a formal set of rules was adopted. Other countries accepted these rules, and soon international matches were held. At this time, Great Britain ruled colonies all over the world, and British traders, soldiers, and sailors introduced the game to many parts of Asia, Africa, and the Americas.

The *Fédération Internationale de Football Association* (FIFA) was formed in 1904. It is still the governing body of the sport. By 1930, there were professional football leagues in many countries. The first World Cup tournament was held in Uruguay in 1930. It has been held every four years since then.

A Big Boom

Today, about 18 million people play soccer in the United States. It is the fastest growing team sport in the country. Major League Soccer (MLS) was started in 1996, after other professional soccer leagues had failed. The goal of MLS is to make soccer into a mainstream sport like football, baseball, and basketball.

---

traders, people who buy and sell goods
mainstream, popular; accepted

One big boost was the 1999 Women's World Cup played at the Rose Bowl in Palo Alto, California. The U.S. Women's National Team beat China in front of a crowd of 90,185, the largest number of people at a women's sports event ever. The teams were scoreless in regulation time, scoreless in overtime, and the U.S. finally won 5-4 in penalty kicks. Brandi Chastain scored the winning point, and her picture was on the cover of many sports magazines and newspapers. People who had never followed soccer watched this game on television, and the sport began to attract many new fans.

---

regulation time, the normal period of time in which a soccer game is played; 90 minutes
overtime, the period of time added to the end of a sports game to give one of the two teams a chance to win
penalty kicks, chances to kick the ball into the goal that are given because the other team has not obeyed a rule

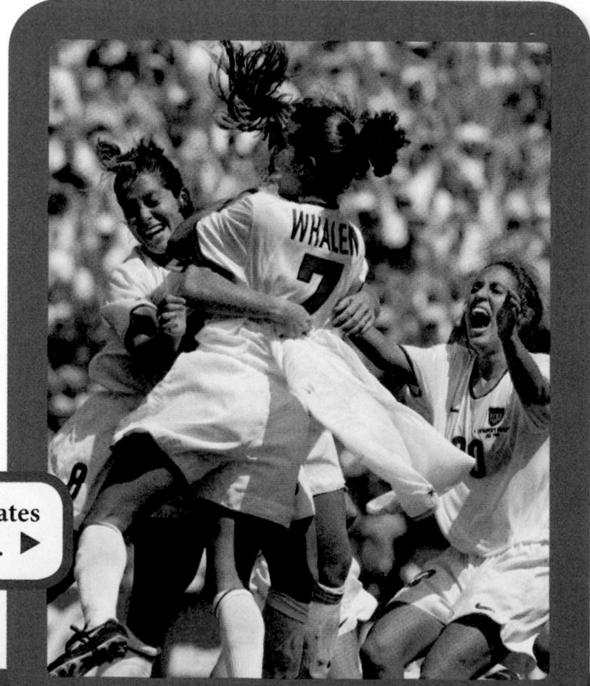

The U.S. Women's National Team celebrates its World Cup win over China. ▶

Something Bigger Than Winning

Most athletes play sports because they want to win. Why else would the players put in hours of practice and travel? Why would they sacrifice their social life and money and sleep to help their team get better and better?

But, if winning is the only goal, most teams will feel like losers, because there can be only one winner at the end of each season.

▲ The Fugees soccer team

Is there something about soccer—as it's played in the United States at this time in history—that goes beyond winning and losing? The answer doesn't come from the game, but from the people who play it. The wave of immigrants to the United States in the last ten to fifteen years has been a big part of the soccer boom. These newcomers have arrived from Central and South America, Africa, and parts of Asia. Many have come from countries torn apart by war, poverty, and natural disasters. Soccer is important to people already in the United States, but it has an even deeper meaning to many recent refugees. For them, soccer can sometimes be a lifeline.

One example of this is a team in Clarkston, Georgia, a small town outside of Atlanta. In 2004, a soccer team was organized. It is made up entirely of refugees. In fact, the team calls itself the Fugees (as in re**fugees**). The players are all in this country legally, brought by a resettlement agency because of housing and low-paying jobs nearby.

The reporter Warren St. John wrote about the Fugees in the *New York Times*. The boys, all between eight and thirteen, have come from Sudan, Somalia, Bosnia, Iraq, and Afghanistan. Some lived for years in refugee camps. Some have been separated from their families. Some watched their loved ones taken away to prison. One boy saw his father murdered in their home. They have been through a lot in their young lives.

BEFORE YOU GO ON

1 Where was the first World Cup tournament held?

2 Who are the Fugees?

On Your Own
Why do you think that soccer has an even deeper meaning to many recent refugees?

---

refugees, people who have left their country, especially because of a war

lifeline, something that someone depends on completely

resettlement agency, organization that helps refugees adjust to life in the United States

▲ The Fugees, led by Coach Luma Mufleh, stretch before a game.

One day a young coach named Luma Mufleh put up a sign announcing tryouts for a soccer team. The team was to be for refugees only, and she was going to be the coach. Those who made the team had to sign a contract accepting certain responsibilities on and off the field. They were going to have to work really hard, but they would have the chance to do something they loved. Before they played their first game, the boys had already "won" several important things: respect, a group they could belong to, and the chance to do really well at something.

The season wasn't perfect. The Fugees did not win every game. The tragedies they had experienced in the past did not suddenly disappear. But other teams admired the way the Fugees played. Parents from the wealthier teams helped the Fugees buy balls, uniforms, and cleated shoes. The boys on the team learned to work together. They had come from different countries, but they all shared a love of soccer. They got to know one another through the sport, and the sport is helping them all to bridge the gap from their old world to their new one.

Throughout U.S. cities and towns soccer is working its magic. It may be "the simplest game," but soccer can have a powerful effect on people's lives. No other sport crosses over so many cultural, racial, and ethnic boundaries as soccer.

---

tryouts, times when people who want to be on a sports team are tested so that the best can be chosen
tragedies, events that cause a lot of sadness

wealthier, richer, having more money
cleated shoes, sneakers that have short pieces of rubber, plastic, or metal attached to the bottom of them, in order to prevent someone from slipping
bridge the gap, reduce or get rid of the difference between two things

A Different Ending Every Time

It's true that all sports are different, but they all have one thing in common: Every game is like a story written right there on the spot. It's never the same story, and no one knows the ending ahead of time.

You might lose today, but there will be another game tomorrow. Soccer has attracted millions of fans and created millions of players. Most will never make it to the professional leagues, but they'll probably make some friends, have fun, and experience the satisfaction of working hard to meet a goal. That's not bad for a simple game!

▲ The Fugees play as a team.

---

on the spot, immediately, without careful planning
satisfaction, feeling of happiness or pleasure because of an achievement

ABOUT THE AUTHOR

Jane Schwartz writes on many subjects and in many different genres. She is best known for *Ruffian: Burning from the Start*, a nonfiction book about a famous racehorse who suffered a fatal injury. She has also written *Caught*, a novel about a young girl growing up in Brooklyn during the 1950s, and *Grammar Power*, a humorous grammar book. In addition, she writes articles for the *New York Times* and *Sports Illustrated*, and she writes poetry. When she is not busy writing, Schwartz loves to travel.

BEFORE YOU GO ON

- What three things did the Fugees "win" before their first game?
- According to the author, what boundaries does soccer cross over?
- **On Your Own** What does the author compare games to? Do you agree with her? Why?

There was ease in Casey's manner as he stepped into his place;
There was pride in Casey's bearing and a smile on Casey's face.
And when, responding to the cheers, he lightly doffed his hat,
No stranger in the crowd could doubt 'twas Casey at the bat.

Ten thousand eyes were on him as he rubbed his hands with dirt.
Five thousand tongues applauded when he wiped them on his shirt.
Then while the writhing pitcher ground the ball into his hip,
Defiance flashed in Casey's eye, a sneer curled Casey's lip.

And now the leather-covered sphere came hurtling through the air,
And Casey stood a-watching it in haughty grandeur there.
Close by the sturdy batsman the ball unheeded sped—
"That ain't my style," said Casey. "Strike one!" the umpire said.

From the benches, black with people, there went up a muffled roar,
Like the beating of the storm-waves on a stern and distant shore;
"Kill him! Kill the umpire!" shouted someone on the stand;
And it's likely they'd have killed him had not Casey raised his hand.

With a smile of Christian charity great Casey's visage shone;
He stilled the rising tumult; he bade the game go on;
He signaled to the pitcher, and once more the sphereoid flew;
But Casey still ignored it, and the umpire said "Strike two!"

"Fraud!" cried the maddened thousands, and echo answered "Fraud!"
But one scornful look from Casey and the audience was awed.
They saw his face grow stern and cold, they saw his muscles strain,
And they knew that Casey wouldn't let that ball go by again.

Literary Check
*What is the **rhyme scheme** of the first stanza on this page?*

---

bearing, way of moving, standing, or behaving
doffed, took off or tipped
writhing, angry; violently twisting
defiance, bold refusal to obey or give in
visage, face
tumult, noisy and excited situation, often caused by a large crowd

The sneer has fled from Casey's lip, the teeth are clenched in hate;
He pounds with cruel violence his bat upon the plate.
And now the pitcher holds the ball, and now he lets it go,
And now the air is shattered by the force of Casey's blow.

Oh, somewhere in this favored land the sun is shining bright,
The band is playing somewhere, and somewhere hearts are light,
And somewhere men are laughing, and little children shout;
But there is no joy in Mudville—mighty Casey has struck out.

—Ernest Lawrence Thayer

---

clenched, held together tightly

ABOUT THE POET

Ernest Lawrence Thayer was an American poet who wrote during the 1880s and 1890s. Thayer began his writing career at Harvard, as editor of the school newspaper. He spent most of his career writing humorous pieces for the *San Francisco Examiner,* a paper owned by a fellow Harvard classmate, William Randolph Hearst. "Casey at the Bat" was originally written for the newspaper. However, it didn't become popular until months after it was written, when it was recited on Broadway in front of players from professional baseball teams.

BEFORE YOU GO ON

1. What does Casey do right after he comes to bat?
2. What does the crowd yell at the umpire?

On Your Own
How do you feel about Casey? Is he mighty or not?

Swift Things Are Beautiful

Swift things are beautiful:
Swallows and deer,
And lightning that falls
Bright-veined and clear,
Rivers and meteors,
Wind in the wheat,
The strong-withered horse,
The runner's sure feet.

And slow things are beautiful:
The closing of day,
The pause of the wave
That curves downward to spray,
The ember that crumbles,
The opening flower,
And the ox that moves on
In the quiet of power.

—Elizabeth Coatsworth

swift, very fast
meteors, pieces of rock or metal that make a bright line in the night sky when they fall through Earth's atmosphere
withered, referring to the withers, or ridge between a horse's shoulders, the highest part of a horse's back
sure, steady; able to walk or run without sliding or falling
ember, piece of wood or coal that stays red and very hot after a fire stops burning
ox, large bull or cow

ABOUT THE POET

Elizabeth Coatsworth was born in Buffalo, New York, in 1893. As a young child, she lived for a time in Europe and Egypt. She began writing when she was twenty years old and continued until she was in her eighties. Coatsworth wrote over ninety books for children and adults, including poetry, novels, and nonfiction. Her 1930 book *The Cat Who Went to Heaven* won the Newbery Medal.

Buffalo Dusk

The buffaloes are gone.
And those who saw the buffaloes are gone.
Those who saw the buffaloes by thousands and how they
pawed the **prairie sod** into dust with their great hoofs,
their great heads down pawing on in a great **pageant**
of **dusk**,
Those who saw the buffaloes are gone.
And the buffaloes are gone.

—Carl Sandburg

---

prairie sod, grass that covers a large, wide-open space
pageant, public show or display
dusk, time just before it gets dark

Literary Check

How does the ***repetition*** *of the word* gone *make you feel?*

About the Poet

Carl Sandburg is considered by many to be one of the greatest American writers. Although he is best known for his poetry, Sandburg also wrote nonfiction and folklore. Sandburg won the Pulitzer Prize twice: first in 1926 for a biography titled *Abraham Lincoln: The Prairie Years* and later in 1951 for *The Complete Poems of Carl Sandburg.*

Before You Go On

1. What slow animal is described in the poem on page 222?
2. What do the buffaloes do at dusk in the poem on page 223?

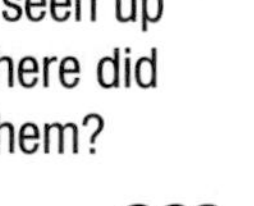

On Your Own
Which of the animals in these two poems have you seen up close? Where did you see them?

READING 2

Review and Practice

DRAMATIC READING

Work in small groups to reread, discuss, and interpret "Casey at the Bat," "Swift Things Are Beautiful," and "Buffalo Dusk." Describe what you visualize as you read each poem line by line. How do the authors use rhyme and rhythm? What images do the poems create in your mind? Then with the rest of the class, read the poems aloud.

One of the best ways to understand a poem is to memorize it, or learn it by heart. Start by saying two lines of the poem you like best. Then memorize the next two lines. Keep going as far into the poem as you can. The part you memorize will be yours forever.

Speaking TIP

Have fun. The more you enjoy reading the poems aloud, the more your classmates will enjoy the poems, too.

COMPREHENSION

Right There

1. In "Casey at the Bat," what is the score in the baseball game when Casey comes to bat?
2. What swift things are mentioned in "Swift Things Are Beautiful"?

Think and Search

3. In "Casey at the Bat," what happens when Flynn comes to bat? What happens when Jimmy Blake comes to bat?
4. In what ways are the moods of each of the three poems different? Which one contains humor and suspense? Which one expresses a serious and thoughtful mood? Which one expresses sadness?

Author and You

5. Why do you think that Carl Sandburg chose to write about buffaloes in "Buffalo Dusk"?
6. Why do you think that Ernest Lawrence Thayer chose to write about a baseball player who strikes out? Why does he call Casey "mighty"?

On Your Own

7. Which fast-moving things do you think are beautiful? Explain.
8. What animal would you like to write a poem about? What three things about that animal would you include in your poem?

DISCUSSION

Discuss in pairs or small groups.

1. "Casey at the Bat" was written in 1888. Why do you think "Casey at the Bat" is still a popular poem?
2. If you were writing a poem about slow things that are beautiful, what five things would you include in your poem?

Q What do we learn through winning and losing? What did you learn about winning and losing from each of the three poems? Which poem taught you the most? Why?

Listening TIP

Evaluate what your classmates say and how they say it. Often a speaker's manner and body language can be more or less persuasive than the content of what the person is saying.

RESPONSE TO LITERATURE

"Swift Things Are Beautiful" describes both swift and slow things. Write a short poem of your own in which you describe two things that are swift and two things that are slow. Use a graphic organizer like the one below to list your ideas. Share your poem with a partner.

Swift Things	Why They Are Beautiful	Slow Things	Why They Are Beautiful

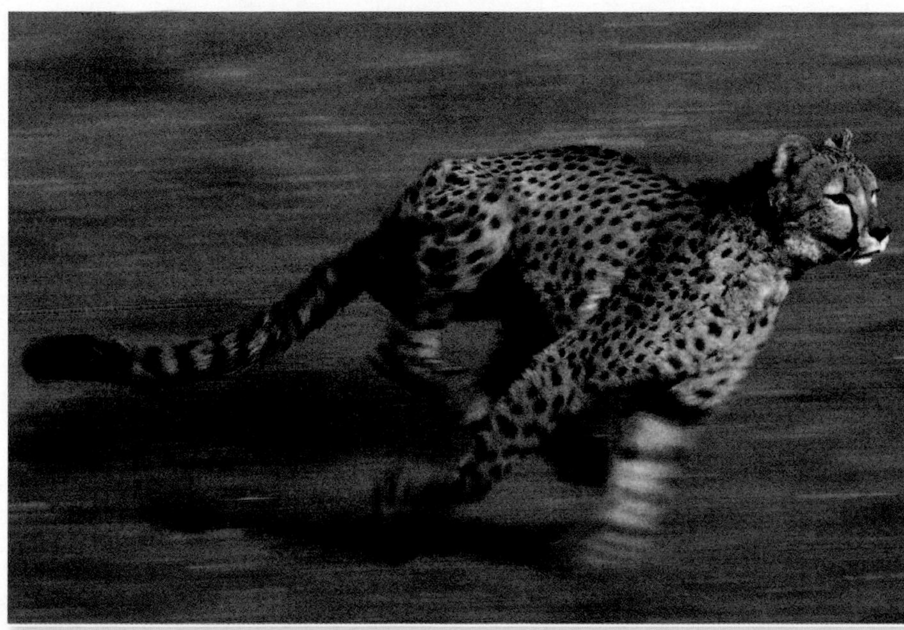

◀ Cheetahs are very swift.

Grammar and Writing

GRAMMAR, USAGE, AND MECHANICS

Simple Past: More Irregular Verbs

Remember to use the simple past to talk about completed actions or conditions that happened at a specific time in the past. Many common verbs in English are irregular. They do not follow regular rules. Some are formed in surprising ways.

The only way to learn the simple past of irregular verbs is to memorize them. However, there are "groupings" that can be helpful in memorizing irregular verbs. Study the examples in the chart below. Some are from "Casey at the Bat."

Base Form	Simple Past
know throw	knew threw
come become overcome	came became overcame
bring think	brought thought
stand understand	stood understood
let put hit	let put hit

Base Form	Simple Past
sleep keep	slept kept
ring sing begin	rang sang began
shake take	shook took
wake break	woke broke
rise ride write	rose rode wrote

Practice

Work with a partner. Copy these sentences into your notebook. Then fill in the blanks with the simple past of the verb in parentheses.

1. The pitcher _______ the ball to Casey. (throw)
2. Flynn _______ he could hit the ball. (think)
3. Jimmy's hand _______ when he held the bat. (shake)
4. Everyone _______ that Casey wanted to hit the ball. (know)
5. No one in Mudville _______ that night. (sing)
6. A reporter _______ an article about the big game. (write)

WRITING AN EXPOSITORY PARAGRAPH

Write a Response to Literature

On this page, you'll write an expository paragraph that explains your response to one of the poems you just read. You'll use a graphic organizer like the one at the right to gather examples and details.

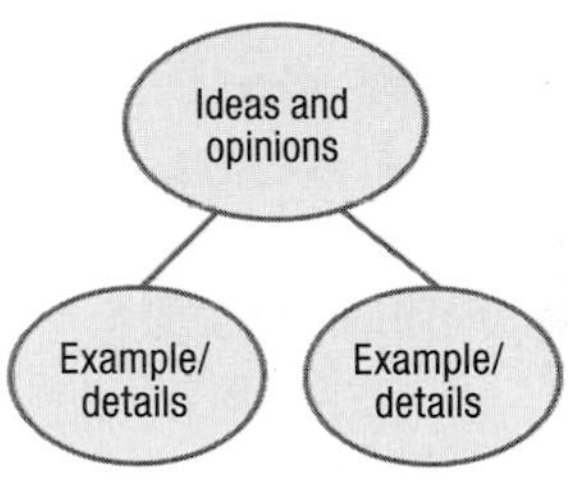

In a response, you give your ideas and opinions about the meaning of a story, poem, or other type of literature. You use examples and other details from the text to support your response. In addition, you show your understanding of the text and give your thoughts and feelings about it.

Here is a model of a response to a poem. Notice how the writer explains his interpretation of and reaction to the poem.

Andrew C. Dubin

"Buffalo Dusk"

"Buffalo Dusk," by Carl Sandburg, is a peaceful, yet very upsetting poem. It is peaceful because Sandburg talks about buffaloes and how they once lived and roamed free on the prairies. He also mentions "those who saw the buffaloes." These are the Native Americans, who also lived freely. The poem is upsetting because Sandburg tells how both the buffaloes and the Native Americans are gone. Reading this makes me angry and upset. The buffaloes were hunted so much, they nearly died out. Without the buffaloes, the Native Americans had no source of food or clothing and began to disappear as well. Some Native Americans and buffaloes did survive, but far fewer of either are alive today compared to 200 years ago. For this reason, the poem is very powerful and also very sad.

Practice

Write a response to "Casey at the Bat" that explains what the poem is about and describes the impact it had on you and why. Include your ideas, opinions, and feelings. Provide reasons and examples to support your opinions. Use a word web to gather examples and details from the poem. Be sure to form the simple past of irregular verbs correctly.

Writing Checklist

IDEAS:

- ☑ I explained my reaction to the poem by providing good examples from the text.

VOICE:

- ☑ My response clearly states my point of view.

READING 3

Prepare to Read

What You Will Learn

Reading

- Vocabulary building: *Literary terms, word study*
- Reading strategy: *Identify author's purpose*
- Text type: *Literature (fable and myth)*

Grammar, Usage, and Mechanics
Adverbs with *-ly*

Writing
Write to compare and contrast

THE BIG QUESTION

What do we learn through winning and losing? What can ancient stories teach us about winning and losing? Every culture has stories that teach a lesson. Many of these stories have animal characters that talk, think, and act as if they were human. You may know the story "The Grasshopper and the Ant." Who is the winner in this story?

> All summer long, Grasshopper relaxed, chirping and singing all day. Ant went by carrying an ear of corn to her nest. "Why work so hard?" Grasshopper said to Ant. "It's summer. Come and relax with me." "I can't," Ant replied. "I'm preparing my nest for winter." Grasshopper laughed and began singing again. "Why worry about winter? We have plenty to eat." When winter came, Grasshopper had nothing to eat and was dying of hunger. He watched the ants eating the food they had gathered in summer. Then Grasshopper realized: It is best to prepare for the future in the present.

Work with a partner. Discuss stories you know that teach a lesson or have animal characters that act like human beings. Compare and contrast them.

BUILD BACKGROUND

Almost every culture in the world has fables and myths. These stories are traditionally passed down from one generation to the next. They are wonderful to listen to or read. They often contain wise messages and advice.

"The Hare and the Tortoise" is a fable from ancient Greece about a race between two animals. The main characters are very different from each other. Their character traits lead one to victory and the other to defeat.

"Orpheus and Eurydice" is a myth that is also from ancient Greece. Like many myths, it tells a story and explains how something in nature came into existence.

◀ "The Hare and the Tortoise" is a fable that teaches a lesson.

VOCABULARY

Learn Literary Words

A **fable** is a short story that teaches a lesson called a **moral**. The moral is sometimes stated at the end of the fable in a short sentence. At other times, the moral is implied. You, the reader, must figure it out yourself. You may have heard the word *proverb*. The morals at the ends of fables are like proverbs, or short statements of advice. Here are the titles of two other fables and the morals they teach.

Literary Words

fable
moral
personification
myth

Fable	Moral
"The Lion and the Mouse"	A little friend can be a big help.
"The Wolf in Sheep's Clothing"	Don't be fooled by outward appearances.

As you learned earlier, animal characters in a fable talk and act like human beings. When writers create animal characters that have human traits, this is called **personification**. Most fables, such as the one you are about to read, contain examples of personification.

A **myth** is a story from long ago that has been passed on by word of mouth. Myths often try to explain cultural beliefs and why certain things occur in the natural world, such as thunder and lightning. Many myths also tell stories about the actions of gods and heroes.

▲ The little mouse was a big help to the trapped lion.

Place	Myth	What It Explains
Greece	"Poseidon, the God of the Sea"	earthquakes, shipwrecks, storms
Hawaii	"Pele, Goddess of Fire"	fire and volcanoes

Practice

Work with a partner to discuss these morals and proverbs. Explain what each one means to you. Write your explanations in your notebook.

1. Absence makes the heart grow fonder.
2. Look before you leap.
3. Evil wishes, like chickens, come home to roost.
4. Little by little does the trick.

Learn Academic Words

Study the **red** words and their meanings. You will find these words useful when talking and writing about literature. Write each word and its meaning in your notebook. After you read "The Hare and the Tortoise" and "Orpheus and Eurydice," try to use these words to respond to the text.

Academic Words

- define
- instruct
- objective
- style

define = show or describe what something is or means	➡	One way to **define** a word is to use a synonym, another word that has the same meaning.
instruct = teach someone or show him or her how to do something	➡	The teacher planned to **instruct** the class on how to write a fable. His outline helped him teach the lesson.
objective = something that you are working hard to achieve	➡	The author's **objective** was to entertain. She wanted readers to enjoy the story.
style = a way of doing, making, or painting something that is typical of a particular period	➡	The artist who drew pictures for the fable had a good **style**. He drew funny, colorful characters.

Practice

Work with a partner to answer the questions. Try to include the **red** word in your answer. Write the sentences in your notebook.

1. What would you say if you were asked to **define** what a fable is?
2. Who would you ask to **instruct** you in how to write a short story?
3. What would be your **objective** if you were running in a race?
4. What kind of writing **style** do you like best?

This woman is dressed in the style of the Hawaiian ◀ goddess Pele.

Word Study: Spellings for *r*-Controlled Vowels

When a vowel is followed by an *r*, the vowel stands for a special sound, called an *r*-controlled vowel. The letters *er*, *ir*, and *ur* all stand for the same *r*-controlled vowel sound. It is the /ər/ sound you hear in *her*, *bird*, and *hurt*. The letters *ar* stand for the *r*-controlled vowel sound you hear in *car*. The letters *or* stand for the *r*-controlled vowel sound you hear in *for*.

▲ This bird is perching on a fern.

/är/ as in car	/ər/ as in her	/ər/ as in bird	/ôr/ as in for	/ər/ as in hurt
start	fern	third	horse	turn
dark	certain	first	tortoise	burst

Practice

Workbook Page 113

Work with a partner. Copy the chart above into your notebook. Sort the words from the box below by their sound-spelling and add them to the chart. Then add other words with *r*-controlled vowels.

artist	corner	curve	nerve	short
circle	curled	large	person	thirst

READING STRATEGY IDENTIFY AUTHOR'S PURPOSE

Identifying an author's purpose (or reason for writing) can make you a better reader because you understand *why* the author wrote the text. Authors can choose to write to inform, to entertain, or to persuade. Sometimes an author has more than one purpose for writing. To identify an author's purpose, ask yourself these questions:

- Is this entertaining? Am I enjoying reading it?
- Am I learning new information? Is something being explained?
- Is the author trying to persuade me about something?

As you read "The Hare and the Tortoise" and "Orpheus and Eurydice," identify the author's purpose.

Workbook Page 114

READING 3

LITERATURE

FABLE AND MYTH

Set a purpose for reading Is speed the most important thing in a race? How does the night sky remind us of Orpheus and his loss? Read the classic fable and myth to answer these questions.

The Hare and the Tortoise

Aesop

On a hot, sunny day, Hare saw Tortoise plodding along on the road. Hare teased Tortoise because she was walking so slowly.

Tortoise laughed. "You can tease me if you like, but I bet I can get to the end of the field before you can. Do you want to race?"

Hare agreed, thinking that he could easily win. He ran off. Tortoise plodded steadily after him.

Before long, Hare began to feel hot and tired. "I'll take a short nap," he thought. "If Tortoise passes me, I can catch up to her." Hare lay down and fell asleep.

Tortoise plodded on steadily, one foot after another.

The day was hot. Hare slept and slept in the heat. He slept for a longer time than he wanted. And Tortoise plodded on, slowly and steadily.

Finally, Hare woke up. He had slept longer than he wanted, but he still felt confident that he could reach the finish line before Tortoise.

He looked around. Tortoise was nowhere in sight. "Ha! Tortoise isn't even here yet!" he thought.

Hare started to run again. He leaped easily over roots and rocks. As he ran around the last corner and stopped to rest, he was amazed to see Tortoise, still plodding steadily on, one foot after another, nearer and nearer the finish line.

Now Hare ran as fast as he could. He almost flew! But it was too late. He threw himself over the finish line, but Tortoise was there first.

"So what do you say?" asked Tortoise. But Hare was too tired to answer.

MORAL: Slow and steady wins the race.

LITERARY CHECK

*How might the **moral** of this fable apply to other areas of life besides a race?*

---

plodding, walking slowly
teased, made jokes and laughed at in order to embarrass
steadily, moving in a continuous, gradual way
nap, short sleep
catch up to, come from behind and reach by going fast
confident, sure
finish line, line at which a race ends

ABOUT THE AUTHOR

Aesop was a slave in ancient Greece. He was a great storyteller. In many of his fables, Aesop uses personification to teach people lessons. Some historians believe that Aesop gained his freedom because of his stories. His fables are still popular today.

BEFORE YOU GO ON

1. What kind of character is Hare? Describe Hare's traits.
2. What is Tortoise like? How is she different from Hare?

On Your Own
Who did you want to win the race? Why?

▲ Orpheus leading Eurydice

Orpheus and Eurydice

In ancient times, no one played more beautiful music or sang more lovely songs than Orpheus. The god Apollo gave Orpheus a lyre made out of a turtle shell. When Orpheus played on the lyre and sang, everyone—gods, humans, and wild creatures—stopped and listened. The trees and stones danced. Even the rivers stopped flowing to listen to his song.

Literary Check
What examples of ***personification*** *can you find in the first paragraph?*

Orpheus was married to a wood nymph named Eurydice. He loved her more than anything else in the world. One day Eurydice was running across a meadow, and failed to notice a poisonous snake. The snake bit her ankle, and she died. Orpheus was left grief-stricken and alone. From that time on, Orpheus played such sad songs that gods, nymphs—anyone

---

Apollo, Greek god of the sun, medicine, poetry, music, and prophecy
lyre, musical instrument with strings across a U-shaped frame, used especially in ancient Greece
wood nymph, spirit of nature who, according to ancient Greek and Roman stories, appeared as a young girl living in trees, mountains, and streams
grief-stricken, feeling very sad because of something that has happened

who heard the music—felt sorry for him. Soon, Orpheus could not bear his grief any longer. He decided to travel to the Underworld to find his beloved Eurydice. The god Hades and his wife Persephone ruled this underground kingdom of the dead.

As Orpheus came near the secret cave that led to the Underworld, he grew hopeful. He whispered to himself, "I will play such lovely songs that maybe Hades himself will return Eurydice to me."

A fierce three-headed guard dog, called Cerberus, stood in front of the entrance to the cave. Orpheus was determined to find Eurydice. He did not turn back. He played on his lyre until Cerberus fell fast asleep, letting him pass. Next, Orpheus came to the river Styx. Here, the boatman Charon **ferries** dead souls to the Underworld. At first, Charon refused to take Orpheus across the water. But when he heard the lovely music Orpheus made, he was **entranced** and ferried Orpheus to the other side.

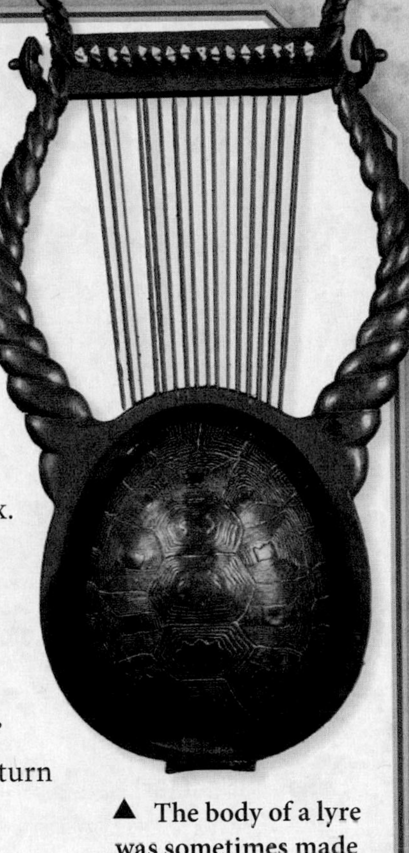

▲ **The body of a lyre was sometimes made out of a turtle shell.**

At last, Orpheus entered the Underworld and stood before Hades and Persephone. "I beg you, please, let Eurydice come back with me," Orpheus pleaded. The Lord of the Underworld said, "No. I cannot return her to you."

Bold Orpheus did not give up. He played **passionately** on his lyre. Hades softened, and Persephone was moved to tears. Suddenly, the Lord of the Underworld understood Orpheus's grief.

"I will let Eurydice go," Hades said, "on one **condition**. You cannot turn around to look back at her until you reach the light of the living world above."

Orpheus agreed. Eurydice followed Orpheus up the steep path out of the Underworld. They had almost reached the cave entrance, when Orpheus was overwhelmed by a desire to see his wife's face. He glanced back and she cried out. Then Eurydice vanished into the mist. She was caught in the Underworld forever.

Orpheus was **desolate** and remained so for the rest of his life. When he died, the gods hung his lyre in the night sky. To this day, if you look at the night sky, you can see the **constellation** called Lyra. It is a reminder of the sad story of Orpheus and Eurydice.

---

ferries, carries a short distance from one place to another in a boat
entranced, focused so much on something that other things go unnoticed
passionately, with very strong feeling
condition, something that is stated in an agreement that must be done
desolate, very sad and lonely
constellation, group of stars that forms a particular pattern and has a name

LITERARY CHECK

What aspect of nature does the ***myth*** *of Orpheus explain?*

BEFORE YOU GO ON

1. What great skill does Orpheus have?
2. What is the Underworld, and why does Orpheus go there?

On Your Own
Why is Orpheus desolate at the end of the story?

READING 3 Review and Practice

READER'S THEATER

Act out this scene between Hare and Tortoise.

Hare: Everyone knows that I am the fastest animal in the forest. No one can run as fast as I can. That's why they call me Speedy.

Tortoise: You think you are so fast. You just like to brag.

Hare: Well, how about having a race to prove that I am the fastest animal of all? I can beat anyone. I can certainly beat you. You are such a slowpoke.

Tortoise: Okay, let's race. But I wouldn't be so sure I'd win if I were you. I may not be so fast, but I am steady.

Hare: Ha! Steady doesn't matter at all. Speed is the only important thing in a race.

Tortoise: We'll just see about that. Let's get some friends to watch us and time us.

Hare: I'll ask Mouse to time us. He's good at keeping time because he likes to run up and down clocks.

Tortoise: Here we go! Let the steadiest animal win!

Hare: Yes, here we go! Let the fastest animal win!

Speaking TIP

Speak naturally and with feeling. Try to convey the humor of the situation with your voice.

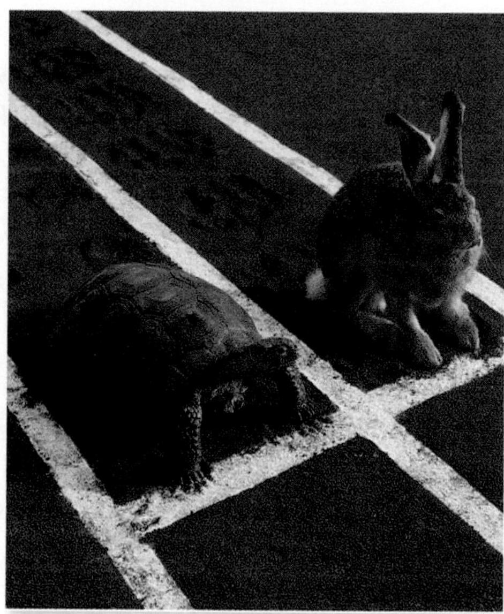

▲ Hare and Tortoise at the starting line

COMPREHENSION

Right There

1. What is the moral of the fable "The Hare and the Tortoise"?
2. What instrument does Orpheus play in the myth "Orpheus and Eurydice"? Who gave it to him?

Think and Search

3. Why does Hare take a nap and sleep longer than he planned to?
4. How does Orpheus use his music to find Eurydice in the Underworld?

Author and You

5. Why does Hare lose the race? Why do you think that Aesop created a character like Hare?
6. Why do you think that Orpheus was unable to obey the instructions he received from Hades?

On Your Own

7. Why are fables a good way to teach important lessons?
8. Why do all cultures have myths that try to explain aspects of nature?

DISCUSSION

Discuss in pairs or small groups.

1. How does Aesop use personification in "The Hare and the Tortoise"?
2. What did you learn about loss from reading "Orpheus and Eurydice"?
3. How are the fable and myth you read similar? How are they different?

Q What do we learn through winning and losing? Why do you think that winning and losing are often themes in traditional stories, such as myths and fables? How are winning and losing experiences that everyone can relate to?

Listening TIP

As you listen, write down key points that your classmates make. This will help you recall and participate in the discussion.

RESPONSE TO LITERATURE

Write a brief fable of your own. Use animals as your main characters and give them human traits. Be sure to use dialogue and personification to make your story lively and appealing.

When you are done writing, read your fable to a small group of classmates. Don't read the moral. See whether your friends can identify the moral on their own.

Orpheus and Eurydice with the messenger of the gods, who guided dead souls to the Underworld ▶

Grammar and Writing

GRAMMAR, USAGE, AND MECHANICS

Adverbs with *-ly*

Writers use adverbs to make their writing clear and exact. An adverb usually describes the action of a verb. An adverb can appear at the beginning, middle, or end of a sentence. It can be placed before or after the verb. Place a comma after an adverb when it comes at the beginning of a sentence.

Slowly, (adverb) the tortoise moved (verb) along the beach.
The tortoise moved (verb) **slowly** (adverb) along the beach.
The tortoise **slowly** (adverb) moved (verb) along the beach.

▲ A tortoise moves very slowly.

Adding *-ly* to an adjective forms many adverbs.

Adjective	Adverb
happy	happily
quick	quickly
swift	swiftly

Don't confuse adverbs that end with *-ly* with adjectives that end in *-y*.

Adjectives: pretty, merry, sleepy, cloudy, windy, rainy

Practice

Work with a partner. In your notebook, write sentences for each adverb.

1. gladly
2. easily
3. steadily
4. suddenly
5. wisely
6. carefully

WRITING AN EXPOSITORY PARAGRAPH

Write to Compare and Contrast

On this page, you will compare and contrast two things. You'll use a Venn diagram like the one at the right to help you structure your writing. When you compare, you show how two people, places, or things are alike. When you contrast, you show how they are different. To compare and contrast, select two topics that are alike and different in important ways. First, explain how the two items are alike. Then explain how they are different.

Here is a model of how to compare and contrast. Notice how the writer presents similarities in the first paragraph and differences in the second paragraph.

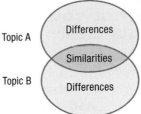

Topic A — Differences
Similarities
Topic B — Differences

Wendy Willner

"The Hare and the Tortoise" and "Orpheus and Eurydice"

The fable by Aesop and the myth of Orpheus have several similarities. First, they are both ancient Greek stories about a series of events that occur between two main characters. In each story, one character acts without thinking. Hare does not think deeply before carelessly napping. Orpheus does not think when he looks back at Eurydice. Both characters suffer a loss because of their mistakes.

There are also differences between the two stories. "The Hare and the Tortoise" is a fable with a moral: Slow and steady wins the race. "Orpheus and Eurydice" is a how-and-why myth that explains how Lyra became a constellation. Each story has a very different ending, too. Hare may have lost the race but can still live happily ever after. Orpheus stays madly in love with Eurydice, so he is sad for the rest of his life.

Practice

Write two paragraphs that compare and contrast two people, places, or things. Choose topics that have points of similarity and difference, such as Orpheus and Hare. Tell how the two things are alike in the first paragraph and how they are different in the second paragraph. List your ideas in a Venn diagram. Be sure to use adverbs that end in *-ly* correctly.

ORGANIZATION:

☑ I explained all the similarities and then all the differences.

WORD CHOICE:

☑ I used specific details and examples to support my comparison and contrast.

READING 4

Prepare to Read

What You Will Learn

Reading

- Vocabulary building: *Context, dictionary skills, word study*
- Reading strategy: *Recognize cause and effect*
- Text type: *Informational text (science)*

Grammar, Usage, and Mechanics
Showing cause and effect: *because, because of,* and *so*

Writing
Write a cause-and-effect explanation

THE BIG QUESTION

What can we learn through winning and losing? You are going to read about three kinds of birds that were lost forever. What might cause a type of bird to die out? How would this affect other animals, including humans?

Think about what you know about birds. Make a two-column chart in your notebook with the headings *Birds* and *Facts*. Work in small groups to list the names of birds you know, such as robins, toucans, penguins, and cardinals. Write any facts you know about each bird; for example, robins eat worms. Then discuss what might happen to cause these birds to die out. Discuss how this would affect other animals.

▲ A toucan

BUILD BACKGROUND

"Going, Going, Gone?" and **"Ivory-Billed Woodpeckers Make Noise"** are science articles. The first article explains why three kinds of birds died out. The second suggests that a type of bird once thought to have died out may actually still exist.

▲ A penguin

In "Buffalo Dusk" you learned that humans were responsible for killing off most of the buffaloes in North America. If laws had not been passed to protect buffaloes, they would have become extinct, or lost forever. Why do specific kinds of animals become extinct? They may not be able to find the food they need. People or other creatures may destroy their habitats. Disease might wipe them out. In the case of dinosaurs, meteors may have struck Earth and killed off these creatures.

▲ A cardinal

VOCABULARY

Learn Key Words

Read these sentences. Use the context to figure out the meaning of the **red** words. Use a dictionary to check your answers. Then write each word and its meaning in your notebook.

1. The **conservationists** at the park protected the lions by keeping them in a safe area.
2. After the **destruction** of the forest, the animals had nowhere to live. Their homes had been ruined.
3. Dinosaurs have become **extinct**. They are all gone now.
4. The birds' **habitats** in the nature preserve look like their original rain forest homes. There is food to eat, and there are trees to live in.
5. The student took a class in **ornithology** because he wanted to know all about birds.
6. The cat is a **predator** that likes to attack birds.

Key Words

conservationists
destruction
extinct
habitats
ornithology
predator

Practice

Work with a partner to answer these questions. Try to include the **red** word in your answer. Write the sentences in your notebook.

1. How do **conservationists** protect animals?
2. What natural disasters might cause **destruction** in a town?
3. What do you think caused dinosaurs to become **extinct**?
4. What do you think the **habitats** of penguins look like?
5. What sort of people would teach classes in **ornithology**?
6. What animal might be a **predator** of a cat?

Serious bird-watchers often read books on ornithology. ▶

Learn Academic Words

Study the **red** words and their meanings. You will find these words useful when talking and writing about informational texts. Write each word and its meaning in your notebook. After you read "Going, Going, Gone?" and "Ivory-Billed Woodpeckers Make Noise," try to use these words to respond to the text.

Academic Words

environment
estimate
factors
statistics

environment = the land, water, and air in which people, animals, and plants live	➡	Oil spills and other changes in the **environment** had a bad effect on the birds that lived there.
estimate (verb) = judge the value or size of something	➡	Rico and Li **estimate** that more than 100 birds live in the region. It is a logical guess.
factors = several things that influence or cause a situation	➡	Many **factors** caused the birds to move to a new area. One reason was the weather.
statistics = a collection of numbers that represents facts or measurements	➡	The **statistics** show how the number of birds has gone up and down over the years.

Practice

Write the sentences in your notebook. Choose a **red** word from the box above to complete each sentence. Then take turns reading the sentences aloud with a partner.

1. People gather _______ about the number of animals in a certain place.
2. There are many _______ that help to keep an animal safe.
3. Sometimes it's better to _______ than to count every single item.
4. People and other living creatures need a certain _______ in order to survive.

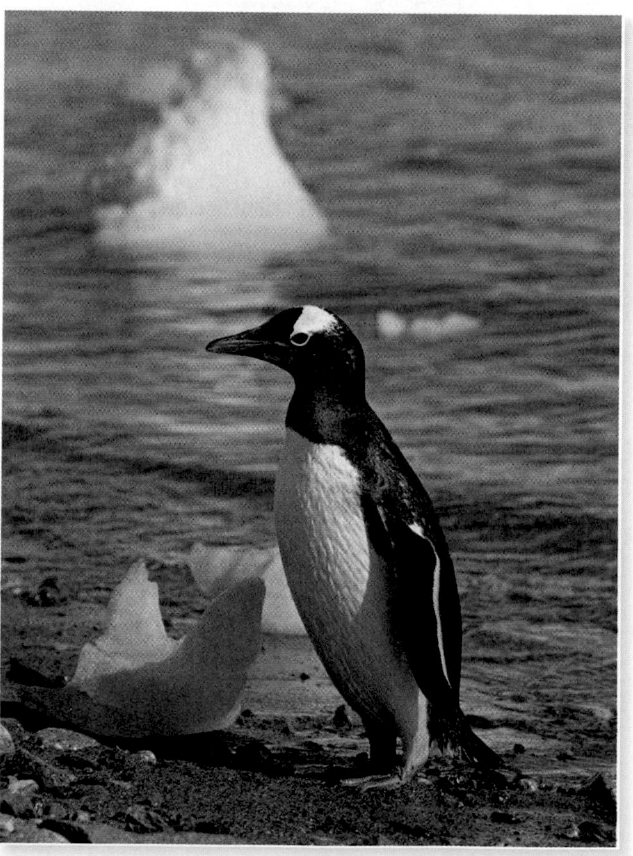

Gentoo penguins like this one live in the cold environment of Antarctica. ▶

Word Study: Homophones

A homophone is a word that sounds the same as another word but has a different meaning and a different spelling, such as *hair* and *hare*. Homophones can be confusing when you read or hear them. To figure out which meaning is being used, check the spelling and use context clues. If you still can't figure out which meaning is correct, look up the word in a dictionary.

▲ The sailor could see the sea.

Homophone	Meaning
one **won**	number that comes before two simple past of *win*
prey **pray**	hunt another animal for food speak to a god
sea **see**	the ocean use your eyes to notice

Practice

Work with a partner. Define each pair of homophones. Then use each word in a sentence to show its meaning. Check your answers in a dictionary. Write the words and definitions in your notebook.

break/brake	main/mane	tale/tail
hour/our	seen/scene	weather/whether

READING STRATEGY RECOGNIZE CAUSE AND EFFECT

Recognizing a cause and an effect helps you understand explanations in texts. An effect is "what happened." A cause is "why it happened." To recognize causes and effects, follow the steps in this example:

- Read this sentence: *The bird died because it didn't have food.*
- Look for what happened. (The bird died.) This is the effect.
- Look for the reason why it happened. (It didn't have food.) This is the cause.
- Look for words that signal cause and effect, such as *so, because, because of, therefore,* and *as a result.*

As you read the next two articles, look for the causes and effects. Use a graphic organizer to help you.

READING 4

INFORMATIONAL TEXT

SCIENCE

Set a purpose for reading Why did the birds in these paintings become extinct or almost extinct? Read to find out the causes. Do you think that people learned anything from this loss? Analyze the effects.

Going, Going, Gone?

When a species, or kind of animal, becomes extinct, it is lost forever. These online science articles both deal with birds that have become extinct. You will find out the effects that certain events and actions had on the dodo, the passenger pigeon, and the Carolina parakeet. You will also find out why some bird lovers now feel hopeful about a bird that was thought to be extinct. As you read, consider what can be done to prevent other living things from becoming extinct in the future.

More than eighty kinds of birds have died out, or become extinct, in the last 300 years. Some vanished because of natural causes. Humans killed off most of them. They hunted the birds too much and destroyed the birds' habitats. Read on for more details on the search for the ivory-billed woodpecker. (It might not be extinct as once thought.) Then check out the stories behind three extinct birds.

The Ivory-Billed Woodpecker

A team of bird experts is walking through mud and swamps in Louisiana's Pearl River forest. They hope to find the mysterious ivory-billed woodpecker. Experts believed this bird had been extinct for more than fifty years. A college student's sighting of unusual-looking birds sparked hopes that it might still be alive.

Loggers cut down trees in the Pearl River forest during the early 1800s. But some trees have grown back. There are now many old cypress, sweet gum, and oak trees that would serve as a good home for ivory-billed woodpeckers. The birds were known to eat the fat grubs that live under the bark of these trees. The researchers have already found trees with areas of bark that have been chipped off, as if by a large woodpecker. Only time will tell if it is an ivory-billed one.

---

loggers, people whose job it is to cut down trees

grubs, insects when they are in the form of small, soft white worms

The Dodo

The dodo was the first bird to be wiped out by people during modern times. Dodos were large, flightless birds. They were first seen around 1600 on Mauritius, an island in the Indian Ocean. Less than eighty years later, the dodo was extinct. The dodo's heavy, clumsy body made it an easy target for sailors, who hunted it for food. As forests were destroyed, so was the dodo's food supply. And the cats, rats, pigs, and other predators unleashed by sailors **preyed on** the dodos. Together these factors led to the dodo's extinction.

The Passenger Pigeon

These pigeons once lived in the eastern United States. They flew across this area in flocks so huge that they darkened the sky. In 1808 a single flock in Kentucky was estimated to contain over 2 billion birds. Today the passenger pigeon is extinct because of human activities. Settlers moving West during the nineteenth century cleared huge numbers of eastern chestnut and oak trees to make room for farms and towns. These trees were the passenger pigeon's main source of food. The birds were seen as a threat to crops, so people killed the birds. They were also hunted for food. All of these factors wiped out the passenger pigeon. The last one, which lived in the Cincinnati Zoological Garden, died on September 1, 1914.

preyed on, hunted and ate

The Carolina Parakeet

This colorful bird was the only parrot native to the eastern United States. It had green feathers with a yellow head and orange cheek patches and forehead. The largest Carolina parakeets were 33 centimeters (13 in.) long, including their tail feathers. They once lived throughout the Southeast, as far north as Virginia and as far west as Texas. Parrots are among the smartest of birds. However, farmers thought these fruit-eaters were **pests**. So they shot them from the skies. The Carolina parakeet became extinct in the 1920s. As a result, all that's left are stuffed examples of this bird in museums.

pests, small animals or insects that harm people or destroy things, especially crops or food supplies

BEFORE YOU GO ON

1. What caused the passenger pigeon to become extinct?
2. Why did farmers kill the Carolina parakeet?

On Your Own
Why should we try to prevent species (kinds) of birds from becoming extinct?

Ivory-Billed Woodpeckers Make Noise

Jill Egan

Bird lovers were chirping back in April of 2005. Why? Scientists from Cornell University announced they'd rediscovered the ivory-billed woodpecker. The rare bird was thought to have been extinct since 1944. It was rediscovered at Cache River National Wildlife Refuge in eastern Arkansas.

Wildlife Refuge, protective environment for animals

In July, a small group of bird experts said that they weren't sure the ivory-billed woodpecker had really been rediscovered. They said a blurry videotape of the bird wasn't enough evidence. Researchers then decided to send them more proof. They shared a sound recording of the ivory-billed woodpecker's one-of-a-kind double-rap.

one-of-a-kind, unique, or very special because there is nothing else like it

The ivory-billed woodpecker ▶

The unique sounds made believers out of the bird experts. "The thrilling new sound recordings provide clear and convincing evidence that the ivory-billed woodpecker is not extinct," said Richard Prum, a scientist from Yale University.

The ivorybill is the largest woodpecker in the United States. It has a wingspan of about 91 centimeters (3 ft.). The ivorybill began to disappear because loggers cut down forests across the Southeast between 1880 and the 1940s. Soon after the ivorybill was rediscovered, the U.S. government announced a $10 million plan to protect the rare bird.

Conservationists are trying to help the woodpecker by killing trees. Sound strange? The woodpecker feeds on beetle larvae found under the bark of dead trees. When the trees are killed, more beetles will likely be attracted to the trees. With more food for the woodpeckers, the species will have a better chance at recovering.

Only about thirty-five to fifty trees will be cut on four 4-acre sections of land. There are 2,000 to 2,800 trees on each section. In about two or three years, scientists hope the trees will have lots of beetles for the woodpeckers. Then the double-rap of the ivorybill will be a common sound.

---

larvae, young insects with soft, tube-shaped bodies, which will eventually become adult insects with wings

BEFORE YOU GO ON

1. What caused bird lovers to be happy?
2. What effect did loggers have on the ivory-billed woodpecker?

On Your Own
How is losing a species different from losing a competition?

READING 4

Review and Practice

COMPREHENSION

Right There

1. Which bird was the first one to be wiped out by people during modern times?
2. Where was the ivory-billed woodpecker rediscovered?

Think and Search

3. What factors contributed to the extinction of the passenger pigeon?
4. What two things helped to convince bird experts that the ivory-billed woodpecker was not extinct?

Author and You

5. Why does the author use a question mark rather than a period in the title "Going, Going, Gone?"
6. What could you have said to farmers to protect the Carolina parakeet from becoming extinct?

▲ The green turtle, giant panda, and Bengal tiger are in danger of becoming extinct.

On Your Own

7. Which animals do you know of that are in danger of becoming extinct? Are changes to the animals' environment part of the cause? Explain.
8. How can people help protect animals and plants from extinction?

IN YOUR OWN WORDS

Imagine that you are telling a classmate about "Going, Going, Gone?" and "Ivory-Billed Woodpeckers Make Noise." For each article, make a three-column chart with these headings in your notebook: *Section, Main Ideas,* and *Important Details.* Use the charts to organize the information in each article. Then share your summaries with a classmate.

Speaking TIP

Use words that help your classmate visualize the main ideas and important details.

DISCUSSION

Discuss in pairs or small groups.

1. How are the four kinds of birds in "Going, Going, Gone?" similar and different?
2. Do you believe that the ivory-billed woodpecker is extinct or not? Why?

Q What do we learn through winning and losing? Imagine that you could bring back the dodo, passenger pigeon, or Carolina parakeet. Which one would you choose? Why? What lessons would people need to learn to make sure the bird didn't die out again?

Listening TIP

When people want to persuade you to do something, they often give only arguments that support their position or point of view. As you listen to your classmates' ideas, think about the opposite point of view. Then draw your own conclusions.

READ FOR FLUENCY

It is often easier to read a text if you understand the difficult words and phrases. Work with a partner. Choose a paragraph from the reading. Identify the words and phrases you do not know or have trouble pronouncing. Look up the difficult words in a dictionary.

Take turns pronouncing the words and phrases with your partner. If necessary, ask your teacher to model the correct pronunciation. Then take turns reading the paragraph aloud. Give each other feedback on your reading.

▲ Huge flocks of passenger pigeons used to fill the sky.

EXTENSION

Endangered species are kinds of animals that are in danger of becoming extinct. Learn more about how people around the world are working to protect endangered species. Use encyclopedias, reference books, and reliable websites. Copy the chart below into your notebook. Use it to organize the information you find. Share your findings with the class.

Ways to Protect Endangered Animals			
Placing Animals in Preserves	Protecting Habitats	Breeding Animals	Passing Protective Laws

Grammar and Writing

GRAMMAR, USAGE, AND MECHANICS

Showing Cause and Effect: *because, because of,* and *so*

Writers use expressions such as *because, because of,* and *so* to signal cause and effect. However, these signal words are each used differently in a sentence. *Because* and *so* are followed by a clause. *Because of* is followed by a noun or noun phrase. Look at the examples from "Going, Going, Gone?" and "Ivory-Billed Woodpeckers Make Noise." Notice the difference in structures and punctuation.

because (subordinating conjunction) + clause	The ivorybill began to disappear **because** loggers cut down forests across the Southeast between 1880 and the 1940s.
because of (preposition) + noun or noun phrase	Today the passenger pigeon is extinct **because of** human activities.
so (coordinating conjunction) + clause	The birds were seen as a threat to crops, **so** people killed the birds.

Practice

Work with a partner. Copy the sentences into your notebook. Then fill in the blanks with *because, because of,* or *so*.

1. Passenger pigeons were killed ______ they were seen as a threat to crops.
2. Loggers cut down trees in the Pearl River forest, ______ ivory-billed woodpeckers lost their homes.
3. Carolina parakeets are beautiful ______ their colorful feathers.
4. A recording of the ivory-billed woodpecker's sound was sent, ______ bird experts were able to listen to the sound.
5. Dodo birds are extinct ______ their food supply was destroyed.
6. The last passenger pigeon died on September 1, 1914, ______ now passenger pigeons are extinct.

▲ Because of its heavy body, the dodo was an easy target.

WRITING AN EXPOSITORY PARAGRAPH

Write a Cause-and-Effect Explanation

Certain texts are structured according to causes and effects. On this page, you'll write a cause-and-effect paragraph that tells why the ivory-billed woodpecker was nearly wiped out. You'll use a graphic organizer like the one at the right to help you organize your paragraph. To organize your writing by cause and effect:

- Think about why something happened. Use *because* to signal a cause.
- Think about what happened. Use *so* to signal an effect.
- List the chain of causes and effects that led to what happened.

Here is a model of a cause-and-effect paragraph about the passenger pigeon. Notice how the writer presents causes and effects and uses signal words.

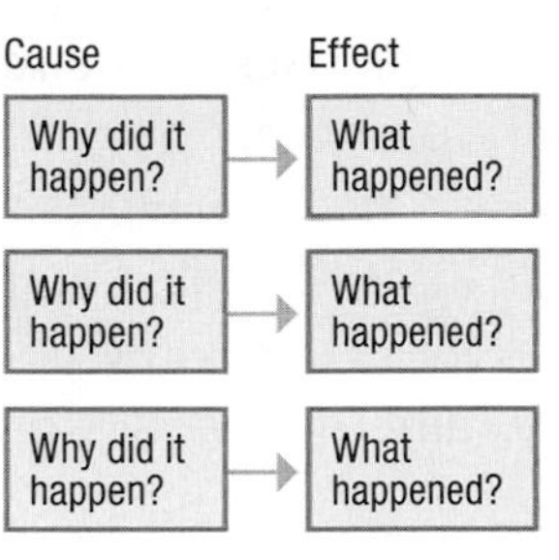

Tamar Honig

What Happened to the Passenger Pigeon?

At one time, passenger pigeons flew in abundance. Now, they can no longer be found because of human actions. These birds, native to the eastern United States, became extinct in the early 1900s. Several factors caused their extinction. The birds lost their habitat because people cleared a great number of oak and eastern chestnut trees to build towns and farms. In doing so, people wiped out the bird's main source of food. The birds were also viewed as a danger to crops, so people killed them. In addition, passenger pigeons were hunted for food. As a result of these causes, their population gradually decreased until fewer and fewer were left. The last passenger pigeon died in the Cincinnati Zoological Garden in 1914.

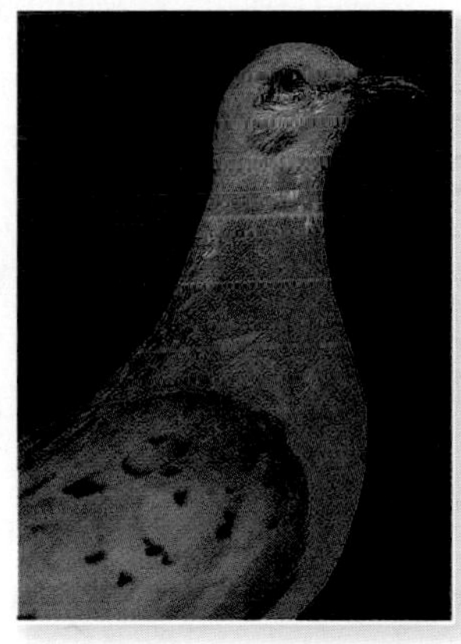

Practice

Write a cause-and-effect paragraph that gives reasons why the ivory-billed woodpecker was nearly wiped out. Show how the causes and effects are related to each other. Use a cause-and-effect chart to list your ideas about what happened and why. Include signal words such as *because, because of, so,* and *as a result,* and be sure to use them correctly.

SENTENCE FLUENCY:

☑ I used signal words to show causes and effects.

ORGANIZATION:

☑ I presented the causes and effects in a logical order.

Link the Readings

Critical Thinking

Look back at the readings in this unit. Think about what they all have in common. They all have something to do with winning or losing. Yet they do not all have the same purpose. The purpose of one reading might be to inform, while the purpose of another might be to entertain or persuade. In addition, the content of each reading relates to winning or losing in different ways. Copy the chart into your notebook and complete it.

Title of Reading	Purpose	Big Question Link
"Soccer: The World Sport"		
"Casey at the Bat," "Swift Things Are Beautiful," "Buffalo Dusk"	*to entertain*	
"The Hare and the Tortoise" "Orpheus and Eurydice"		
"Going, Going, Gone?" "Ivory-Billed Woodpeckers Make Noise"		*explains what happens when a species is lost*

Discussion

Discuss in pairs or small groups.

- How does the author's purpose in "Soccer: the World Sport" differ from the author's purpose in "The Hare and the Tortoise"?

Q What do we learn through winning and losing? Is it always important to win? What sorts of lessons can you learn from losing? Can you learn as much from winning as you can from losing? Explain.

Fluency Check

Work with a partner. Choose a paragraph from one of the readings. Take turns reading it for one minute. Count the total number of words you read. Practice saying the words you had trouble reading. Take turns reading the paragraph three more times. Did you read more words each time? Copy the chart below into your notebook and record your speeds.

	1st Speed	2nd Speed	3rd Speed	4th Speed
Words Per Minute				

Projects

Work in pairs or small groups. Choose one of these projects.

1 Working with some classmates, define what "winning" and "losing" mean to you. Talk about what character traits it takes to be a real winner.

2 You read about soccer and its popularity around the world. Organize a game of soccer. Invite everyone in the class to play. First, explain the rules and practice a little. Then have fun playing a complete game!

3 Perform "The Hare and the Tortoise" as a play. Work with several classmates. First, rewrite the fable as a script. Then create simple costumes and props. Learn the lines and rehearse the play. When everyone is ready, perform the play for the class.

4 Find out more about buffaloes. Why did they almost become extinct? How did they come back? Research this topic, and write a brief report about buffaloes. Use visuals and present your report to the class. Be sure to mention your sources in your report.

Further Reading

To find out more about the theme of this unit, choose from these reading suggestions.

Moby Dick, Herman Melville
In this Penguin Reader® adaptation of the classic novel, Captain Ahab and his men hunt for Moby Dick, the most dangerous whale in the ocean.

Black Star, Bright Dawn, Scott O'Dell
When her father is injured, Bright Dawn takes his place in the Iditarod, a 1,000-mile dogsled race through Alaska's frozen wilderness. She must learn to keep going despite her fears.

Sasha Cohen: Fire on Ice: Autobiography of a Champion Figure Skater, Sasha Cohen
The much admired skater describes the hard work and challenges she faced that made her a National Champion and an Olympic silver medalist.

Put It All Together

LISTENING & SPEAKING WORKSHOP

TV Sports Report

You will explain what happened at a sports event as if you were a TV newscaster on the scene.

1 THINK ABOUT IT Think about the baseball game in "Casey at the Bat" and the footrace in "The Hare and the Tortoise." How would a TV sports reporter at the scene tell what happened?

Work in small groups. Discuss what kinds of sports you like to watch in person or on TV. Work together to develop a list of sports events you would like to tell about on TV. For example:

- A championship soccer match
- A World Series baseball game
- An Olympic skating competition

2 GATHER AND ORGANIZE INFORMATION Choose a sports event from your group's list. Write down what you would like to find out about it. Think about how a TV sports reporter would describe it. Watch a TV news show and get ideas from the sports reporters.

Research Go to the library and read newspaper articles about your sports event, or look for information about it on the Internet. If possible, watch the event on TV or in person. Take notes on the information you find. Include details that show why the event was exciting, surprising, or special.

Order Your Notes Arrange your notes in a logical way. For example, you could use a timeline to arrange them in time order, from the beginning of the event to the end. Put extra information, such as descriptive details and quotes from players, in a separate section.

Use Visuals TV sports reporters often show video clips of the events they describe. Make or find posters or other visuals to show during your report, such as drawings of team logos or photographs of the star players. Be sure your visuals can be seen from the back of the room.

Prepare a Script Use your notes to write a script for a TV sports report. Include enough details to explain what happened and to convey the excitement or other emotions felt by people at the event.

3 PRACTICE AND PRESENT

Read your script aloud, over and over, until you know it well. Practice giving your sports report and showing your visuals to a friend or family member. Keep practicing until you can look at the audience while you talk, glancing at your script only occasionally.

Deliver Your TV Sports Report Speak loudly enough so that everyone in the class can hear you. Say each word carefully so that it is clear. Look at the audience as you speak, and don't hide behind your script! Hold up your visuals so that everyone can see them.

4 EVALUATE THE PRESENTATION

A good way to improve your speaking and listening skills is to evaluate each presentation you give and hear. When you evaluate yourself, you think about what you did well and what you can do better. Use this checklist to help you judge your TV sports report and the sports reports of your classmates.

- ☑ Did the speaker clearly tell the results and other details of the sports event?
- ☑ Did the speaker provide enough description to show why the event was exciting, surprising, or special?
- ☑ Could you hear the speaker easily?
- ☑ Could you understand the speaker's words?
- ☑ What suggestions do you have for improving the presentation?

Speaking TIPS

Always face the audience (or an imaginary TV camera) when you speak. Ask if people can hear you clearly.

Pronounce names and numbers carefully. Write these important details on your visuals so that the audience can both see them and hear them.

Listening TIP

Take notes as you listen. Do you understand who played and what happened in this sports event? Do you know why it was exciting or special? Ask questions after the report if you need more information.

WRITING WORKSHOP

Expository Essay

In this unit, you have been learning the skills of expository writing. Now you will use your skills to write an expository essay. An expository essay is a group of paragraphs that gives information about a specific topic. A good expository essay begins with a paragraph that introduces the writer's topic and focus. Each body paragraph presents a main idea that helps develop the topic. Main ideas are supported by facts and examples. To organize information, the writer uses a method that suits the topic, such as the 5Ws, cause and effect, or comparison and contrast. A conclusion sums up the essay's important ideas in a way that readers will remember.

Your assignment for this workshop is to write a five-paragraph expository essay about a topic that interests you.

1 PREWRITE Brainstorm a list of topics in your notebook. You might focus on some aspect of winning and losing. Winning and losing is relevant to many topics in human life and in the natural world. After selecting a topic, think about your readers. What might they already know about your topic? What would you like them to learn from your essay?

List and Organize Ideas and Details Use a graphic organizer such as a Venn diagram, a 5Ws chart, or a cause-and-effect chart to organize your information. A student named Tamar decided to write about extinct and endangered bird species. Here is her cause-and-effect chart:

Cause	*Effect*
Passenger Pigeon *1. Food supply destroyed by people* *2. Killed for food and to protect crops*	*Extinct*
Great Auk *1. Climate change* *2. Hunted for its valuable feathers*	*Extinct*
Whooping Crane *1. Wetlands habitat destroyed* *2. Hunted for food and sport*	*Endangered*

2 DRAFT Use the model on page 259 and your graphic organizer to help you write a first draft. Remember to include an introductory paragraph, three body paragraphs, and a concluding paragraph.

3 REVISE Read over your draft. As you do so, ask yourself the questions in the writing checklist. Use the questions to help you revise your essay.

SIX TRAITS OF WRITING CHECKLIST

- ☑ **IDEAS:** Do I present a main idea in each body paragraph?
- ☑ **ORGANIZATION:** Do I include an introduction and a conclusion?
- ☑ **VOICE:** Does my writing show my knowledge of the topic?
- ☑ **WORD CHOICE:** Do I use words accurately?
- ☑ **SENTENCE FLUENCY:** Do my sentences begin in different ways?
- ☑ **CONVENTIONS:** Does my writing follow the rules of grammar, usage, and mechanics?

Here are the changes Tamar plans to make when she revises her first draft:

Extinct and Endangered Birds

It may seem that there are plenty of birds in the world, [but] Several bird species are endangered, and others already [have] becomed extinct. It is important to realize that when a bird species dies out, it's gone forever In addition, we're always in danger of losing more birds.

When european explorers first ~~comed~~ [came] to this continent, passenger pigeons were abundant. Today, this species no longer exists. [One reason is that] People chopped down forests to build houses, towns, and farms. In doing so, they wiped out the passenger pigeon's food supply. Also, passenger pigeons were shot, [because] They were viewed as a threat to crops. Huge numbers were hunted for food as well. As a result, their population decreased. Eventually, none remained.

Another extinct bird is the great auk, a flightless bird that lived in the North Atlantic. Climate change may have helped cause the great auk's extinction. During a period known as "the little ice age, the climate turned colder. ^so Many birds died. However, one of the most important causes of the bird's disappearance is that people hunted the great auk for its valuable feathers ^and rare eggs. They killed as many birds ^and took as many eggs as they could. Mainly because of these human activities^, the species did not survive.

The whooping crane, the largest bird in North America, is endangered. It has been hunted for food and also shot for sport. Wetlands, which are its habitat, often have been turned into farmlands and towns. Some of the reasons it is endangered are familiar. Collisions with power lines have killed many birds. Fortunately, the whooping crane, although endangered, still exists.

These three bird species are just a few among the many that are extinct or in danger of becoming so. If people work hard, we may be able to help prevent more birds from becoming extinct. Once a bird species becomes extinct, it ^sadly has been ~~losed~~ ^lost forever.

4 EDIT AND PROOFREAD

Copy your revised draft onto a clean sheet of paper. Read it again. Correct any errors in grammar, word usage, mechanics, and spelling. Here are the additional changes Tamar plans to make when she prepares her final draft.

Tamar Honig

Extinct and Endangered Birds

It may seem that there are plenty of birds in the world, but several bird species are endangered, and others already have become extinct. It is important to realize that when a bird species dies out, it's gone forever. In addition, we're always in danger of losing more birds.

When european explorers first came to this continent, passenger pigeons were abundant. Today, this species no longer exists. One reason is that people chopped down forests to build houses, towns, and farms. In doing so, they wiped out the passenger pigeon's food supply. Also, passenger pigeons were shot because they were viewed as a threat to crops. Huge numbers were hunted for food, as well. As a result, their population decreased. Eventually, none remained.

Another extinct bird is the great auk, a flightless bird that lived in the North Atlantic. Climate change may have helped cause the great auk's extinction. During a period known as "the little ice age," the climate turned colder, so many birds died. However, one of the most important causes of the bird's disappearance is that people hunted the great auk for its valuable feathers and rare eggs. They killed as many birds and took as many eggs as they could. Mainly because of these human activities, the species did not survive.

The whooping crane, the largest bird in North America, is endangered. Some of the reasons it is endangered are familiar. It has been hunted for food and also shot for sport. Wetlands, which are its habitat, often have been turned into farmlands and towns. Collisions with power lines have killed many birds. Fortunately, the whooping crane, although endangered, still exists.

These three bird species are just a few among the many that are extinct or in danger of becoming so. If people work hard, we may be able to help prevent more birds from becoming extinct. Once a bird species becomes extinct, it sadly has been lost forever.

5 PUBLISH Prepare your final draft. Share your essay with your teacher and classmates.

Learn about Art with the Smithsonian American Art Museum

BASEBALL IN AMERICA

Americans love to watch and play many different sports. Baseball, basketball, hockey, and football are all very popular. In these games, one team will win and another will lose. Everyone loves a winning team, but we don't always cheer for the winner. Sometimes the losing team has played a great game. Then we might cheer for the loser, too.

Mark Sfirri, *Rejects from the Bat Factory* (1996)

Artist Mark Sfirri's ten-year-old son wanted a new baseball bat. Sfirri agreed to make him one. As he worked, Sfirri realized that he could do a lot with the wood and shape of the bat as an artist. So he made his son a regular bat first. Then he made the five bats hanging in *Rejects from the Bat Factory.*

Sfirri made his bats out of different kinds of unusual wood. A wood called curly maple has a wavy pattern of red and yellow colors in it. Zebrawood has stripes. Sfirri used a method called turning to create the bats. Turning allows a woodworker to give pieces of wood a rounded shape by rotating them against a cutting tool. The bat on the far left still has a ball "stuck" in it. The bat fourth from the left has a dent!

Sfirri wanted to create a fun set of bats, but he also wanted to show how we often value things that aren't perfect. Sometimes a "loser" can be a real "winner."

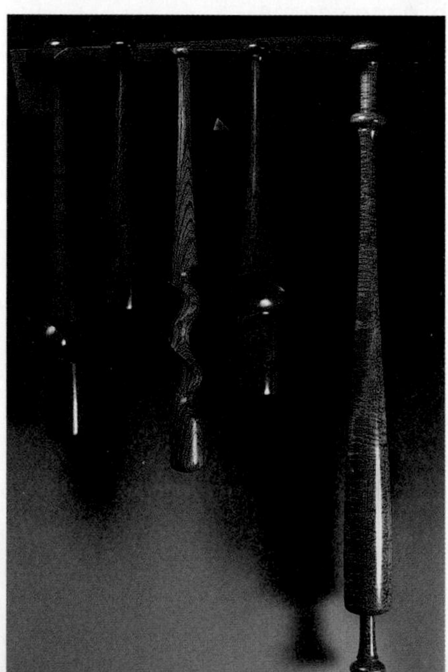

◀ **Mark Sfirri, *Rejects from the Bat Factory*, 1996, wood, 15⅜ x 36½ in., Smithsonian American Art Museum**

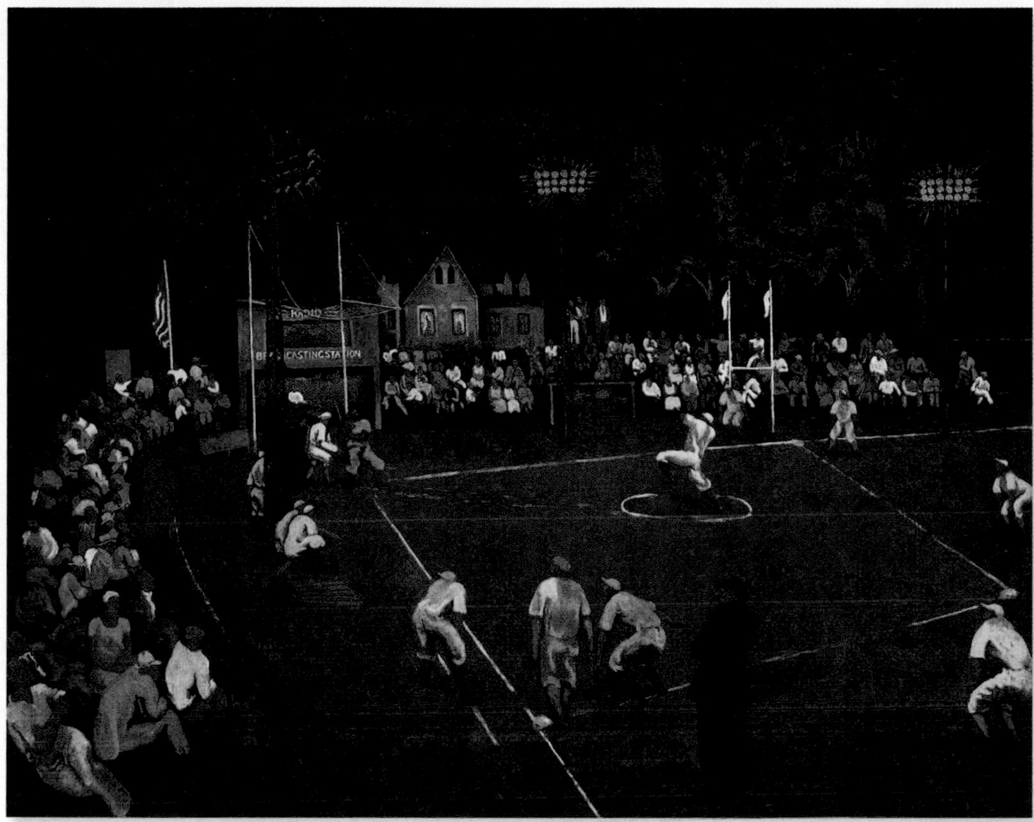

▲ **Morris Kantor, *Baseball at Night*, 1934, oil, 37 x 47¼ in., Smithsonian American Art Museum**

Morris Kantor, *Baseball at Night* (1934)

Morris Kantor captures the charm of a small-town baseball game in *Baseball at Night*. The crowd fills the stands. The players in the field are ready for the next play. The pitcher steps toward the batter, and . . . .

The painting doesn't show what happens next, but you can use your imagination. Kantor puts all of the important elements in his painting: the players, the tall umpire dressed in black, the crowd, the lights that light up the field, and the warm lights from the house behind the stands. Night lights had just begun to be added to fields at this time. Now everyone is out to enjoy the game!

Both of these artists focus on the fun of team sports, where winning is just one part of a much larger story.

Apply What You Learned

1. How do both of these artworks show the fun side of a sport like baseball?
2. What kind of artwork would you make to capture the feeling of another sport, such as basketball or soccer?

Big Question
What would you show in a painting to illustrate the ideas of winning and losing?

Workbook
Pages 127–128

UNIT 5

How are courage and imagination linked?

This unit is about courage and imagination. You'll read about an orphan who helps a grieving family and about kids who create art in order to promote peace. You'll read about an effort to save burrowing owls from destruction and about a Kenyan woman who created a simple method of improving living conditions in her native country. As you read, you'll practice the literary and academic language you need to use in school.

Listening and Speaking

At the end of this unit, you'll give a **how-to demonstration** that explains the steps involved in doing something.

Writing

In this unit you'll practice **expository writing,** or writing that explains a topic. You'll write four expository paragraphs and an expository essay.

QuickWrite

Write several sentences about a time when you used courage and imagination to solve a problem.

READING 1

Prepare to Read

What You Will Learn

Reading

- Vocabulary building: *Literary terms, dictionary skills, word study*
- Reading strategy: *Analyze text structure 1*
- Text type: *Literature (play)*

Grammar, Usage, and Mechanics

More adverbs with *-ly*

Writing

Write a formal e-mail

THE BIG QUESTION

How are courage and imagination linked? Why does it take imagination to create a garden? You have to choose which plants to grow and where to plant them. You have to be able to imagine what the garden will look like after it grows and flowers.

Think about what you know about gardens. Maybe you have seen photographs and drawings of gardens in books and magazines, or perhaps you have seen gardens in your own neighborhood. You might even have grown flowers, herbs, or vegetables in your own garden or apartment.

Work with a partner. Talk about what you know about gardens. Use this chart to get you started. Add more columns and rows if you need them. Then share what you know with the class.

Why People Plant Gardens	What Plants I Like

▲ A wild English garden

BUILD BACKGROUND

You will read an adapted version of the play ***The Secret Garden***. The play is based on the novel *The Secret Garden*, written by Frances Hodgson Burnett. The book has been popular since it was first published in 1911. The story takes place in the early 1900s in the English countryside.

In the play, the actors tell the story through their dialogue and actions. We get to know the characters by what they say and do. When the play opens, the orphaned girl Mary Lennox has just arrived in England to live with Mr. Craven. Mary had been living in India with her parents. This is a difficult time for Mary because her parents died within days of each other. Mr. Craven was her father's best friend, so he agreed to take care of Mary. Mr. Craven has a very large house with many gardens. Mary is curious about the gardens.

VOCABULARY

Learn Literary Words

Playwrights, or people who write plays, usually begin by **setting the scene**. They give important details about the time and place of each section of the play. This helps readers and actors to visualize each scene. Study this example from *The Secret Garden*. How has the writer helped you visualize the opening scene?

Literary Words
- setting the scene
- list of characters
- stage directions

> Early 1900s. Bedroom in Misselthwaite Manor, England.
> Bed center; table next to it holds tray of food.

At the beginning of a play, you will also find a **list of characters**. Below is a list of characters from the *The Secret Garden*.

Characters		
Mary Lennox	Ben Weatherstaff	Mr. Archibald Craven
Martha Sowerby	Dickon Sowerby	Colin Craven

Stage directions are notes included in a play that tell how the play should be performed. These directions are in brackets and set in italics near the character's name. Stage directions tell actors what they should do and how they should look and act. They may also tell about the scenery and costumes. Study the stage directions below. How do they help you understand the characters and what is happening? How do they help you act out the dialogue?

> **Mary:** [*Puzzled*] How can a garden be locked?
> **Martha:** It can be if there's a high wall around it. [*She exits.*]
> **Mary:** [*Sighing*] How I wish I were back in India! [*Curtain*]

Practice

Take turns reading the lines above with a partner. Pay close attention to the stage directions. Act out each line, using the stage directions as your guide. Use a dictionary to look up any words that you don't know.

Learn Academic Words

Study the **red** words and their meanings. You will find these words useful when talking and writing about literature. Write each word and its meaning in your notebook. After you read *The Secret Garden*, try to use these words to respond to the text.

Academic Words

approach
convey
cooperate
drama

approach = move closer to someone or something	➡	The girl wanted to **approach** the lamb, but she was afraid of coming too close to the animal.
convey = communicate a message or information, with or without using words	➡	Birds **convey** their fear by flying away. Everyone understands their message.
cooperate = work with someone else to achieve something that you both want	➡	When people **cooperate**, they get the job done faster.
drama = a play for the theater, television, radio, and so forth	➡	The class **drama** was a big success. Everyone enjoyed watching the play.

Practice

Work with a partner to answer the questions. Try to include the **red** word in your answer. Write the sentences in your notebook.

1. How would you **approach** a bird in a garden?
2. How do dogs and cats **convey** their feelings?
3. What happens when someone won't **cooperate** with you? What do you do?
4. What do you like about watching or acting in a **drama**?

Some students love to study drama and perform. ▶

Word Study: Spelling Words with *oo*

In English, the letters *oo* can stand for either a short sound /o͝o/ or a long sound /o͞o/. For example, *The Secret Garden* has many words with the short sound of *oo*, such as *book*. It also contains words with the long sound of *oo*, such as *room*. Notice the /o͝o/ and /o͞o/ sounds and their spellings in the chart below.

oo* as in *book	***oo* as in *moon***
g**oo**d-bye	l**oo**se
t**oo**k	n**oo**n
underst**oo**d	ch**oo**se

Practice

Work with a partner. Copy the chart above into your notebook. Say a word from the chart, and ask your partner to spell it aloud. Then have your partner say the next word. Continue until you can spell all of the words correctly. Then work with your partner to spell the following words: *blooming, cook, afternoon, goodness, gloomy, wood, shook,* and *tools*. Add them to the chart under the correct heading.

READING STRATEGY ANALYZE TEXT STRUCTURE 1

Analyzing text structure can help you understand what kind of text you're reading. It can also help you set a purpose for reading. Different kinds of writing, or genres, have different kinds of text structures. Read these descriptions to help you understand the various types of text structures:

- Stories and novels are written in sentences and paragraphs. Dialogue is enclosed within quotation marks.
- Poems are usually written in lines and groups of lines, called stanzas. The punctuation in poems may not follow the same rules as it does in other kinds of writing.
- Plays are mainly written in dialogue. The characters' names are given, followed by colons (:) and the words the speakers say. Stage directions are usually in brackets ([ ]) and set in italics. Many plays are divided into numbered scenes.

Preview the text structure of *The Secret Garden*. Describe it to a partner.

READING 1

LITERATURE

PLAY

Set a purpose for reading How will certain characters' courage and imagination change life at Misselthwaite Manor? Read the play to find out.

The Secret Garden

Frances Hodgson Burnett,
adapted by David C. Jones

In this classic play, the orphaned girl Mary Lennox comes from India to live at Misselthwaite Manor, England. She finds the place gloomy until she hears about a long-lost garden. Then she has a wonderful idea.

CHARACTERS
MARY LENNOX
MARTHA SOWERBY
BEN WEATHERSTAFF
DICKON SOWERBY
MR. ARCHIBALD CRAVEN
COLIN CRAVEN

Scene 1

Time: *Early 1900s.*

Setting: *Bedroom in Misselthwaite Manor, England. Bed center; table next to it holds tray of food.*

At rise: *Mary is alone, looking around.*

MARY: What a dreary place. I know I'm not going to like it here. [*Martha enters.*]

MARTHA: Good afternoon, miss.

MARY: [*Imperiously*] Good afternoon. Are you going to be my servant?

MARTHA: I'm to do a bit of cleaning up and bring you your food.

MARY: I don't like English food.

MARTHA: [*Sharply*] I've nine little brothers and sisters who would be glad to eat this food in a minute.

MARY: [*Surprised*] My goodness! You have nine brothers and sisters?

---

dreary, very dull and causing sadness
servant, someone paid to clean and cook for someone else

Martha: Yes. We have to take care of each other since Father died. Thank goodness for Dickon. He's a big help.

Mary: Who's Dickon?

Martha: My oldest brother. He's a rare boy. He talks to the animals, and when he plays his pipes, they all stop to listen. Everyone loves him. Well, I must be off now. I have a lot of work to do.

Mary: But what will I do?

Martha: You could go play in one of the gardens—except for the one that's locked.

Mary: [*Puzzled*] How can a garden be locked?

Martha: It can be if there's a high wall around it. [*She exits.*]

Mary: [*Sighing*] How I wish I were back in India! [*Curtain*]

Scene 2

Setting: *The mansion gardens. There are flowerbeds, bushes, etc., around the stage. Fence covered with ivy, brambles, etc., is upright.*

At rise: *Ben Weatherstaff is working with a hoe. Mary enters.*

Ben: [*Looking up*] Well, well. You must be Mistress Mary, quite contrary.

Mary: I am not contrary—and who are you?

Ben: I'm Ben Weatherstaff, the gardener. I've worked for Mr. Craven for many, many years.

Mary: And where's this locked garden I've heard about?

Ben: Why, you're standing next to it.

Mary: But where is the entrance?

Ben: Well, the gate is somewhere under all those brambles and ivy that have grown and covered it. It's been locked up so long.

Mary: But why was it ever locked? I never heard of such a thing.

Ben: Well, it was Mr. and Mrs. Craven's favorite spot, and they spent many a happy hour in it, reading and laughing together like two lovebirds. Mrs. Craven used to sit reading on a high branch of one of the big trees, but one day the branch broke and she fell to her death. After that, Mr. Craven had the gate locked, and he hasn't entered the garden since.

---

pipes, tube-shaped musical instruments, such as flutes
mansion, very large house
brambles, wild plants with thorns and berries
upright, straight up
contrary, deliberately doing or saying the opposite of what others want
lovebirds, people who show by their behavior that they love each other very much

Literary Check

Which two people on the ***list of characters*** *are mentioned in the dialogue but have not yet appeared at the end of page 269?*

BEFORE YOU GO ON

1. What is Mary's first reaction to Misselthwaite Manor?
2. Who is Dickon?

On Your Own
How do most people feel when they are in an unfamiliar place far from home?

MARY: [*Resolutely*] Well, I shall find the entrance and go in there to play.

BEN: You won't be able to go in without the key.

MARY: [*Surprised*] There's a key? Where is it?

BEN: No one knows. Mr. Craven was so heartbroken he took the key one day and threw it as far as he could. No one has ever found it.

MARY: I'll find it. You'll see.

BEN: [*Wryly*] Well, good luck, Mistress Mary. You'll need it. [*Laughs and exits. After a moment, Dickon enters, carrying animals.*]

DICKON: Hello. You must be Miss Mary.

MARY: How did you know my name? And who are you?

DICKON: They call me Dickon. And I know about you because my sister, Martha, told me all about you.

MARY: Is it true you speak to animals?

DICKON: Aye. Say hello to my friends. This is Cert, the crow. [*Cawing sound is heard.*] The fox is Captain, and the lamb, Lady. [*Bleating is heard.*]

MARY: Those are strange names for animals.

DICKON: It's what they asked to be called.

MARY: [*Scoffing*] Animals and birds can't talk.

DICKON: Sure they can. You just have to know how to listen. [*Looks offstage*] Look! Here comes my friend, Robin. [*Robin enters.*]

ROBIN: Hello Dickon, Who is your friend?

MARY: [*Astonished*] Why, he does talk!

DICKON: See? You just have to want to listen to them. [*Curtain*]

Scene 3

Setting: *Colin's bedroom. There is a bed center, a large portrait covered with sheet, and a window.*

At rise: *Colin is in bed, covered completely with blankets. Mary wanders on stage, doesn't notice Colin.*

MARY: [*To herself*] I thought that the library was here somewhere. [*Notices bed*] Oh! [*Colin sits up.*]

COLIN: [*Frightened*] Are you a ghost?

MARY: Of course not. Do I look like a ghost? Who are you, and why are you in bed? It's two in the afternoon!

LITERARY CHECK

*Why is **setting the scene** important at the beginning of Scene 3? What information does the playwright provide about the place? How does this help you visualize where Mary is now?*

---

resolutely, in a very determined way
bleating, the sound that a sheep or goat makes: "baa"
scoffing, laughing at or talking to in a scornful way
astonished, very surprised

COLIN: I'm Colin Craven. My father is the master of this manor.

MARY: Why didn't anyone tell me he had a son?

COLIN: Because no one is allowed to talk about me.

MARY: Why not?

COLIN: Because I'm going to have a hump on my back, just like my father.

MARY: Don't you ever leave this room?

COLIN: No. If people look at me, I get sick.

MARY: That's ridiculous! I'm looking at you and you're not getting sick.

COLIN: Well, I might.

MARY: Save yourself the trouble. I'm leaving.

COLIN: [*Pleading*] No, don't go! Tell me about India. I hear that's where you're from.

MARY: You can read about India in books.

COLIN: Reading gives me a headache.

MARY: Well, if I were your father I'd make you read so you can learn about things.

COLIN: [*Stubbornly*] No one can make me do anything I don't want to do.

MARY: Well, why not?

COLIN: Because I'm sick and I'm dying!

MARY: Well, do you want to live?

COLIN: Not if I have a hump on my back like my father. [*Cries*]

MARY: [*Disgusted*] I'm leaving. You cry too much! [*Mary exits. Quick curtain*]

---

pleading, begging

BEFORE YOU GO ON

1. Who are Dickon's friends?
2. What does Colin beg Mary to do?

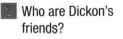

On Your Own
Do you think that animals can communicate with people? Explain.

Scene 4

Setting: *Mr. Craven's library, with desk center, and bookshelves on walls.*

At rise: *Mary enters library where Mr. Craven is sitting.*

MARY: [*Timidly*] You sent for me, sir?

MR. CRAVEN: Yes. Come closer, my dear. Don't be afraid. I'm quite harmless.

MARY: [*Boldly*] You don't frighten me.

MR. CRAVEN: [*Kindly*] You look just like your father. He was my best friend, you know, and when he died, and I learned you had no living relatives, I felt it my duty to care for you.

MARY: Yes. And I'm truly thankful, sir.

MR. CRAVEN: I wish I could do more for you, but I have been ill, you know.

MARY: I'm sorry.

MR. CRAVEN: Are you being taken good care of?

MARY: Martha has been very kind to me.

MR. CRAVEN: But are you happy here? Is there anything you need or want?

MARY: I wonder if I could have a place to make a garden? I love gardens so.

MR. CRAVEN: [*Pleased*] You do? [*Distantly*] There was once someone very dear to me who loved gardens, too. Yes, of course. Choose any part of the garden you wish, and I will see that you get all the tools you need. Now, child, leave me—I wish to be alone.

MARY: Thank you, Mr. Craven. [*Nervously*] And . . . and try not to be so sad. [*Runs out. Curtain*]

LITERARY CHECK

Reread Scene 4, paying special attention to the ***stage directions****. How does Mary behave at first with Mr. Craven? How does her attitude change?*

Scene 5

Setting: *Same as Scene 2.*

At rise: *Mary and Dickon, holding Robin, are looking at fence covered with brambles.*

MARY: Oh, Dickon, if only we could find the entrance to this locked garden. Mr. Craven said I could have any garden I wish—and I want this one.

DICKON: But even if we found the door, we'd still need the key.

ROBIN: Key . . . Now, where did I see a key?

DICKON: You saw a key, Robin?

ROBIN: Yes. I was flying around the other day, and I spotted a rusty old key.

---

relatives, members of your family
dear to, much loved by

Mary: [*Excitedly*] Oh, Robin, think—please! Where was it?

Robin: [*Thinking*] Over there. Near that bush, I think. [*Mary and Dickon search.*]

Dickon: Look! Here it is! [*Holds up key*] Now if we only knew where the gate was.

Robin: Oh, I know that, too.

Mary: Well, why didn't you tell us?

Robin: You never asked me.

Dickon: Show us where it is, Robin.

Robin: It's over here, behind this ivy. [*They rush over to fence.*]

Mary: [*Finding door*] Yes, yes! Here it is. Quick, Dickon. Try the key!

Dickon: Very well. [*He tries the key.*] It's turning . . . but very slowly. It's very rusty. There! I think I've got it. Now, we'll just give a little push, and—[*Curtain goes up, revealing a dead garden.*]

Mary: [*Excited*] This is it! The locked garden! [*Disappointed*] Oh, but look! Nothing is growing. Everything is dead.

Dickon: It just needs some care, and lots of water. [*Gestures*] See, these rose bushes are alive. Soon they'll be blooming. [*Curtain*]

Scene 6

Setting: *Same as Scene 3.*

At rise: *Colin is in bed. Mary and Dickon enter, holding animals.*

Mary: Hello, Colin. This is my friend, Dickon. He brought his animals to show you.

Colin: Where were you, Mary? I've missed you. Hello, Dickon. I've heard all about you.

Dickon: Hello! Want to hold Lady? She's a nice and gentle lamb. [*Baaing is heard.*]

Colin: Oh, yes, thank you. [*Holds lamb*] I'm glad you came. I have so few visitors—only Mary and Martha. Not even Father comes to see me.

Dickon: Why not?

Colin: Because he doesn't want to see the hump on my back.

Mary: Let me see. [*Looks at Colin's back*] Why, there's no hump there, Colin. Only a knobby spine like mine.

---

knobby spine, backbone with hard parts that stick out from under the surface

BEFORE YOU GO ON

1. Why does Mr. Craven decide to take care of Mary?
2. Who helps Mary and Dickon find the key to the garden?

On Your Own
What do you think Mary and Dickon will do next?

Colin: [*Amazed*] You mean I don't have a hump, and I'm not dying?

Mary: Of course not! It's all in your mind.

Dickon: Roses won't grow where there are only **thistles**.

Colin: What does that mean?

Mary: It means that you can't have happy thoughts if you always have **gloomy** ones.

Colin: You're right. I must find something to do to keep me happy.

Mary: Dickon and I have a secret. I'll tell you if you promise not to tell anyone else!

Colin: I promise.

Mary: We have found the garden that your mother and father used to love so much, and we're going to make it beautiful again—just the way it used to be.

Colin: [*Excited*] Really? Oh, I wish I could help, but I can't walk.

Dickon: I could take you out into the garden in your wheelchair. You could sit on the ground and plant seeds and pull weeds.

Colin: Do you really think I could?

Mary: Of course you could! In fact, you shall! We'll start tomorrow.

Colin: [*Delighted*] That's wonderful!

Mary: We have to go now. We'll see you tomorrow. [*Dickon and Mary exit.*]

Colin: [*Calling off*] Good-bye! Thanks for coming. [*He looks at the picture.*] Oh, Mother. Forgive me for covering you up. [*He gets out of bed and tries to walk toward the picture, but falls.*] If only I could walk . . . I will walk. I'll practice a little bit each day, and when Father comes home I'll show him I'm not an invalid anymore! [*Curtain*]

Scene 7

Time: *Two months later.*

Setting: *The mansion gardens. There are flowerbeds, bushes, etc., around the stage. Fence covered with ivy, brambles, etc., is upright.*

At rise: *Mr. Craven is on stage alone.*

Ben: [*Entering*] Mr. Craven! Welcome home. Mary wants to see you right away. She's in the locked garden, sir.

Mr. Craven: [*Amazed*] The garden? How is that? I thought the key was lost forever.

---

thistles, wild plants with purple flowers and leaves that have sharp points
gloomy, sad and hopeless

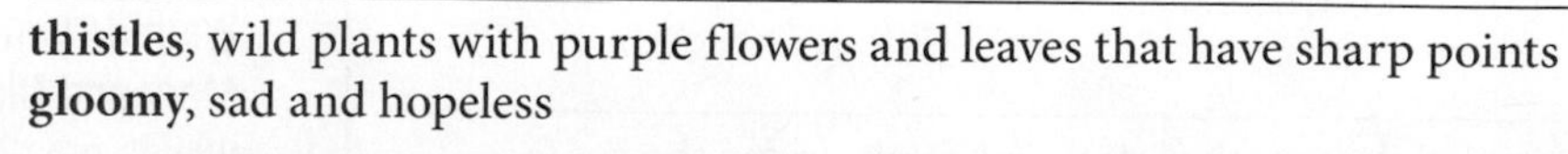

Ben: Come, I'll show you. The entrance is this way. [*Curtain goes up, reveals a beautiful garden. Mary, pushing Colin in a wheelchair, enters, followed by Dickon.*]

Mary and Colin: Surprise!

Mr. Craven: Why, it's beautiful! You've planted my favorite flowers!

Ben: Just the way it was when your wife was alive, sir. The children worked very hard.

Mary: Ben helped, too. He told us how it used to look and pruned all the dead wood.

Mr. Craven: And Colin! You have color in your cheeks, and you've gained weight.

Colin: And that's not all, Father. [*He gets out of the wheelchair.*] I . . . can walk. [*He walks with difficulty to Mr. Craven, and they embrace. Ben and Dickon watch happily.*]

Mr. Craven: My son! [*Mary embraces them, too.*] My children. You have made me very happy! And you have brought love back into our garden.

Colin: Our secret garden!

Mary: Yes, but now it needn't be a secret any longer. [*Curtain*]

---

pruned, cut back some of the branches of a tree or bush to make it grow better
embrace, hug; put their arms around each other in a caring way

ABOUT THE AUTHOR AND PLAYWRIGHT

Frances Hodgson Burnett was born in England in 1849. Her family moved to Knoxville, Tennessee, after her father's death. To help support her siblings, she began to write short stories for magazines. Later, she wrote many novels and children's books, including *Little Lord Fauntleroy* and *A Little Princess*.

David C. Jones has written more than a dozen plays for *PLAYS Magazine* with fellow-writer Lewis Mahlmann. He and Mahlmann also published several books through *PLAYS Magazine*, including *Puppet Plays from Favorite Stories* and *Folk Tales for Puppets*.

BEFORE YOU GO ON

1. What does Mary help Colin understand about his back?
2. What makes Mr. Craven happy at the end of the play?

On Your Own
Do you agree with Dickon that "roses won't grow where there are only thistles"? Why or why not?

READING 1

Review and Practice

READER'S THEATER

Speaking TIP

Vary the volume of your voice to keep your audience interested.

Act out the following scene between Colin, Mary, and Mr. Craven.

Mary: Mr. Craven, Colin has a big surprise for you. [*Colin stands.*]

Mr. Craven: Colin, my boy! You are standing on your own!

Colin: Yes, I am, Father. It feels great to finally get out of my room and into the fresh air of this garden.

Mr. Craven: But how did you build your strength?

Colin: Mary and Dickon took me out to the garden. I practiced walking a little bit each day. I couldn't have done it without their help.

Mr. Craven: I'm so proud of you, son. [*Colin and Mr. Craven hug each other.*]

Mary: Congratulations, Colin. You worked very hard. I always knew you could do it.

COMPREHENSION

Right There

1. Which garden is the only one Mary is told that she can't play in?
2. Why does Dickon name the animals?

Think and Search

3. What causes Mr. Craven to toss away the key to the garden?
4. What do the children do to fix the garden?

Author and You

5. Why is the garden called "a secret garden"?
6. What are Colin's feelings about life in the beginning of the play? How do they change by the end?

On Your Own

7. Other authors write stories about characters who talk to animals. If you could talk to animals, which ones would you choose? Why?
8. Do you think that planting a beautiful garden can improve life in a city or town? Explain.

DISCUSSION

Listening TIP

Look at each speaker as he or she speaks to show that you are interested.

Discuss in pairs or small groups.

1. What part of *The Secret Garden* did you like best? Why?
2. Do you think the children should have restored the garden or left it as it was in memory of Mrs. Craven? Why?
3. This play is called *The Secret Garden.* What would be another good title for this drama? Why?

Q How are courage and imagination linked? Which character in *The Secret Garden* has the most imagination? Which character has the most courage? How does each character affect the other people in the play? How do the characters work together?

RESPONSE TO LITERATURE

Imagine that you are Mary Lennox. What was your life like in India? How do you feel about moving to England? Write a diary entry in which you describe your feelings about the changes in your life. You may want to use a graphic organizer like this one:

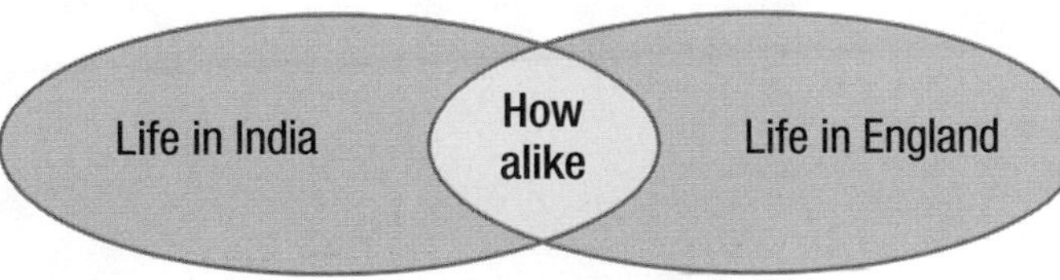

When you are done writing, share your diary entry with a classmate. Talk about the details in the play that helped you understand Mary's feelings.

Grammar and Writing

GRAMMAR, USAGE, AND MECHANICS

More Adverbs with *-ly*

An adverb usually describes the action of a verb. Many adverbs end with *-ly*. An adverb often answers the question *How?*

Question	Answer
How did Mary speak?	Mary spoke **imperiously**.
How did Martha answer?	Martha answered **sharply**.
How did Colin walk?	Colin walked **carefully**.

Stage directions may include adverbs with *-ly* to help an actor read his or her lines correctly.

Mary: [*Excitedly*] Oh, Robin, think—please! Where was it?
Mary: [*Timidly*] You sent for me, sir?
Mr. Craven: [*Kindly*] You look just like your father.

Practice

Work with a partner. Use your imagination to write a sentence for each of the adverbs in the box below. Look up any words you don't know in a dictionary. Write the sentences in your notebook. Then take turns reading your sentences to your partner. Compare your sentences.

happily	sadly	thoughtfully
nervously	stubbornly	wryly

WRITING AN EXPOSITORY PARAGRAPH

Write a Formal E-mail

On this page, you'll write an expository paragraph that states a problem and presents a solution. The paragraph will be part of a formal e-mail. You'll use a graphic organizer like the one at the right to list the problem and solution.

Problem	Solution

To develop and structure a problem-and-solution paragraph, first, clearly state what is happening and why it is a problem. Then give one or more suggestions about how to solve the problem. Also, explain why your solution will work.

Here is a model of an e-mail about a problem. Notice how the writer first states the problem and then presents a solution.

From: Angelina Xing <axing@coldmail.com>
Date: Tue, 6 Oct 2009 10:29:31
To: Mayor's Office <mayor@briarcliff.gov>
Subject: Law Park in Briarcliff Manor

Dear Mayor:

I am writing to you to address a problem I see with Law Park in Briarcliff Manor. The park's main feature is a monument dedicated to the memory of soldiers who served our country in World War II. However, the bare surroundings don't express the importance of the monument. My suggestion is to start a community garden in Law Park to make a beautiful setting for the monument. The community could work independently on creating the garden. If only one percent of the population actively works on this project, there will be more than enough people to keep the garden alive all year long. The whole town could benefit from improving this special place. Thank you very much for taking the time to consider my idea.

Sincerely,
Angelina Xing

Practice

Workbook Page 135

Write a formal e-mail to your community's mayor about a problem you want to solve in your neighborhood. Use a problem-solution chart to list your ideas. Be sure to use adverbs correctly.

IDEAS:

☑ I clearly stated the problem and solution.

VOICE:

☑ I used the correct type of language and format for a formal e-mail.

READING 2

Prepare to Read

What You Will Learn

Reading

- Vocabulary building: *Context, dictionary skills, word study*
- Reading strategy: *Classify*
- Text type: *Informational text (social studies/art)*

Grammar, Usage, and Mechanics

More uses of the present perfect

Writing

Write a paragraph that classifies something

THE BIG QUESTION

How are courage and imagination linked? Think of some situations in which a person needs to have imagination to do something. These can be situations at school or at home, with your family or friends, or when you are by yourself. Do you think it sometimes takes courage to have imagination? If so, why? Discuss with a partner.

BUILD BACKGROUND

"**Kids' Guernica**" is a photo-essay about a mural project that began in 1995. It explains how one person's imagination and courage led him to organize an international art project for peace. The title of the project and the ideas for it were based on Picasso's painting *Guernica*. Picasso painted *Guernica* in 1937 during the Spanish Civil War (1936–1939).

In 1936, General Francisco Franco led a revolt against the Spanish Republic. Franco's side received help from the Nazi dictator Adolf Hitler, the leader of Germany. After much chaos and violence, Franco's side won, and he became the dictator of Spain until 1975. As you will read, one of Franco's violent actions during the Spanish Civil War inspired Picasso to create *Guernica*.

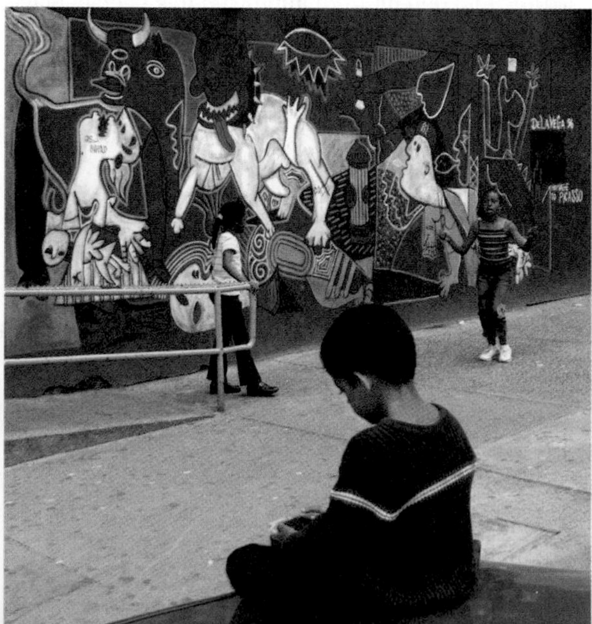

The figures on this wall in New York City imitate those in Picasso's *Guernica*. ▶

VOCABULARY

Learn Key Words

Read the sentences. Use the context to figure out the meaning of the **red** words. Use a dictionary to check your answers. Then write each word and its meaning in your notebook.

1. People honor the **anniversary** of World War II. Every year they hold a ceremony on the date the war ended.
2. The **atomic bomb** is very destructive. It releases energy in a powerful explosion.
3. Many artists paint on **canvases**. These strong, heavy pieces of cloth are stretched on wooden frames.
4. War causes great **chaos**. In the confusion, it is difficult for people to live normal lives.
5. Reading about great acts can be an **inspiration** to do great things yourself.
6. The artist made a **mural**. The huge painting covered a whole wall.

Key Words

- anniversary
- atomic bomb
- canvases
- chaos
- inspiration
- mural

Practice

Write the sentences in your notebook. Choose a **red** word from the box above to complete each sentence. Then take turns reading the sentences aloud with a partner.

1. The children painted a ______ on the wall of the playground.
   a. chaos b. mural c. anniversary
2. The soldiers celebrated the ______ of the end of the war.
   a. chaos b. inspiration c. anniversary
3. The woman got her ______ to become a writer from a novel she read when she was young.
   a. inspiration b. canvases c. chaos
4. The fear and violence of war created ______ in the capital city.
   a. chaos b. mural c. atomic bomb
5. The art museum was filled with ______ painted by Pablo Picasso.
   a. canvases b. chaos c. anniversary
6. The ______ is a powerful explosive weapon that causes enormous damage.
   a. chaos b. mural c. atomic bomb

▲ An oil painting on canvas by Picasso

Learn Academic Words

Study the **red** words and their meanings. You will find these words useful when talking and writing about informational texts. Write each word and its meaning in your notebook. After you read "Kids' Guernica," try to use these words to respond to the text.

Academic Words

circumstances
construct
react
region

circumstances = the facts or conditions that affect a situation, action, or event	➡	The meeting had to be canceled because of difficult **circumstances**. The streets were covered with deep snow.
construct = build something large such as a building, bridge, or sculpture	➡	Chris and Luz plan to **construct** a class peace project. They will build it with sticks and paper.
react = behave in a particular way because of what someone has done or said to you	➡	The students usually **react** to one another's speeches by clapping loudly.
region = a fairly large area of a state, country, and so on	➡	The travelers visited the whole **region** even though it was a large area to travel through.

Practice

Work with a partner to answer these questions. Try to include the **red** word in your answer. Write the sentences in your notebook.

1. Under what **circumstances** would you want to join a club?
2. What do sculptors do before they **construct** a work of art?
3. How do you **react** to surprises?
4. What is the weather like in your **region** during winter?

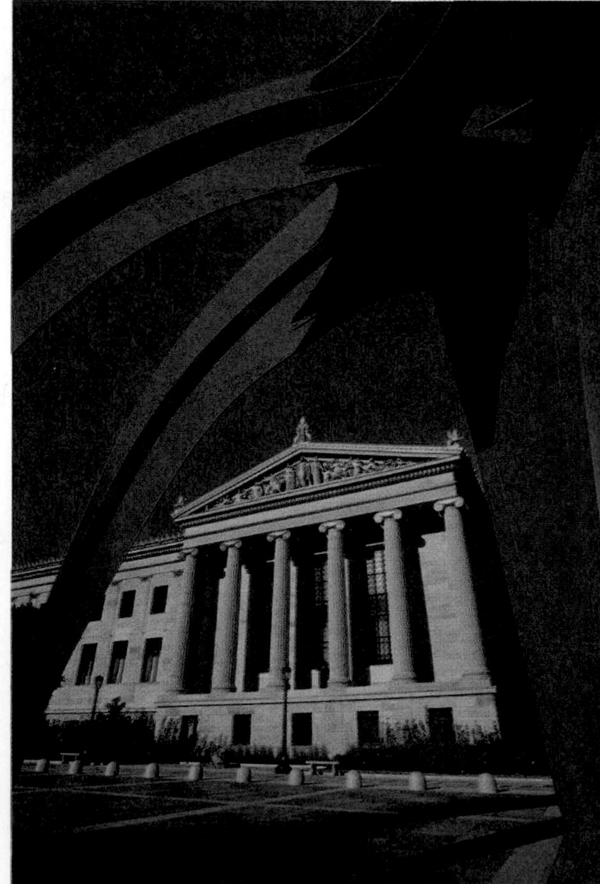

Alexander Calder used red metal ▶ arches to contruct this sculpture.

Word Study: Spelling Words with *ea*

Two vowels can work as a team to stand for one vowel sound. The vowel team *ea* often stands for the long vowel sound /ē/. The vowel team *ea* can also stand for the short vowel sound /e/. In a few words, *ea* stands for the long vowel sound /ā/. Study the chart.

Single- and Multisyllabic Words with *ea*		
/ē/ spelled *ea*	/e/ spelled *ea*	/ā/ spelled *ea*
p**ea**ce	spr**ea**d	st**ea**k
be-n**ea**th	w**ea**lth-y	gr**ea**t-est

In multisyllabic words, or words with more than one syllable, the letters *ea* can also stand for two separate sounds because the letter *e* is part of one syllable and the letter *a* is part of another.

ar-**e**-**a**	cr**e**-**a**te	i-d**e**-**a**	Ko-r**e**-**a**

Practice

Work with a partner. Copy the chart above into your notebook. Say a word from the chart, and ask your partner to spell it aloud. Then have your partner say the next word. Continue until you can spell all of the words correctly. Now practice spelling these words with your partner: *neat, dead, daybreak, breath,* and *breathe.* Add them to the chart under the correct headings.

READING STRATEGY CLASSIFY

Classifying helps you understand, organize, and remember what you read. When you classify, you arrange things into groups with common characteristics. For example, you could classify the texts in this book into these categories: articles, stories, poems, photo-essays, and so on. Classifying words is a good way to learn and remember their meanings. To classify words in a text, follow the steps in this example:

- As you read, think of categories that many words fall into. In "Kids' Guernica," many words relate to the categories "war" and "art."
- Ask yourself: "Which words relate to these categories?" Group the words according to category.

As you read "Kids' Guernica," find words that relate to "war" and "art."

READING 2

INFORMATIONAL TEXT

SOCIAL STUDIES/ART

Set a purpose for reading How can one person's courage and imagination inspire other people to work for peace? Read this photo-essay to find out how and why young people around the world are creating works of art to encourage world peace.

Kids' Guernica

In Kyoto, Japan, in 1995, Yasuda Tadashi started an international art project for peace. Its name was Kids' Guernica. Using the Internet, Tadashi organized schools around the world to participate. The goal was to have children in different parts of the world create peace paintings on huge canvases. The model for the project was one of the most famous paintings of the twentieth century.

Spanish artist Pablo Picasso (1881–1973) had painted *Guernica* in 1937 to protest the brutal bombing of a town in Northern Spain during the Spanish Civil War (1936–1939). Guernica had been an independent and democratic town. Around 7,000 people lived there. On April 26, 1937, Spanish dictator Francisco Franco ordered Nazi planes to bomb the town. It was 4:00 P.M. on a busy market day. About 1,650 innocent people were killed, and 889 were injured. Picasso was shocked by the black-and-white photographs he saw in the newspapers. He quickly sketched the first images for a mural. His final painting shows the horror and chaos of war.

participate, do a particular activity
brutal, very cruel and violent
independent, free and not controlled by another country
democratic, controlled by leaders who are elected by the people of a country
Nazi planes, planes flown by members of the National Socialist Party of Adolf Hitler, which controlled Germany from 1938 to 1945

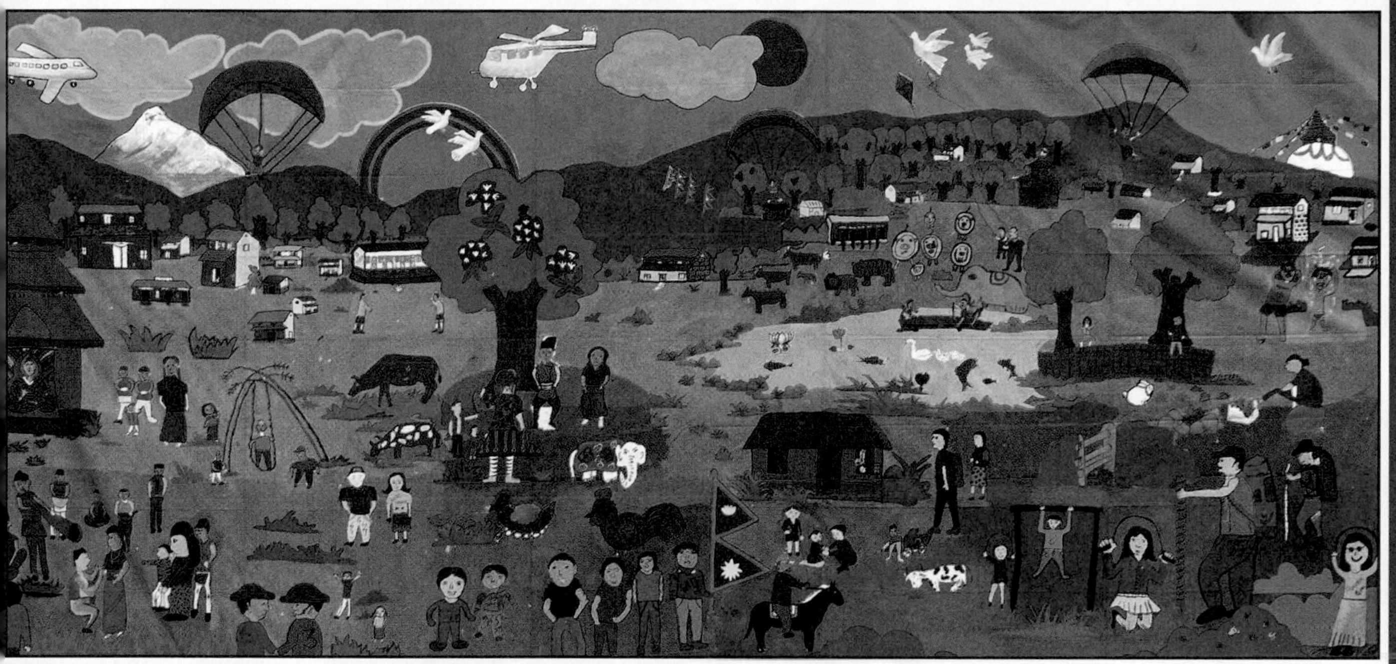

▲ Children created this mural for the Kids' Guernica project in Nepal.

Pablo Picasso painted *Guernica* in 1937. The mural makes a powerful statement about war. ▼

Picasso's symbols
bull = the brutality of war
horse = the people
electric light = an all-seeing God
flower = hope

BEFORE YOU GO ON

1. Who started the Kids' Guernica project?
2. What did Francisco Franco do to the people of Guernica?

On Your Own
Do you think that works of art can stop violence and war? Explain.

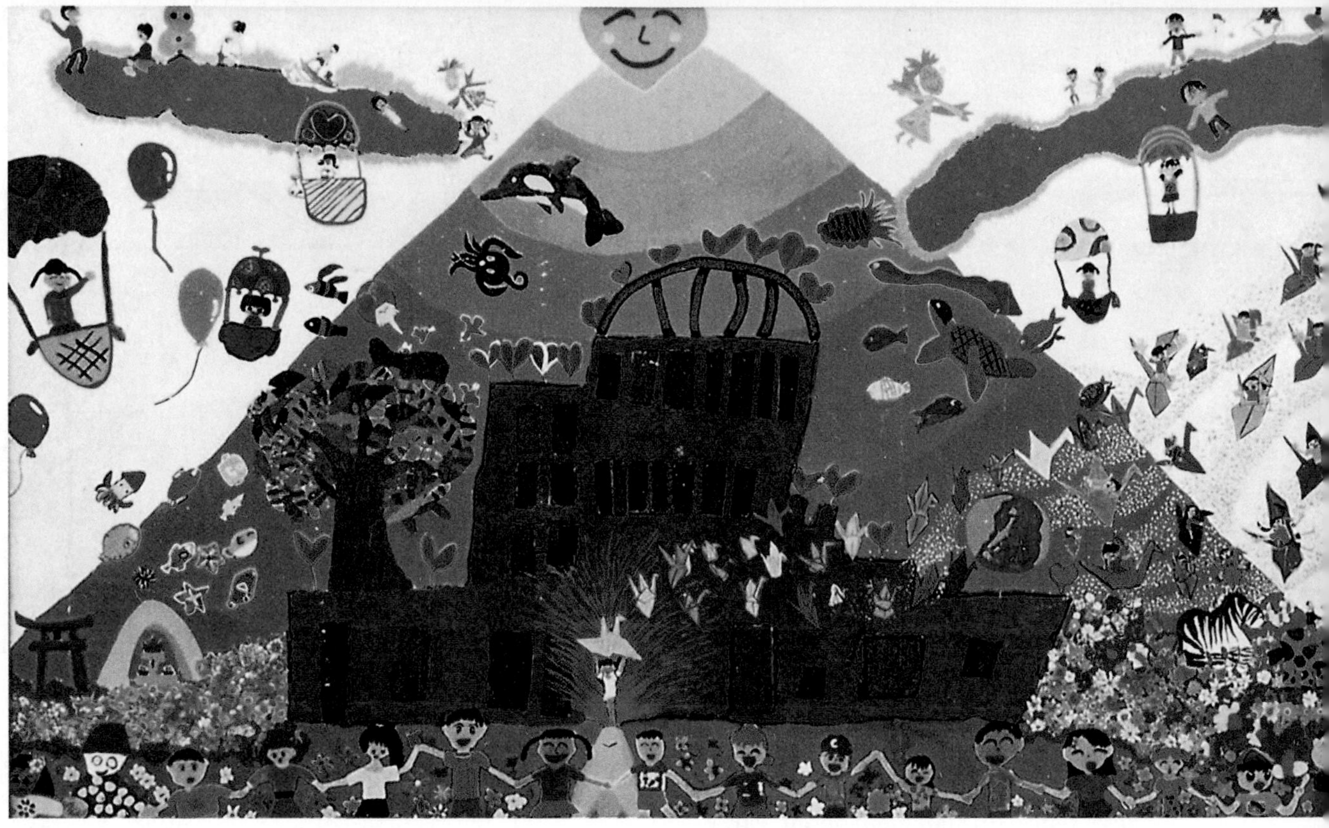

▲ *Hiroshima*, by students participating in Kids' Guernica. The mural shows a bombed building in Hiroshima now known as the Atomic Bomb Dome.

Tadashi was inspired by Picasso's painting. Since 1995, he has organized children throughout the world to paint murals for peace that are the same size as the painting *Guernica*. The original painting is 3.5 × 7.8 meters (11.5 × 25.5 ft.).

The ruins known as the Atomic Bomb Dome ▼

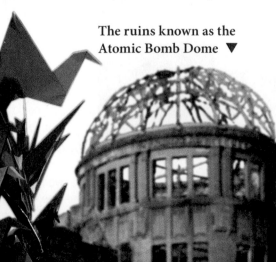

Children participate in workshops in their schools and create their own paintings.

The Kids' Guernica project often takes place in areas that have been torn apart by war. Hiroshima, Japan, is one example. In 1945, the United States dropped an atomic bomb on Hiroshima, ending World War II. The city was completely destroyed. In 1999, forty-one students from four elementary schools in Hiroshima participated in the Kids' Guernica art project. These schools are all located in the area where the bomb exploded. The students created their mural in memory of the 140,000 people who died. Their mural also expresses hope for peace in the future.

▲ Girls creating a mural for the Kids' Guernica project in Bali

The Kids' Guernica project has traveled all over the world. Children across the globe have used art to express their messages of peace. They have made murals in places such as Israel, Palestine, Afghanistan, Korea, and Kuwait. They have tried to spread peace on every continent. In 2004, children involved in the project made a mural for the United Nations building in Geneva, Switzerland. In 2005, the Kids' Guernica project celebrated its tenth anniversary with an art show in Bali, Indonesia. And in 2006 and 2007, participants in the project created murals in Kastelli, Crete, and Chios, Greece. So far, more than 500 children from schools in Cambodia, Sri Lanka, Chile, Nepal, India, Algeria, Germany, the United States, Australia, China, Canada, France, Italy, and other countries have participated.

The people involved in the Kids' Guernica project hope that their paintings will make the world a better place. They want to spread their powerful message around the globe. They say that the project will go on until there is world peace.

BEFORE YOU GO ON

1. What happened in Hiroshima in 1945?
2. When will the Kids' Guernica project end?

On Your Own
In your opinion, does it take courage and imagination to be part of the Kids' Guernica project? Why?

READING 2

Review and Practice

COMPREHENSION

Right There

1. When and where did Yasuda Tadashi start an international art project for peace?
2. About how many children have participated in Kids' Guernica?

Think and Search

3. Why did Picasso paint *Guernica*?
4. Which countries have had children participate in Kids' Guernica?

Author and You

5. Why do you think that Picasso wanted to show the chaos and horror of war in his mural?
6. Why do you think that the text of "Kids' Guernica" is illustrated with so many photographs and works of art?

On Your Own

7. In what ways can people around the world use their imagination to work for peace?
8. If you were participating in the Kids' Guernica project, what would you paint on your mural? Why?

Speaking TIP

Be ready to answer questions and share your opinions with your classmates.

IN YOUR OWN WORDS

Imagine that you are telling a classmate about "Kids' Guernica." You want to include all the main ideas and important details in the photo-essay. Complete the chart below to help you organize your ideas. Then share your summary with a classmate.

Section	Main Idea	Important Details
Introduction (first paragraph)		
Picasso paints *Guernica* in protest		
Kids' Guernica project since 1995		
Conclusion (last paragraph)		

DISCUSSION

Discuss in pairs or small groups.

1. How did the bombing of Guernica affect Picasso? Why do you think he reacted this way?
2. Name some places around the world where the Kids' Guernica project has traveled. How are these places alike? How are they different?
3. What places do you think the Kids' Guernica project should visit in the future? Why?

Q How are courage and imagination linked? Think of other courageous and imaginative projects that might help to spread world peace. What would the projects be? Would the projects use art or something else imaginative? Explain.

Listening TIP

Do not interrupt your classmates when they are speaking. Save your questions until a speaker is finished.

READ FOR FLUENCY

Reading with feeling helps make what you read more interesting. Work with a partner. Choose a paragraph from the reading. Read the paragraph to yourselves. Ask each other how you felt after reading the paragraph. Did you feel happy or sad?

Take turns reading the paragraph aloud to each other with a tone of voice that represents how you felt when you read it the first time. Give each other feedback.

EXTENSION

In "Kids' Guernica," you read about people who make art to bring about peace. Picasso created his mural *Guernica* during the Spanish Civil War. Find out more about the Spanish Civil War. Use encyclopedias, reference books, and reliable websites. Share your findings with the class.

▲ A painting of poet Antonio Machado during the Spanish Civil War

Grammar and Writing

GRAMMAR, USAGE, AND MECHANICS

More Uses of the Present Perfect

Sometimes when you write, you will use the present perfect to talk about the past. The present perfect refers to an action that happened at an indefinite time in the past. The present perfect also is used to describe an action that started in the past and continues into the present. In addition, you can use the present perfect to ask questions with the word *ever.*

Use of the Present Perfect	Example
Actions that happened at an indefinite time	Children in different places **have made** murals.
Actions that started in the past and continue into the present (with *for* or *since*)	He **has organized** children to paint murals for peace since 1995.
Actions with *ever* to ask if the person has done something "at any time" or "in your entire life"	**Have** you **ever visited** Hiroshima, Japan?

Practice

Work with a partner. Copy the sentences below into your notebook. Choose the correct verb to complete each sentence. Then take turns reading the sentences aloud with a partner.

1. The students at my school (participated / have participated) in an art project since 2005.
2. My teacher (was / has been) in charge of one event on May 3.
3. We (worked / have worked) on many special projects since the fall.
4. The art club (was / has been) the most popular club for many years.
5. The children (painted / have painted) murals outdoors in June.
6. Picasso (created / has created) these paintings on plates during the 1940s and 1950s.

WRITING AN EXPOSITORY PARAGRAPH

Write a Paragraph That Classifies Something

Paintings	Plates	Sculptures

Grouping information by category is an effective way to organize ideas and details. On this page, you'll use categories to organize a paragraph. You'll use a graphic organizer like the one on the right to classify your ideas and details. Suppose you want to write a paragraph about Picasso's artwork. You could categorize the information by subject, style, or the materials used. Choose the categories that best suit your purpose. Then describe the features of each category.

Here is a model of an expository paragraph that discusses three categories of work by Picasso. Notice how the writer presents the three categories first. Then he discusses each type of art one at a time.

Koji Mori

Picasso's Paintings, Plates, and Sculptures

I have seen and enjoyed three types of artwork by Picasso: his paintings, plates, and sculptures. His paintings on canvas are his most well-known works. Like all paintings, they are two dimensional. Picasso's come in a wide range of styles including realistic portraits and abstract works. Picasso did a second type of artwork that I like very much: paintings and sculpted designs on three-dimensional objects such as plates. The subjects of these paintings include images of people and birds. The third type of artwork, and my own personal favorite, are Picasso's sculptures. These three-dimensional artworks were made from all kinds of materials. Picasso used wood, clay, metal, stone, or a combination of materials. His sculptures exhibit a wide range of subjects, from realistic figures of people, animals, and birds to abstract works.

Practice

Write a paragraph about three types of art that you enjoy. List your categories on a chart. Explain the features of each category. Tell why you like each type of art. Be sure to use the present perfect correctly.

ORGANIZATION:

☑ I presented each category one at a time.

WORD CHOICE:

☑ I chose words carefully to explain the features of each category.

READING 3 Prepare to Read

What You Will Learn

Reading

- Vocabulary building: *Literary terms, dictionary skills, word study*
- Reading strategy: *Summarize*
- Text type: *Literature (novel excerpt)*

Grammar, Usage, and Mechanics
Quoted versus reported speech

Writing
Write a plot summary

THE BIG QUESTION

How are courage and imagination linked? Why might people care enough about birds and animals to take risks to protect them? Why might courage and imagination be necessary to convince people that birds and animals have rights, too? Discuss with a partner.

The next reading involves efforts to save a unique type of owl. Explore with your partner what you know about owls. Where do they live? What do they eat? Why might it be important to protect their habitats? In your notebook, copy and fill in the first two columns of the K-W-L-H chart below.

K What do I **know**?	W What do I **want** to know?	L What did I **learn**?	H **How** did I learn it?

As you read the excerpt from *Hoot* and complete the activities after the reading, fill out the rest of the K-W-L-H chart with your partner.

▲ Burrowing owls live in holes in the ground.

BUILD BACKGROUND

In the comic novel ***Hoot,*** burrowing owls play an important role. These tiny owls with big yellow eyes are quite different from most owls. Burrowing owls are very small, only 23 centimeters (9 in.) tall. They hunt throughout the day, not just at night, and they don't live in trees. They make their nests in underground holes, or burrows. They often use burrows made by prairie dogs or other animals. Burrowing owls eat mice, like other owls do, but they also eat beetles, moths, grasshoppers, frogs, and lizards. They even eat scorpions.

VOCABULARY

Learn Literary Words

Everyone likes a funny story! **Humor** is anything that amuses people or makes them laugh. Writers create humor with the words they choose and the images these words create.

Sometimes writers exaggerate a scene or a character's traits to make something seem funny. Read these examples from *Hoot*. What is humorous about each sentence?

Literary Words

humor
colorful language

> Mr. Muckle's cheeks turned purple.
> The chamber-of-commerce guy looked like he'd swallowed a bar of soap.

Writers often use **colorful language**, such as idioms, hyperbole, and slang, to make their stories humorous. Slang is very informal language that certain people use. Colorful expressions can be used to create a silly character or to make the dialogue between characters amusing. Here are some examples of colorful language that you will read in *Hoot*.

> *dorky*: silly-looking or strange-looking
> *hotshot*: someone who is very successful and confident
> *twerp*: an annoying or stupid person
> *noggin*: head or brain

Practice

Write a funny paragraph about a "hotshot" who tries to convince a "dorky" friend of his to do something silly. You may want to use some of the words above in your paragraph and add some colorful expressions of your own. Share your paragraph with a partner.

Learn Academic Words

Study the **red** words and their meanings. You will find these words useful when talking and writing about literature. Write each word and its meaning in your notebook. After you read the excerpt from *Hoot*, try to use these words to respond to the text.

Academic Words

demonstrate
deny
image
site

demonstrate = protest or support something in public with a lot of other people	➡	The students decided to **demonstrate** against the builders who were destroying the owls' habitat.
deny = say that something is not true	➡	The builders will **deny** that the burrowing owls live here. However, we know they're lying.
image = a picture that you can see through a camera, on television, or in a mirror; a picture that you have in your mind	➡	The protester drew the **image** of a burrowing owl on her poster. The picture looked real.
site = a place where something is being built or will be built	➡	The protest took place at the construction **site**, where the owls lived.

Practice

Write the sentences in your notebook. Choose a **red** word from the box above to complete each sentence. Then take turns reading the sentences aloud with a partner.

1. What possible motive could the company have for constructing a restaurant on this ______?
   a. site **b.** image
2. The boy is afraid of admitting the truth, so he will ______ what he did.
   a. demonstrate **b.** deny
3. Roy's ______ of the owls was blurry.
   a. site **b.** image
4. Many people plan to ______ against the new law, because they think that it is unfair.
   a. demonstrate **b.** deny

▲ People demonstrate on Earth Day to protect our planet.

Word Study: Prefixes *mega-*, *tele-*, *re-*

A prefix is a word part added to the beginning of a word that changes the word's meaning. Knowing the meanings of prefixes can help you figure out the meaning of many unfamiliar words. Study the chart.

Prefix	+ Base Word	= New Word
mega- (large; one million)	ton	megaton ("1 million tons")
tele- (distance; distant)	communication	telecommunication ("communication over a large distance by electronic means")
re- (again; backward)	capture	recapture ("capture again")

Practice

Work with a partner. Use what you have learned about prefixes to figure out the meanings of the words below. Copy the items below into your notebook. Write your own definitions for each word. Then check the meanings in a dictionary. Discuss how learning about prefixes can expand your vocabulary.

1. mega- + phone = ____________
2. tele- + scope = ____________
3. re- + viewing = ____________

▲ A telescope

Reading Strategy SUMMARIZE

Summarizing helps you remember and understand a text. When you summarize fiction, you write a few sentences about what happened. You tell the goals of the characters, how they tried to reach their goals, and whether they succeeded. When you summarize nonfiction, you write a few sentences about the main ideas. To summarize, follow these steps:

- As you read, stop from time to time to summarize parts of the text.
- Write a sentence or two about the most important event or idea in that section. Leave out unimportant events, ideas, and details.
- After reading, summarize the most important points of the whole text.

As you read the excerpt from "Hoot," stop to summarize the plot. When you finish reading, summarize the entire excerpt in a short paragraph.

READING 3

LITERATURE

NOVEL

Set a purpose for reading What will happen when the Mother Paula Company starts to build a restaurant on lands inhabited by burrowing owls? Read to find out whether anyone will have the courage and imagination to help save the owls and their habitat.

from HOOT

Carl Hiaasen

Chuck E. Muckle plans to build a new Mother Paula's restaurant on lands that are home to burrowing owls. The special groundbreaking ceremony is about to begin, and many people have gathered for the occasion. Three kids, Roy, Mullet Fingers, and his stepsister, Beatrice, are also on the scene. They are determined to save the tiny owls from the developers.

At a quarter past twelve, the door of the construction trailer swung open. First to emerge was a policeman whom Roy recognized as Officer Delinko; then the bald construction foreman with the rotten temper; then a snooty-looking guy with silver hair and dorky sunglasses.

The last to come out was the woman who played Mother Paula on the TV commercials. She wore a shiny gray wig, wire-rimmed glasses, and a calico apron. A few people clapped in recognition, and she waved halfheartedly.

The group marched to a rectangular clearing that had been roped off in the center of the construction site. A megaphone was handed to the silvery-haired guy, who said his name was Chuck E. Muckle, a vice-president from Mother Paula's company headquarters. He really thought he was hot snot, Roy could tell.

LITERARY CHECK

*What **colorful language** does the author use to describe Chuck E. Muckle?*

---

temper, tendency to become suddenly angry
commercials, advertisements
calico, light cotton cloth with a small pattern
halfheartedly, without interest or enthusiasm

Ignoring the foreman and the police officer, Mr. Muckle proceeded with great enthusiasm to introduce some local big shots—the mayor, a city councilman, and the head of the chamber of commerce.

"I can't tell you how proud and delighted we are to make Coconut Cove the home of our 469th family-style restaurant," Mr. Muckle said. "Mr. Mayor, Councilman Grandy, all of you terrific folks who've come out on this gorgeous Florida day . . . I'm here to promise you that Mother Paula will be a good citizen, a good friend, and a good neighbor to everybody!"

"Unless you're an owl," Roy said.

Mr. Muckle didn't hear it. . . . He snickered nervously. "Mother Paula, dearest, I think it's time. Shall we do the deed?"

They all posed side by side—the company V.P., the mayor, Mother Paula, Councilman Grandy, and the boss of the chamber of commerce—for the television crew and the news photographer.

Gold-painted shovels were handed out, and on Mr. Muckle's signal all the dignitaries smiled, leaned over, and dug up a scoopful of sand. . . .

As soon as the photo pose ended, Mr. Muckle tossed down his gold shovel and snatched up the megaphone. "Before the bulldozers and backhoes get rolling," he said, "Mother Paula herself wants to say a few words."

Mother Paula didn't look overjoyed to have the megaphone shoved in her hand. "You've got a real nice town," she said. "I'll see you next spring at the grand opening—"

"Oh no, you won't!"

This time the words came out of Roy's mouth as a shout, and nobody was more stunned than he. A tremor rippled through the audience and Beatrice edged closer, half expecting somebody to come after him.

The actress playing Mother Paula seemed miffed, peering over her cheap wire-rimmed glasses into the crowd.

"Now, who said that?"

Roy found himself raising his right arm. "I did, Mother Paula," he called out. "If you hurt a single one of our owls, I'm not eating any more of your stupid pancakes."

"What're you talking about? What owls?"

---

foreman, person who is in charge of a group of workers
proceeded, continued
snickered, laughed quietly in a way that is not nice at something that is not supposed to be funny
deed, action
dignitaries, people who have important official positions
backhoes, large digging machines
tremor, tense feeling or shudder

BEFORE YOU GO ON

1. Which characters pose for the television crew and news photographer?
2. Who is playing Mother Paula at the ceremony?

On Your Own
Summarize the main events in the story so far.

Chuck Muckle lunged for the megaphone, but Mother Paula threw an elbow and caught him square in the gut. "Back off, Chuckie Cheeseball," she huffed.

"Go on, check it out for yourself," Roy said, gesturing around. "Wherever you see one of those holes, there's an owl den underneath. It's where they build their nests and lay their eggs. It's their home."

Mr. Muckle's cheeks turned purple. The mayor looked lost, Councilman Grandy looked like he was about to faint, and the chamber-of-commerce guy looked like he'd swallowed a bar of soap.

By now, the parents in the crowd were talking loudly and pointing at the den holes. A few of the schoolkids started chanting in support of Roy, and Beatrice's soccer teammates began waving their hand-lettered signs.

One said: MOTHER PAULA DOESN'T GIVE A HOOT ABOUT OWLS!

Another read: BIRD KILLERS GO HOME!

And still a third sign said: SAVE THE OWLS, BURY THE BUTTERMILKS!

As the news photographer snapped pictures of the protesters, Mother Paula pleaded, "But I don't want to hurt your owls! Really, I wouldn't hurt a flea!"

Chuck Muckle finally recaptured the megaphone and boomed a harsh scolding at Roy: "Young fellow, you'd better get your facts straight before making such outrageous and slanderous charges. There are no owls here, not one! Those old burrows have been abandoned for years."

Literary Check

*How do these sentences—"Back off, Chuckie Cheeseball" and "Mother Paula doesn't give a hoot about owls"—add to the **humor** of the story?*

---

lunged for, made a sudden forceful movement toward
threw an elbow, stuck out an elbow to stop someone
give a hoot, care
scolding, statement that someone has done something wrong
slanderous, untrue
abandoned, not used or taken care of

"Yeah?" Roy reached into his backpack and whipped out his mother's camera. "I've got proof!" he shouted. "Right here."

The kids in the crowd hooted and hurrahed. Chuck Muckle's face went gray and slack. He held out his arms and lurched toward Roy. "Lemme see that!"

Scooting out of reach, Roy switched on the digital camera and held his breath. He had no idea what he was about to see.

He pressed the button to display the first photograph that Mullet Fingers had taken. The instant that the blurred, crooked image appeared in the viewfinder, Roy knew he was in trouble.

It was a picture of a finger.

Anxiously he clicked to the second frame, what he saw was no less discouraging: a dirty bare foot. It appeared to be a boy's foot, and Roy knew whose it was.

Beatrice's stepbrother had many special talents, but nature photography obviously wasn't one of them. . . .

Roy was crushed—the pictures taken by Beatrice's stepbrother were worthless. The **authorities** in charge of protecting the burrowing owls would never block the construction of the pancake house based on such fuzzy evidence. . . .

Then a young voice rose up: "Wait, it ain't over! Not by a mile it ain't."

This time it wasn't Roy.

"Uh-oh," said Beatrice, lifting her eyes.

A girl in the rear of the crowd let out a shriek, and everybody wheeled at once to look. At first glance the object on the ground could have been mistaken for a kickball, but it was actually . . . a boy's head.

His matted hair was blond, his face was caramel-brown, and his eyes were wide and unblinking. A kite string led from his pursed lips to the handle of a large tin bucket a few feet away.

The big shots came hurrying out of the crowd, with Beatrice and Roy at their heels. They all stopped to **gape** at the head on the ground.

"What now?" moaned the construction foreman.

Chuck Muckle **thundered**: "Is this somebody's idea of a sick joke?"

"Good heavens," cried the mayor, "is he dead?"

The boy wasn't the least bit dead. He smiled up at his stepsister and winked slyly at Roy. Somehow he'd fit his entire skinny body down the opening of an owl burrow, so that only his noggin stuck out.

"Yo, Mother Paula," he said.

---

scooting, moving quickly
authorities, people or organization
gape, look at something for a long time, with their mouths open because they are shocked
thundered, yelled in a loud voice

LITERARY CHECK

*What is **humorous** about this scene in the story?*

BEFORE YOU GO ON

1. Who are the people demonstrating against Mother Paula's?
2. Where is Mullet Fingers and what does he have in his mouth?

On Your Own
Summarize the most important events on pages 298–299.

The actress stepped forward hesitantly. Her wig looked slightly crooked and her makeup was beginning to melt in the humidity.

"What is it?" she asked uneasily.

"You bury those birds," Mullet Fingers said, "you gotta bury me, too."

"But no, I love birds! All birds!"

"Officer Delinko? Where are you!" Chuck Muckle motioned for the policeman to come forward. "Arrest this impertinent little creep right now."

"For what?"

"Trespassing, obviously."

"But your company advertised this event as open to the public," Officer Delinko pointed out. "If I arrest the boy, I'll have to arrest everyone else on the property, too."

Roy watched as a vein in Mr. Muckle's neck swelled up and began to pulse like a garden hose. "I'll be speaking to Chief Deacon about you first thing tomorrow," Mr. Muckle hissed under his breath at the patrolman. "That gives you one whole night to work on your sorry excuse for a résumé."

Next he turned his withering gaze upon the forlorn foreman. "Mr. Branitt, please uproot this . . . this stringy *weed*."

"Wouldn't try that," Beatrice's stepbrother warned though clenched jaws.

"Really. And why not?" Chuck Muckle said.

The boy smiled. "Roy, do me a favor. Check out what's in the bucket."

Roy was happy to oblige.

"What do you see?" the boy asked.

"Cottonmouth moccasins," Roy replied.

"How many?"

"Nine or ten."

"They look happy, Roy?"

"Not really."

"What do you think's gonna happen if I tip that thing over?" With his tongue Mullet Fingers displayed the string that connected him to the bucket.

"Somebody could get hurt pretty bad," Roy said, playing along. He had been mildly surprised (though relieved) to see that the reptiles in the bucket were made of rubber.

---

motioned, gave directions using his hand(s)
impertinent, impolite, disrespectful
sorry excuse, worthless or poor excuse
withering gaze, look that makes someone feel stupid or embarrassed
forlorn, sad and lonely
oblige, do what he asked
cottonmouth moccasins, venomous water snakes that live in the southeastern United States

Mr. Muckle stewed. "This is ridiculous—Branitt, do what I told you. Get that kid outta my sight!"

The foreman backed away. "Not me. I don't much care for snakes."

"Really? Then you're fired." Once again the vice-president turned to confront Officer Delinko. "Make yourself useful. Shoot the damn things."

"No, sir, not around all these people. Too dangerous."

The policeman approached the boy and dropped to one knee.

"How'd you get here?" he asked.

"Hopped the fence last night. Then I hid under the backhoe," the boy said. . . . "Man, you don't understand. The owls got no chance against those machines."

"I do understand. I honestly do," Officer Delinko said. "One more question: You serious about the cottonmouths?"

"Serious as a heart attack."

"Can I have a look inside the bucket?"

The boy's eyes flickered. "It's your funeral," he said.

Roy whispered to Beatrice: "We've gotta do something quick. Those snakes aren't real."

"Oh, great."

As the policeman approached the tin bucket, Beatrice shouted, "Don't do it! You might get bit—"

Officer Delinko didn't flinch. He peeked over the rim for what seemed to Roy and Beatrice like an eternity.

Jig's up, Roy thought glumly. No way he won't notice they're fake.

Yet the patrolman didn't say a word as he backed away from the bucket.

"Well?" Mr. Muckle demanded. "What do we do?"

"Kid's for real. If I were you, I'd negotiate," said Officer Delinko.

"Ha! I don't negotiate with juvenile delinquents." With a snarl, Chuck Muckle snatched the gold-painted shovel from Councilman Grandy's hands and charged toward the bucket.

"Don't!" hollered the boy in the owl hole, spitting the string.

But the man from Mother Paula's was unstoppable. With a wild swing of the shovel he knocked over the bucket, and commenced flailing and hacking at the snakes in a blind, slobbering fury. He didn't stop until they were in pieces.

Little rubber pieces.

---

stewed, became angry because something bad has just happened
glumly, unhappily
negotiate, discuss something in order to reach an agreement
snarl, angry growl like an animal
flailing, waving his arms and legs in a fast but uncontrolled way
slobbering fury, state of extreme anger

BEFORE YOU GO ON

1. What does Chuck E. Muckle ask Officer Delinko to do to Mullet Fingers?
2. Why doesn't Officer Delinko flinch when he looks in the bucket?

On Your Own
What do you think will happen next?

Exhausted, Chuck Muckle leaned over and squinted at the mutilated toy snakes. His expression reflected both disbelief and humiliation. . . .

"Hey, them snakes're fake!" Curly piped. "They ain't even real."

Roy leaned toward Beatrice and whispered, "Another Einstein."

Chuck Muckle pivoted in slow motion. Ominously he pointed the blade of the shovel at the boy in the owl burrow.

"You!" he bellowed, stalking forward.

Roy jumped in front of him.

"Outta my way, kid," Chuck Muckle said. "I don't have time for any more of your nonsense. Move it *now*!"

It was clear that the Mother Paula's bigshot had totally lost his cool, and possibly his marbles.

"What're you doing?" Roy asked, knowing he probably wouldn't get a calm, patient answer.

"I said, *Get outta my way*! I'm gonna dig that little twerp out of the ground myself."

Beatrice Leep darted forward and stood next to Roy, taking his right hand. An anxious murmur swept through the crowd.

"Aw, that's real cute. Just like Romeo and Juliet," Chuck Muckle taunted. He dropped his voice and said, "Game over, kiddies. On the count of three, I'm going to start using this shovel—or better yet, how about I get Baldy over here to crank up the bulldozer?"

The foreman scowled. "Thought you said I was fired." . . .

Roy turned to see that Beatrice had been joined by the entire soccer team, linking arms in a silent chain. They were tall, strong girls who weren't the least bit intimidated by Chuck Muckle's blustery threats.

Chuck Muckle realized it, too. "Stop this foolishness right now!" he begged. "There's no need for an ugly mob scene."

Roy watched in wonderment as more and more kids slipped out of the crowd and began joining hands, forming a human barricade around Beatrice's self-buried stepbrother. None of the parents made a move to stop them.

The TV cameraman announced that the demonstration was being broadcast live on the noon news, while the photographer from the paper swooped in for a close-up of Mr. Muckle, looking drained, defeated, and suddenly very old. He braced himself on the ceremonial shovel as if it were a cane.

---

mutilated, severely damaged
bellowed, shouted loudly in a deep voice
Romeo and Juliet, two young lovers in a Shakespeare play
taunted, joked to anger or upset someone
blustery, loud and bullying
swooped in, moved in very quickly

"Didn't any of you people hear me?" he rasped. "This event is over! Done! You can all go home now." . . .

Roy was in an eerie yet tranquil daze.

Some girl started singing a famous old folk song called "This Land Is Your Land." It was Beatrice, of all people, and her voice was surprisingly lovely and soft. Before long, the other kids were singing along, too. Roy shut his eyes and felt like he was floating on the sunny slope of a cloud.

"Excuse me, hotshot. Got room for one more?"

Roy blinked open his eyes and broke into a grin.

"Yes, ma'am," he said.

Mother Paula stepped between him and Garrett to join the circle. Her voice was gravelly, but she could carry a tune just fine. . . .

Overhead, a small dusky-colored bird was flying in marvelous daring corkscrews. Roy and Beatrice watched in delight as it banked lower and lower, finishing with a radical dive toward the burrow at the center of the circle.

Everybody whirled to see where the bird had landed. All of a sudden the singing stopped.

There was Mullet Fingers, trying not to giggle, the daredevil owl perched calmly on the crown of his head.

"Don't worry, little guy," the boy said. "You're safe for now."

---

rasped, spoke in a rough, unpleasant way
tranquil, pleasantly calm
banked, sloped to one side while turning
radical, wonderful
daredevil, bold and not caring about danger

ABOUT THE AUTHOR

Carl Hiaasen is a best-selling author of young adult novels and a proud lifelong resident of Florida. After graduating from the University of Florida, Hiaasen began working at the *Miami Herald* as a reporter. He still contributes a weekly column to the paper today, in addition to writing novels. *Hoot*, one of Hiaasen's most popular novels, was a Newbery Honor book. It was so successful that it was made into a movie.

BEFORE YOU GO ON

1. What do Roy, Beatrice, and the other demonstrators do to protect Mullet Fingers?
2. How does Chuck E. Muckle look at the end?

On Your Own
How do Roy, Mullet Fingers, and Beatrice show courage and imagination?

READING 3 Review and Practice

READER'S THEATER

Use realistic voices and facial expressions to communicate different emotions.

Act out the following scene between Roy and Beatrice.

Roy: Bea, did you hear what just happened? Mother Paula's decided to build a new restaurant in our town!

Beatrice: Oh, that's cool.

Roy: No, it's not! They want to build it where the burrowing owls live over by Coconut Cove! They've got the mayor and the city council on their side.

Beatrice: Those poor little owls! We have to do something!

Roy: What can we do? They start building next week.

Beatrice: Hmm . . . I know! We have to get out and tell people. Once they know about the owls, they definitely won't want the restaurant there.

Roy: But how can we tell the whole town?

Beatrice: We'll bring signs and posters to the groundbreaking ceremony. The whole town will show up, and then we'll let them know what's *really* going on!

COMPREHENSION

Workbook Page 147

Right There

1. Who is Chuck E. Muckle?
2. What kind of snakes does Roy say are in the bucket?

Think and Search

3. Roy wants to show that the owls still live in their burrows. What proof does he have? Why isn't it any good?
4. What kind of snakes does Mullet Fingers use to stop Chuck Muckle from breaking ground for the new restaurant? Why does this plan work?

Author and You

5. Do you think that the author agrees with Roy and Mullet Fingers or with Chuck Muckle? What makes you think so?
6. Why does Mother Paula decide to demonstrate with the kids and other community members at the end of the excerpt?

On Your Own

7. Is it a good idea for human beings to try to take care of wildlife? Why?
8. Have you or someone close to you ever felt so strongly about an issue that you decided to demonstrate about it? Explain.

DISCUSSION

Discuss in pairs or small groups.

1. Which part of the excerpt from *Hoot* did you find the most humorous? Why?
2. In what ways can writers add humor to a story? Give some examples of humorous stories, television shows, and movies.
3. In what ways can builders be more careful when preparing to build on sites where birds and animals live?

Q How are courage and imagination linked? Do you think that it is important to fight for animals' rights? Would you be willing to work to preserve animals and their habitats? If so, how could you use your imagination to come up with ways to help animals?

Listening TIP

When listening to your classmates, pay attention to the examples they use to illustrate their ideas. Think about how these ideas are similar to or different from your own.

RESPONSE TO LITERATURE

Hoot is a humorous novel about saving burrowing owls. The author shows Chuck E. Muckle as a silly character with the wrong ideas and motives. But think about the problem of the burrowing owls from Chuck E. Muckle's point of view. After all, he can't open his new restaurant. He might even lose his job. Retell part of the story from Chuck E. Muckle's point of view. Suggest how he might solve his problem. When you are finished writing, share your paragraph with a partner. Discuss how Chuck E. Muckle must feel about what is happening to him.

A burrowing owl ▶

Grammar and Writing

GRAMMAR, USAGE, AND MECHANICS

Quoted versus Reported Speech

Quoted speech is used to state exactly what someone said. A writer uses quotation marks around the speaker's words. Reported speech is used to tell another person what someone said without using his or her exact words. A writer does not use quotation marks in reported speech.

Notice that the verb changes from present to past in reported speech. The word *that* is often added to reported speech.

Quoted speech: "I **love** birds," Mother Paula said.
Reported speech: Mother Paula said that she **loved** birds.

Quoted speech: "This event **is** over," Mr. Muckle said.
Reported speech: Mr. Muckle said that the event **was** over.

Quoted speech: "You **have** a real nice town," she said.
Reported speech: She said that you **had** a real nice town.

Quoted speech: Roy said, "I **want** those pictures."
Reported speech: He said that he **wanted** those pictures.

Practice

Work with a partner. Write each sentence in your notebook. Label each sentence *quoted speech* or *reported speech*. Underline the present verb in the quoted speech and the past verb in the reported speech.

1. Roy said, "I want to save the owls." ______
2. Roy said that he wanted to save the owls. ______
3. The policeman said that everything was ready. ______
4. The policeman said, "Everything is ready." ______
5. Mr. Muckle said, "I need the gold shovel." ______
6. Mr. Muckle said that he needed the gold shovel. ______

WRITING AN EXPOSITORY PARAGRAPH

Write a Plot Summary

On this page, you will write a plot summary. You'll use a graphic organizer like the one at the right to organize your ideas. As you know, a plot is what happens in a story. It includes a problem or conflict and the outcome. When you summarize a plot, you say in a few sentences what happened. You introduce the main characters and the setting. You tell the goals of the characters, how they tried to reach them, and whether they succeeded.

Below is a plot summary of the excerpt you just read from *Hoot*. Notice that the writer describes the setting and the main characters in the first two sentences. Then he presents the main events in chronological order. He ends by telling the outcome.

Main characters and setting:
Characters' goals:
Main events: 1. 2. 3.
Outcome:

Brandon Saiz

Hoot: A Summary of the Excerpt

Hoot is a funny novel set in Coconut Cove, Florida. The main characters are three teenagers: Roy, Beatrice, and her stepbrother, Mullet Fingers. They want to stop Mother Paula's, a pancake chain, from building a new restaurant on land that is home to burrowing owls. The excerpt begins at the groundbreaking ceremony for the new restaurant. Everyone in town is there, including the vice president of the restaurant chain, Chuck E. Muckle. First, Roy tries to stop the builders by speaking out. Mr. Muckle tries to shut Roy up, by saying that he'd better get his facts straight. Next, Roy tries to convince the crowd by showing photos of the owls, but the photos are unclear. Finally, Mullet Fingers appears. He has buried his body in an owl burrow. He and Roy play a prank on Mr. Muckle that involves a bucket of snakes. The snakes turn out to be fake, and Muckle ends up looking foolish. Through their courage and creativity, the main characters save the burrowing owls.

Writing Checklist

IDEAS:

☑ I included only the most important events in my plot summary.

ORGANIZATION:

☑ I first introduced the characters and setting. Then I presented the main events in time order.

Practice

Write a paragraph that summarizes the plot of a story, novel, movie, or television show. Use a plot-summary chart to list information about the plot. Then write your summary. Be sure to use reported and quoted speech correctly.

READING 4

Prepare to Read

What You Will Learn

Reading

- Vocabulary building: *Context, dictionary skills, word study*
- Reading strategy: *Follow steps in a process*
- Text type: *Informational texts (science) (instructions)*

Grammar, Usage, and Mechanics
Imperatives

Writing
Write how-to instructions

THE BIG QUESTION

How are courage and imagination linked? Why might courage and imagination be needed to improve our environment? Do you think that one person really can make a difference? How might planting trees make a big difference to people throughout a country? Discuss with a partner.

▲ A beech tree forest

BUILD BACKGROUND

"A Tree Grows in Kenya: The Story of Wangari Maathai" is a biographical science article about an environmentalist from Kenya. An environmentalist is someone who works to protect the natural world. The woman you will be reading about, Wangari Maathai, has done a lot to improve the environment of Kenya, her home country. You will see how she used her imagination and courage to change the land around her.

Kenya is a country in eastern Africa. The southeastern part of the country borders the Indian Ocean. Kenya was once a colony ruled by the British. In 1963, Kenya won its independence from Britain. In 1964, Kenya became an independent republic.

Today Kenya is a popular place for travelers to visit. It has wildlife parks, mountains, sophisticated cities, and beaches. Imagine going on a safari and seeing lions, elephants, zebras, and wildebeests.

VOCABULARY

Learn Key Words

Read the sentences. Use the context to figure out the meaning of the **red** words. Use a dictionary to check your answers. Then write each word and its meaning in your notebook.

1. The **campaign** to save the forest was successful. The series of actions helped to save the forest.
2. The **committee** has six members. The group is preparing a report on Kenya.
3. North America is a **continent**, one of the seven main areas of land in the world.
4. A **democratic** government is controlled by leaders who are elected by the people of the country.
5. Wood is a **natural** material. It is not man-made.
6. Fruit gives us the **nutrition** we need. It has many of the vitamins and minerals we need to stay healthy.

Key Words

campaign
committee
continent
democratic
natural
nutrition

Practice

Write the sentences in your notebook. Choose a **red** word from the box above to complete each sentence. Then take turns reading the sentences aloud with a partner.

1. If you live in a ______ country, you elect leaders by voting for them.
2. Water is one important ______ resource. Others are minerals and land.
3. Trees get the ______ they need to grow from water, sun, and soil.
4. The girl started a ______ to save trees. She planned six events.
5. The planting ______ is in charge of planting trees.
6. Kenya and the United States are not located on the same ______.

Learn Academic Words

Study the **red** words and their meanings. You will find these words useful when talking and writing about informational texts. Write each word and its meaning in your notebook. After you read "A Tree Grows in Kenya: The Story of Wangari Maathai," try to use these words to respond to the text.

Academic Words

aspect
finance
resource
sustain
technology
welfare

aspect = one of the parts or features of a situation, idea, or problem	➡	People try to think of every **aspect** of a problem and try to solve each part.
finance = provide money for something	➡	The club needed to **finance** a trip, so they raised money with a bake sale.
resource = something such as land, minerals, or natural energy that exists in a country and can be used in order to increase its wealth	➡	A waterfall is a natural **resource**. It makes power that can be turned into electricity.
sustain = make it possible for someone or something to continue to exist over time	➡	Trees **sustain** life for many animals. They make life for these animals possible.
technology = a combination of all the knowledge, equipment, or methods used in scientific or industrial work	➡	Computers and cars are examples of modern **technology**. We use these machines daily.
welfare = health, comfort, and happiness	➡	Trees are good for our **welfare**. They add to our health and happiness.

Practice

Work with a partner to answer the questions. Try to include the **red** word in your answer. Write the sentences in your notebook.

1. What **aspect** of nature would you like to photograph?
2. How might you **finance** a campaign to save a forest?
3. Which **resource** do you think helps a country become wealthier—gold or oil? Why?
4. How do forests help to **sustain** life?
5. What types of **technology** are used to communicate across continents?
6. How is a diet rich in fresh fruits and vegetables good for people's **welfare**?

Forests help to sustain life in many ways. ▶

Word Analysis: Suffixes *-ic*, *-ist*, *-able*

A suffix is a letter or group of letters placed at the end of a base word. It can change a word's part of speech and its meaning. If you know the meaning of a suffix, it can help you understand the meaning of the new word. Study the examples in the chart below. If a base word ends in *e*, remember to drop the *e* before adding the suffix.

▲ Wind energy is a sustainable resource.

Word	Suffix	New Word (Part of Speech and Meaning)
democrat (noun)	-*ic*	democratic (adjective) (having the characteristics of a democrat)
environmental (adjective)	-*ist*	environmentalist (noun) (person who works for the environment)
sustain (verb)	-*able*	sustainable (adjective) (capable of being sustained)

Practice

Copy the chart above into your notebook. Work with a partner. Add these words and the suffixes to the chart to create new words:

poet + ic	art + ist	understand + able

Identify each new word's part of speech. Then define each word using what you know about suffixes. Check the dictionary to make sure that your answers are correct.

Reading Strategy | FOLLOW STEPS IN A PROCESS

Learning how to follow steps in a process will help you read and understand instructions. The steps are usually arranged in chronological order, from first to last. The author often numbers the steps to make them easier to follow. When you read instructions, follow these steps:

- Look for numbers.
- Look for time-order words such as *first, second, then, next,* and *last.*
- Read the steps from first to last.
- Restate the steps to make sure that you can follow them in the correct order.

As you read "How to Plant a Tree," follow the steps above to understand the steps in the process.

READING 4

INFORMATIONAL TEXT

SCIENCE

Set a purpose for reading Why might something as simple as planting a tree require courage and imagination? As you read this article, think about how a simple action can have a big effect. Then find out how to plant a tree yourself.

A Tree Grows in Kenya:

The Story of Wangari Maathai

In October 2004, Wangari Maathai (wan-GAH-ree mah-DHEYE), an environmentalist from Kenya, Africa, received an unexpected phone call. The person on the phone told her that she had won the Nobel Peace Prize. Each year, the Nobel committee chooses someone whose work for peace is judged to be the most important to the world. This was an incredible honor and an enormous surprise for Maathai. She was very excited. In an interview with *Time* magazine, she said, "I think what the Nobel committee is doing is going beyond war and looking at what **humanity** can do to prevent war. Sustainable management of our natural resources will promote peace." She was pleased that the judges had recognized the deep connection between environmentalism and peace. "If we conserved our resources better," she said, "fighting would not occur."

humanity, people in general

Maathai's love of the environment began when she was very young. She was born in the **highland** village of Nyeri in Kenya in 1940. As a child she enjoyed the lush, green forests around her. Her parents were farmers, so she grew up close to the natural world. In her Nobel prize speech, she said:

> *I would visit a stream next to our home to fetch water for my mother. I would drink water straight from the stream. Playing among the arrowroot leaves, I tried in vain to pick up the strands of frogs' eggs, believing they were beads. But every time I put my little fingers under them they would break. Later, I saw thousands of **tadpoles**: black, energetic, and wriggling through the clear water against the background of the brown earth. This is the world I **inherited** from my parents.*

highland, mountain
tadpoles, small creatures with long tails that live in water and grow into frogs or toads
inherited, received

Maathai was an excellent student. She won a scholarship to attend a college in the United States. She studied hard and received a degree in biology. Then she worked toward more advanced degrees at the University of Pittsburgh and University of Nairobi in Kenya. In 1971, she earned a doctoral degree. She was honored to be the first woman in East and Central Africa to earn such an advanced degree.

At first, Maathai taught at the University of Nairobi. Soon she wanted to do more than teach. While in the United States, she had been deeply impressed by the democratic freedom that people enjoyed. She wanted the Kenyan people to enjoy similar freedom and a better quality of life.

Maathai was concerned that the luxuriant forests of her childhood were rapidly disappearing because of excessive logging and other practices. She wanted the people of her village, especially the women, to have more of a voice in government. Maathai decided that it was time for a change.

It is said that "a journey of a thousand miles begins with a single step." Maathai took one step to change the world around her: She planted nine trees in her backyard. With this simple act, she planted the seed of her campaign to save the forests of Africa!

In 1976, Maathai interviewed many farmers in the Kenyan countryside. Most of them were women, and they often had the same concerns. They needed more firewood, which was their main source of energy. They needed clean water for drinking, cooking, and bathing. They needed to be able to grow their own food. In addition, they needed to be able to make more money so that they could become self-sufficient.

Maathai knew that the destruction of the forests was at the root of these problems. She decided to put her knowledge and creativity to work. Trees were needed to stop soil erosion. They were also important sources of firewood for cooking. Why not encourage farmers in Kenya to plant as many trees as possible? This would be a simple way to improve the farmers' living conditions. And this method wouldn't require expensive tools or large sums of money.

In 1977, Maathai founded the Green Belt Movement. A greenbelt is a band of farmland or parks surrounding a village. Maathai hoped to see belts of green trees again throughout Kenya. The goals of the Green Belt Movement were to encourage Kenyan farmers to plant trees and to conserve the environment. This, in turn, would help farmers, and women in particular, to improve their living conditions.

---

scholarship, money given to help pay for a person's education
luxuriant, healthy, thick, and strong
excessive, much more than reasonable or necessary

self-sufficient, able to provide for themselves
erosion, destruction and wearing away because of wind and rain

BEFORE YOU GO ON

1. Where in Kenya did Wangari Maathai grow up?
2. What did Maathai study in college?

On Your Own
Have you ever thought of a simple solution to a big problem? Explain.

At first, her idea wasn't very popular. As Maathai said, "It took me a lot of days and nights to convince people that women could improve their environment without much technology or . . . financial resources." Although it took a long time, the movement achieved its goal. Within thirty years, the women of Kenya had planted 30 million trees. The Green Belt Movement did other things to improve the quality of Kenyan life. Members also promoted better education and nutrition throughout the country.

When Maathai started her campaign to plant trees, she was working at the grass-roots level. This means that she worked directly with the local people. Sometimes, she also worked directly with the government to bring about change. For example, in the 1980s, Kenyan President Daniel arap Moi planned to build a sixty-two-story skyscraper. This plan would have destroyed Uhuru Park, a beautiful park in Nairobi, the nation's capital. Maathai had visited Uhuru Park many times. It was one of the only green spaces available in the city for public use. Families often went there on weekends to relax, play, and enjoy time together. To save this precious green space, she led protests against the government. President Moi called her "a threat to the order and security of the country." Maathai was arrested by the police and treated badly, but she never gave up the fight. Because of her courage and persistence, she eventually succeeded in preserving the park.

Wangari Maathai strongly believes that solutions to most of the world's problems will come from the people themselves. She is now a national hero in Kenya. If young Kenyan girls are strong-willed and outspoken, people say they are "like Wangari." "Like Wangari" has become an expression of admiration and affection.

Today, Wangari Maathai and the members of the Green Belt Movement continue to plant trees throughout many countries in Africa, as well as in Haiti and the United States. They have educated thousands of people along the way. As the Nobel committee said, "Maathai is a strong voice speaking for the best forces in Africa to promote peace and good living conditions on the continent. She thinks globally and acts locally."

---

financial resources, money or access to money
skyscraper, very tall building
precious, valuable and important

persistence, determination
strong-willed, determined to achieve goals
outspoken, expressing opinions honestly and directly
admiration, approval and respect

▼ Uhuru Park

How to Plant a Tree

What You Need

- Something to dig with, like a shovel or spade.
- A tree! You can buy a tree at a garden center. In some places, state or community foresters have trees that they'll give to anyone who wants to plant them. When you buy your tree, you'll notice that all of its roots are wrapped up with fabric in a little ball. This is called the rootball.
- A watering can and some water.

What to Do

1. First, choose a site. Pick a place that gets enough sun, where your tree will be happy. Don't plant close to power or telephone wires.
2. Dig a hole as deep as the rootball and three times as wide.
3. Unwrap the rootball and spread out the roots. If they're tangled up, straighten them out.
4. Put the tree in the hole. The soil should come up as high on the tree as it was before you got it. Usually this will be to the top of the rootball. Be sure that the tree is straight.
5. Fill in the space around the rootball gently but firmly with soil. Pack down the soil with your hands and feet. Be sure that there are no air pockets.
6. Make a little dam around the base of the tree about as wide as the hole. This will keep the water close to the tree.
7. After it's planted, your tree will be very thirsty, so give it lots of water.
8. If you need more help, call your local garden store or contact a community park or forest agency.

Some Tips to Keep in Mind

- If you want to plant your tree in a park or other public place, make sure you ask for permission. Some places may have rules about what kind of trees can be planted there.
- Your tree is just a baby, and like any baby, you need to take care of it. You should water it every week. Most trees need 7.5 to 11 liters (2–3 gal.) of water per week.

BEFORE YOU GO ON

1. What did the Green Belt Movement promote besides planting trees?
2. What park did Maathai help to save in Kenya?

On Your Own
What do you think of Wangari Maathai? How did she show courage and imagination?

READING 4

Review and Practice

COMPREHENSION

Right There

1. What was the first step Wangari Maathai took to change the world?
2. What are the goals of the Green Belt Movement?

Think and Search

3. What education did Maathai receive? What degrees did she earn?
4. What concerns did the women farmers of Kenya have?

Author and You

5. How did Wangari's childhood affect the way she thought when she was growing up?
6. Why did the Nobel committee award her the peace prize?

On Your Own

7. Suppose that you could award the Nobel Prize. To whom would you give the prize and why?
8. Why are city parks important to people who live near them?

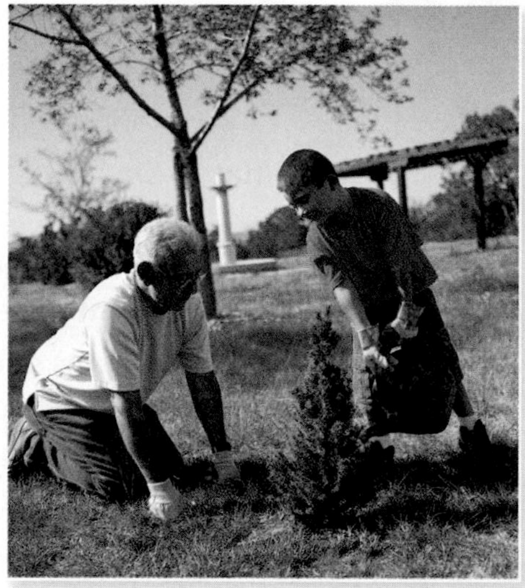

IN YOUR OWN WORDS

Imagine that you are telling a small group of friends about this biographical article. Tell your friends three facts about Maathai's life and work. Use the chart below to help you list your facts and write a brief summary of the article's main points. Then share your summary with a classmate. Compare and contrast your summaries.

Speaking TIP

Communicate your interest in what you are saying so that your partner will be interested, too.

A Tree Grows in Kenya: The Story of Wangari Maathai
Fact 1:
Fact 2:
Fact 3:
Overall summary:

DISCUSSION

Discuss in pairs or small groups.

1. In what ways is Wangari Maathai an admirable person?
2. Maathai spent time living and studying in the United States. How do you think this affected her life and her goals?
3. A Nobel Prize winner receives more than $1 million. How would you have advised Maathai to spend the money?

Q **How are courage and imagination linked?** What is the meaning of the saying, "A journey of a thousand miles begins with a single step"? What role does courage play in that journey? What role does imagination play?

Listening TIP

Listen for supporting details and reasons. Ask yourself, "Did the speaker explain why these ideas are important?"

▲ Elie Wiesel

READ FOR FLUENCY

When we read aloud to communicate meaning, we group words into phrases, pause or slow down to make important points, and emphasize important words. Pause for a short time when you reach a comma and for a longer time when you reach a period. Pay attention to rising and falling intonation at the end of sentences.

Work with a partner. Choose a paragraph from the reading. Discuss which words seem important for communicating meaning. Practice pronouncing difficult words. Give each other feedback.

▲ Nelson Mandela

EXTENSION

Learn more about other Nobel Peace Prize winners. Choose one recent winner and report on his or her life and accomplishments. Here are some Nobel winners to choose from: Muhammad Yunus, Shirin Ebadi, Kim Dae Jung, Jody Williams, Nelson Mandela, F. W. de Klerk, Aung San Suu Kyi, and Elie Wiesel. Use encyclopedias, reference books, and reliable websites. Copy and complete the following diagram to organize your ideas. Report your findings to the class.

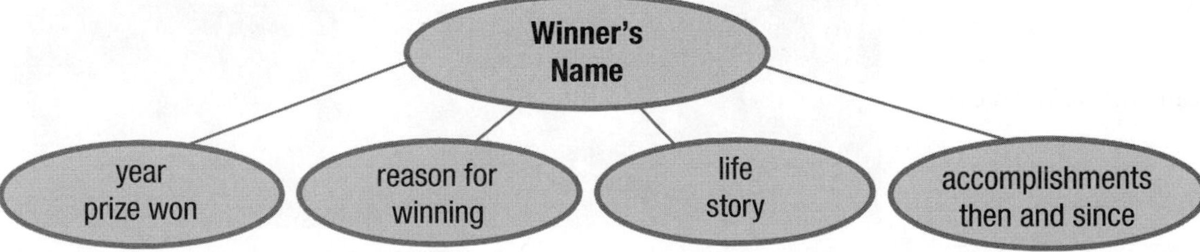

Grammar and Writing

GRAMMAR, USAGE, AND MECHANICS

Imperatives

An imperative is the form of a verb used for giving instructions. An imperative sentence ends with a period or an exclamation mark.

Use imperatives to make your how-to instructions direct and clear. Study these examples from "How to Plant a Tree."

> **Dig** a hole as deep as the rootball.
> **Pack** down the soil with your hands and feet.
> **Put** the tree in the hole.

Practice

Work with a partner. Copy the sentences into your notebook. Rewrite them as imperatives. Do not state the subject.

1. You will pick a place that gets enough sun.
2. You will plant far from any power or telephone lines.
3. You can straighten the roots if they are tangled.
4. You will make sure that the tree is straight.
5. You should be sure that there are no air pockets.
6. You can give the tree lots of water after it is planted.

Notice the beautiful palm trees. ▶

WRITING AN EXPOSITORY PARAGRAPH

Write How-to Instructions

On this page, you will write a paragraph on how to do something step by step. When you wrote a plot summary, you presented events in a chronological sequence. You can organize your "how-to" paragraph in the same way. You can use a graphic organizer like the one at the right to put the steps in a process in a clear order.

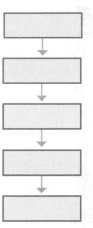

Sometimes you will need to explain how to do something by writing instructions. To make your instructions clear and easy to follow:

- Present the steps in order from first to last.
- Use words that signal time order, such as *first, later,* and *last*.
- Use imperatives to make your instructions clear and direct.

Below is a model of how-to instructions for taking care of a young tree. Notice how the student has put the steps in chronological order and used time-order words and imperatives.

Danielle Christian

Caring for a Newly Planted Tree

After planting a new tree, the first thing you need to do is water it. Water the tree where the roots are located, just under the tree. Make sure that you widen the watering area as the tree grows. It is better to give regular deep soakings rather than water the tree lightly every day. Never water too little or too much! Next, make sure you place mulch, or decaying leaves, around the tree. Do not put a protective covering around the tree; that will prevent water and air from reaching the roots. Don't fertilize the tree unless it is lacking in nutrients. Finally, keep checking the tree to make sure that it is healthy and growing well. Check for any diseases or insects that might hurt the tree. If you think there are any problems, call a professional to come and check the tree out immediately.

Practice

Workbook
Page 156

Give step-by-step instructions that explain how to do something, such as how to build a tree house or create a family recipe book. List your ideas in a steps-in-a-process chart. Be sure to use imperatives to make your instructions easy to follow.

Writing Checklist

ORGANIZATION:

☑ I organized my instructions in chronological order.

SENTENCE FLUENCY:

☑ I used imperatives to make each step clear.

Link the Readings

Critical Thinking

Look back at the readings in this unit. Think about what they all have in common. They all have something to do with courage and imagination. Yet they do not all have the same purpose. The purpose of one reading might be to inform, while the purpose of another might be to entertain or persuade. In addition, the content of each reading relates to courage and imagination in different ways. Now copy the chart below into your notebook and complete it.

Title of Reading	Purpose	Big Question Link
From *The Secret Garden*	*to entertain*	
"Kids' Guernica"		
From *Hoot*		
"A Tree Grows in Kenya"	*to inform*	*tells the story of an environmentalist who won the Nobel Peace Prize*
"How to Plant a Tree"		

Discussion

Discuss in pairs or small groups.

- What conclusion can you draw about the imagination and courage of the people and characters in the readings? Do the real people and fictional characters share certain traits? Explain.

Q How are courage and imagination linked? Think about the readings. In what ways do you think courage and imagination are linked? How do the people and situations in the readings demonstrate the link between the two traits?

Fluency Check

Work with a partner. Choose a paragraph from one of the readings. Take turns reading it for one minute. Count the total number of words you read. Practice saying the words you had trouble reading. Take turns reading the paragraph three more times. Did you read more words each time? Copy the chart below into your notebook and record your speeds.

	1st Speed	2nd Speed	3rd Speed	4th Speed
Words Per Minute				

Projects

Work in pairs or small groups. Choose one of these projects.

1 Mary Lennox in *The Secret Garden* was born and raised in India. When her parents die, she moves to England. Create a poster showing all the countries controlled by Great Britain in the early 1900s when the story was written.

2 "A Tree Grows in Kenya: The Story of Wangari Maathai" is about the country of Kenya. Find out more about this country's history. Make a fact file about Kenya with interesting facts about the country. Share your file with a partner.

3 Create a painting or other artwork that could be part of the Kids' Guernica project. Display your art in the classroom. Tell your classmates how your artwork stands for peace.

4 You read only one chapter of *Hoot*. What do you think happens at the end of the novel? Write a plot summary of the ending. Then read the book to see if your prediction is correct.

5 You learned how to plant a tree. Now, grow some seeds. Save the seeds from the fruits you eat, such as apples and avocados. Plant different kinds of seeds in different containers. Write down when each type of seed starts to grow and how fast it grows.

Further Reading

To find out more about the theme of this unit, choose from these reading suggestions.

The Gift of the Magi and Other Stories, O. Henry
This Penguin Reader® adaptation includes the classic story of a poor couple who use their imaginations to buy each other a special holiday gift.

The Lotus Seed, Sherry Garland
Fleeing her war-torn country, a Vietnamese girl takes a lotus seed to remind her of her homeland. Later, when her grandson plants the seed, a pink lotus blossom grows.

Flash, Carl Hiaasen
This book, by the author of *Hoot*, also tackles environmental issues with a touch of humor.

Put It All Together

LISTENING & SPEAKING WORKSHOP

How-To Demonstration

With a group, you will tell and show the class how to do something.

1 THINK ABOUT IT Reread "A Tree Grows in Kenya: The Story of Wangari Maathai" and "How to Plant a Tree."

In small groups, discuss how Wangari Maathai helped the environment and the people of Kenya. Review the steps involved in planting a tree. Practice listing the steps you follow to perform another simple activity, such as making a sandwich or brushing your teeth.

Work together to develop a list of ideas for a how-to demonstration. Think of interesting activities your group could show the class, using props or pictures. For example:

- How to play the flute
- How to make an origami flower
- How to build a birdhouse
- How to wash a car

2 GATHER AND ORGANIZE INFORMATION As a group, choose a topic from your list. Write down what you already know about how to do the activity. Try to write step-by-step instructions. Also write down any questions you have.

Research Go to the library, search the Internet, or ask an adult for more information about how to perform the activity. Look for answers to your questions. Take notes on what you find.

Order Your Notes Organize your notes, using a sequence-of-events chart to show the order of the steps in your activity. Decide which step(s) each group member will present. Assign one person to give a short introduction that tells what activity your group will demonstrate.

Use Visuals Find or make props that you can use to show the key steps in the process that you will demonstrate. You may also want to create posters, models, or other visuals to help you explain the steps.

3 PRACTICE AND PRESENT

Use your sequence-of-events chart as an outline for your how-to demonstration. As a group, practice your demonstration several times. Use your visuals to help explain each step in the activity. When possible, act out the steps with props. Work on making smooth transitions between speakers. If possible, ask a classmate or friend to listen and give your group feedback. Or you can tape-record your presentation and listen for parts that need more work.

Deliver Your How-to Demonstration Speak loudly enough so that everyone in the class can hear you. Make eye contact with people as you speak. Emphasize important points by changing your tone of voice, slowing down, and using actions or visuals to help show your meaning. At the end of the demonstration, give your audience a chance to ask questions.

4 EVALUATE THE PRESENTATION

A good way to improve your speaking and listening skills is to evaluate each presentation you give and hear. When you evaluate yourself, you think about what you did well and what you can do better. Use this checklist to help you judge your group's how-to demonstration and the demonstrations of your classmates.

- ☑ Did the group present each step in the how-to demonstration clearly?
- ☑ Were the steps presented in a logical order?
- ☑ Did the demonstration give you enough information to do the activity on your own?
- ☑ Did the group members use props and other visuals effectively?
- ☑ What suggestions do you have for improving the demonstration?

Speaking TIPS

Make note cards to remind yourself of important ideas and details in the step(s) you are presenting. Add words or symbols that tell you when to speak and what props or visuals to use.

To show order and to help with transitions, use numbers and time-order words such as *first*, *then*, and *next*.

Listening TIPS

Watch and listen carefully. Give the speakers your full attention.

Think about what you are hearing. Does it make sense? Would you be able to explain the steps to someone else? Write down questions and ask them at the end of the demonstration.

WRITING WORKSHOP

Expository Essay

You have learned that an expository essay gives readers information about a topic. One type of expository essay explains how to solve a problem or how to do an activity. In this type of expository essay, the writer organizes information by using a problem-solution method or by including step-by-step instructions. The writer begins with a paragraph that states the essay's purpose and topic. Body paragraphs develop the topic with facts, details, and examples. This information explains solutions to the problem or instructions for the activity. The essay concludes with a summary of what the writer has explained.

Your assignment for this workshop is to write an expository essay that presents a problem and explains how it was solved.

1 PREWRITE Brainstorm a list of topics for your essay in your notebook. Think about something you accomplished that made you really happy or proud. Maybe it was a problem that took imagination to solve. Maybe it was a problem that took courage and daring to solve. Maybe you discovered a solution that will help readers solve a similar problem in their own lives. Choose a topic that you can write about with enthusiasm.

List and Organize Ideas and Details Use a graphic organizer such as a problem-solution chart to gather ideas and facts for your essay. A student named Danielle wanted to attract more wildlife to her backyard. Here is the problem-solution chart she prepared.

Problem	*Solution*
Wanted to attract more wildlife to my yard	*Figured out what lives in area, like butterflies and hummingbirds* *Found out facts about things they need for food and shelter* *Asked permission to add things like feeders* *Stopped doing things that might scare wildlife away* *Now, see hummingbirds in my yard*

2 DRAFT Use the model on page 327 and your graphic organizer to help you write a first draft. Remember to use time-order words such as *first, then,* and *next* to explain the sequence of events. Time-order words can help readers better understand the steps involved in solving the problem.

3 **REVISE** Read over your draft. As you do so, ask yourself the questions in the writing checklist. Use the questions to help you revise your essay.

SIX TRAITS OF WRITING CHECKLIST

- ✔ **IDEAS:** Do my explanations, details, and examples tell how a problem was solved?
- ✔ **ORGANIZATION:** Do I present information in a logical order?
- ✔ **VOICE:** Does my writing express my personality?
- ✔ **WORD CHOICE:** Do I use words that tell the time order of events?
- ✔ **SENTENCE FLUENCY:** Do I use the imperative correctly?
- ✔ **CONVENTIONS:** Does my writing follow the rules of grammar, usage, and mechanics?

Here are the changes Danielle plans to make when she revises her first draft:

Wildlife Report

Last year, my friend ~~digged~~ [dug] a hole in her backyard to plant a flower. Out of the hole jumped a big toad! When she excited[ly] told me [that a toad lived in her garden], I decided to try to attract more birds and other animals to my yard. I ~~done~~ [did] it and you can do it, too.

[First,] You need to know what appeals to the wildlife in your region. Which birds and animals can be found [nearby?] What food and shelter do they like? [Books and websites can tell you these facts.] Then ask permission to add some of these things to your yard. Once you have permission, you can create a little habitat. [For example,] Hummingbirds visit my area every summer. I learned that they love nectar plants, so I planted a red hibiscus. A hummingbird feeder works, too. Birdbaths provide many birds with water and a place to splash and play. Some creatures are very private, so you can build hiding places for them with piles of dirt brush, or rocks.

There are some other general tips for attracting wildlife. Try not to use chemical pesticides. Don't place nests where barking dogs may scare the birds away. Don't put lots of food in bird feeders all at once. Instead, put in only a small amount of food every day. Predators may come and eat the leftovers.

Finally
You don't need to live in the country to attract wildlife. I have a little backyard in a town. If you don't have a yard, you may be able to volunteer at a neighborhood park or community garden. you may have a window large enough for a bird feeder. Maybe your schoolyard can be turned into a garden! Remember to ask permission.

Right now I'm looking at a yellow butterfly on a green bush. Have you ever wanted to invite wildlife to visit you? If you learn the facts and do some work, you will probably see lots of wildlife!

4 EDIT AND PROOFREAD

Copy your revised essay onto a clean sheet of paper. Read it again. Correct any errors in grammar, word usage, mechanics, and spelling. Here are the additional changes Danielle plans to make when she prepares her final draft.

Danielle Christian

Wildlife Report

Last year, my friend dug a hole in her backyard to plant a flower. Out of the hole jumped a big toad! When she excitedly told me that a toad lived in her garden, I decided to try to attract more birds and other animals to my yard. I did it and you can do it, too.

First, you need to know what appeals to the wildlife in your region. Which birds and animals can be found nearby? What food and shelter do they like? Books and websites can tell you these facts. Then ask permission to add some of these things to your yard. Once you have permission, you can create a little habitat. For example, hummingbirds visit my area every summer. I learned that they love brightly colored nectar plants, so I planted a red hibiscus. A hummingbird feeder works, too. Birdbaths provide many birds with water and a place to splash and play. Some creatures are very private, so you can build hiding places for them with piles of dirt brush, or rocks

There are some other general tips for attracting wildlife. Try not to use chemical pesticides. Don't place nests where barking dogs may scare the birds away. Don't put lots of food in bird feeders all at once. Predators may come and eat the leftovers. Instead, put in only a small amount of food every day.

Finally, you don't need to live in the country to attract wildlife. I have a little backyard in a town. If you don't have a yard, you may be able to volunteer at a neighborhood park or community garden. you may have a window large enough for a bird feeder. Maybe your schoolyard can be turned into a garden! Remember to ask permission.

Right now I'm looking at a yellow butterfly on a green bush. Have you ever wanted to invite wildlife to visit you? If you learn the facts and do some work, you will probably see lots of wildlife!

5 PUBLISH Prepare your final draft. Share your essay with your teacher and classmates.

Learn about Art with the Smithsonian American Art Museum

Dignity Through Art

It takes courage to follow your imagination. You can't worry about what other people think. You have to follow where your imagination takes you. Some artists become famous because they follow their imaginations. They do things that most other people would not think about doing.

James Hampton, *The Throne of the Third Heaven of the Nations' Millennium General Assembly* (about 1950–64)

Gold and silver foil cover every object in James Hampton's *The Throne of the Third Heaven of the Nations' Millennium General Assembly.* When the light hits it, you feel as though you are looking at something from another world. This sculpture once filled an empty garage which became the artist's studio behind his small apartment in Washington, D.C. Art experts believe that Hampton started the piece in 1950 and worked on it for hours nearly every day for fourteen years. When Hampton finished it, the sculpture comprised dozens of parts, including a central unit that rose as high as 4.6 meters (15 ft.) and was 8.2 meters (27 ft.) across. The sculpture contains about 180 separate glittering objects!

Hampton had little money and was not trained as an artist. He could not afford to make a throne out of real gold and silver. But he wanted to celebrate his deep religious beliefs. He worked as a janitor at night. At his job, he picked up objects that he would later turn into parts of his artwork. He collected old lightbulbs, wood furniture, jelly glasses, pieces of a mirror, and many other objects. He carefully wrapped every single object in foil.

A throne that is 2.13 meters (7 ft.) high sits at the center of the sculpture. At the top of the throne, Hampton made a sign with the words FEAR NOT in foil. He added to his religious ideas by making altars and tablets with writings from the Bible. He also included many angels' wings. He made the wings from paper and cardboard covered with foil.

▲ **James Hampton, *The Throne of the Third Heaven of the Nations' Millennium General Assembly*, about 1950–64, mixed media, 10½ x 27 x 14½ ft., Smithsonian American Art Museum**

Hampton's artwork was virtually unknown until shortly after his death. However, he left behind a lot of his own writing in journals. He wrote in a code that only he understood, so no one knows what it says. Perhaps it's best that his feelings are kept private.

Hampton had the courage to follow his own artistic ideas, even though he was poor and had few resources to work with.

Apply What You Learned

1. Why did James Hampton use found objects to make his artwork?
2. Why do you think that James Hampton used a secret code in his journals?

Big Question
How did James Hampton show courage, imagination, and dignity through his artwork?

Workbook
Pages 159–160

UNIT 6

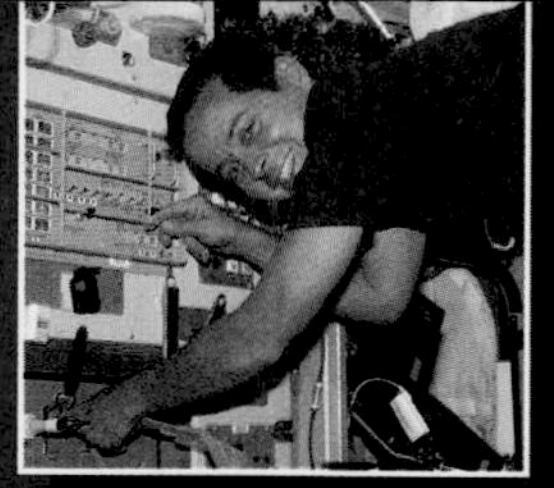

THE BIG QUESTION

What is your vision of life in the future?

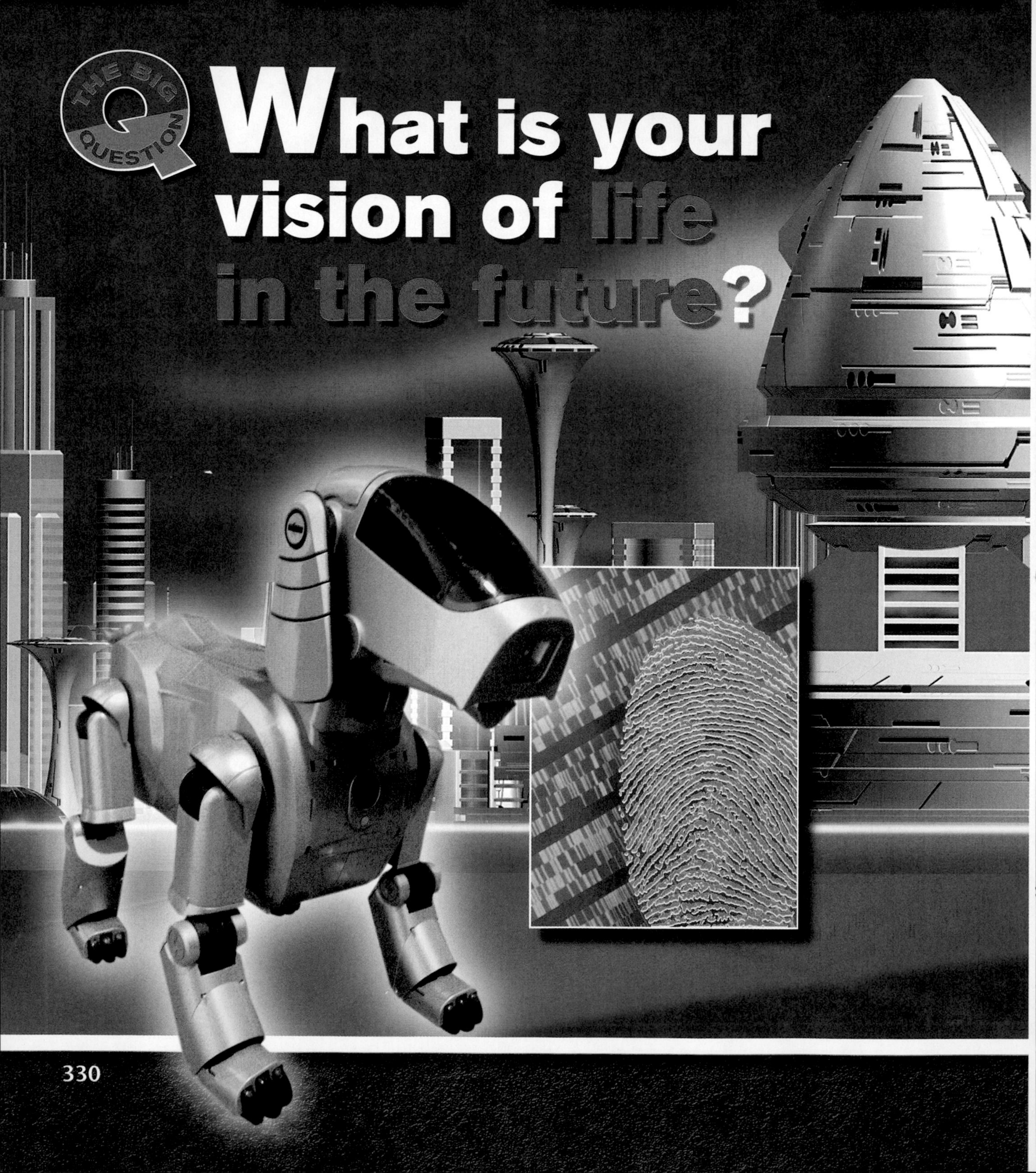

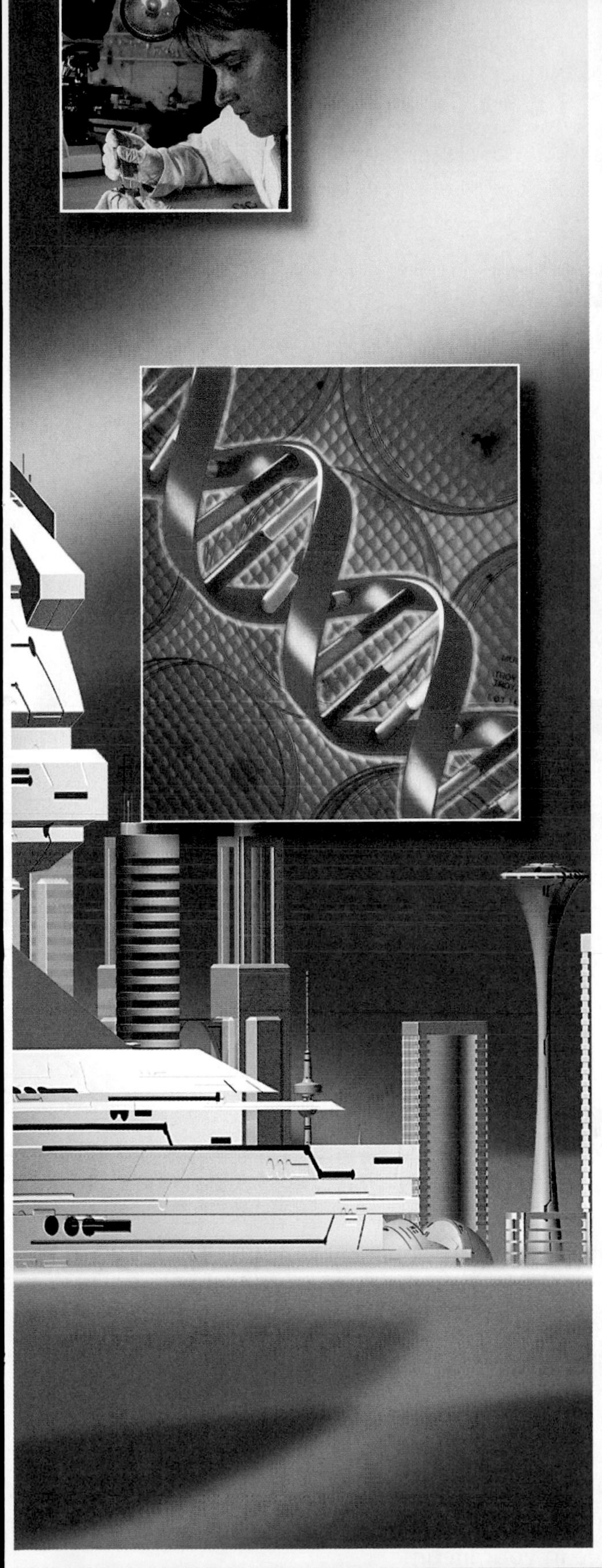

This unit is about life in the future. You will explore life in the years to come. You will read about how Earth and space look to an astronaut and how Earth might look to a visitor. You will read about a group of friends who travel to the year 2095 and about scientists who are unlocking the secrets of DNA. As you read, you will practice the literary and academic language you need to use in school.

READING 1: Social Studies Article

- "Life in the Future"

READING 2: Poetry and Interview

- "Southbound on the Freeway" and "Cardinal Ideograms" by May Swenson
- "Interview with an Astronaut: Dan Bursch"

READING 3: Novel Excerpt

- From *The Time Warp Trio: 2095* by Jon Scieszka

READING 4: Science Article

- "Genetic Fingerprints"

Listening and Speaking

At the end of this unit, you will give a **speech** on life in the future.

Writing

In this unit you will practice writing parts of a **research report** (a special kind of expository writing). You will choose a topic, do research, and write about it. At the end of the unit, you will develop one of your topics into a research report.

QuickWrite

Write several sentences about a prediction you made in the past.

READING 1

Prepare to Read

What You Will Learn

Reading

- Vocabulary building: *Context, dictionary skills, word study*
- Reading strategy: *Take notes*
- Text type: *Informational text (social studies)*

Grammar, Usage, and Mechanics
Different ways of expressing predictions

Writing
Write an introductory paragraph

THE BIG QUESTION

What is your vision of life in the future? What will our world be like one hundred years from now? What will travel, home life, medicine, and technology be like? Work in small groups. Study the picture below. Then create a word web with your ideas about life in the future. Share your ideas with other groups. Find out what your classmates think.

▲ *Exploration of Mars* by Chesley Bonestell

BUILD BACKGROUND

"Life in the Future" is a nonfiction article that explores what life might be like ten, twenty, thirty, or more years from now. The article uses facts to describe inventions and advances that people are developing for the future. People have always tried to predict what will happen in the future. We sometimes call people who try to predict what will happen in years to come "futurists." In Italy, there was a futurist movement in the early 1900s. It inspired new forms of art, architecture, and writing. In the United States, organizations were formed to "think about" the future during the 1940s. As you read the selection, think about why people are fascinated by a time that hasn't come yet. Think also about the inventions you would like to see in your lifetime.

▲ A futurist sculpture by Umberto Boccioni

VOCABULARY

Learn Key Words

Read the sentences. Use the context to figure out the meaning of the **red** words. Use a dictionary to check your answers. Then write each word and its meaning in your notebook.

Key Words

artificial
canyons
frontier
mass-produced
robots
volcanoes

1. In the future, doctors will use more **artificial** body parts to replace real body parts.
2. The airplane flew into the deep **canyons**. The pilot had to steer away from the steep cliffs surrounding the plane.
3. Space is called a **frontier** because it is far away from Earth. We have explored Earth but we are just beginning to explore space.
4. Now many cars at a time are made in factories. They are **mass-produced**. The first cars were produced one at a time.
5. In the future, dangerous work will be done by machines called **robots**.
6. Scientists study active **volcanoes** and watch as they send out red-hot lava.

▲ Mount Etna is an active volcano in Sicily.

Practice

Write the sentences in your notebook. Choose a **red** word from the box above to complete each sentence. Then take turns reading the sentences aloud with a partner.

1. The power of the erupting _______ surprised the movie audience.
2. In the United States in the 1800s, the area beyond the Appalachian Mountains was called the _______.
3. Car parts are _______ at factories.
4. Some people would like to have _______ do their housework.
5. Real plants need sunshine and water, but _______ plants do not.
6. The planet Mars has many deep _______ with steep rocky cliffs.

Learn Academic Words

Study the **red** words and their meanings. You will find these words useful when talking and writing about informational texts. Write each word and its meaning in your notebook. After you read "Life in the Future," try to use these words to respond to the text.

Academic Words

function
occupation
research
trend

function = the usual purpose of a thing, or the job that someone usually does	➡	The **function** of a brake is to stop a car. That's the brake's purpose.
occupation = job or profession	➡	An astronaut's **occupation** is exploring space.
research = serious study of a subject that is intended to discover new facts about it	➡	Scientists do **research** to predict the future. They study many books to gather information.
trend = the way a situation is generally developing or changing	➡	The **trend** is toward smaller cars. People want cars that use less gas.

Practice

Work with a partner to answer the questions. Try to include the **red** word in your answer. Write the sentences in your notebook.

1. What is a computer's **function** now? What might its purpose be in the future?
2. What **occupation** would you like to have twenty years from now? Why?
3. How would you **research** a topic like future inventions? What sources would you use to find factual information?
4. What **trend** do you predict for schools in the future? Would this be a good development or not?

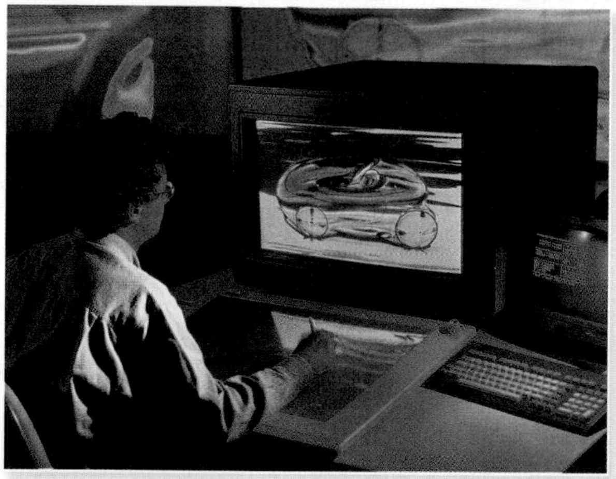

▲ Using computers to design cars is the current trend in the automotive world.

Word Study: Spelling the Diphthongs /oi/ and /ou/

Some English words, such as *boil* and *round* contain two vowel sounds that are said quickly so that the sounds glide into one another. Together the two sounds form a vowel sound called a diphthong. In the word *boil*, the letters *oi* stand for the diphthong /oi/. In the word *round*, the letters *ou* stand for the diphthong /ou/.

Below are some examples of words with the diphthongs /oi/ and /ou/. As you read each word, say it aloud. Listen to how the two vowel sounds glide into one another in one syllable.

/oi/ as in *coin*	/oi/ as in *boy*	/ou/ as in *ground*	/ou/ as in *how*
b**oi**l	j**oy**	f**ou**nd	n**ow**
v**oi**ce	enj**oy**	sh**ou**t	d**ow**n
p**oi**nts	t**oy**	**ou**r	d**ow**nstage

Practice

Work with a partner. Copy the chart above into your notebook. Say a word from the chart, and ask your partner to spell it aloud. Then have your partner say the next word. Continue until you can spell all of the words correctly. Now work with your partner to spell these words: *house, soil, destroy, mountain, royal, cow, noise, how, loyal, toil, brown, sound.* Add them to the chart under the correct headings.

Reading Strategy | TAKE NOTES

Taking notes keeps you focused on what you are reading, and it helps you organize and remember new information. Notes are also a useful tool to refer back to when answering questions about a reading selection. To take notes, follow these steps:

- In your notebook, make two columns, one for main ideas and one for details.
- Think about your purpose for reading the text.
- Look for key dates, names, places, and events.
- Write short notes about the most important facts and details you may need to know.

As you read "Life in the Future," think about the information you want to remember. Take notes while you read. Review your notes and check that they are correct.

INFORMATIONAL TEXT

SOCIAL STUDIES

Set a purpose for reading What will cities, travel, medicine, and other aspects of life be like in the future? As you read, contrast the writer's vision of the future with your own. Do you think that the writer's description of the future is accurate? Why?

Life in the Future

Imagine traveling in a time machine into the future. What do you think life will be like? This timeline shows some predictions about the future.

A robot ▶

▲ A robotic dog

◀ An artificial leg

▼ A robotic bug

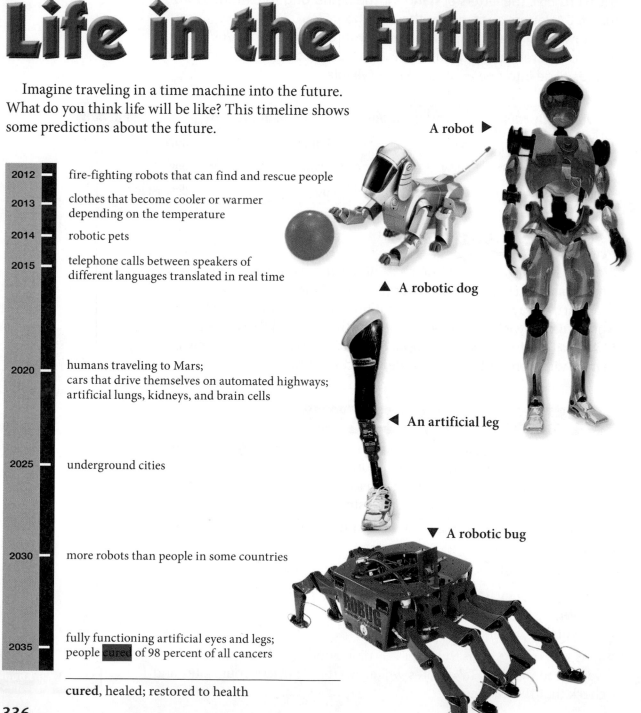

2012	fire-fighting robots that can find and rescue people
2013	clothes that become cooler or warmer depending on the temperature
2014	robotic pets
2015	telephone calls between speakers of different languages translated in real time
2020	humans traveling to Mars; cars that drive themselves on automated highways; artificial lungs, kidneys, and brain cells
2025	underground cities
2030	more robots than people in some countries
2035	fully functioning artificial eyes and legs; people **cured** of 98 percent of all cancers

cured, healed; restored to health

The Growing World

The world's population is growing very fast. In 1800, the population was about 1 billion. Now it is over 6.5 billion. One reason for this fast growth is that the birthrate is higher than the death rate. That is, there are more people being born than there are people dying. Also, medical advances and better living conditions help people live longer. Scientists predict that in the year 2100, the population will be 11 billion.

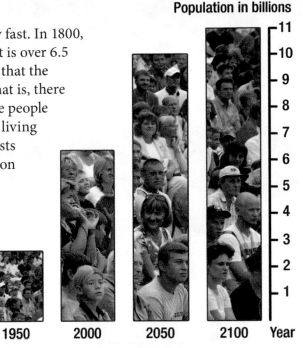

▲ A bar graph showing world population growth

Future Cities

As the population grows, it will be necessary to rebuild existing cities and build new ones. Some apartment buildings will be like small cities. Architects have created a model for an apartment building in Tokyo. It will be 840 meters (2,750 ft.) high and will have 180 floors. A population of 60,000 will be able to live there. High-speed elevators will carry sixty people at a time. The building will have stores, restaurants, and cinemas. People won't ever have to leave!

elevators, machines in a building that carry people from one floor to another

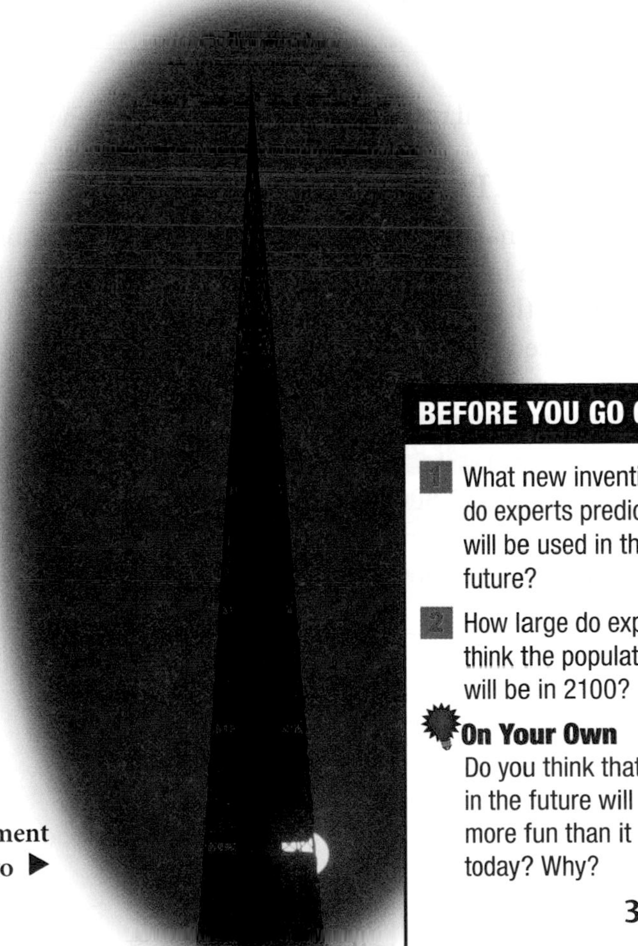

A model for an apartment building in Tokyo ▶

BEFORE YOU GO ON

1. What new inventions do experts predict will be used in the future?
2. How large do experts think the population will be in 2100?

On Your Own
Do you think that life in the future will be more fun than it is today? Why?

Learn Academic Words

Study the **red** words and their meanings. You will find these words useful when talking and writing about literature. Write each word and its meaning in your notebook. After you read "Southbound on the Freeway," "Cardinal Ideograms," and "Interview with an Astronaut: Dan Bursch," try to use these words to respond to the text.

Academic Words

complex
interpretation
published
section

complex = complicated	➡	A computer is a **complex** tool because it is made of many parts. A wrench is a simple tool.
interpretation = an explanation	➡	Everyone had a different **interpretation** of the poem. Each of us had a different reaction to the poet's metaphors.
published = printed and sold	➡	A new book of poems was **published**. The poet was happy to see her poems in print in the bookstore.
section = a part of something	➡	I looked in the nonfiction **section** of the library for a book about our space program.

Practice

Work with a partner to answer the questions. Try to include the **red** word in your answer. Write the sentences in your notebook.

1. What kind of **complex** cars do you think you will see in the future?
2. Why might your **interpretation** of a poem be different from your friend's ideas?
3. What subject would you write about if you could have a book **published**?
4. In what **section** might a bookstore put up this sign: *Ages 3 to 5*?

▲ A wrench is a simple tool.

A race car is a complex machine. ▶

Word Study: Greek and Latin Roots

▲ A unicycle

As you have learned, many English words come from Greek and Latin word parts called roots. Sometimes knowing the meaning of a root word can help you figure out the meaning of a new word. Knowing the meaning of a prefix can help, too.

Take, for example, the word *cycle*. It contains the root *cycl*, meaning "round." What happens when you add the following prefixes to *cycle*?

The prefix *uni-* means one.	A unicycle has **one** round wheel.
The prefix *bi-* means two.	A bicycle has **two** round wheels.
The prefix *tri-* means three.	A tricycle has **three** round wheels.

Practice

Work with a partner. Copy the chart below into your notebook. Talk about meanings of the word parts, and discuss what the new word means. Use a dictionary to check the meanings. List other words you know of that contain the roots *spec* and *verse* in your notebook. Add them to the chart.

Prefix	+ Root	= New Word
re- ("again")	spec ("see")	respect
uni- ("one")	verse ("turn")	universe

Reading Strategy | ANALYZE TEXT STRUCTURE 2

Analyzing text structure can help you identify what kind of text you're reading. Poems and interviews each have a special text structure.

To analyze the text structure of a poem, follow these steps:

- Look for rhyming patterns and stanzas.
- Look for punctuation that shows you where to pause, such as commas, periods, dashes, or line breaks.

To analyze the text structure of an interview, follow these steps:

- Find speakers' names; they will be bold and followed by a colon (:).
- Look for name changes that signal different speakers.

Preview the text structures of the poems and interview. Discuss them with a partner.

READING 2

LITERATURE

POETRY AND INTERVIEW

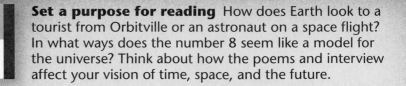

Set a purpose for reading How does Earth look to a tourist from Orbitville or an astronaut on a space flight? In what ways does the number 8 seem like a model for the universe? Think about how the poems and interview affect your vision of time, space, and the future.

Southbound on the Freeway

May Swenson

A tourist came in from Orbitville,
parked in the air, and said:

The creatures of this star
are made of metal and glass.

Through the transparent parts
you can see their guts.

Their feet are round and roll
on diagrams—or long

measuring tapes—dark
with white lines.

They have four eyes.
The two in the back are red.

---

transparent, clear and easy to see through

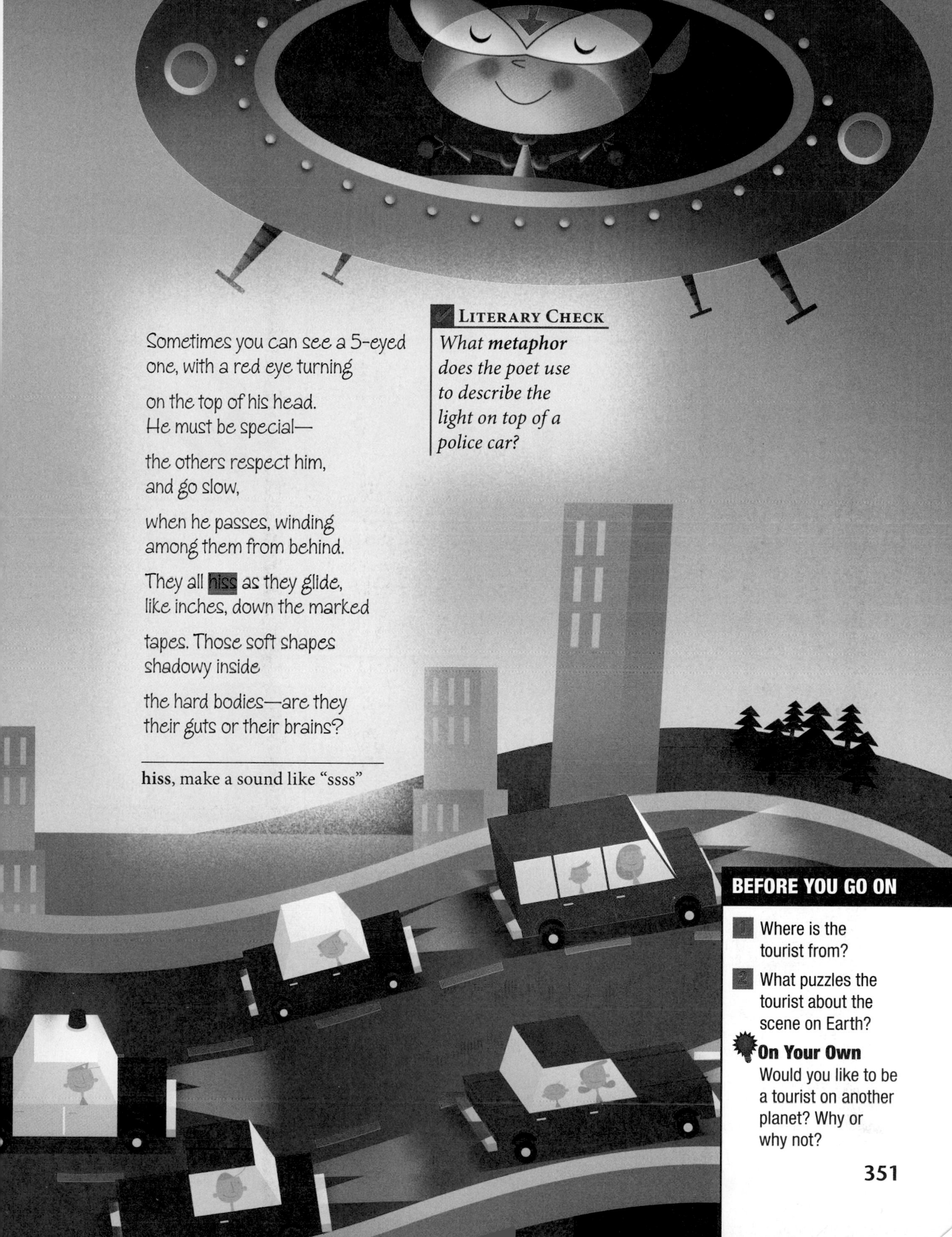

Sometimes you can see a 5-eyed
one, with a red eye turning

on the top of his head.
He must be special—

the others respect him,
and go slow,

when he passes, winding
among them from behind.

They all **hiss** as they glide,
like inches, down the marked

tapes. Those soft shapes
shadowy inside

the hard bodies—are they
their guts or their brains?

---

hiss, make a sound like "ssss"

LITERARY CHECK

*What **metaphor** does the poet use to describe the light on top of a police car?*

BEFORE YOU GO ON

1. Where is the tourist from?
2. What puzzles the tourist about the scene on Earth?

On Your Own
Would you like to be a tourist on another planet? Why or why not?

Cardinal Ideograms*

May Swenson

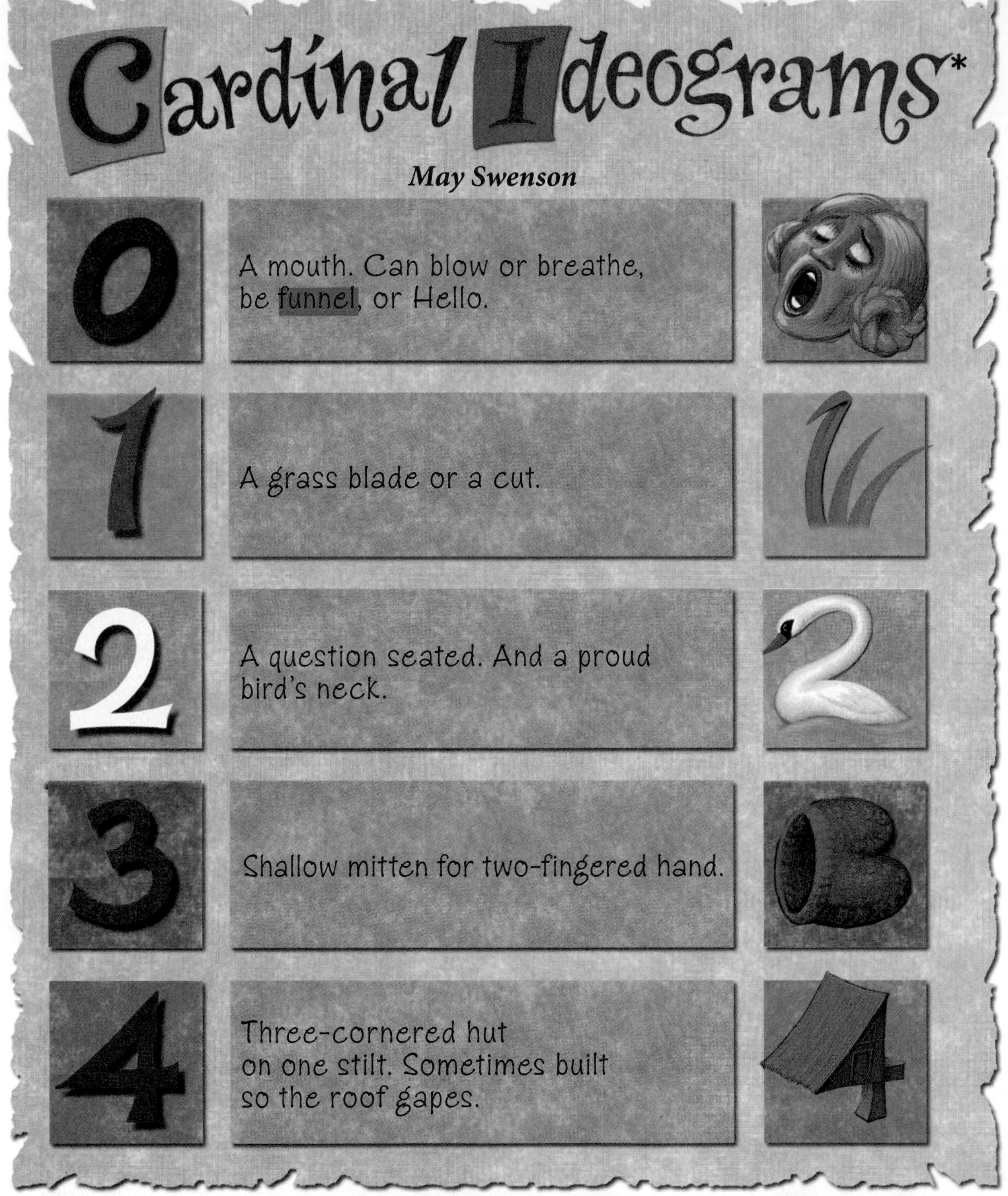

0 A mouth. Can blow or breathe,
be funnel, or Hello.

1 A grass blade or a cut.

2 A question seated. And a proud
bird's neck.

3 Shallow mitten for two-fingered hand.

4 Three-cornered hut
on one stilt. Sometimes built
so the roof gapes.

funnel, a tube with a wide top used for pouring things

* This excerpt from "Cardinal Ideograms" contains eight of the ten stanzas from the original poem. Cardinal numbers are any of the numbers 0, 1, 2, 3, and so on. Ideograms are written signs that stand for an idea or thing.

5

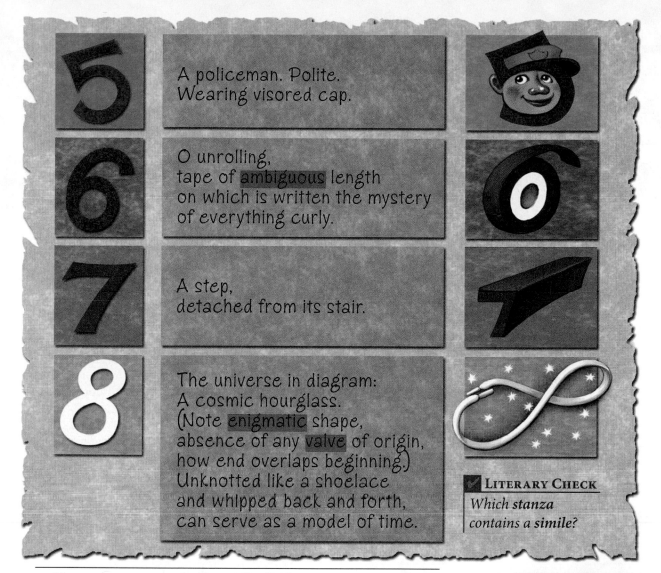

A policeman. Polite.
Wearing visored cap.

6

O unrolling,
tape of ambiguous length
on which is written the mystery
of everything curly.

7

A step,
detached from its stair.

8

The universe in diagram:
A cosmic hourglass.
(Note enigmatic shape,
absence of any valve of origin,
how end overlaps beginning.)
Unknotted like a shoelace
and whipped back and forth,
can serve as a model of time.

LITERARY CHECK
Which stanza contains a simile?

---

ambiguous, uncertain or hard to understand
enigmatic, mysterious and hard to explain
valve, part of a pipe that opens and closes to control the flow of liquid, air, or gas passing through it

ABOUT THE POET

May Swenson (1913–1989) was born in Utah. She came from a very large family and was the oldest of ten children. English was her second language; Swedish was spoken at home. She attended Utah State University and later taught poetry there. Swenson also worked as an editor and was the Chancellor of the Academy of American Poets. Her poetry won many awards, including the Bollingen Prize and the Shelley Memorial Award.

BEFORE YOU GO ON

1. What does the poem compare the cardinal number 3 to?
2. What reasons does the poem give for calling the cardinal number 8 enigmatic, or mysterious?

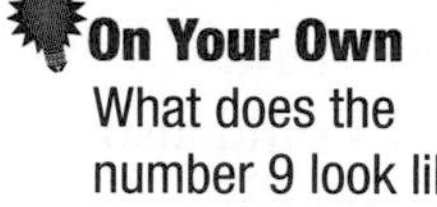

On Your Own
What does the number 9 look like to you? Create your own cardinal ideogram.

▲ The International Space Station

Interview with an Astronaut: Dan Bursch

Dan Bursch has made three space flights and has been in space for 746 hours. He lived on the International Space Station from December 5, 2001, until June 19, 2002. Before this expedition, he ***chatted*** *online with some students on www.discovery.com.*

Dan Bursch: I would just like to say welcome to everyone tonight. Thank you for spending your Sunday evening with me. . . .

Cody: I am ten years old, and I would like to know what the food is like. I would also like for you to trade me just one day in the space station and you can go to my school.

---

chatted, talked informally

▲ Astronaut Dan Bursch works in the weightless environment of space.

Dan Bursch: Food is very important for us up in space, as it is here on Earth. In fact, one of the things that I will be starting tomorrow . . . is food tasting. We are selecting our menu for the four- to six-month flight that I will have in space. What is different about my next mission on the space station is that we will have a mixture of American and Russian food, so that will certainly make it different. . . . Perhaps I can come to your school someday and perhaps in fifteen years or so you can go to space!

Gary TX: What kind of work do you do when you are at the space station?

Dan Bursch: We have a crew of three—myself, Carl Walz (another American astronaut), and Yuri. He is a Russian cosmonaut. He will be our commander. We divide up the work because there is a lot of work to be done. . . .

selecting, choosing
cosmonaut, Russian astronaut
commander, leader

BEFORE YOU GO ON

1. Who are the people interviewing Dan Bursch?
2. What is different about the menu on this trip?

On Your Own
Would you like to spend a day on the space station? Why or why not?

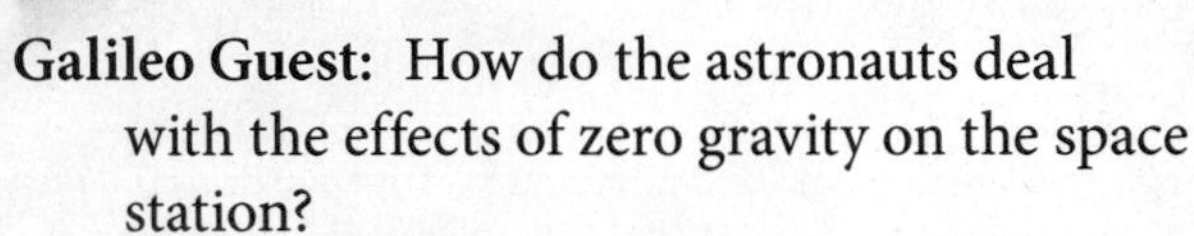

Galileo Guest: How do the astronauts deal with the effects of zero gravity on the space station?

Dan Bursch: Learning to work in space without feeling gravity is always a challenge. . . . Getting used to not feeling gravity usually takes a day or two.

International: What is it like working with scientists and other astronauts from all around the world? Do you all get along? Do you have fun?

▲ **The space shuttle *Discovery* blasts off into space.**

Dan Bursch: This job is particularly interesting just because of that fact. . . . In the astronaut office, the range of different kinds of people is pretty wide. . . . But we all share one common goal, and that is to fly and live and work in space. . . .

Hollifeld: Can you see the lights of the world's cities from space?

Dan Bursch: Yes. We spend half of our time while in orbit on the dark side of the planet. If there is a thin cloud layer, you see kind of a glow like from a lampshade that dampens the light a little bit. But when it is clear—when there are no clouds—the lights are spectacular. . . .

Venus: What is the first time you go into space like? Is it hard to learn to use the tools or get used to things floating around?

Dan Bursch: I remember my first flight in 1993 on [the space shuttle]

---

get along, act friendly
in orbit, circling around Earth
spectacular, wonderful and exciting to see
floating around, moving around freely in the air

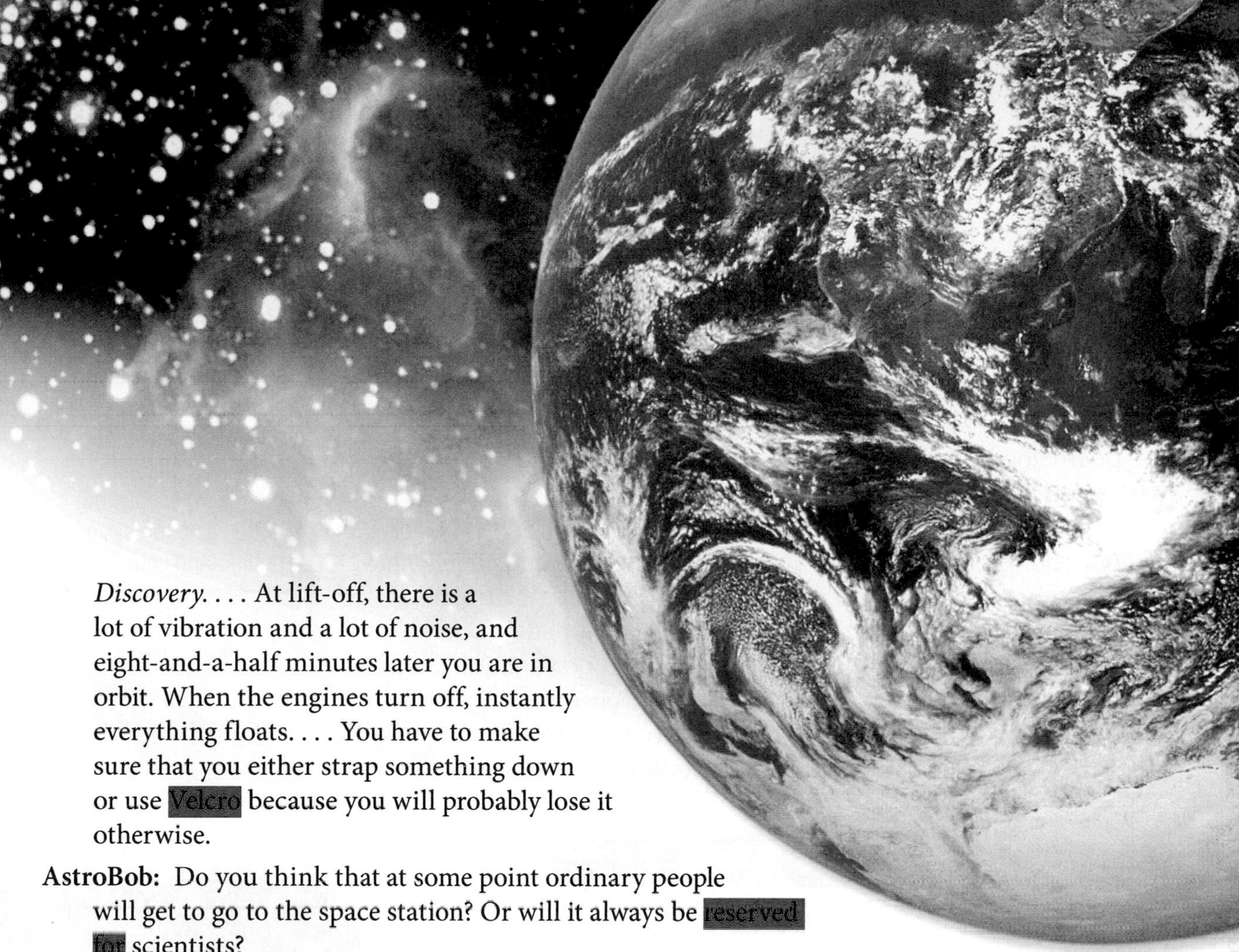

Discovery. . . . At lift-off, there is a lot of vibration and a lot of noise, and eight-and-a-half minutes later you are in orbit. When the engines turn off, instantly everything floats. . . . You have to make sure that you either strap something down or use Velcro because you will probably lose it otherwise.

AstroBob: Do you think that at some point ordinary people will get to go to the space station? Or will it always be reserved for scientists?

Dan Bursch: I think that is certainly a goal that we should try to reach. If it will be in my lifetime, I don't know. . . . When airplanes first came out, they were reserved at first for just the very daring or risk takers. And now anybody can fly on an airplane. So, I don't think it is a question of IF the opportunity will come . . . it is simply a matter of WHEN.

Sandy Fay: What kinds of things do they hope the space station will be good for once it is completed?

Dan Bursch: . . . I see the biggest challenge and the biggest thing that we are learning is two former enemies learning how to work together and build such a large and complex structure in space. And not just two former enemies, but all of the over one dozen countries that are working together . . .

Discovery.com: Thank you, Dan, for chatting with us tonight.

Velcro, a material that can stick to itself to fasten things together
reserved for, set aside for
daring, brave

▲ **Planet Earth, as seen from space**

BEFORE YOU GO ON

1. How do astronauts make sure that none of their things float away while in space?
2. For Dan Bursch, what is the biggest challenge of the space station?

On Your Own
What question would you like to ask Dan Bursch about the future?

READING 2

Review and Practice

DRAMATIC READING

One of the best ways to understand a poem is to memorize it, or learn it by heart. Work in groups of six to reread, discuss, and interpret "Southbound on the Freeway." Describe what you visualize as you read the poem line by line. Identify any metaphors, similes, or vivid sensory words you find. Work together to interpret any difficult words or phrasing. Use a dictionary or ask your teacher for help if necessary.

After your group has reread and examined the poem carefully, have each member of your group memorize one or two of the poem's stanzas. Then recite the entire poem, with each student reciting the stanzas that he or she memorized. Comment on one another's oral reading and make helpful suggestions for improvements. Practice reciting the poem with your group. Then hold a "poetry slam" with the whole class in which each group competes for the best oral reading.

Speaking TIP

Face the audience when you say your lines. Speak clearly and loudly. If you turn away from the audience too much, people may not be able to hear or understand you.

COMPREHENSION

Right There

1. Where does the tourist come from in "Southbound on the Freeway"?
2. How long does it take astronaut Dan Bursch to get used to not feeling gravity?

Think and Search

3. What two things does the poet compare to the number 2 in "Cardinal Ideograms"?
4. What does Earth look like from space according to Dan Bursch?

Author and You

5. What does the tourist think the people on Earth look like in "Southbound on the Freeway"? What is the tourist's interpretation of Earth's complex people?
6. Why would it be important for astronauts to cooperate with each other while they are in space?

▲ Astronauts cooperate with each other to repair the International Space Station.

▲ The space shuttle, docked with the International Space Station

On Your Own

7. What do you think the number 8 looks like? Compare the number 8 to different things.
8. What kinds of food would you choose for a six-month journey into space? Explain your reasons.

DISCUSSION

Discuss in pairs or small groups.

1. How are "Southbound on the Freeway" and "Cardinal Ideograms" similar? How are they different?
2. Which of the metaphors in "Cardinal Ideograms" did you think was most interesting or accurate? Why?
3. Dan Bursch talks about the challenges of living on the space station, such as dealing with gravity and working with others. What would be your biggest challenge on the space station? Why?

Q What is your vision of life in the future? Imagine that you are going to the space station at some point in the future. What would you take with you? What do you think you would see?

***Listening* TIP**

Listen to the verbs and adjectives your classmates use when they speak. Try to visualize, or picture in your mind, what each speaker is describing.

RESPONSE TO LITERATURE

If you were a tourist from Orbitville visiting Earth, what aspects of Earth would you find most confusing? What aspects would you find most amazing? Write an e-mail to send to your home planet telling what strange and interesting things you discovered on Earth. When you have finished your e-mail, share it with a classmate.

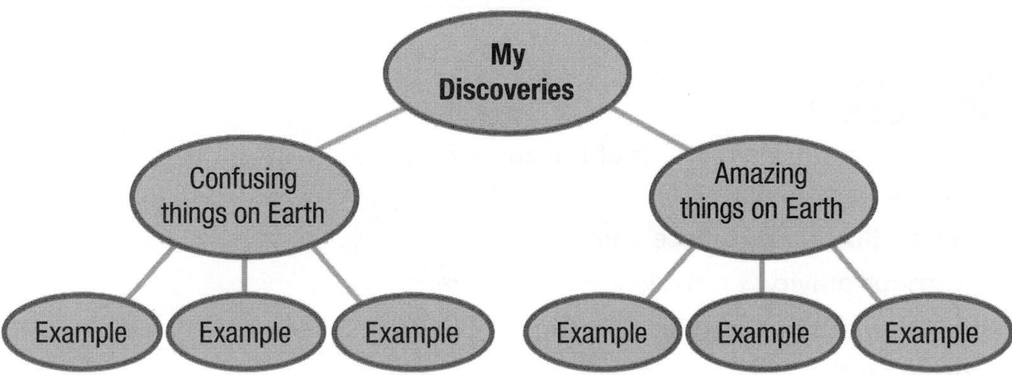

Grammar and Writing

GRAMMAR, USAGE, AND MECHANICS

Different Ways of Asking Questions

In English, there are different ways of asking questions. Knowing the different ways will help you get the information you need. In each case, use the method that best helps you get the facts, details, and opinions that you are looking for. You can ask questions using the 5Ws: *Who? Where? When? What? Why?* You can also ask questions that start with *How?*

- **Who** were the first astronauts?
- **Where** do you want to travel in space?
- **When** did you decide to become an astronaut?
- **What** is it like working with scientists and astronauts from all around the world?
- **Why** is it important that we travel into space?
- **How** long does it take to become an astronaut?

You can also ask *yes/no* questions using the words *can* and *do.*

- **Can** you see the lights of the world's cities from space?
- **Do** you all get along?
- **Do** you have fun?

In addition, you can ask a question in statement form.

- I would like to know if astronaut training is difficult.
- I want to ask you whether you think people will ever live on other planets.

Practice

Work with a partner. Write a question for each of the answers. Try to use different ways of asking questions.

1. The interview with Dan Bursch took place online.
2. Learning to work without gravity is a challenge for astronauts.
3. The lights from the planet look spectacular.
4. Yuri is a Russian cosmonaut.
5. Someday maybe everyone will visit a space station.

WRITING A RESEARCH REPORT

Support a Main Idea with Examples

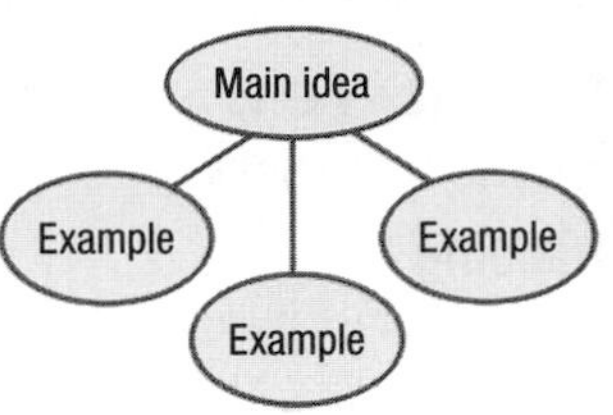

Using examples is often the best way to explain an idea clearly. Examples are bits of information that explain or describe a point. They can include facts, dates, numbers, and descriptions of events. On this page, you will support a main idea with examples, using a graphic organizer like the one at the right.

To find examples, you can do research and take notes. Suppose that your main idea is the following: *Astronauts must go through difficult training before going into space.* In your research, you might find specific examples to support this idea. For example, an astronaut must spend 1,000 hours flying in a jet aircraft and take a class in aircraft safety.

Here is a model of a paragraph that uses examples to support a main idea. Notice the different kinds of examples the writer uses.

Koji Mori

Mars

What do scientists know about the red planet? Mars is the fourth planet from the sun and the seventh largest planet in our solar system. It has two moons, Deimos and Phobos. Temperatures on Mars oan get extremely cold because of the planet's thin atmosphere. The temperature can drop to -133 degrees Celsius (-207 degrees Fahrenheit). Huge dust storms also take place on the planet. Despite the extreme weather, Mars is more like Earth than any other planet in our solar system. In fact, scientists think that there is frozen water at the poles on Mars, especially at the south polar region. There may be enough ice to cover the entire planet.

Practice

Write a paragraph about space missions or astronauts in which your main idea is supported by three short examples. List your ideas in a main idea/examples web. Try to begin your paragraph with an interesting question that is connected to your main idea.

Writing Checklist

IDEAS:

☑ I chose specific examples that explain and support my main idea.

CONVENTIONS:

☑ I corrected all errors in spelling, capitalization, and punctuation.

READING 3

Prepare to Read

What You Will Learn

Reading

- Vocabulary building: *Literary terms, dictionary skills, word study*
- Reading strategy: *Skim*
- Text type: *Literature (novel excerpt)*

Grammar, Usage, and Mechanics
Using punctuation

Writing
Include quotations and citations

THE BIG QUESTION

What is your vision of life in the future? Some people think the future will be wonderful, thanks to machines that will save us time and effort. They think that there will be new ways to communicate and connect people all over the world. Others think that the future will not be so bright. They predict the world will be overcrowded and that wars will be fought over natural resources.

Work with a partner. Debate whether the future will be positive or negative. Decide whether the future holds great things or not-so-great things, or a combination of both. Put all of your ideas together and write a statement about the future. Share your statement with other pairs.

▲ An artist's idea of two future cities, with protective domes

BUILD BACKGROUND

The Time Warp Trio: 2095 is a science fiction novel about traveling into the future. The novel takes place at two different times: 1995 and 2095. To create this science fiction story, author Jon Scieszka combined real things with imaginary, or fantastic, things. He made up the characters and their adventures. One part of the setting is real: the American Museum of Natural History. This famous museum is located in New York City opposite Central Park. And a statue of Theodore Roosevelt, the twenty-sixth president of the United States, really does stand outside the museum. Roosevelt loved nature and was a great friend of the museum. He was a strong believer in preserving the environment.

VOCABULARY

Learn Literary Words

Literary Words
- science fiction
- setting

Writers of **science fiction** often imagine what life in the future might be like. They base their plots on ideas and predictions about science and technology. Science fiction usually takes place in the future or involves time travel. It may be about an ideal society or fantastic creatures, inventions, and places. For example, in *The War of the Worlds*, author H. G. Wells tells a story about visitors from Mars.

Setting is the time and place when an event or story occurs. Sometimes writers tell you the setting. Other times, you have to figure it out from clues such as the characters' speech, clothing, or ways of traveling.

Read this excerpt from *The Best New Thing*, by Isaac Asimov. How do you know that this selection is science fiction? Which paragraph reveals the setting?

> Rada lived on a little world, far out in space. Her father and her mother and her brother, Jonathan, lived there too. So did other men and women.
>
> Rada was the only little girl on the little world. Jonny was the only little boy. They had lived there all their lives. Rada's father and other men worked on the spaceships. They made sure everything was all right before the spaceships went on their way back to Earth or to other planets.

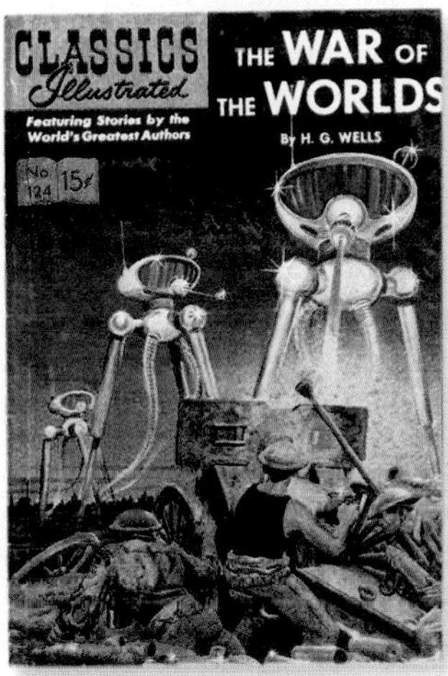

▲ *The War of the Worlds* is a classic science fiction novel about visitors from space.

Practice

With a partner, take turns reading aloud the descriptions below. Do you think that each is a setting for a science fiction novel? Explain your reasoning to your partner.

1. The story takes place on Mars in the year 2891. Humans live in a big dome. Martians live on the surface of the planet. The Martians and humans get along well but do not interact much.
2. The year is 1850. The place is Austin, Texas. The novel tells the real life story of a ranching family whose members are close and loving.

In your notebook, write a paragraph describing the setting for a science fiction story of your own. Share it with a partner.

Learn Academic Words

Study the **red** words and their meanings. You will find these words useful when talking and writing about literature. Write each word and its meaning in your notebook. After you read the excerpt from *The Time Warp Trio: 2095*, try to use these words to respond to the text.

Academic Words

shift
specific
strategies
techniques

shift = a change in the way most people think about something, or in the way something is done	➡	There was a huge **shift** in their ideas about nature after their visit to the natural history museum.
specific = detailed and exact	➡	Tell me more about your trip. You told me some general things, but I'd like to hear some **specific** details.
strategies = sets of plans and skills used in order to gain success or achieve an aim	➡	Her **strategies** for preparing for an exam are to study with friends and get a good night's sleep.
techniques = special methods of doing something	➡	There are many **techniques** that science fiction writers use to create believable stories.

Practice

Work with a partner to answer these questions. Try to include the **red** word in your answer. Write the sentences in your notebook.

1. Do you think that we will see a **shift** in how we use natural resources in the future? Explain.
2. What **specific** facts about the future would you like to know?
3. What **strategies** do you use to help you remember new words?
4. What **techniques** do you use to help you take good photographs?

▲ A popular study strategy is to have a friend quiz you on facts.

Word Study: Schwa spelled *a, e, i, o, u*

In many English words, the letters *a, e, i, o,* and *u* can stand for the sound you hear when you say "uh." The "uh" sound is called a schwa. The symbol for the schwa is the letter *e* turned upside down /ə/. In multisyllabic words, the schwa occurs only in an unstressed syllable. Recognizing and pronouncing /ə/ will help you spell many words correctly. Study the chart. Notice that the schwa occurs only in an unstressed syllable.

/ə/ spelled *a*	/ə/ spelled *e*	/ə/ spelled *i*	/ə/ spelled *o*	/ə/ spelled *u*
a-'maze	'tak-**en**	'an-**i**-mal	'les-s**o**n	'care-f**u**l
'so-f**a**	'trav-**e**l	ex-'per-**i**-ment	'com-m**o**n	'Ve-n**u**s

Practice

Work with a partner to spell these words: *alike, museum, uniforms, lion, happen.* Write five headings in your notebook: *a, e, i, o, u.* Say a word from the list slowly and clearly, syllable by syllable. Listen for the schwa. Ask your partner to spell the word aloud. Then have your partner say the next word. Continue until you can spell all of the words correctly. Write the words under the correct headings in your notebook. If you have trouble finding the schwa, check the word's pronunciation in a dictionary.

Reading Strategy SKIM

Skimming helps you get an idea of what a text is about. Skimming will also help you make and confirm predictions and become an active reader. To skim a text, follow these steps:

- Glance at the title, text, and illustrations to see what the plot, characters, and setting will be like.
- Read through the first page quickly.
- Make predictions about what you think will happen in the selection.

Skim the excerpt from *The Time Warp Trio: 2095* and make predictions. Then read the selection carefully. Confirm or revise your predictions.

READING

3

LITERATURE

NOVEL

Set a purpose for reading What would it be like to travel into the future? Read to find out how Sam, Fred, and Joe travel to the year 2095. How did they get there? How will they get back home?

from

THE TIME WARP TRIO: 2095

Jon Scieszka

Sam, Fred, and Joe are three friends. They are visiting the American Museum of Natural History in New York City in the year 1995. Joe, the narrator, has The Book, *a time-travel guide given to him by his uncle, who is also named Joe. Without meaning to, Joe does something that transports him and his two friends into the year 2095. As this excerpt begins, the trio of friends is running away from a security robot called a Sellbot.*

We jumped over the twitching Sellbot and ran down a flight of stairs. We had almost made it to the lobby, when the sound of a buzzer filled the halls.

The museum doors opened. A tidal wave of people came flooding in, and we were right in its path.

We dodged the first bunch of teenagers. They had corkscrew, spike, and Mohawk hair in every color you can think of. But the most amazing thing was that no one was touching the ground.

"They're flying. People in the future have figured out how to fly," said Sam.

A solid river of people flowed past us. An old man in an aluminum suit. A woman with leopard-patterned skin. A class in shiny school uniforms. Everyone was floating about a foot above the floor.

"How do they do that?" I said.

"Look closely," said Sam. "Everyone has a small disk with a green triangle and a red square."

"Hey, you're right," I said.

"I'm always right," said Sam. "That is obviously the antigravity disk that kid was talking about. Now let's get out of here before another Sellbot tracks us down."

Fred grabbed my belt. Sam grabbed Fred's belt. And we fought our way outside. We stopped at the statue of Teddy Roosevelt sitting on his horse looking out over Central Park. We stood and looked out with him.

"Wow," said Fred. "I see it but I don't believe it."

The sidewalk was full of floating people of every shape and color. There were people with green skin, blue skin, purple skin, orange, striped, plaid, dotted, and you-name-it skin. The street was packed three high and three deep with floating bullet-shaped things that must have been antigravity cars. And all around the trees of Central Park, towering buildings spread up and out like gigantic mechanical trees taller than the clouds.

---

flight of stairs, group of steps from one floor to the next
tidal wave of people, large crowd of people
antigravity disk, small item that fights the force of gravity, allowing one to float above the ground
tracks us down, finds us
you-name-it skin, every kind of skin

LITERARY CHECK

What details confirm that this is a ***science fiction*** *selection?*

BEFORE YOU GO ON

1. What do the people of the future look like?
2. What is the most amazing thing about people in the future?

On Your Own
Imagine that you could travel to any time period. Which one would you choose?

Layers and layers of antigravity cars and lines of people snaked around a hundred stories above us. New York was bigger, busier, and noisier than ever. . . .

Now wearing antigravity disks, the boys fly through the streets of New York, still chased by the Sellbot and three futuristic girls who look strangely familiar. Joe's uncle has appeared out of nowhere to help. The girls catch up, and Joe is surprised to see that one of the girls looks very much like his sister.

"Come on," said the girl who looked like my sister. "Follow us."

Sam looked at Fred. Fred looked at me. I looked at Uncle Joe.

"Do we have any choice?" I asked.

We **took off** and followed the girls around the buildings, over crowds of crazily colored people, past streamlined **pods** and more talking, blinking, singing 3-D ads, until I had no idea where we were.

We finally stopped in front of a building too tall to believe.

"Here's my house," said the **lead girl**.

Fred, Sam, and I looked up and up and up at the building that disappeared in the clouds.

The girl led us through a triangle door that opened at her voice. She put her hand over a blinking red handprint on the wall. And in five seconds we were all transported to a room that must have been five miles above New York City.

The girls flopped down on cushions. "This is my room," said the girl who looked like my sister.

We stood nervously in one corner.

"So you're not **killer time cops**?" I said.

---

took off, left quickly
pods, long vehicles
lead girl, girl at the front of the others
killer time cops, secret police who catch time travelers

The three girls looked at me like I was crazy.

"Of course not," said one.

"Whatever gave you that idea?" said another.

Then we all started asking questions.

"Who are you guys?"

"How did you know we'd be at the museum?"

"Do you have anything to eat?"

The girls laughed. The one who led us there pushed a green dot on a small table. A bowl of something looking like dried green dog food appeared with a pile of liquid filled plastic balls.

"Here's some Vitagorp and Unicola," said the girl who looked like my sister. "Now let me try to explain things from the beginning."

We copied the girls and sucked on the plastic ball things the same way they did. Fred ate a handful of the green dog food.

"I'm Joanie. This is Samantha. That's Frieda."

"But everybody calls me Freddi," said the girl with the baseball hat.

"And we have these names," Joanie continued, "because we were named after our great-grandfathers—Joe, Sam, and Fred."

"Or in other words—you," said Samantha.

Everything suddenly made sense. That's why they looked so much like us.

"Of course," said Uncle Joe, dusting off his top hat. "Your great-grandkids have to make sure you get back to 1995. Otherwise you won't have kids. Then your kids won't have kids. Then your kids' kids won't have—"

"Us," said Samantha. "Your great-grandkids. And we knew you would be at the museum because you wrote us a note." Samantha handed me a yellowed sheet of paper that had been sealed in plastic. It was our Museum Worksheet from 1995. On the back was a note in my handwriting that said:

Girls,

Meet us under Teddy Roosevelt's statue at the Museum of Natural History, September 28, 2095.

Sincerely,

Joe, Sam, Fred

"How did you get our worksheet from 1995?" asked Sam.

"I got it from my mom," said Joanie. "And she got it from her mom."

"But we didn't write that," I said.

"You will," said Samantha, "if we can get you back to 1995."

Vitagorp and Unicola, imaginary food and drink of the future

top hat, tall black hat

BEFORE YOU GO ON

1. Who are the three girls?
2. How do the girls know the boys will be at the museum?

On Your Own
Imagine that you are Joe. How do you feel at this point in the story?

"Saved by our own great-grandkids with a note we haven't written yet?" said Sam. "I told you something like this was going to happen. Now we're probably going to blow up."

"Wow," said Fred, eating more Vitagorp. "Our own great-grandkids. So what team is that on your hat? I've never seen that logo."

"That's the Yankees," said Freddi. "They changed it when Grandma was pitching."

"Your grandma? Fred's daughter?" I said. "A pitcher for the Yankees?"

"Not just a pitcher. She was a great pitcher," said Freddi. "2.79 lifetime ERA, 275 wins, 3 no-hitters, and the Cy Young award in '37."

"Forget your granny's stats," said Sam. "We could be genius inventors back in 1995 if we could reconstruct these levitation devices."

"What did he just say?" asked Freddi.

"He wants to know how the antigravity disks work," said Samantha. "A truly amazing discovery. More surprising than Charles Goodyear's accidental discovery of vulcanized rubber. More revolutionary than Alexander Graham Bell's first telephone. But all I can tell you is that the antigravity power comes from the chemical BHT. And it was discovered in a breakfast accident."

"What's a breakfast accident?" said Sam. "A head-on collision with a bowl of cornflakes? And who found out BHT could make things fly?"

"You did," said Samantha. "That's why we can't tell you more. You know the Time Warp Info-Speed Limit posted in *The Book*. Anyone traveling through time with too much information from another time blows up."

Sam's eyes nearly bugged out of his head. "I knew it. Don't tell me another word."

"Hey, wait a minute," I said. "Where did you say that info-speed limit was?"

Samantha looked at me like I was an insect.

"In *The Book*, of course."

"How do you know about *The Book*?"

"I got it for my birthday last year," said Joanie.

---

blow up, explode
logo, brand name or label
granny's stats, Grandma's *statistics*—facts about how well Grandma played
levitation devices, machines that let you float off the ground
head-on collision, violent crash
bugged out, popped out

"And since then we've been all over time," said Freddi. "We've met cavewomen, Ann the Pirate, Calamity Jane. . . ."

"And don't forget Cleopatra and the underground cities of Venus," said Samantha.

"But if you have *The Book*, that means we're saved," said Sam.

Samantha gave Sam her look. "If you remember the Time Warpers' Tips, you know nothing can be in two places at once. Of course our *Book* disappeared as soon as your *Book* appeared."

"So now we have to help you get *The Book* back to the past," said Freddi, "so we can have it in the future."

"Of course," said Sam.

"We knew that," said Fred.

"Uh, right . . ." I said, trying to talk my way out of this mess. "We knew that would happen, but we uh . . . " I looked around at Sam, Fred, Samantha, Freddi, and Joanie. Then I spotted Uncle Joe. "We thought we could really learn some tricks about finding *The Book* from Uncle Joe!"

Uncle Joe looked up from something he was fiddling with in his lap. "*The Book*? Oh, I never could get it to work the way your mother did. That's why I gave it to you for your birthday."

"Oh, great," said Sam. "We're *doomed*."

"But that's also why I put this together." Uncle Joe held up the thing he had been fiddling with in his lap. It was an old-fashioned pocket watch. "My Time Warp Watch."

"We're saved!" yelled Sam.

Calamity Jane, an American frontier woman from the 1800s famous for her unconventional behavior and courage
Cleopatra, an ancient Egyptian queen
spotted, saw
fiddling with, playing with
doomed, in a hopeless situation

ABOUT THE AUTHOR

Jon Scieszka has written many books for kids. Other books in the Time Warp Trio series include *The Good, the Bad, and the Goofy; Knights of the Kitchen Table; The Not-So-Jolly Roger;* and *Your Mother Was a Neanderthal.*

BEFORE YOU GO ON

1. Which character discovers the antigravity disk but doesn't know it?
2. What will happen to the boys if they learn too much information while visiting the future?

On Your Own
Do you think that any of the inventions described in this selection will really exist in the future? Explain.

READING 3 Review and Practice

READER'S THEATER

Speak clearly and slowly. Use gestures to emphasize your character's emotions.

Act out the following scene between Joe and Joanie.

Joe: You look so much like my sister. This is very strange, Joanie.

Joanie: Well, I was named after my great-grandfather Joe. Samantha, Frieda, and I were named after our great-grandfathers.

Joe: Well, that explains why you look like you are part of my family. You are! I am your great-grandfather!

Joanie: This means that all three of you—Sam, Fred, and you, Joe—must get back to your own time, 1995.

Joe: Why does that matter so much?

Joanie: If you don't get back, you won't be able to have kids when you grow up. Then your kids won't have kids, and . . .

Joe: I understand now! If we don't get back, you, Samantha, and Frieda won't be born. If we don't get back, we will change the future.

Joanie: We must find a way to get all of you back to 1995—and fast!

COMPREHENSION

Right There

1. Under what statue do the boys meet the girls at the American Museum of Natural History?
2. Where does the antigravity power come from?

Think and Search

3. Who are some of the people the girls have visited?
4. What are the Sellbots?

Author and You

5. Describe the tone of this story. For example, is it serious or funny?
6. Do you think the author's view of the future is positive or negative? Expain.

On Your Own

7. What specific strategies would you use to write a believable story about the future? How would you make your story realistic and futuristic at the same time?
8. Imagine that you could travel in time. Would you go ahead to the future or back to the past? Why?

DISCUSSION

Discuss in pairs or small groups.

1. Why do the girls—Frieda, Joanie, and Samantha—help the boys?
2. How is the year 2095 different from the year 1995? How is it similar?
3. Describe the skin of people in the future. Why do you think the author included this detail in the novel?

Q **What is your vision of life in the future?** Is Jon Scieszka's vision of the future realistic and believable? Why or why not?

Listening TIP

When your classmates speak, listen for supporting details and reasons. Ask yourself, "Did the speaker explain why these ideas are important?"

RESPONSE TO LITERATURE

The Book has directions for time travel. But nothing can be in two places at the same time. As a result, the girls' copy of *The Book* disappeared as soon as the boys' copy of *The Book* appeared. Help the boys get back to 1995. Write directions for time travel. When you have finished writing, share your instructions with a classmate. Talk about the steps in the process.

Grammar and Writing

GRAMMAR, USAGE, AND MECHANICS

Using Punctuation

Good writers use proper punctuation. It's important to punctuate your writing correctly so that readers understand what you want to say.

End marks are punctuation marks that come at the end of sentences. There are three kinds of end marks: periods, question marks, and exclamation points.

Use a period to end a statement or to end an imperative.

The girls flopped down on cushions**.**	Look closely**.**

Use a question mark to end a question.

> What do you know about wormholes, or space-time warps**?**

Use an exclamation point to end a sentence that expresses strong feeling.

> We're saved**!**

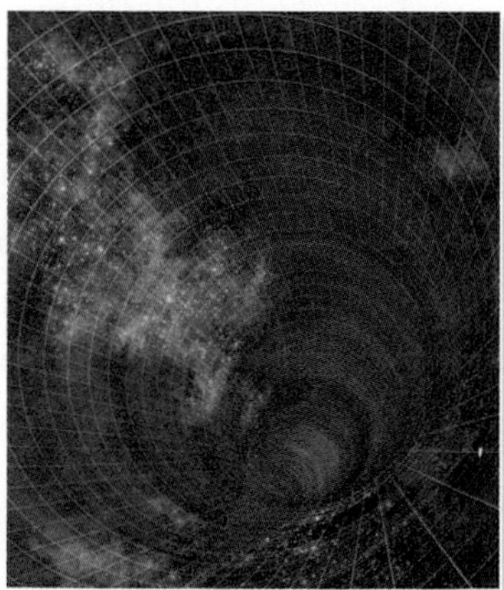

▲ This computer art shows how a wormhole might look.

A comma separates, or sets off, parts of a sentence, for instance, certain words or phrases. Use commas to separate nouns or phrases in a series, to separate introductory words and phrases, and to set off a speaker's quoted words in a sentence.

> I looked around at Sam**,** Fred**,** Samantha**,** Freddi**,** and Joanie.
> Hey**,** wait a minute.
> "Of course not**,**" said one.

Practice

Copy the sentences below into your notebook. Add proper punctuation to each. Then compare your sentences with a partner's.

1. The museum doors opened
2. "I'm always right" said Sam
3. Do we have any choice
4. That's amazing

Include Quotations and Citations

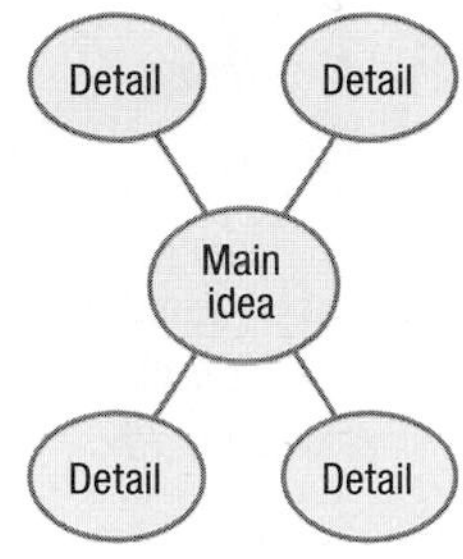

An effective research report should include what other people have said or researched about your topic. On this page, you'll practice using quotations to support an idea or explain a topic in a research report. Use a graphic organizer like the one at the right to help you.

Whenever you copy material word for word from another person's writing or speech, you must acknowledge the person by placing his or her words within quotation marks. After the quotation, you must also provide a citation, that is, information about the source of the quote. (See pages 455–456 for how to create citations for various sources.)

Here is a model of a paragraph with a quotation and a citation. The writer uses a quotation to support his main idea.

Andrew C. Dubin

Wormholes and Black Holes

Time travel is a popular topic in science fiction. Authors sometimes have their characters use wormholes as a way to travel through time. Wormholes are two black holes that are connected. Researchers say that wormholes "are more science fiction than they are science fact" (NASA). Wormholes are popular in science fiction, but there is no proof that they even exist. Researchers can prove that black holes exist, though. A black hole is the last stage in the life of a star. The force of gravity in black holes is very strong. Black holes and wormholes are related, but black holes are science fact, and wormholes are science fiction.

Works Consulted List

"Black Holes." NASA Goddard Space Flight Center. September 2006. 28 March 2009 <http://imagine.gsfc.nasa.gov/docs/science/know_12/black_holes.html>.

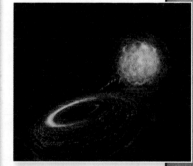

Practice

Write a paragraph about time travel or science fiction. List your ideas in a main idea/details web like the one above. Be sure to use quotations, citations, and punctuation correctly.

Writing Checklist

SENTENCE FLUENCY:

☑ I introduced my quotations and made sure that they flowed smoothly within my paragraph.

CONVENTIONS:

☑ I punctuated my citations correctly.

READING 4

Prepare to Read

What You Will Learn

Reading

- Vocabulary building: *Context, dictionary skills, word study*
- Reading strategy: *Make generalizations*
- Text type: *Informational text (science)*

Grammar, Usage, and Mechanics

Using quotation marks

Writing

Include paraphrases and citations

THE BIG QUESTION

What is your vision of life in the future? Do you ever imagine what your great-grandkids will look and be like? Think about Sam, Fred, and Joe from the last reading. They figured out that the futuristic girls who looked "strangely familiar" were their great-grandkids because the girls looked like them. The girls had inherited some of their great-grandparents' genetic traits. Certain physical traits, such as eye and hair color, straight or curly hair, and the shape of a person's face, are passed on from one generation to the next.

What physical or character traits do you want to pass on to future generations? Why do you think that these traits would be helpful to people in the future? Discuss with a partner.

BUILD BACKGROUND

"Genetic Fingerprints" is a science article that explains facts about DNA—the chemical instructions that tell a plant or animal what it needs to grow and work.

People have long wondered how certain traits are passed down from person to person, from animal to animal, and from plant to plant. Why do children look like their parents? Why are some horses faster than others?

In 1865, a monk named Gregor Mendel discovered that traits are passed down through tiny bits of material he called "genes." He studied pea plants and learned that certain traits were passed down from one plant to the next. It wasn't until 1953, however, that two scientists, James Watson and Francis Crick, figured out the structure of DNA and linked it to how traits are passed down. Some people have called this the biggest scientific discovery of all time.

▲ Gregor Mendel discovered the laws of heredity by studying pea plants.

VOCABULARY

Learn Key Words

Read the sentences. Use the context to figure out the meaning of the **red** words. Use a dictionary to check your answers. Then write each word and its meaning in your notebook.

1. **Cells** are the smallest living things. Scientists use microscopes to study cells.
2. The **defendant** was charged with a crime. The jury had to decide whether he was guilty or not guilty.
3. The **forensic** evidence was used in court. Fingerprints were one of many pieces of evidence used.
4. **Genes** carry traits, such as eye and hair color, that are passed down from one generation to the next.
5. People **inherit** qualities from both parents. A girl may be tall like her mother and have curly hair like her father.
6. Fingerprints have **whorls** that look like circles and swirls. Each person has a different pattern of whorls.

Key Words

cells
defendant
forensic
genes
inherit
whorls

Practice

Write the sentences in your notebook. Complete each sentence using the **red** word. Then take turns reading the sentences aloud with a partner.

1. The researcher was studying . . . (**cells**)
2. A lawyer was hired to help . . . (**defendant**)
3. At the trial, different kinds of . . . (**forensic**)
4. The baby developed an illness because . . . (**genes**)
5. Some children . . . (**inherit**)
6. The police matched one set of fingerprints to the . . . (**whorls**)

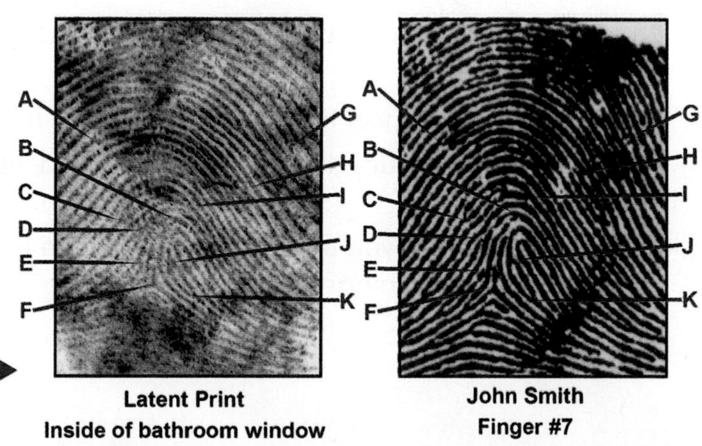

A fingerprint whorl comparison ▶

Learn Academic Words

Study the **red** words and their meanings. You will find these words useful when talking and writing about informational texts. Write each word and its meaning in your notebook. After you read "Genetic Fingerprints," try to use these words to respond to the text.

Academic Words

generation
legislation
medical
policy
procedure

generation = all the people who are about the same age, especially in a family	➡	My grandfather's **generation** believed in the value of hard work.
legislation = a law or set of laws	➡	New **legislation** has been passed about DNA. These laws allow DNA evidence to be used in court.
medical = relating to medicine and the treatment of disease or injury	➡	**Medical** people work to prevent some diseases and treat other ones.
policy = a way of doing things that has been officially agreed upon and chosen by a political party or an organization	➡	The lab has a firm **policy** about DNA testing. The rules can be found in the lab's guidebook.
procedure = the correct or normal way of doing something	➡	Lawyers follow a careful **procedure** during a trial.

Practice

Work with a partner to answer the questions. Try to include the **red** word in your answer. Write the sentences in your notebook.

1. Who is in your **generation**? Name six people.
2. What type of **legislation** do you think is important to young people?
3. What job in the **medical** field would you like to have?
4. What **policy** does your school have to keep students and teachers safe?
5. What **procedure** do you follow when you begin to write a story? What things do you do first?

▲ Three generations of a family

Word Study: Multiple-Meaning Words

You have learned that many English words have multiple meanings. To figure out which meaning fits, look at the context in which you found the word. Are there any clues in the words and sentences surrounding the word? See which meaning makes most sense in the sentence. Also, identify the word's part of speech. It may be an important clue. If necessary, look up the word in a dictionary.

Word and Meaning	Part of Speech	Sentence
matches: two or more things or people that go well together	Verb	The tie **matches** the shirt.
matches: pieces of wood or cardboard with a flammable tip used to start a fire	Noun	The campers used **matches** to start the campfire.
matches: games or contests	Noun	We played two tennis **matches**.

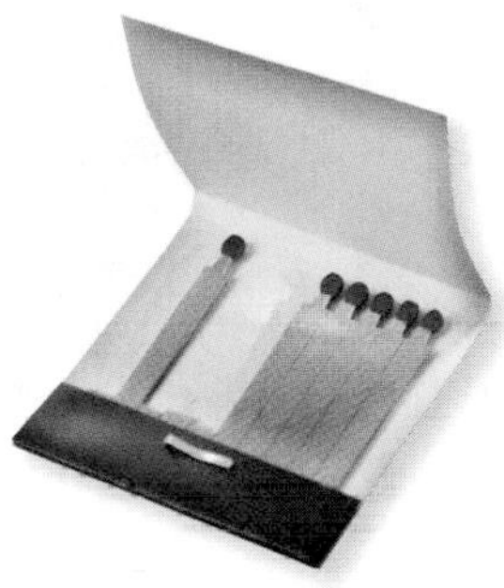

▲ A book of matches

Practice

Work with a partner to explore the different meanings of these words: *tissue, tests, code, suspect, serve,* and *commit.* Start by looking up each word in a dictionary. Then use each word in two sentences to show two of the word's meanings. Write the sentences in your notebook.

READING STRATEGY MAKE GENERALIZATIONS

Making generalizations helps you apply what you read to other situations. A generalization is a statement or rule that applies to most examples and can be supported by facts. Suppose you read this sentence: *Baby polar bears, baby elephants, and baby giraffes look like their mothers, only smaller.* The following would be a good generalization:

Generalization: Many baby animals look like their parents.

Be careful not to make a false generalization—one that cannot be supported by facts. Why is the following generalization false?

False Generalization: All baby animals look like their parents.

Make generalizations when you read "Genetic Fingerprints." Combine facts from the text with what you already know to make a generalization. Be sure that you can support the generalization with facts.

READING 4

INFORMATIONAL TEXT

SCIENCE

Set a purpose for reading What surprising discoveries have been made about DNA and DNA fingerprinting? How might these discoveries affect the future? Read the article to find out.

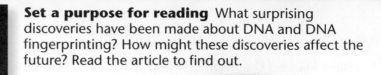

Genetic Fingerprints

Your fingerprints are unlike anyone else's. They have a pattern of ridges and whorls that is unique to you. The same is true of your DNA "fingerprints." You can't see them with the naked eye, but they have a pattern that is unique to you. Your DNA fingerprint exists in every cell of your body, and it is yours and yours alone.

The Wonders of DNA

Within the cells of your body, there is a chemical set of instructions, called DNA (deoxyribonucleic acid). These instructions tell a plant's or animal's body what it needs to grow and work.

You inherit about 80,000 genes from your parents. All 80,000 genes are present in each individual cell of your body. These genes contain the instructions that make you human.

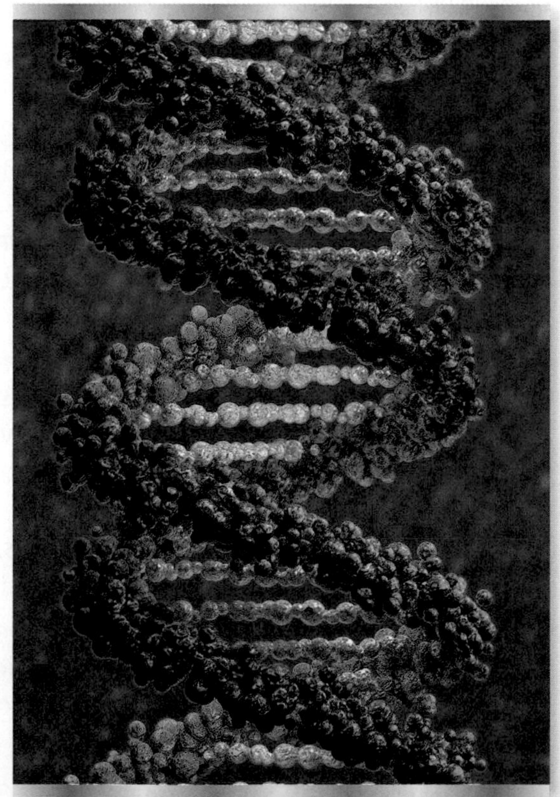

▲ A DNA double helix

Discovery of the DNA Fingerprint

In 1984, Sir Alec Jeffreys discovered how to make a DNA fingerprint. It happened by accident. He had been studying the differences in human DNA.

DNA is like a long, twisted ladder. The rungs of the ladder have a unique pattern of genes for each person. This unique arrangement of genes is what makes human beings different from one another.

Jeffreys took pieces of DNA. He marked them with a radioactive substance. Then he made images of these DNA fragments on X-ray film. When he developed the pictures, he was surprised at what he saw.

> Instead of a few isolated images . . . [he] saw long strings of images arranged in patterns. Dark bands—some thick, some thin—were stacked in patterns that looked a great deal like the bar codes found on products in the supermarkets (Fridell 18).

fragments, small pieces of something

Here in visual form was a code that could be used to identify every living thing. This DNA "fingerprint" was a picture of a person's unique genetic code. Now scientists had solid evidence that they could use to uniquely identify people through their genes. Your DNA fingerprint, Alec Jeffreys said, "does not belong to anyone on the face of the planet who ever has been or ever will be."

▲ A scientist examines a DNA sequence.

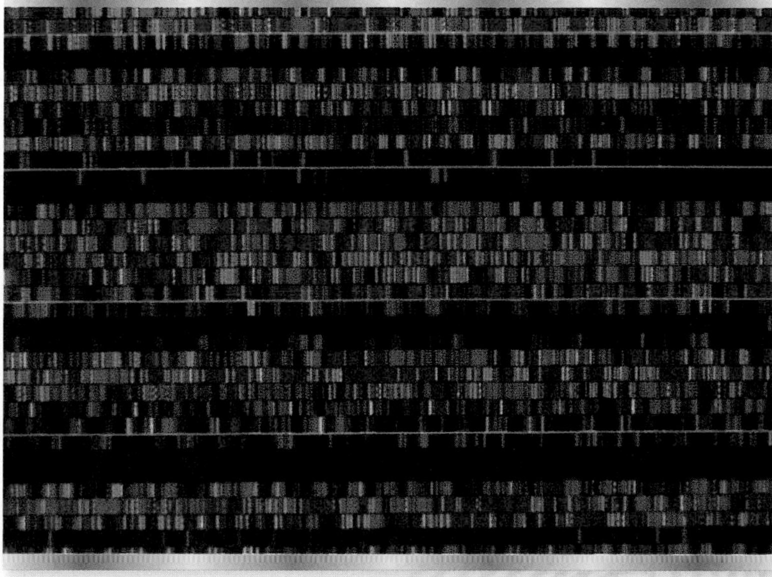

◀ This human DNA sequence is displayed as a series of colored bands.

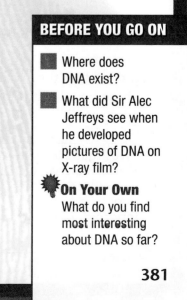

BEFORE YOU GO ON

1. Where does DNA exist?
2. What did Sir Alec Jeffreys see when he developed pictures of DNA on X-ray film?

On Your Own
What do you find most interesting about DNA so far?

◀ A man walks out of court after his conviction is overturned because of DNA evidence.

DNA and Justice

Once DNA fingerprinting was discovered, it was used to identify people. Forensic scientists study crimes by looking at evidence. They use various scientific tests. Since the 1980s, they have used DNA fingerprints to investigate and solve crimes. They take a sample of blood, hair, or other body tissue found at the scene of a crime. This tissue contains DNA. The scientists check to see whether the DNA from a crime scene matches a sample of the suspect's DNA. This way they can figure out whether the suspect could have possibly committed a crime.

In recent years, many people have been released from prison after DNA tests proved that they were "wholly innocent." These people had not committed any crime at all.

investigate, look into, research
tissue, material, such as skin and muscle
committed a crime, done something wrong or illegal
innocent, not guilty

In 1992, the Innocence Project was founded. It serves defendants who could be proved innocent through DNA testing. Since that time, innocence organizations have spread throughout the United States.

Law students at the Wisconsin Innocence Project investigate about twenty to thirty criminal cases at a time. In 2001, the project was responsible for the release of a Texas prisoner, Chris Ochoa. He was serving a life sentence for a 1988 murder. DNA tests on samples found on the victim proved that Ochoa did not commit the crime. He was innocent. Chris Ochoa had spent twelve years in prison for a crime he didn't commit. He is not alone. As of 2008, more than 200 people previously convicted of serious crimes have been found innocent because of DNA testing.

DNA testing is now a very important tool in criminal investigation. It is going to be more important in the future. More forensic scientists are going to use DNA tests to help make sure the right people are punished for their crimes.

Other Uses of DNA Fingerprints

DNA is also being used in many other ways. For example, in India, chefs were having trouble identifying the type of rice they were cooking. Each type had to be soaked and cooked differently. So a rice producer used DNA fingerprinting to identify specific types. Now the chefs know how to cook each type correctly. Medical researchers have used DNA tests to identify and fight bacteria that cause food-related illnesses. DNA has also been used to investigate objects from the past. For instance, archaeologists have used DNA to help piece together the remains of the Dead Sea Scrolls. DNA fingerprinting has been used to identify family members who have been separated from one another because of wars or natural disasters. As DNA fingerprinting becomes increasingly popular, it will be used for many other purposes in the future.

bacteria, very small living things, some of which cause illness or disease

Dead Sea Scrolls, ancient texts, approximately 2,000 years old, discovered in caves near the Dead Sea

Work Cited

Fridell, Ron. *DNA Fingerprinting: The Ultimate Identity*. New York: Franklin Watts, 2001.

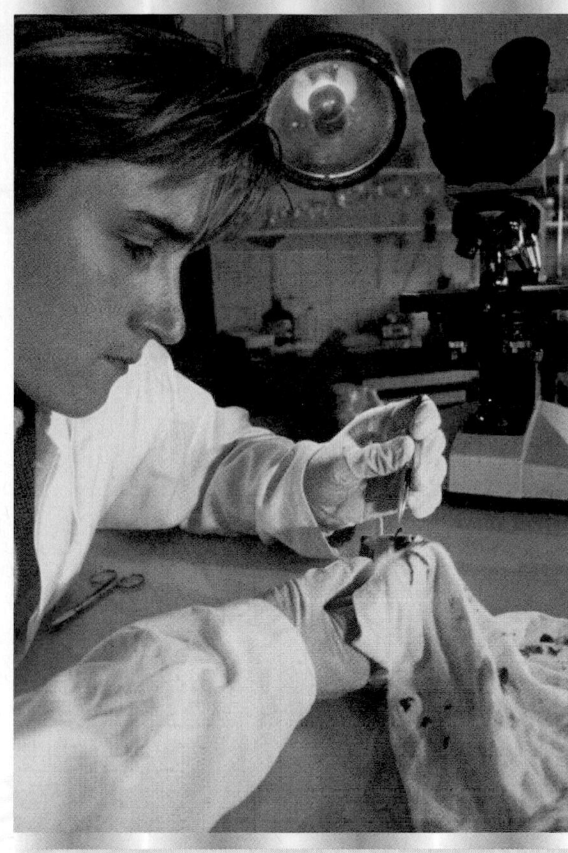

▲ A forensic scientist extracts DNA evidence from a piece of clothing.

Scientists clean fragments of the Dead Sea Scrolls. ▼

BEFORE YOU GO ON

1. What can scientists test to find DNA?
2. What group of people does the Innocence Project serve?

On Your Own
What uses would you like to see for DNA fingerprints in the future?

READING 4

Review and Practice

COMPREHENSION

Right There

1. What is DNA?
2. About how many genes do you inherit from your parents?

Think and Search

3. What procedure did Sir Alec Jeffreys use to make a DNA fingerprint?
4. What is one way that DNA is being used in India?

Author and You

5. In what ways does DNA prove that each person is unique?
6. How do you think people reacted to Jeffreys's discovery of the DNA fingerprint?

On Your Own

7. Would you want to work for the Innocence Project? Why or why not?
8. Do you think that DNA will have a greater effect on scientists or lawyers? Explain your opinion.

▲ **Each person has a unique fingerprint.**

IN YOUR OWN WORDS

Summarize "Genetic Fingerprints" for a friend. Include all the main ideas and important details in your summary. Make your summary interesting so that your friend will want to read the article. Use the following chart to help you organize your ideas. Then share your summary of the article with a classmate.

Speaking TIP

Ask your friend whether he or she has any questions about your summary. Receiving feedback will help you improve.

Section	Main Idea	Important Details
The Wonders of DNA		
Discovery of DNA Fingerprints		
DNA and Justice		
Other Uses of DNA Fingerprints		

DISCUSSION

Discuss in pairs or small groups.

1. Why was the discovery of DNA so important?
2. How has DNA changed the legal field?

Q What is your vision of life in the future? What are some other ways that people might use DNA in the future? Could there be some negative uses? Explain.

Listening TIP

Listen carefully to other people's ideas so that you understand what they're saying.

READ FOR FLUENCY

When we read aloud to communicate meaning, we group words into phrases, pause or slow down to make important points, and emphasize important words. Pause for a short time when you reach a comma and for a longer time when you reach a period. Pay attention to rising and falling intonation at the end of sentences.

Work with a partner. Choose a paragraph from the reading. Discuss which words seem important for communicating meaning. Practice pronouncing difficult words. Take turns reading the paragraph aloud and give each other feedback.

EXTENSION

You read about Sir Alec Jeffreys's important contribution to DNA research. Many other scientists contributed to our current understanding of DNA as well. Make a timeline showing at least five people who made important discoveries about DNA and heredity. Use encyclopedias, reference books, and reliable websites. Copy the following timeline into your notebook. Use it to help you organize your ideas.

▲ Scientists James Watson and Francis Crick discovered the structure of DNA.

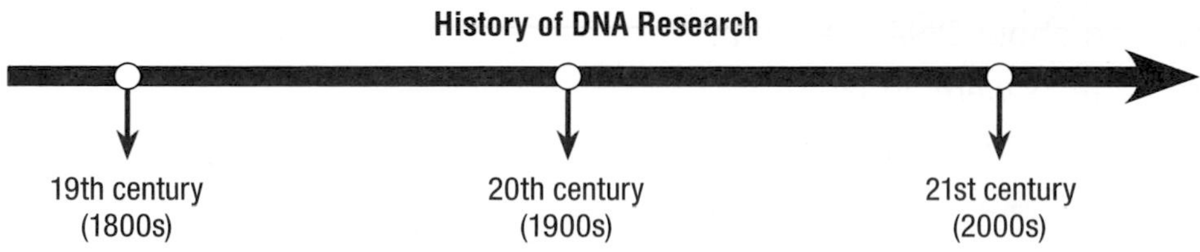

Grammar and Writing

GRAMMAR, USAGE, AND MECHANICS

Using Quotation Marks

Knowing how to use quotation marks correctly will help you write stories, essays, and research reports. In dialogue in narratives, enclose a character's exact words or thoughts in quotation marks. In expository writing, place quotation marks around a person's exact words. For long quotations of more than five lines, indent and single-space the quotes, and do not use quotation marks.

"I'm hungry," Fred said.
"Your DNA fingerprint," Jeffreys said, "does not belong to anyone on the face of the planet who ever has been or ever will be."

In addition, use quotation marks to enclose special or technical terms, unfamiliar slang, and any other unusual expressions. Also, use quotation marks to set off a word or phrase that defines another word and to set off the titles of short written works such as articles, poems, and short stories.

DNA tests proved they were "wholly innocent."
Generation means "all the people who are about the same age."
"Genetic Fingerprints"
"Mending Wall" by Robert Frost

Practice

Copy the sentences below into your notebook. Add quotation marks where they are needed.

1. I have read about DNA before, he said.
2. I read a short story called A Family History.
3. The word *legislation* means a law or set of laws.
4. The student said, Learning about DNA is exciting.
5. The scientist felt that the tests were useless.
6. He's written an article called DNA for Beginners.

Include Paraphrases and Citations

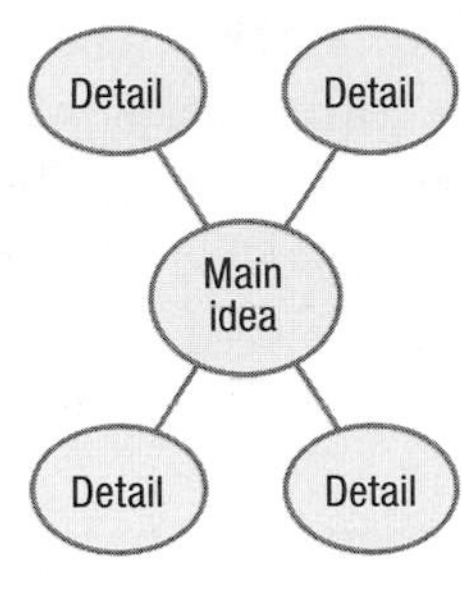

To support your own ideas in a research report, you can quote information directly from a source, or you can put the information into your own words. When you put other people's ideas into your own words, you are paraphrasing. On this page, you will learn how to paraphrase information from other sources. You will use a graphic organizer like the one at the right to organize your information.

To paraphrase, read a source several times, then put it away. Write what you learned in your own words. Check your paraphrase against the original source for accuracy. When you write research reports, you should include more paraphrases than quotations. Whether you quote or paraphrase, provide a citation.

Here is a model paragraph in which the writer paraphrases information and includes a citation.

Angelina Xing

Fraternal and Identical Twins

There are two types of twins, identical and fraternal. The word identical means "exactly the same." Identical twins have the same DNA and look almost exactly alike. Identical twins are also always the same sex. Giving birth to identical twins occurs less frequently than giving birth to fraternal twins. According to doctors, approximately two-thirds of twin pregnancies are fraternal (Iannelli). Fraternal twins are actually quite different from each other. Most of the time, they don't look alike at all. Fraternal twins are sometimes the same sex, and other times, they're not. They also have different blood types and different DNA.

Works Consulted List

Iannelli, Vincent. "Facts about Twins." Keep Kids Healthy. May 2003. 15 March 2009 <http://www.keepkidshealthy.com/twins/expecting_twins.html>.

Practice

Write a paragraph about DNA that includes a paraphrase and a citation. Use reliable sources and a main idea/details web to organize the information. Use quotation marks if and when they are needed.

Writing Checklist

IDEAS:

☑ I used paraphrases that clearly support my main idea.

ORGANIZATION:

☑ I included a citation within and at the end of my paragraph.

Link the Readings

Critical Thinking

Look back at the readings in this unit. Think about what they all have in common. They all tell about the future. Yet they do not all have the same purpose. The purpose of one reading might be to inform, while the purpose of another might be to entertain or persuade. In addition, the content of each reading relates to the future in different ways. Now copy the chart below into your notebook and complete it.

Title of Reading	Purpose	Big Question Link
"Life in the Future"		
"Southbound on the Freeway" "Cardinal Ideograms" "Interview with Dan Bursch"		
From *The Time Warp Trio: 2095*	*to entertain*	
"Genetic Fingerprints"		*tells about how our knowledge of DNA will help fight disease in the future*

Discussion

Discuss in pairs or small groups.

- How does the purpose of "Life in the Future" differ from the purpose of *The Time Warp Trio: 2095*?
- **Q** **What is your vision of life in the future?** Think about the readings in this unit. What picture of the future does each one show? Is the picture positive or negative? What's your opinion? Does life in the future look positive, negative, or both? Explain.

Fluency Check

Work with a partner. Choose a paragraph from one of the readings. Take turns reading it for one minute. Count the total number of words you read. Practice saying the words you had trouble reading. Take turns reading the paragraph three more times. Did you read more words each time? Copy the chart below into your notebook and record your speeds.

	1st Speed	2nd Speed	3rd Speed	4th Speed
Words Per Minute				

Projects

1 You have read a lot about the future. What do you think the future will look like? Paint a picture of your town or city 100 years from now.

2 You read an interview with an astronaut. What training do astronauts need? Go to the NASA website to find out the requirements for being a U.S. astronaut. Share your findings in an oral report. Include handouts or other visuals.

3 *The Time Warp Trio: 2095* is part of a series of books about the travels of Sam, Fred, and Joe. Read another book in the series, such as *Tut Tut* or *It's All Greek to Me.* Then give a brief book report to the class. You might want to read the entire series!

4 Make a model of the DNA double helix. You may use any material you like, such as marshmallows and sticks or Styrofoam and clay. Label each part of the model. Present your model to the class.

5 Working with some classmates, adapt *The Time Warp Trio: 2095* as a brief play. Choose any part of the novel you like, rewrite it as a script, and act it out for the class. Include some costumes and simple props, too.

Further Reading

To find out more about the theme of this unit, choose from these reading suggestions.

Hulk, Based on the Motion Picture Story by James Schamus
In this Penguin Reader® adaptation, Bruce knows he's different. When he gets angry, his body changes. It grows and turns green. But where did he come from?

Tomorrowland: Ten Stories About the Future, Michael Cart
This collection of short stories, written by current writers, explores many aspects of life in the future.

Tuck Everlasting, Natalie Babbitt
The Tuck family discovers a spring with "unusual" properties. A conflict arises when others learn the spring's secret.

Put It All Together

LISTENING & SPEAKING WORKSHOP

Speech

You will give a speech that expresses your vision of life in the future.

1 THINK ABOUT IT In small groups, discuss the texts you read in this unit. Did any influence your vision of life in the future? Discuss your own predictions about life in the future. For instance, discuss what you think future schools will be like. Work together to develop a list of topics for a speech about the future. Here are some examples:

- space tourism
- new technology for communications
- homes of the future
- environmental issues in the future

2 GATHER AND ORGANIZE INFORMATION Choose a topic from your group's list. Write down what you already know about the topic. Look at an encyclopedia or a website to find out more about it. Decide what the focus of your speech will be.

Research Use the library or the Internet to find more information about your topic. Look for interesting facts, examples, and details that support your main idea or prediction about the topic. Take notes on what you find. Be sure to write down the sources of the information you wish to include.

Order Your Notes Decide on the main idea or prediction for your speech; for example: *In the future, people will live in "smart houses." Computers will turn the lights on and off, lock the doors, and water the plants.* Arrange your note cards in logical order and prepare an outline for your speech. Your outline should include your main idea and the facts, examples, and details that you will use to support it. Think of an interesting way to begin your speech. Plan a conclusion that summarizes your findings.

Prepare a Script Use your outline and note cards to write a script for your speech.

Use Visuals To make your speech more interesting and effective, find or make visuals such as posters and models that illustrate your ideas and predictions. Your visuals should be big enough for everyone to see easily. Decide when to show your visuals, and mark reminders in your speech.

3 PRACTICE AND PRESENT

Practice reading your speech aloud until you know it very well. Keep practicing until you can speak smoothly, looking just occasionally at your script. Have a friend or family member listen as you practice giving your speech. Ask whether your words and ideas are understandable. Keep practicing until you feel comfortable and confident saying your speech while looking at your audience.

Deliver Your Speech Speak clearly and loudly enough so that everyone in the class can hear you. Glance at your script as needed, but remember to look up and make eye contact with your listeners. Be careful not to hide behind your visuals or turn away from the audience while speaking. At the end of your speech, ask the audience members whether they have any questions.

4 EVALUATE THE PRESENTATION

A good way to improve your speaking and listening skills is by evaluating each presentation you give and hear. Use this checklist to help you judge your speech and the speeches of your classmates.

- ☑ Was the speaker's main idea or prediction clear?
- ☑ Do you agree with the speaker's main idea or prediction? Why or why not?
- ☑ Was the speaker easy to hear and understand?
- ☑ Did you enjoy listening to the speech? Why or why not?
- ☑ What suggestions do you have for improving the speech?

Speaking TIPS

Use words such as *may*, *might*, *will*, *could*, *would*, *perhaps*, and *probably* to explain your predictions for the future.

Make sure your voice and body language show your enthusiasm for your topic. If you're having fun, your audience will enjoy the speech, too.

Listening TIPS

Try to visualize, or picture in your mind, what the speaker is describing.

Think about the speaker's reasons for his or her prediction. Do they seem logical and possible? Are they supported by research?

WRITING WORKSHOP

Research Report

In a research report, you explain a topic you have studied in depth. You include research gathered from several different sources. If you use an exact quotation from a source, you put the words in quotation marks and include a citation. You list all your sources at the end of your report. A good research report begins with a paragraph that introduces the writer's topic and states a controlling idea or focus. Each body paragraph presents a main idea that develops the topic. Main ideas are supported by facts, details, and examples. A concluding paragraph sums up what the writer has explained.

Your assignment for this workshop is to write a five-paragraph research report about a topic related to life in the future.

1 PREWRITE Select a topic that interests you. You might write about medicine, education, transportation, architecture, or any other area of human life that will probably be different in the future from the way it is now. Then ask yourself, "What do I want to know about my topic?" Use this question to guide your research. Consult sources such as books, magazines, encyclopedias, and websites. Take notes on note cards.

List and Organize Ideas and Details Create an outline to organize your ideas. A student named Brandon decided to write about future transportation. Here is the outline he prepared.

I. Introduction
- *A. Huge advances made in the last 200 years*
- *B. More advances coming in the future*

II. Hybrid cars
- *A. Already have better gas mileage than before*
- *B. Stronger batteries needed to become main energy source*

III. Faster and more fuel-efficient airplane
- *A. Flying wing*
- *B. Shaped like triangle*

IV. Other flying vehicles
- *A. SoloTrek EFV*
- *B. Urban Aeronautics X-Hawk*

V. Safer, faster, more fuel-efficient modern vehicles
- *A. Will be even better in the future*
- *B. Designed for environment-friendly society*

2 DRAFT Use the model on pages 396–397 and your outline to help you write a draft of your report. Be sure to use your own words when you write your report. If you use exact words from a source, make sure to use quotation marks correctly. List all of your sources accurately at the end of your report.

Citing Sources Look at the style, punctuation, and order of information in the following sources. Use these examples as models.

Book
Stanchak, John. Civil War. New York: Dorling Kindersley, 2000.

Magazine article
Kirn, Walter. "Lewis and Clark: The Journey That Changed America Forever." Time 8 July 2002: 36–41.

Internet website
Smith, Gene. "The Structure of the Milky Way." Gene Smith's Astronomy Tutorial. 28 April 1999. Center for Astrophysics & Space Sciences, University of California, San Diego. 20 July 2009 <http://casswww.ucsd.edu/public/tutorial/MW.html>.

Encyclopedia article
Siple, Paul A. "Antarctica." World Book Encyclopedia. 1991 ed.

3 REVISE Read over your draft. As you do so, ask yourself the questions in the writing checklist. Use the questions to help you revise your report.

SIX TRAITS OF WRITING CHECKLIST

- ✔ **IDEAS:** Does my first paragraph introduce my topic and focus?
- ✔ **ORGANIZATION:** Do facts, examples, and details support the main idea in each paragraph?
- ✔ **VOICE:** Is my tone serious and suited to the topic?
- ✔ **WORD CHOICE:** Do I use words that clearly express my meaning?
- ✔ **SENTENCE FLUENCY:** Do my sentences vary in length and type?
- ✔ **CONVENTIONS:** Does my writing follow the rules of grammar, usage, and mechanics?

Here are the changes Brandon plans to make when he revises his first draft:

Transportation of the Future

In the last 200 years, transportation technology has made astonishing advances. Steamships replaced sailing ships. Railroads were created. Automobiles were invented. The Wright brothers made the first airplane flight. Astronauts traveled to the moon! What ~~can~~ will transportation be like in the future? Transportation technology ~~may~~ will continue to advance, perhaps more than we can imagine today. We will see improvements in hybrid and electric cars, airplanes, and personal jetpacks.

Car companies are already making hybrid or fuel efficient cars that have improved gas mileage. However, Batteries must become stronger and cheaper in order to become the main energy source for cars. electric cars today must use gasoline power as a backup. ~~They~~ can go only 50 to 100 miles between charges, so they According to scientist Joshua Cunningham, "Gasoline will remain a dominant fuel until at least 2050" (Layton, Nice).

Many airlines are trying to make their jets faster and more fuel efficient. A group called Greener By design predicts that a new kind of plane, the flying wing, will be carrying passengers by 2025. These planes will be made of plastic and shaped like a triangle. Passengers will sit in rows of up to 40 seats across.

Several new flying vehicles ~~will~~ may be in the sky in the next few decades. Inventors are close to creating a jetpack that can go as high as a plane and maneuver better than a helicopter. The SoloTrek EFV is one example. According to its inventor, Michael Moshier, one day it will "fly at altitudes of nearly 8,000 feet . . . and reach speeds of up to 80 mph" (Sieberg). An emergency vehicle by Urban Aeronautics, known as the X-Hawk, will go places that cannot be reached by helicopters or other emergency vehicles.

Modern vehicles are becoming safer, faster, and more fuel-efficient. In the future, people will have access to even better transportation. This new technology will be specially designed to work in a fast-paced, environment-friendly society.

Works Consulted List

"Future Planes Might Be 'Flying Wings'." Future Planes. 5 April 2007. 23 March 2009 <http://futureplanes.blogspot.com/>.

Layton, Julia, and Karim Nice. "How Hybrid Cars Work." How Stuff Works. 23 March 2009 <http://auto.howstuffworks.com/hybrid-car.htm>.

Sieberg, Daniel. "Personal 'Jetpack' Gets off the Ground." CNN Sci-Tech. 6 February 2002. 24 March 2009 <http://archives.cnn.com/2002/TECH/ptech/02/06/solotrek.jetpack/index.html>.

Stearns, Peter N., general editor. "The Modern Period: Transportation and Communication." The Encyclopedia of World History. 2001 ed.

4 EDIT AND PROOFREAD

Copy your revised report onto a clean sheet of paper. Read it again. Correct any errors in grammar, word usage, mechanics, and spelling. Here are the additional changes Brandon plans to make when he prepares his final draft.

Brandon Saiz

Transportation of the Future

In the last 200 years, transportation technology has made astonishing advances. Steamships replaced sailing ships. Railroads were created. Automobiles were invented. The Wright brothers made the first airplane flight. Astronauts traveled to the moon! What will transportation be like in the future? Transportation technology will continue to advance, perhaps more than we can imagine today. We will see improvements in hybrid and electric cars, airplanes, and personal jetpacks.

Car companies are already making hybrid or fuel efficient cars that have improved gas mileage. However, batteries must become stronger and cheaper in order to become the main energy source for cars. electric cars today can go only 50 to 100 miles between charges, so they must use gasoline power as a backup. According to scientist Joshua Cunningham, "Gasoline will remain a dominant fuel until at least 2050" (Layton, Nice).

Many airlines are trying to make their jets faster and more fuel efficient. A group called Greener By design predicts that a new kind of plane, the flying wing, will be carrying passengers by 2025. These planes will be made of plastic and shaped like a triangle. Passengers will sit in rows of up to 40 seats across.

Several new flying vehicles may be in the sky in the next few decades. Inventors are close to creating a jetpack that can go as high as a plane and maneuver better than a helicopter. The SoloTrek EFV is one example. According to its inventor, Michael Moshier, one day it will "fly at altitudes of nearly 8,000 feet . . . and reach speeds of up to 80 mph" (Sieberg). An emergency vehicle by Urban Aeronautics, known as the X-Hawk, will go places that cannot be reached by helicopters or other emergency vehicles.

Modern vehicles are becoming safer, faster, and more fuel-efficient. In the future, people will have access to even better transportation. This new technology will be specially designed to work in a fast-paced, environment-friendly society.

Works Consulted List

"Future Planes Might Be 'Flying Wings'." Future Planes. 5 April 2007. 23 March 2009 <http://futureplanes.blogspot.com/>.

Layton, Julia, and Karim Nice. "How Hybrid Cars Work." How Stuff Works. 23 March 2009 <http://auto.howstuffworks.com/hybrid-car.htm>.

Sieberg, Daniel. "Personal 'Jetpack' Gets off the Ground." CNN Sci-Tech. 6 February 2002. 24 March 2009 <http://archives.cnn.com/2002/TECH/ptech/02/06/solotrek.jetpack/index.html>.

Stearns, Peter N., general editor. "The Modern Period: Transportation and Communication." The Encyclopedia of World History. 2001 ed.

5 PUBLISH Prepare your final draft. Share your research report with your teacher and classmates.

Learn about Art with the Smithsonian American Art Museum

IMAGINING THE FUTURE

No one can see into the future, but most of us can imagine it. Artists often show the future in their work. Sometimes they show people zooming around in flying jackets across strange-looking cities. Other times, they just try to capture a futuristic mood.

Alexander A. Maldonado, *San Francisco to New York in One Hour* (1969)

In Alexander A. Maldonado's vision of the future, people are able to travel thousands of miles quickly. In *San Francisco to New York in One Hour,* vehicles zip through underground tubes. The tops of these tunnels are round. The overall image looks like a big stadium with a parking lot packed with cars and buses. The artist surrounded his brightly colored painting with a wooden frame. This makes you feel as though you are looking through a window into the future.

A Mexican American who lived in California for most of his adult life, Maldonado continued to have strong ties to his native Mexico. One of the tunnel stations in the painting travels from the United States to Mexico (notice the Mexican flag on the upper right building), a speedy route between the artist's past as a child and where he built his future.

▲ **Alexander A. Maldonado, *San Francisco to New York in One Hour,* 1969, oil, 18 x 24 in., Smithsonian American Art Museum**

▲ Harry Bertoia, *Sculpture Group Symbolizing World's Communication in the Atomic Age*, 1959, brass and bronze, 142¼ x 231¼ x 81 in., Smithsonian American Art Museum

Harry Bertoia, *Sculpture Group Symbolizing World's Communication in the Atomic Age* (1959)

Harry Bertoia's *Sculpture Group Symbolizing World's Communication in the Atomic Age* is made up of one large 2.4-meter (8-ft.) sculpture and three smaller sculptures. Bertoia worked with metals such as brass and copper. Then he added light so that the objects seem to glow like the planets and stars. In the larger piece to the left, he put together squares of metal attached to poles, which formed a circle shaped like the sun.

Even though Bertoia lived at a time when computers and television were new, he felt that electronics and atomic energy already dominated American culture. When you look at his bright sculpture, it's easy to imagine that you're in outer space or inside a TV.

Any future that someone can imagine is always based on what we find in our present. Both of these artists used images we understand today to imagine a different world tomorrow.

Apply What You Learned

1. What is similar in the way each of these artists views the future? In what way are their artworks different?
2. What do you think Alexander Maldonado wanted to express in his painting?

Big Question
If you were asked to imagine the future in an artwork, what would you create?

Workbook
Pages 191–192

Contents
Handbooks and Resources

Study Skills and Language Learning

HOW TO LEARN LANGUAGE

Learning a language takes time, but, just like learning to swim, it can be fun. Whether you're learning English for the first time or adding to your knowledge of English by learning academic or content-area words, you're giving yourself a better chance of success in your studies and in your everyday life.

Learning any language is a skill that requires you to be active. You listen, speak, read, and write when you learn a language. Here are some tips that will help you learn English more actively and efficiently.

Listening

1. Set a purpose for listening. Think about what you hope to learn from today's class. Listen for these things as your teacher and classmates speak.
2. Listen actively. You can think faster than others can speak. This is useful because it allows you to anticipate what will be said next. Take notes as you listen. Write down only what is most important, and keep your notes short.
3. If you find something difficult to understand, listen more carefully. Do not give up and stop listening. Write down questions to ask afterward.
4. The more you listen, the faster you will learn. Use the radio, television, and Internet to practice your listening skills.

Speaking

1. Pay attention to sentence structure as you speak. Are you saying the words in the correct order?
2. Think about what you are saying. Don't worry about speaking fast. It's more important to communicate what you mean.
3. Practice speaking as much as you can, both in class and in your free time. Consider reading aloud to improve your pronunciation. If possible, record yourself speaking.
4. Do not be afraid of making mistakes. Everyone makes mistakes!

Reading

1. Read every day. Read as many different things as possible: Books, magazines, newspapers, and websites will all help you improve your comprehension and increase your vocabulary.
2. Try to understand what you are reading as a whole, rather than focusing on individual words. If you find a word you do not know, see if you can figure out its meaning from the context of the sentence before you look it up in a dictionary. Make a list of new vocabulary words and review it regularly.
3. Read texts more than once. Often your comprehension of a passage will improve if you read it twice or three times.
4. Try reading literature, poems, and plays aloud. This will help you understand them. It will also give you practice pronouncing new words.

Writing

1. Write something every day to improve your writing fluency. You can write about anything that interests you. Consider keeping a diary or a journal so that you can monitor your progress as time passes.
2. Plan your writing before you begin. Use graphic organizers to help you organize your ideas.
3. Be aware of sentence structure and grammar. Always write a first draft. Then go back and check for errors before you write your final version.

HOW TO BUILD VOCABULARY

1. Improving Your Vocabulary

Listening and Speaking

The most common ways to increase your vocabulary are listening, reading, and taking part in conversations. One of the most important skills in language learning is listening. Listen for new words when talking with others, joining in discussions, listening to the radio or audio books, or watching television.

You can find out the meanings of the words by asking, listening for clues, and looking up the words in a dictionary. Don't be embarrassed about asking what a word means. It shows that you are listening and that you want to learn. Whenever you can, use the new words you learn in conversation.

Reading Aloud

Listening to texts read aloud is another good way to build your vocabulary. There are many audio books available, and most libraries have a collection of them. When you listen to an audio book, you hear how new words are pronounced and how they are used. If you have a printed copy of the book, read along as you listen so that you can both see and hear new words.

Reading Often

Usually, people use a larger variety of words when they write than when they speak. The more you read, the more new words you'll find. When you see new words over and over again, they will become familiar to you and you'll begin to use them. Read from different sources—books, newspapers, magazines, Internet websites—in order to find a wide variety of words.

2. Figuring Out What a Word Means

Using Context Clues

When you come across a new word, you may not always need to use a dictionary. You might be able to figure out its meaning using the context, or the words in the sentence or paragraph in which you found it. Sometimes the surrounding words contain clues to tell you what the new word means.

Here are some tips for using context clues:

- Read the sentence, leaving out the word you don't know.
- Find clues in the sentence to figure out the new word's meaning.
- Read the sentence again, but replace the word you don't know with another possible meaning.
- Check your possible meaning by looking up the word in the dictionary. Write the word and its definition in your vocabulary notebook.

3. Practicing Your New Words

To make a word part of your vocabulary, study its definition, use it in your writing and speaking, and review it to make sure that you really understand its meaning.

Use one or more of these ways to remember the meanings of new words.

Keep a Vocabulary Notebook

Keep a notebook for vocabulary words. Divide your pages into three columns: the new words; hint words that help you remember their meanings; and their definitions. Test yourself by covering either the second or third column.

Word	Hint	Definition
zoology	zoo	study of animals
fortunate	fortune	lucky
quizzical	quiz	questioning

Make Flashcards

On the front of an index card, write a word you want to remember. On the back, write the meaning. You can also write a sentence that uses the word in context. Test yourself by flipping through the cards. Enter any hard words in your vocabulary notebook. As you learn the meanings, remove these cards and add new ones.

Say the Word Aloud

A useful strategy for building vocabulary is to say the new word aloud. Do not worry that there is no one to say the word to. Just say the word loud and clear several times. This will make you feel more confident and help you to use the word in conversation.

Record Yourself

Record your vocabulary words. Leave a ten-second space after each word, and then say the meaning and a sentence using the word. Play the recording. Fill in the blank space with the meaning and a sentence. Replay the recording until you memorize the word.

HOW TO USE REFERENCE BOOKS

The Dictionary

When you look up a word in the dictionary, you find the word and information about it. The word and the information about it are called a dictionary entry. Each entry tells you the word's spelling, pronunciation, part of speech, and meaning. Many English words have more than one meaning. Some words, such as *handle*, can be both a noun and a verb. For such words, the meanings, or definitions, are numbered. Sometimes example sentences are given in italics to help you understand how the word is used.

Here is part of a dictionary page with its important features labeled.

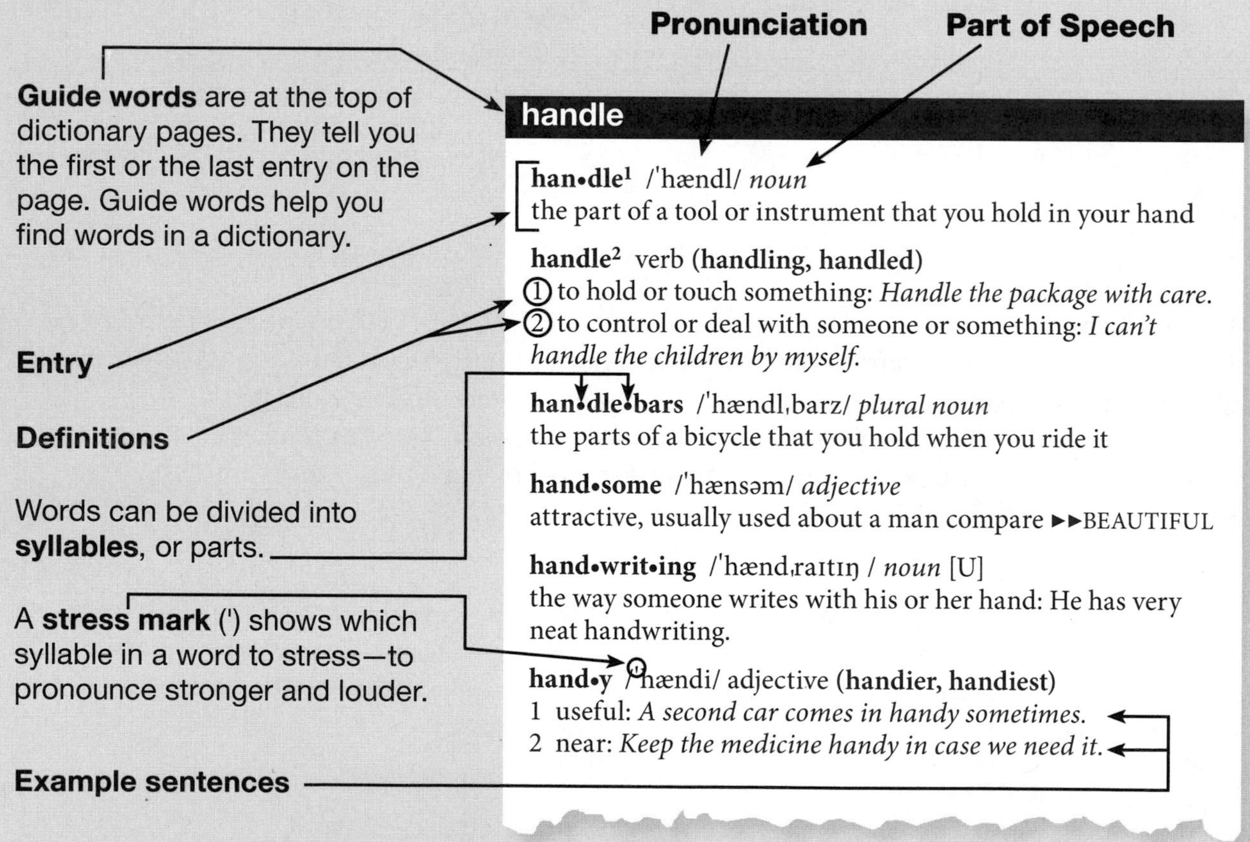

Pronunciation
Part of Speech
Guide words are at the top of dictionary pages. They tell you the first or the last entry on the page. Guide words help you find words in a dictionary.
Entry
Definitions
Words can be divided into **syllables**, or parts.
A **stress mark** (') shows which syllable in a word to stress—to pronounce stronger and louder.
Example sentences
handle
han•dle¹ /'hændl/ *noun*
the part of a tool or instrument that you hold in your hand
handle² verb (**handling, handled**)
① to hold or touch something: *Handle the package with care.*
② to control or deal with someone or something: *I can't handle the children by myself.*
han•dle•bars /'hændl,barz/ *plural noun*
the parts of a bicycle that you hold when you ride it
hand•some /'hænsəm/ *adjective*
attractive, usually used about a man compare ►►BEAUTIFUL
hand•writ•ing /'hænd,raɪtɪŋ / *noun* [U]
the way someone writes with his or her hand: He has very neat handwriting.
hand•y /'hændi/ adjective (**handier, handiest**)
1 useful: *A second car comes in handy sometimes.*
2 near: *Keep the medicine handy in case we need it.*

The Thesaurus

A thesaurus is a kind of dictionary. It is a specialized dictionary that lists synonyms, or words with similar meanings, for words. You can use a print thesaurus (a book) or an online thesaurus on the Internet.

A thesaurus is a useful writing tool because it can help you avoid repeating the same word. It can also help you choose more precise words. Using a thesaurus regularly can help build your vocabulary by increasing the number of words you know that are related by an idea or concept.

In a thesaurus, words may either be arranged alphabetically or be grouped by theme. When the arrangement is by theme, you first have to look up the word in the index to find out in which grouping its synonyms will appear. When the thesaurus is arranged alphabetically, you simply look up the word as you would in a dictionary.

The entry below is from a thesaurus that is arranged alphabetically.

sad *adjective* Tending to cause sadness or low spirits : blue, cheerless, depressed, depressing, dismal, dispiriting, downcast, gloomy, heartbreaking, joyless, melancholy, miserable, poignant, sorrowful, unhappy. See **happy** (antonym) in index.
—See also **depressed, sorrowful**.

Choose synonyms carefully. You can see from the thesaurus entry above that there are many synonyms for the word *sad*. However, not all of these words may be the ones you want to use. For example, *depressed* can mean that you have an illness called depression, but it can also mean that you feel sad. If you are not sure what a word means, look it up in a dictionary to check that it is, in fact, the word you want to use.

HOW TO TAKE TESTS

In this section, you will learn some ways to improve your test-taking skills.

1. Taking Tests

Objective tests are tests in which each question has only one correct answer. To prepare for these tests, you should study the material that the test covers.

Preview the Test

1. Write your name on each sheet of paper you will hand in.
2. Look over the test to get an idea of the kinds of questions being asked.
3. Find out whether you lose points for incorrect answers. If you do, do not guess at answers.
4. Decide how much time you need to spend on each section of the test.
5. Use the time well. Give the most time to questions that are hardest or worth the most points.

Answer the Questions

1. Answer the easy questions first. Put a check next to harder questions and come back to them later.
2. If permitted, use scratch paper to write down your ideas.
3. Read each question at least twice before answering.
4. Answer all questions on the test (unless guessing can cost you points).
5. Do not change your first answer without a good reason.

Proofread Your Answers

1. Check that you followed the directions completely.
2. Reread questions and answers. Make sure you answered all the questions.

2. Answering Different Kinds of Questions

This section tells you about different kinds of test questions and gives you specific strategies for answering them.

True-or-False Questions

True-or-false questions ask you to decide whether or not a statement is true.

1. If a statement seems true, make sure that it is *all* true.
2. Pay special attention to the word *not*. It often changes the meaning of a statement entirely.
3. Pay attention to words that have a general meaning, such as *all, always, never, no, none,* and *only*. They often make a statement false.
4. Pay attention to words that qualify, such as *generally, much, many, most, often, sometimes,* and *usually*. They often make a statement true.

Multiple-Choice Questions

This kind of question asks you to choose from four or five possible answers.

1. Try to answer the question before reading the choices. If your answer is one of the choices, choose that answer.
2. Eliminate answers you know are wrong. Cross them out if you are allowed to write on the test paper.

Matching Questions

Matching questions ask you to match items in one group with items in another group.

1. Count each group to see whether any items will be left over.
2. Read all the items before you start matching.
3. Match the items you know first, and then match the others. If you can write on the paper, cross out items as you use them.

Fill-In Questions

A fill-in question asks you to give an answer in your own words.

1. Read the question or exercise carefully.
2. If you are completing a sentence, look for clues in the sentence that might help you figure out the answer. If the word *an* is right before the missing word, this means that the missing word begins with a vowel sound.

Short-Answer Questions

Short-answer questions ask you to write one or more sentences in which you give certain information.

1. Scan the question for key words, such as *explain*, *compare*, and *identify.*
2. When you answer the question, give only the information asked for.
3. Answer the question as clearly as possible.

Essay Questions

On many tests, you will have to write one or more essays. Sometimes you are given a choice of questions that you can answer.

1. Look for key words in the question or questions to find out exactly what information you should give.
2. Take a few minutes to think about facts, examples, and other types of information you can put in your essay.
3. Spend most of your time writing your essay so that it is well planned.
4. Leave time at the end of the test to proofread and correct your work.

1. Understanding the Parts of a Book

The Title Page

Every book has a **title page** that states the title, author, and publisher.

The Table of Contents and Headings

Many books have a **table of contents.** The table of contents can be found in the front of the book. It lists the chapters or units in the book. Beside each chapter or unit is the number of the page on which it begins. A **heading** at the top of the first page of each section tells you what that section is about.

The Glossary

While you read, you can look up unfamiliar words in the **glossary** at the back of the book. It lists words alphabetically and gives definitions.

The Index

To find out whether a book includes particular information, use the **index** at the back of the book. It is an alphabetical listing of names, places, and subjects in the book. Page numbers are listed beside each item.

The Bibliography

The **bibliography** is at the end of a nonfiction book or article. It tells you the other books or sources where an author got information to write the book. The sources are listed alphabetically by author. The bibliography is also a good way to find more articles or information about the same subject.

2. Using the Library

The Card Catalog

To find a book in a library, use the **card catalog**—an alphabetical list of authors, subjects, and titles. Each book has a **call number**, which tells you where to find a book on the shelf. Author cards, title cards, and subject cards all give information about a book. Use the **author card** when you want to find a book by an author but do not know the title. The **title card** is useful if you know the title of a book but not the author. When you want to find a book about a particular subject, use the **subject card**.

The Online Library Catalog

The **online library catalog** is a fast way to find a book using a computer. Books can be looked up by author, subject, or title. The online catalog will give you information on the book, as well as its call number.

3. Learning Strategies

Strategy	Description and Examples
Organizational Planning	Setting a learning goal; planning how to carry out a project, write a story, or solve a problem
Predicting	Using parts of a text (such as illustrations or titles) or a real-life situation and your own knowledge to anticipate what will occur next
Self-Management	Seeking or arranging the conditions that help you learn
Using Your Knowledge and Experience	Using knowledge and experience to learn something new, brainstorm, make associations, or write or tell what you know
Monitoring Comprehension	Being aware of how well a task is going, how well you understand what you are hearing or reading, or how well you are conveying ideas
Using/Making Rules	Applying a rule (phonics, decoding, grammar, linguistic, mathematical, scientific, and so on) to understand a text or complete a task; figuring out rules or patterns from examples
Taking Notes	Writing down key information in verbal, graphic, or numerical form, often as concept maps, word webs, timelines, or other graphic organizers
Visualizing	Creating mental pictures and using them to understand and appreciate descriptive writing
Cooperation	Working with classmates to complete a task or project, demonstrate a process or product, share knowledge, solve problems, give and receive feedback, and develop social skills
Making Inferences	Using the context of a text and your own knowledge to guess meanings of unfamiliar words or ideas
Substitution	Using a synonym or paraphrasing when you want to express an idea and do not know the word(s)
Using Resources	Using reference materials (books, dictionaries, encyclopedias, videos, computer programs, the Internet) to find information or complete a task
Classification	Grouping words, ideas, objects, or numbers according to their attributes; constructing graphic organizers to show classifications
Asking Questions	Negotiating meaning by asking for clarification, confirmation, rephrasing, or examples
Summarizing	Making a summary of something you listened to or read; retelling a text in your own words
Self-evaluation	After completing a task, judging how well you did, whether you reached your goal, and how effective your problem-solving procedures were

Grammar Handbook

THE PARTS OF SPEECH

In English there are eight **parts of speech**: nouns, pronouns, adjectives, verbs, adverbs, prepositions, conjunctions, and interjections.

Nouns

Nouns name people, places, or things. There are two kinds of nouns: **common nouns** and **proper nouns**.

A **common noun** is a general person, place, or thing.

person	thing	place

The **student** brings a **notebook** to **class**.

A **proper noun** is a specific person, place, or thing. Proper nouns start with a capital letter.

person	place	thing

Joseph went to **Paris** and saw the **Eiffel Tower.**

A noun that is made up of two words is called a **compound noun**. A compound noun can be one word or two words. Some compound nouns have hyphens.

One word: **newspaper, bathroom**
Two words: **vice president, pet shop**
Hyphens: **sister-in-law, grown-up**

Articles identify nouns. *A*, *an*, and *the* are articles.

A and *an* are called **indefinite articles**. Use the article *a* or *an* to talk about one general person, place, or thing.

Use *an* before a word that begins with a vowel sound.

I have **an** idea.

Use *a* before a word that begins with a consonant sound.

May I borrow **a** pen?

The is called a **definite article**. Use *the* to talk about one or more specific people, places, or things.

Please bring me **the** box from your room. **The** books are in my backpack.

Pronouns

Pronouns are words that take the place of nouns or proper nouns. In this example, the pronoun *she* replaces, or refers to, the proper noun *Angela*.

proper noun
pronoun
Angela is not home. She is babysitting.

Pronouns can be subjects or objects. They can be singular or plural.

	Subject Pronouns	Object Pronouns
Singular	I, you, he, she, it	me, you, him, her, it
Plural	we, you, they	us, you, them

A **subject pronoun** replaces a noun or proper noun that is the subject of a sentence. A **subject** is who or what a sentence is about. In these sentences, *He* replaces *Daniel.*

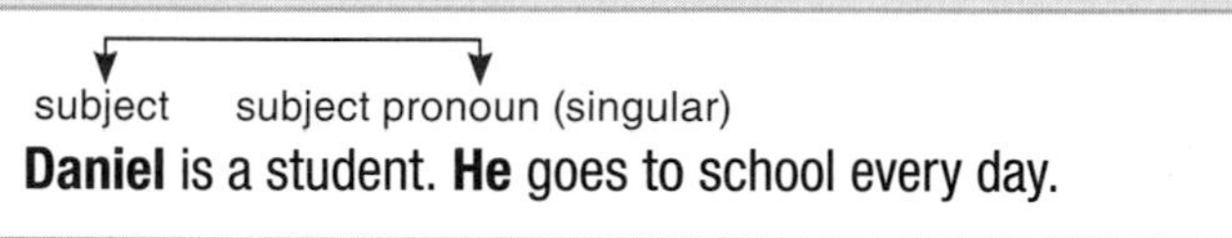

subject
subject pronoun (singular)
Daniel is a student. He goes to school every day.

In these sentences, *We* replaces *Heather* and *I*.

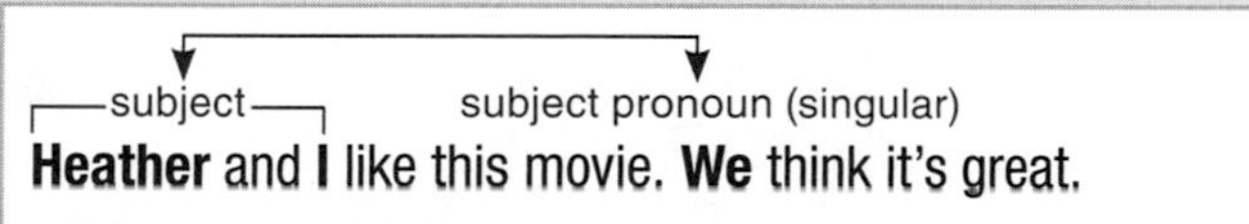

subject
subject pronoun (singular)
Heather and I like this movie. We think it's great.

An **object pronoun** replaces a noun or proper noun that is the object of a verb. A verb tells the action in a sentence. An **object** receives the action of a verb.

In these sentences the verb is *gave*. *Him* replaces *Ed*, which is the object of the verb.

object — object pronoun (singular)

Lauren gave **Ed** the notes. Lauren gave **him** the notes.

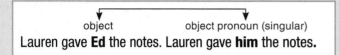

An object pronoun can also replace a noun or proper noun that is the **object of a preposition**. Prepositions are words like *for, to,* or *with*. In these sentences, the preposition is *with*. *Them* replaces *José* and *Yolanda*, which is the object of the preposition.

object of a preposition — object pronoun (plural)

I went to the mall with **José and Yolanda**. I went to the mall with **them**.

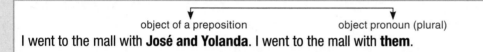

Pronouns can also be possessive. A **possessive pronoun** replaces a noun or proper noun. It shows who owns something.

	Possessive Pronouns
Singular	mine, yours, hers, his
Plural	ours, yours, theirs

In these sentences, *hers* replaces the words *Kyoko's coat*. It shows that Kyoko owns the coat.

It is **Kyoko's coat**. It is **hers**.

Adjectives

Adjectives describe nouns. An adjective usually comes before the noun it describes.

tall grass	**big** truck	**two** kittens

An adjective can also come *after* the noun it describes.

The bag is **heavy**. The books are **new**.

Do not add *-s* to adjectives that describe plural nouns.

the **red** houses	the **funny** jokes	the **smart** teachers

Verbs

Verbs express an action or a state of being.

subject verb Jackie **walks** to school.	subject verb The school **is** near her house.

An **action verb** tells what someone or something does or did. You cannot always see the action of an action verb.

Verbs That Tell Actions You Can See		Verbs That Tell Actions You Cannot See	
dance	swim	know	sense
play	talk	remember	name
sit	write	think	understand

A **linking verb** shows no action. It links the subject with another word that describes the subject.

Linking Verbs		
look	is	appear
smell	are	seem
sound	am	become
taste	were	
feel		

In this sentence, the adjective *tired* tells something about the subject, *dog*. *Seems* is the linking verb.

Our dog **seems** tired.

In this sentence, the noun *friend* tells something about the subject, *brother*. *Is* is the linking verb.

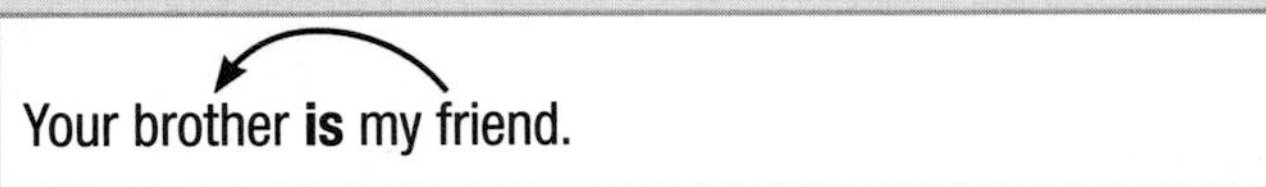
Your brother **is** my friend.

A **helping verb** comes before the main verb. It adds to the main verb's meaning. Helping verbs can be forms of the verbs *be*, *do*, or *have*.

	Helping Verbs
Forms of *be*	am, was, is, were, are
Forms of *do*	do, did, does
Forms of *have*	have, had, has
Other helping verbs	can, must, could, have (to), should, may, will, would

In this sentence, *am* is the helping verb; *walking* is the action verb.

helping verb / action verb

I **am walking** to my science class.

In this sentence, *has* is the helping verb; *completed* is the action verb.

helping verb / action verb

He **has completed** his essay.

In questions, the subject comes between a helping verb and a main verb.

person

Did Liang **give** you the CD?

Adverbs

Adverbs describe the action of verbs. They tell *how* an action happens. Adverbs answer the question *Where*? *When*? *How*? *How much*? or *How often*?

Many adverbs end in *-ly*.

easily	slowly	carefully

Some adverbs do not end in *-ly*.

seldom	fast	very

In this sentence, the adverb *everywhere* modifies the verb *looked*. It answers the question *Where*?

verb adverb
Nicole looked **everywhere** for her cell phone.

In this sentence, the adverb *quickly* modifies the verb *walked*. It answers the question *How*?

verb adverb
They walked home **quickly**.

Adverbs also modify adjectives. They answer the question *How much*? or *How little*?

In this sentence, the adjective *dangerous* modifies the noun *road*. The adverb *very* modifies the adjective *dangerous*.

adverb adjective noun
This is a **very** dangerous road.

Adverbs can also modify other adverbs. In this sentence, the adverb *fast* modifies the verb *runs*. The adverb *quite* modifies the adverb *fast*.

verb adverb adverb
John runs **quite** fast.

Prepositions

Prepositions can show time, place, and direction.

Time	Place	Direction
after	above	across
before	below	down
during	in	into
since	near	to
until	under	up

In this sentence, the preposition *above* shows where the bird flew. It shows place.

preposition
A bird flew **above** my head.

In this sentence, the preposition *across* shows direction.

preposition
The children walked **across** the street.

A **prepositional phrase** starts with a preposition and ends with a noun or pronoun.

In this sentence, the preposition is *near* and the noun is *school.*

prepositional phrase
The library is **near the new school**.

Conjunctions

A **conjunction** joins words, groups of words, and whole sentences.

Conjunctions			
and	for	or	yet
but	nor	so	

In this sentence, the conjunction *and* joins two proper nouns: *Jonah* and *Teresa.*

> noun noun
> Jonah **and** Teresa are in school.

In this sentence, the conjunction *or* joins two prepositional phrases: *to the movies* and *to the mall.*

> prepositional phrase — prepositional phrase
> They want to go to the movies **or** to the mall.

In this sentence, the conjunction *and* joins two independent clauses: *Amanda baked the cookies,* and *Eric made the lemonade.*

> independent clause — independent clause
> Amanda baked the cookies, **and** Eric made the lemonade.

Interjections

Interjections are words or phrases that express emotion.

Interjections that express strong emotion are followed by an exclamation point.

> **Wow!** Did you see that catch?
> **Hey!** Watch out for that ball.

Interjections that express mild emotion are followed by a comma.

> **Gee,** I'm sorry that your team lost.
> **Oh,** it's okay. We'll do better next time.

CLAUSES

Clauses are groups of words with a subject and a verb. Some clauses form complete sentences; they tell a complete thought. Others do not.

This clause is a complete sentence. Clauses that form complete sentences are called **independent clauses**.

subject verb
The dog's **tail wagged**.

This clause is not a complete sentence. Clauses that don't form complete sentences are called **dependent clauses**.

subject verb
when the **boy patted** him.

Independent clauses can be combined with dependent clauses to form a sentence.

In this sentence, *The dog's tail wagged* is an independent clause. *When the boy patted him* is a dependent clause.

independent clause — dependent clause
The dog's tail wagged when the boy patted him.

SENTENCES

Sentences have a subject and a verb, and tell a complete thought. A sentence always begins with a capital letter. It always ends with a period, question mark, or exclamation point.

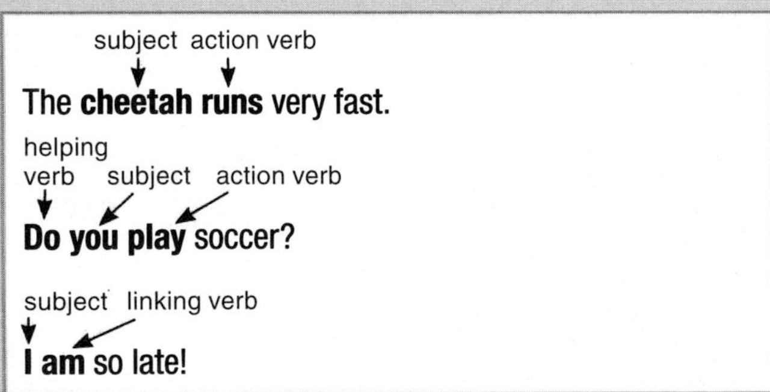

subject
action verb
The cheetah runs very fast.
helping verb
subject
action verb
Do you play soccer?
subject
linking verb
I am so late!

Simple Sentences and Compound Sentences

Some sentences are called simple sentences. Others are called compound sentences. A **simple sentence** has one independent clause. Here is an example.

independent clause
The dog barked at the mail carrier.

Compound sentences are made up of two or more simple sentences, or independent clauses. They are joined together by a **conjunction** such as *and* or *but*.

independent clause		independent clause
The band has a lead singer,	**but**	they need a drummer.

Sentence Types

Sentences have different purposes. There are four types of sentences: declarative, interrogative, imperative, and exclamatory.

Declarative sentences are statements. They end with a period.

> We are going to the beach on Saturday.

Interrogative sentences are questions. They end with a question mark.

> Will you come with us?

Imperative sentences are commands. They usually end with a period. If the command is strong, the sentence may end with an exclamation point.

> Put on your life jacket. Now jump into the water!

Exclamatory sentences express strong feeling. They end with an exclamation point.

> I swam all the way from the boat to the shore!

MECHANICS

End Marks

End marks come at the end of sentences. There are three kinds of end marks: periods, question marks, and exclamation points.

Use a **period** to end a statement (declarative sentence).

> The spacecraft *Magellan* took pictures of Jupiter.

Use a **period** to end a command or request (imperative sentence) that isn't strong enough to need an exclamation point.

> Please change the channel.

Use a **question mark** to end a sentence that asks a question. (interrogative sentence).

> Where does Mrs. Suarez live?

Use an **exclamation point** to end a sentence that expresses strong feeling (exclamatory sentence).

> That was a great party!
> Look at that huge house!

Use an **exclamation point** to end an imperative sentence that gives an urgent command.

> Get away from the edge of the pool!

Periods are also used after initials and many abbreviations.

Use a **period** after a person's initial or abbreviated title.

Ms. Susan Vargas	Mrs. Fiske	J. D. Salinger
Gov. Lise Crawford	Mr. Vargas	Dr. Sapirstein

Use a **period** after the abbreviation of streets, roads, and so on.

Avenue	Ave.	Road	Rd.
Highway	Hwy.	Street	St.

Use a **period** after the abbreviation of many units of measurement. Abbreviations for metric measurements do *not* use periods.

inch	in.	centimeter	cm
foot	ft.	meter	m
pound	lb.	kilogram	kg
gallon	gal.	liter	l

Commas

Commas separate, or set off, parts of a sentence, or phrase.

Use a comma to separate two independent clauses linked by a conjunction. In this sentence, the comma goes before the conjunction *but*.

independent clause — independent clause

We went to the museum**, but** it is not open on Mondays.

Use commas to separate the parts in a series. A series is a group of three or more words, phrases, or very brief clauses.

	Commas in Series
To separate words	Lucio's bike is red**,** white**,** and silver.
To separate phrases	Today, he rode all over the lawn**,** down the sidewalk**,** and up the hill.
To separate clauses	Lucio washed the bike**,** his dad washed the car**,** and his mom washed the dog.

Use a comma to set off an introductory word, phrase, or clause.

	Commas with Introductory Words
To separate words	Yes**,** Stacy likes to go swimming.
To set off a phrase	In a month**,** she may join the swim team again.
To set off a clause	If she joins the swim team**,** I'll miss her at softball practice.

Use commas to set off an interrupting word, phrase, or clause.

	Commas with Interrupting Words
To set off a word	We left, finally, to get some fresh air.
To set off a phrase	Carol's dog, a brown pug, shakes when he gets scared.
To set off a clause	The assignment, I'm sorry to say, was too hard for me.

Use a comma to set off a speaker's quoted words in a sentence.

Jeanne asked, "Where is that book I just had?"
"I just saw it," said Billy, "on the kitchen counter."

In a direct address, one speaker talks directly to another. Use commas to set off the name of the person being addressed.

Thank you, Dee, for helping to put away the dishes.
Phil, why are you late again?

Use a comma between the day and the year.

My cousin was born on September 9, 2003.

If the date appears in the middle of a sentence, use a comma before and after the year.

Daria's mother was born on June 8, 1969, in New Jersey.

Use a comma between a city and a state and between a city and a nation.

My father grew up in Bakersfield, California.
We are traveling to Acapulco, Mexico.

If the names appear in the middle of a sentence, use a comma before *and* after the state or nation.

My friend Carl went to Mumbai, India, last year.

Use a comma after the greeting in a friendly letter. Use a comma after the closing in both a friendly letter and formal letter. Do this in e-mail letters, too.

Dear Margaret,	Sincerely,	Yours truly,

Semicolons and Colons

Semicolons can connect two independent clauses. Use them when the clauses are closely related in meaning or structure.

The team won again; it was their ninth victory. Ana usually studies right after school; Rita prefers to study in the evening.

Colons introduce a list of items or important information.

Use a colon after an independent clause to introduce a list of items. (The clause often includes the words *the following, these, those,* or *this.*)

The following animals live in Costa Rica: monkeys, lemurs, toucans, and jaguars.

Use a colon to introduce important information. If the information is in an independent clause, use a capital letter to begin the first word after the colon.

There is one main rule: Do not talk to anyone during the test. You must remember this: Stay away from the train tracks!

Use a colon to separate hours and minutes when writing the time.

1:30	7:45	11:08

Quotation Marks

Quotation Marks set off direct quotations, dialogue, and some titles. A **direct quotation** is the exact words that somebody said, wrote, or thought.

Commas and periods *always* go inside quotation marks. If a question mark or exclamation point is part of the quotation, it is also placed *inside* the quotation marks.

> "Can you please get ready**?**" Mom asked.
> My sister shouted, "Look out for that bee**!**"

If a question mark or exclamation point is *not* part of the quotation, it goes *outside* the quotation marks. In these cases there is no punctuation before the end quotation marks.

> Did you say, "I can't do this"**?**

Conversation between two or more people is called **dialogue**. Use quotation marks to set off spoken words in dialogue.

> "What a great ride**!**" Pam said. "Let's go on it again."
> Julio shook his head and said, "No way. I'm feeling sick."

Use quotation marks around the titles of short works of writing or other art forms. The following kinds of titles take quotation marks:

Chapters	"The Railroad in the West"
Short Stories	"The Perfect Cat"
Articles	"California in the 1920s"
Songs	"This Land Is Your Land"
Single TV episodes	"Charlie's New Idea"
Short poems	"The Bat"

Titles of all other written work and artwork are underlined or set in italic type. These include books, magazines, newspapers, plays, movies, TV series, and paintings.

Apostrophes

Apostrophes can be used with singular and plural nouns to show ownership or possession. To form the possessive, follow these rules:

For singular nouns, add an apostrophe and an *s*.

Maria**'s** eyes	hamster**'s** cage	the sun**'s** warmth

For singular nouns that end in *s*, add an apostrophe and an *s*.

her boss**'s** office	Carlos**'s** piano	the grass**'s** length

For plural nouns that do not end in *s*, add an apostrophe and an *s*.

women**'s** clothes	men**'s** shoes	children**'s** books

For plural nouns that end in *s*, add an apostrophe.

teachers' lounge	dogs' leashes	kids' playground

Apostrophes are also used in **contractions**. A contraction is a shortened form of two words that have been combined. The apostrophe shows where a letter or letters have been taken away.

I will
I'll be home in one hour.

do not
We **don't** have any milk.

Capitalization

There are five main reasons to use capital letters:

1. To begin a sentence and in a direct quotation
2. To write the word *I*
3. To write a proper noun (the name of a specific person, place, or thing)
4. To write a person's title
5. To write the title of a work (artwork, written work, magazine, newspaper, musical composition, organization)

Use a capital letter to begin the first word in a sentence.

Cows eat grass. **T**hey also eat hay.

Use a capital letter for the first word of a direct quotation. Use the capital letter even if the quotation is in the middle of a sentence.

Carlos said, "**W**e need more lettuce for the sandwiches."

Use a capital letter for the word *I*.

How will **I** ever learn all these things? **I** guess **I** will learn them little by little.

Use a capital letter for a proper noun: the name of a specific person, place, or thing. Capitalize the important words in names.

Robert **E**. **L**ee **M**orocco **T**uesday **T**ropic of **C**ancer

Capital Letters in Place Names	
Streets	Interstate 95, Center Street, Atwood Avenue
City Sections	Greenwich Village, Shaker Heights, East Side
Cities and Towns	Rome, Chicago, Fresno
States	California, North Dakota, Maryland
Regions	Pacific Northwest, Great Plains, Eastern Europe
Nations	China, Dominican Republic, Italy
Continents	North America, Africa, Asia
Mountains	Mount Shasta, Andes Mountains, Rocky Mountains
Deserts	Mojave Desert, Sahara Desert, Gobi Desert
Islands	Fiji Islands, Capri, Virgin Islands
Rivers	Amazon River, Nile River, Mississippi River
Lakes	Lake Superior, Great Bear Lake, Lake Tahoe
Bays	San Francisco Bay, Hudson Bay, Galveston Bay
Seas	Mediterranean Sea, Sea of Japan
Oceans	Pacific Ocean, Atlantic Ocean, Indian Ocean

Capital Letters for Specific Things	
Historical Periods, Events	Renaissance, Battle of Bull Run
Historical Texts	Constitution, Bill of Rights
Days and Months	Monday, October
Holidays	Thanksgiving, Labor Day
Organizations, Schools	Greenpeace, Central High School
Government Bodies	Congress, State Department
Political Parties	Republican Party, Democratic Party
Ethnic Groups	Chinese, Latinos
Languages, Nationalities	Spanish, Canadian
Buildings	Empire State Building, City Hall
Monuments	Lincoln Memorial, Washington Monument
Religions	Hinduism, Christianity, Judaism, Islam
Special Events	Boston Marathon, Ohio State Fair

Use a capital letter for a person's title if the title comes before the name. In the second sentence below, a capital letter is not needed because the title does not come before a name.

> I heard **S**enator Clinton's speech about jobs. The **s**enator may come to our school.

Use a capital letter for the first and last word and all other important words in titles of books, newspapers, magazines, short stories, plays, movies, songs, paintings, and sculptures.

> Lucy wants to read **T**he **L**ord of the **R**ings.
> The newspaper my father reads is **T**he **N**ew **Y**ork **T**imes.
> Did you like the painting called **W**ork in the **F**ields?
> This poem is called "**T**he **B**irch **T**ree."

Reading Handbook

WHAT IS READING COMPREHENSION?

People often think of reading as a passive activity—that you don't have to do much, you just have to take in words—but that is not true. Good readers are active readers.

Reading comprehension involves these skills:

1. Understanding what you are reading.
2. Being part of what you are reading, or engaging with the text.
3. Evaluating what you are reading.
4. Making connections between what you are reading and what you already know.
5. Thinking about your response to what you have read.

Understanding What You Are Reading

One of the first steps is to recognize letters and words. Remember that it does not matter if you do not recognize all the words. You can figure out their meanings later. Try to figure out the meaning of unfamiliar words from the context of the sentence or paragraph. If you cannot figure out the meaning of a word, look it up in a dictionary. Next, you activate the meaning of words as you read them. That is what you are doing now. If you find parts of a text difficult, stop and read them a second time.

Engaging with the Text

Good readers use many different skills and strategies to help them understand and enjoy the text they are reading. When you read, think of it as a conversation between you and the writer. The writer wants to tell you something, and you want to understand his or her message.

Practice using these tips every time you read:

- Predict what will happen next in a story. Use clues you find in the text.
- Ask yourself questions about the main idea or message of the text.
- Monitor your understanding. Stop reading from time to time and think about what you have learned so far.

Evaluating What You Are Reading

The next step is to think about what you are reading. First, think about the author's purpose for writing. What type of text are you reading? If it is an informational text, the author wants to give you information about a subject, for example, about science, social science, or math. If you are reading literature, the author's purpose is probably to entertain you.

When you have decided what the author's purpose is for writing the text, think about what you have learned. Use these questions to help you:

- Is the information useful?
- Have you changed your mind about the subject?
- Did you enjoy the story, poem, or play?

Making Connections

Now connect the events or ideas in a text to your own knowledge or experience. Think about how your knowledge of a subject or your experience of the world can help you understand a text better.

- If the text has sections with headings, notice what these are. Do they give you clues about the main ideas in the text?
- Read the first paragraph. What is the main idea?
- Now read the paragraphs that follow. Make a note of the main ideas.
- Review your notes. How are the ideas connected?

Thinking about Your Response to What You Have Read

You read for a reason, so it is a good idea to think about how the text has helped you. Ask yourself these questions after you read:

- What information have I learned? Can I use it in my other classes?
- How can I connect my own experience or knowledge to the text?
- Did I enjoy reading the text? Why or why not?
- Did I learn any new vocabulary? What was it? How can I use it in conversation or in writing?

WHAT ARE READING STRATEGIES?

Reading strategies are specific things readers do to help them understand texts. Reading is like a conversation between an author and a reader. Authors make decisions about how to effectively communicate through a piece of writing. Readers use specific strategies to help them understand what authors are trying to communicate. Ten of the most common reading strategies are Previewing, Predicting, Skimming, Scanning, Comparing and Contrasting, Identifying Problems and Solutions, Recognizing Cause and Effect, Distinguishing Fact from Opinion, Identifying Main Idea and Details, and Identifying an Author's Purpose.

Viewing and Representing

WHAT ARE VIEWING AND REPRESENTING?

Viewing

Viewing is something you do every day. Much of what you read and watch includes visuals that help you understand information. These visuals can be maps, charts, diagrams, graphs, photographs, illustrations, and so on. They can inform you, explain a topic or an idea, entertain you, or persuade you.

Websites use visuals, too. It is important for you to be able to view visuals critically in order to evaluate what you are seeing or reading.

Representing

Representing is creating a visual to convey an idea. It is important for you to be able to create and use visuals in your own written work and presentations. You can use graphic organizers, diagrams, charts, posters, and artwork to illustrate and explain your ideas. Following are some examples of visuals.

HOW TO READ MAPS AND DIAGRAMS

Maps

Maps help us learn more about our world. They show the location of places such as countries, states, and cities. Some maps show where mountains, rivers, and lakes are located.

Many maps have helpful features. For example, a **compass rose** shows which way is north. A **scale** shows how miles or kilometers are represented on the map. A **key** shows what different colors or symbols represent.

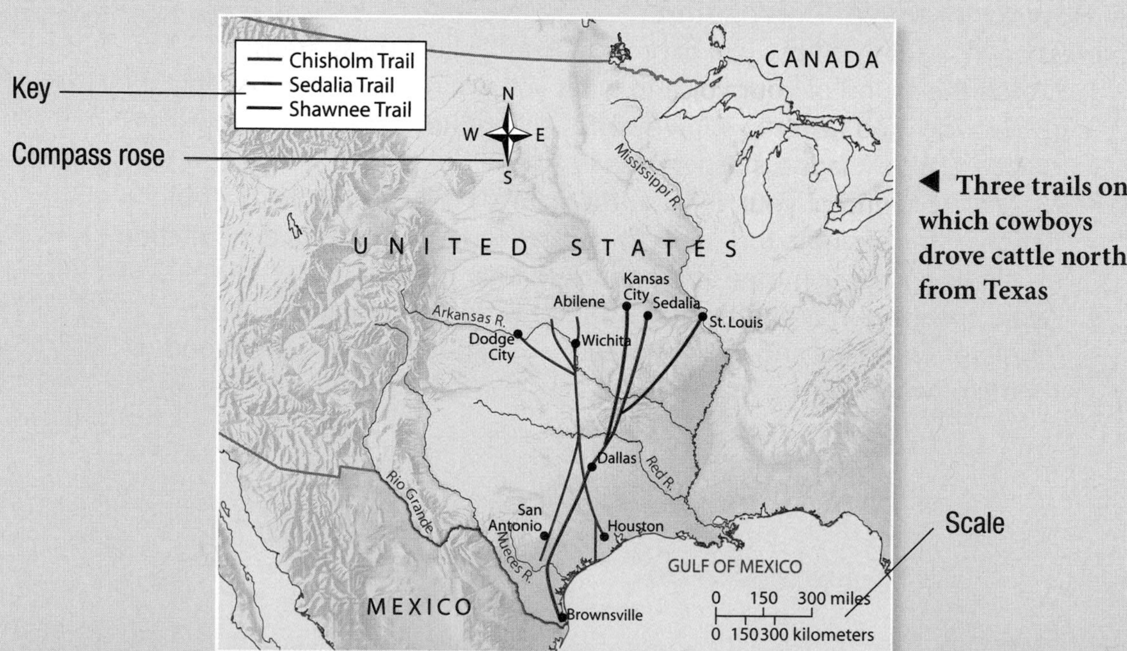

◀ **Three trails on which cowboys drove cattle north from Texas**

Diagrams

Diagrams are drawings or plans used to explain things or show how things work. They are often used in social studies and science books. Some diagrams show pictures of how objects look on the outside or on the inside. Others show the different steps in a process.

This diagram shows what a kernel of corn looks like on the inside.

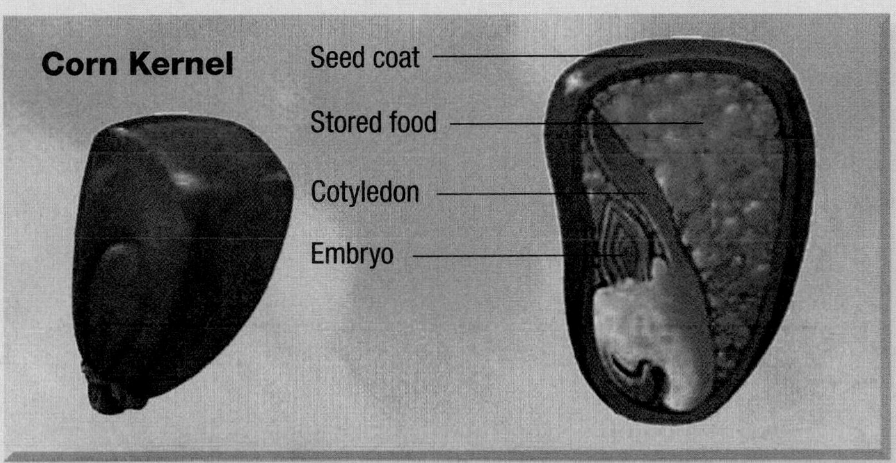

A **flowchart** is a diagram that uses shapes and arrows to show a step-by-step process. The flowchart below shows the steps involved in baking chicken fingers. Each arrow points to the next step.

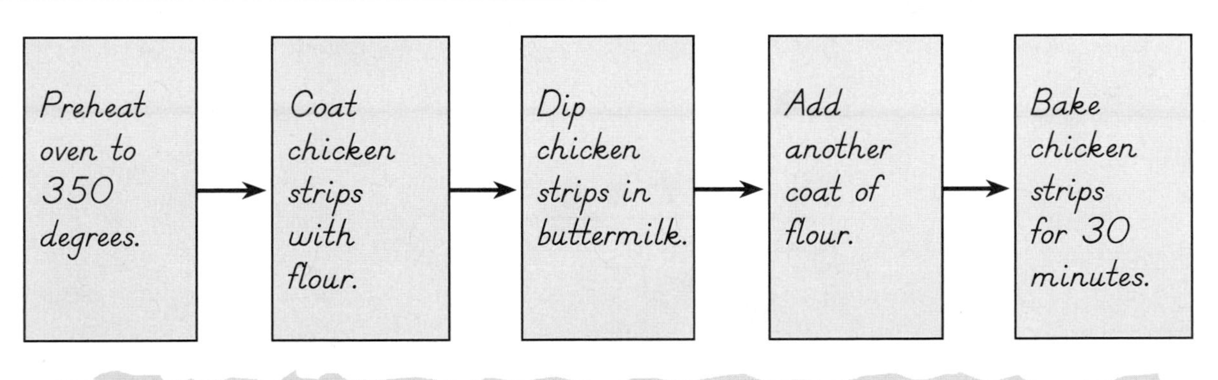

Preheat oven to 350 degrees.
Coat chicken strips with flour.
Dip chicken strips in buttermilk.
Add another coat of flour.
Bake chicken strips for 30 minutes.

HOW TO READ GRAPHS

Graphs organize and explain information. They show how two or more kinds of information are related, or how they are alike. Graphs are often used in math, science, and social studies books. Three common kinds of graphs are **line graphs, bar graphs,** and **circle graphs.**

Line Graphs

A line graph shows how information changes over a period of time. This line graph explains how, over a period of about 100 years, the Native-American population of Central Mexico decreased by more than 20 million people. Can you find the population in the year 1540? What was it in 1580?

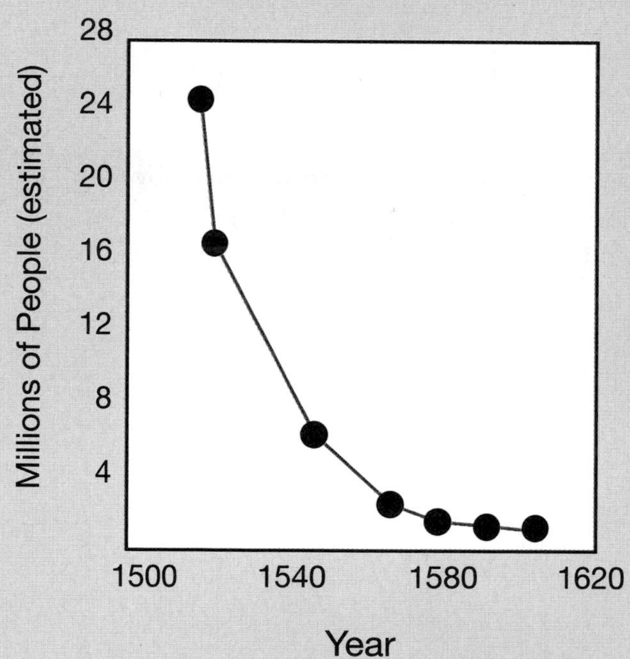

Bar Graphs

We use bar graphs to compare information. For example, this bar graph compares the populations of the thirteen United States in 1790. It shows that, in 1790, Virginia had over ten times as many people as Delaware.

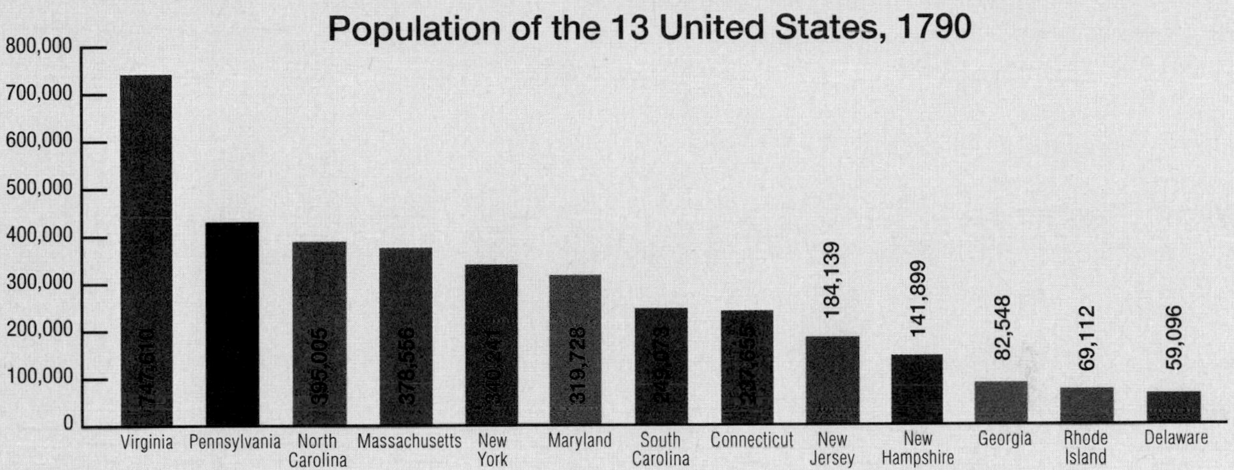

Circle Graphs

A circle graph is sometimes called a pie chart because it looks like a pie cut into slices. Circle graphs are used to show how different parts of a whole thing compare to one another. In a circle graph, all the "slices" add up to 100 percent. This circle graph shows that only 29 percent of the earth's surface is covered by land. It also shows that the continent of Asia takes up 30 percent of the earth's land.

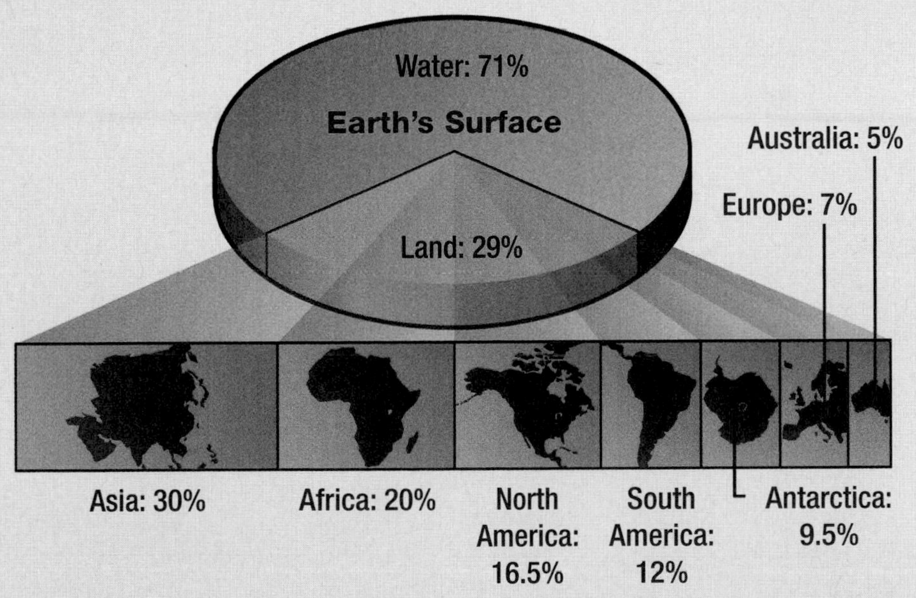

HOW TO USE GRAPHIC ORGANIZERS

A graphic organizer is a diagram that helps you organize information and show relationships among ideas. Because the information is organized visually, a graphic organizer tells you—in a quick snapshot—how ideas are related. Before you make a graphic organizer, think about the information you want to organize. How are the ideas or details related? Choose a format that will show those relationships clearly.

Venn diagrams and **word webs** are commonly used graphic organizers. Here is an example of each.

Venn Diagrams

A Venn diagram shows how two thing are alike and different. The diagram below compares oranges and bananas.

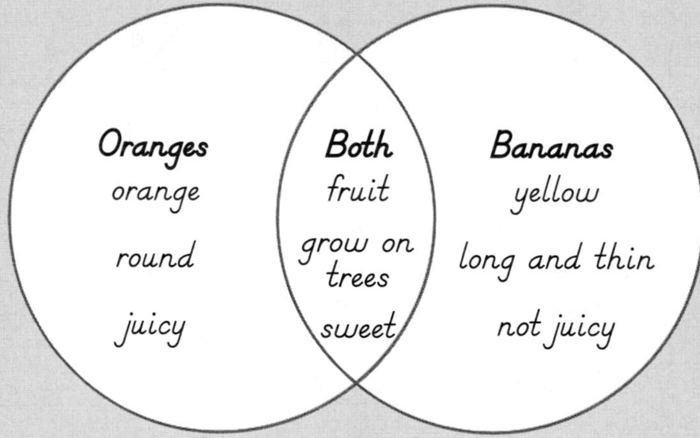

Word Webs

A word web is often used to help a writer describe something. The word web below lists five sensory details that describe popcorn.

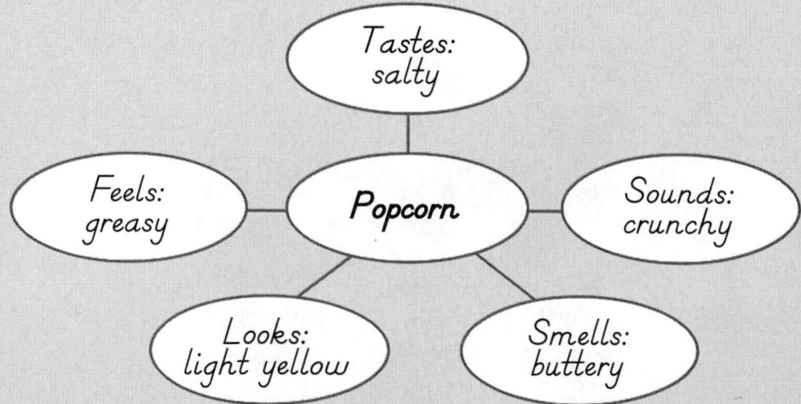

Writing Handbook

MODES OF WRITING

Narration

When writers tell a story, they use narration. There are many kinds of narration. Most include characters, a setting, and a sequence of events. Here are some types of narration.

A **short story** is a short, creative narrative. Most short stories have one or more characters, a setting, and a plot. A few types of short stories are realistic stories, fantasy stories, science-fiction stories, and adventure stories.

Autobiographical writing is a factual story of a writer's own life, told by the writer, usually in the first-person point of view. An autobiography may tell about the person's whole life or only a part of it.

Biographical writing is a factual story of a person's life told by another person. Most biographies are written about famous or admirable people.

Description

Description, or descriptive writing, is writing that gives the reader a mental picture of whatever is being described. To do this, writers choose their words carefully. They use figurative language and include vivid sensory details.

Persuasion

Writers use persuasion to try to persuade people to think or act in a certain way. Forms of persuasive writing include advertisements, essays, letters, editorials, speeches, and public-service announcements.

Exposition

Exposition, or expository writing, is writing that gives information or explains something. The information that writers include in expository writing is factual. Here are some types of expository writing.

A **compare-and-contrast essay** analyzes the similarities and differences between or among things.

A **cause-and-effect essay** explains causes or effects of an event. For example, a writer might examine several causes of a single effect or several effects of a single cause.

Writers use a **problem-and-solution essay** to describe a problem and offer one or more solutions to it.

A **how-to essay** explains how to do or make something. The process is broken down into steps, which are explained in order.

A **summary** is a brief statement that gives the main ideas of an event or a piece of writing. One way to write a summary is to read a text and then reread each paragraph or section. Next put the text aside and write the main ideas in your own words in a sentence or two.

Research Writing

Writers often use research to gather information about topics, including people, places, and things. Good research writing does not simply repeat information. It guides the readers through a topic, showing them why each fact matters and creating a complete picture of the topic. Here are some types of research writing.

Research report A research report presents information gathered from reference books, interviews, or other sources.

Biographical report A biographical report includes dates, details, and main events in a person's life. It can also include information about the time in which the person lived.

Multimedia report A multimedia report presents information through a variety of media, including text, slides, photographs, prerecorded music and sound effects, and digital imaging.

Responses to Literature

A **literary essay** is one type of response to literature. In a literary essay, a writer discusses and interprets what is important in a book, short story, essay, article, or poem.

Literary criticism is another type of response to literature. Literary criticism is the result of a careful examination of one or more literary works. The writer makes a judgment by looking carefully and critically at various important elements in the work.

A book **critique** gives readers a summary of a book, encouraging the reader either to read it or to avoid reading it. A movie critique gives readers a summary of a movie, tells if the writer enjoyed the movie, and then explains the reasons why or why not.

A **comparison of works** compares the features of two or more works.

Creative Writing

Creative writing blends imagination, ideas, and emotions, and allows the writer to present a unique view of the world. Poems, plays, short stories, dramas, and even some cartoons are examples of creative writing.

Practical and Technical Documents

Practical writing is fact-based writing that people do in the workplace or in their day-to-day lives. A business letter, memo, school form, job application, and a letter of inquiry are a few examples of practical writing.

Technical documents are fact-based documents that identify a sequence of activities needed to design a system, operate machinery, follow a procedure, or explain the rules of an organization. You read technical writing every time you read a manual or a set of instructions.

In the following descriptions, you'll find tips for tackling several types of practical and technical writing.

Business letters are formal letters that follow one of several specific formats.

News releases, also called press releases, announce factual information about upcoming events. A writer might send a news release to a local newspaper, local radio station, TV station, or other media that will publicize the information.

Guidelines give information about how people should act or how to do something.

Process explanations are step-by-step explanations of how to do something. The explanation should be clear and specific and can include diagrams or other illustrations. Below is an example.

KEYSTONE

CD-ROM

Usage Instructions

1. Insert the *Keystone* CD-ROM into your CD drive.
2. Open "My Computer."
3. Double-click on your CD-ROM disk drive.
4. Click on the *Keystone* icon. This will launch the program.

THE WRITING PROCESS

The **writing process** is a series of steps that can help you write effectively.

Step 1: Prewrite

During **prewriting**, you collect topic ideas, choose a topic, plan your writing, and gather information.

A good way to get ideas for a topic is to **brainstorm**. Brainstorming means writing a list of all the topic ideas you can think of.

Look at your list of topic ideas. Choose the one that is the most interesting to you. This is your **topic**, the subject you will write about.

Plan your writing by following these steps:

- First, decide on the **type** of writing that works best with your topic. For example, you may want to write a description, a story, or an essay.
- The type of writing is called the **form** of writing.
- Then think about your **audience**. Identifying your audience will help you decide whether to write formally or informally.
- Finally, decide what your reason for writing is. This is your **purpose**. Is your purpose to inform your audience? To entertain them?

How you gather information depends on what you are writing. For example, for a report, you need to do research. For a description, you might list your ideas in a graphic organizer. A student named Becca listed her ideas for a description of her week at art camp in the graphic organizer below.

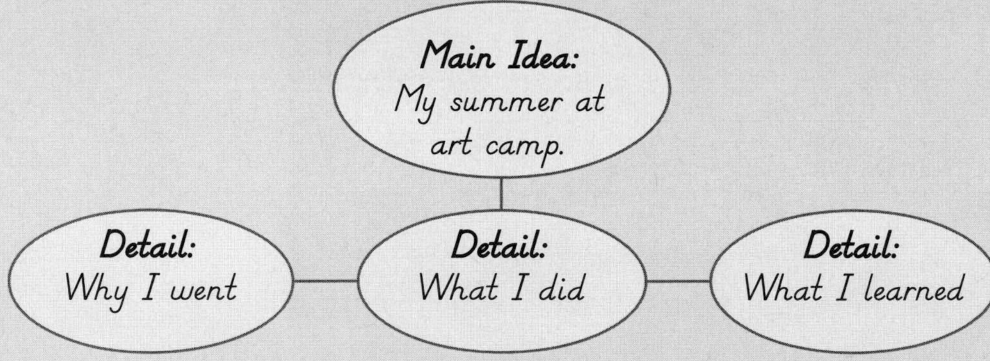

Step 2: Draft

In this step, you start writing. Don't worry too much about spelling and punctuation. Just put your ideas into sentences.

Here is the first paragraph that Becca wrote for her first draft.

> I saw an art contest advertised in the newspaper last spring. I entered my best drawing. I have always loved art. The prize was a week at an art camp in June with 9 other kids. I was very happy when I won.

Step 3: Revise

Now it's time to revise, or make changes. Ask yourself these questions:

- Are my ideas presented in the order that makes the most sense?
- Does my draft have a beginning, a middle, and an end?
- Does each paragraph have a main idea and supporting details?

If you answered *no* to any of these questions, you need to revise. Revising can mean changing the order of paragraphs or sentences. It can mean changing general words for specific words. It can mean correcting errors.

Once you decide what to change, you can mark the corrections on your draft using editing marks. Here's how Becca marked up her first paragraph.

> When I saw an art contest advertised in the newspaper last spring, I entered my best drawing. I have always loved art. The prize was a week at an art camp in June with ~~9~~ nine other kids. I was very ~~happy~~ excited when I won.

Step 4: Edit and Proofread

In this step, you make a second draft that includes the changes you marked on your first draft. You can also add details you may have thought of since writing your first draft. Now you're ready to **proofread**, or check your work for errors and make final corrections.

Here's Becca's first draft after she finished proofreading.

My Week at Art Camp

I have always loved art. When I saw an art contest advertised in the newspaper last spring, I entered my best drawing. The prize was a week at an art camp in June with nine other students. I was very excited when I won.

The camp was located at the Everson museum of art. On the first day, we looked at paintings by different artists. My favorite was by a painter named Monet. He painted colorful land scapes of boats and gardens. On the second day, we began our own paintings. I choose to paint a picture of the duck pond on the campus. I worked hard on my painting because we were going to have an art show of all our work at the end of the week.

I learned alot about painting at camp. I especially liked learning to use watercolors. For example, I found out that you can make interesting designs by sprinkling salt on a wet watercolor painting.

I had a great time at art camp. The show at the end of the week was a big success, and I made some new friends. I hope to go again next year.

Step 5: Publish

Prepare a final copy of your writing to **publish**, or share with your audience. Here are some publishing tips.

- Photocopy and hand out your work to your classmates.
- Attach it to an e-mail and send it to friends.
- Send it to a school newspaper or magazine for possible publication.

Here is the final version of Becca's paper.

My Week at Art Camp

I have always loved art. When I saw an art contest advertised in the newspaper last spring, I entered my best drawing. The prize was a week at an art camp in June with nine other students. I was very excited when I won.

The camp was located at the Everson Museum of Art. On the first day, we looked at paintings by different artists. My favorite was by a painter named Monet. He painted colorful landscapes of boats and gardens. On the second day, we began our own paintings. I chose to paint a picture of the duck pond on the campus. I worked hard on my painting because we were going to have an art show of all our work at the end of the week.

I learned a lot about painting at camp. I especially liked learning to use watercolors. For example, I found out that you can make interesting designs by sprinkling salt on a wet watercolor painting.

I had a great time at art camp. The show at the end of the week was a big success, and I made some new friends. I hope to go again next year.

Once you have shared your work with others, you may want to keep it in a **portfolio**, a folder or envelope with your other writing. Each time you write something, add it to your portfolio. Compare recent work with earlier work. See how your writing is improving.

RUBRICS FOR WRITING

What Is a Rubric?

A **rubric** is a tool, often in the form of a chart or a grid, that helps you assess your work. Rubrics are helpful for writing and speaking assignments.

To help you or others assess your work, a rubric offers several specific criteria to be applied to your work. Then the rubric helps you indicate your range of success or failure according to those specific criteria. Rubrics are often used to evaluate writing for standardized tests.

Using a rubric will save you time, focus your learning, and improve your work. When you know the rubric beforehand, you can keep the specific criteria for the writing in your mind as you write. As you evaluate the essay before giving it to your teacher, you can focus on the specific criteria that your teacher wants you to master—or on areas that you know present challenges for you. Instead of searching through your work randomly for any way to improve or correct it, you will have a clear and helpful focus.

How Are Rubrics Structured?

Rubrics can be structured in several different ways:

1. Your teacher may assign a rubric for a specific assignment.
2. Your teacher may direct you to a rubric in your textbook.
3. Your teacher and your class may structure a rubric for a particular assignment together.
4. You and your classmates may structure a rubric together.
5. You can create your own rubric with your own specific criteria.

How Will a Rubric Help Me?

A rubric will help you assess your work on a scale. Scales vary from rubric to rubric but usually range from 6 to 1, 5 to 1, or 4 to 1, with 6, 5, or 4 being the highest score and 1 being the lowest. If someone else is using the rubric to assess your work, the rubric will give your evaluator a clear range within which to place your work. If you are using the rubric yourself, it will help you improve your work.

What Are the Types of Rubrics?

A **holistic rubric** has general criteria that can apply to a variety of assignments. An **analytic rubric** is specific to a particular assignment. The criteria for evaluation address the specific issues important in that assignment. The following pages show examples of both types of rubrics.

Holistic Rubrics

Holistic rubrics such as this one are sometimes used to assess writing assignments on standardized tests. Notice that the criteria for evaluation are focus, organization, support, and use of conventions.

Points	Criteria
6 Points	• The writing is focused and shows fresh insight into the writing task. • The writing is marked by a sense of completeness and coherence and is organized with a logical progression of ideas. • A main idea is fully developed, and support is specific and substantial. • A mature command of the language is evident. • Sentence structure is varied, and writing is free of fragments. • Virtually no errors in writing conventions appear.
5 Points	• The writing is focused on the task. • The writing is organized and has a logical progression of ideas, though there may be occasional lapses. • A main idea is well developed and supported with relevant detail. • Sentence structure is varied, and the writing is free of fragments. • Writing conventions are followed correctly.
4 Points	• The writing is focused on the task, but unrelated material may intrude. • Clear organizational pattern is present, though lapses occur. • A main idea is adequately supported, but development may be uneven. • Sentence structure is generally fragment free but shows little variation. • Writing conventions are generally followed correctly.
3 Points	• Writing is focused on the task, but unrelated material intrudes. • Organization is evident, but writing may lack a logical progression of ideas. • Support for the main idea is present but is sometimes illogical. • Sentence structure is free of fragments, but there is almost no variation. • The work demonstrates a knowledge of conventions, with misspellings.
2 Points	• The writing is related to the task but generally lacks focus. • There is little evidence of an organizational pattern. • Support for the main idea is generally inadequate, illogical, or absent. • Sentence structure is unvaried, and serious errors may occur. • Errors in writing conventions and spellings are frequent.
1 Point	• The writing may have little connection to the task. • There has been little attempt at organization or development. • The paper seems fragmented, with no clear main idea. • Sentence structure is unvaried, and serious errors appear. • Poor diction and poor command of the language obscure meaning. • Errors in writing conventions and spelling are frequent.
Unscorable	• The response is unrelated to the task or is simply a rewording of the prompt. • The response has been copied from a published work. • The student did not write a response. • The response is illegible. • The words in the response are arranged with no meaning. • There is an insufficient amount of writing to score.

Analytic Rubrics

This analytic rubric is an example of a rubric to assess a persuasive essay. It will help you assess presentation, position, evidence, and arguments.

Presentation	Position	Evidence	Arguments
6 Points Essay clearly and effectively addresses an issue with more than one side.	Essay clearly states a supportable position on the issue.	All evidence is logically organized, well presented, and supports the position.	All reader concerns and counterarguments are effectively addressed.
5 Points Most of essay addresses an issue that has more than one side.	Essay clearly states a position on the issue.	Most evidence is logically organized, well presented, and supports the position.	Most reader concerns and counterarguments are effectively addressed.
4 Points Essay adequately addresses issue that has more than one side.	Essay adequately states a position on the issue.	Many parts of evidence support the position; some evidence is out of order.	Many reader concerns and counterarguments are adequately addressed.
3 Points Essay addresses issue with two sides but does not present second side clearly.	Essay states a position on the issue, but the position is difficult to support.	Some evidence supports the position, but some evidence is out of order.	Some reader concerns and counterarguments are addressed.
2 Points Essay addresses issue with two sides but does not present second side.	Essay states a position on the issue, but the position is not supportable.	Not much evidence supports the position, and what is included is out of order.	A few reader concerns and counterarguments are addressed.
1 Point Essay does not address issue with more than one side.	Essay does not state a position on the issue.	No evidence supports the position.	No reader concerns or counterarguments are addressed.

WRITING LETTERS

Friendly Letters

A friendly letter is less formal than a business letter. It is a letter to a friend, a family member, or anyone with whom the writer wants to communicate in a personal, friendly way. Most friendly letters are made up of five parts: the **date**, the **greeting** (or salutation), the **body**, the **closing**, and the **signature**. The greeting is followed by a comma, and the paragraphs in the body are indented.

The purpose of a friendly letter is usually to share personal news and feelings, to send or to answer an invitation, or to express thanks.

In this letter, Maité tells her friend Julio about her new home.

March 2, 2009

Dear Julio,

I was so happy to receive your letter today. I am feeling much better. My mom and I finally finished decorating my room. We painted the walls green and the ceiling pink. At first, my mom was nervous to paint the ceiling something other than white, but I knew it would look good. Now that my bedroom is finished, Manhattan is starting to feel more like home.

Body

Over the weekend I went to the Museum of Natural History. The whale exhibit made me think of back home and how you and I would spend hours at the beach. I am starting to adjust to city life, but I miss the smell of salt in the air and collecting sea glass on the shore.

My parents said I can spend the summer with my grandparents at their beach house. They said I could invite you for a couple of weeks. We'll go swimming every day. I can't wait!

Your friend, ← **Closing**

Maité ← **Signature**

Business Letters

Business letters follow one of several formats. In **block format**, each part of the letter begins at the left margin. A double space is used between paragraphs. In **modified block format**, some parts of the letter are indented to the center of the page. No matter which format is used, all letters in business format have a date, an inside address, a greeting (or salutation), a body, a closing, and a signature. These parts are shown on the model business letter below, formatted in block style.

June 11, 2009 ← **Date**

Edward Sykes, Vice President
Animal Rights Group ← **Inside Address**
154 Denver Street
Syosset, NY 11791

Dear Mr. Sykes: ← **Greeting**

Many students at Bellevue High School would like to learn about animal rights for a project we're starting next fall. We've read about your program on your website and would like to know more about your activities.

Would you send us some information about your organization? We're specifically interested in learning what we as students can do to help protect animals. About 75 students have expressed interest so far—I think we'll have the people power to make the project a success and have an impact.

Please help us get started. Thank you for your time and consideration.

← **Body**

Sincerely, ← **Closing**

Pedro Rodriguez ← **Signature**

Pedro Rodriguez

The **inside address** shows where the letter will be sent. The **greeting** is punctuated with a colon. The **body** of the letter states the writer's purpose. The **closing** "Sincerely" is common, but "Yours truly" or "Respectfully yours" are also acceptable. The writer types his or her name and writes a **signature**.

FILLING IN FORMS

Forms are preprinted documents with spaces for the user to enter specific information. Some include directions; others assume that users will follow the labels and common conventions. Two common forms in the workplace are fax cover sheets and applications. When you fill out forms, it is important to do the following:

- Fill them out accurately and completely.
- Write neatly in blue or black ink.
- Include only information that is asked for on the form.

Forms usually have limited space in which to write. Because space is limited, you can use standard symbols and abbreviations, such as *$10/hr.* to mean "10 dollars per hour."

FAX COVER SHEET

To: *Mr. Robert Thompson* **From:** *Laura Rivas*

Fax: *(001) 921-9833* **Pages:** *2 (including cover sheet)*

Date: *12/04/09*

Re: *Job Application*

Message:

Dear Mr. Thompson:

Thank you for meeting with me today about the sales associate position at Story Land Bookshop. The following page is my completed application form.

Sincerely,

Laura Rivas

Filling in an Application for Employment

Story Land Bookshop **PRE-EMPLOYMENT QUESTIONNAIRE**
EQUAL OPPORTUNITY EMPLOYER
Date: 12/04/2009

PERSONAL INFORMATION

Name (last name first)		Social Security No.	
Rivas, Laura		145-53-6211	

Present Address	City	State	Zip Code
351 Middleton Road	Osborne	TX	78357

Permanent Address	City	State	Zip Code
Same			

Phone No.	Referred by
(001) 661-1567	Josh Logan

EMPLOYMENT DESIRED

Position	Start Date	Salary Desired
Sales associate	Immediately	$10/hr.

	Yes	No
Are you presently employed?	☐	☑
May we contact your former employer?	☑	☐
Were you ever employed by this company?	☐	☑

EDUCATION

Name and Location of School	Yrs Attended	Did you graduate?
Osborne High School, Osborne, TX	3	Expect to graduate 2010

FORMER EMPLOYERS

Name and Address of Employer	Salary	Position
Blue River Summer Camp	$195 per week	Junior camp
127 Horse Lane		counselor
Millwood, TX 78721		

Date Month and Year	Reason for Leaving
6/20/09 to 9/20/09	Summer ended

CONDUCTING RESEARCH

Reference Skills

There is a wide range of print and electronic references you can use to find many different kinds of information.

Encyclopedias

Encyclopedias contain facts on a great many subjects. They provide basic information to help you start researching a topic. Use encyclopedias for basic facts, background information, and suggestions for additional research.

Periodicals

Periodicals are magazines and journals. Once you've used a periodical index to identify the articles you want to read, ask a librarian to help you locate the periodicals. Often, past issues of magazines are stored electronically on microfilm, a database, or CD-ROMs. The librarian can help you use these resources. Use the table of contents, the titles, and other magazine features to help you find information.

Biographical References

These books provide brief life histories of famous people in many different fields. Biographical references may offer short entries similar to those in dictionaries or longer articles more like those in encyclopedias. Most contain an index to help you locate entries.

Nonfiction Books

Nonfiction books about your topic can also be useful reference tools. Use titles, tables of contents, prefaces, chapter headings, glossaries, indexes, and appendixes to locate the information you need.

Almanacs

Almanacs are published annually. They contain facts and statistics about many subjects, including government, world history, geography, entertainment, business, and sports. To find a subject in a printed almanac, refer to the index in the front or back. In an electronic almanac, you can usually find information by typing a subject or key word.

Electronic Databases

Available on CD-ROMs or online, electronic databases provide quick access to a wealth of information on a topic. Using a search feature, you can easily access any type of data, piece together related information, or look at the information in a different way.

PROOFREADING

All forms of writing—from a letter to a friend to a research paper—are more effective when they are error-free. Once you are satisfied with the content of your writing, polish the grammar, usage, and mechanics.

Challenge yourself to learn and apply the skills of proofreading to everything you write. Review your writing carefully to find and correct all errors. Here are the broad categories that should direct your proofreading:

- ☑ **CHECK YOUR SPELLING:** Use a dictionary or an electronic spelling checker to check any spelling of which you are unsure.

- ☑ **CHECK YOUR GRAMMAR AND USAGE:** Use a writing handbook to correct problems in grammar or usage.

- ☑ **REVIEW CAPITALIZATION AND PUNCTUATION:** Review your draft to be sure you've begun each sentence with a capital letter and used proper end punctuation.

- ☑ **CHECK THE FACTS:** When your writing includes facts gathered from outside sources, confirm the accuracy of your work. Consult reference materials. Check names, dates, and statistics.

Editing Marks		
To:	**Use This Mark:**	**Example:**
add something	^	We ate rice, bean^s and corn.
delete something	ℓ	We ate rice, beans, and corns.
start a new paragraph	¶	¶We ate rice, beans, and corn.
add a comma	^,	We ate rice, beans^, and corn.
add a period	⊙	We ate rice, beans, and corn⊙
switch letters or words	∼	We ate rice, baens, and corn.
change to a capital letter	a with triple underline	we ate rice, beans, and corn.
change to a lowercase letter	A with slash	WE ate rice, beans, and corn.

CITING SOURCES

Proofreading and Preparing Manuscript

Before preparing a final copy, proofread your manuscript.

- Choose a standard, easy-to-read font.
- Type or print on one side of unlined 8 1/2" x 11" paper.
- Set the margins for the side, top, and bottom of your paper at approximately one inch. Most word-processing programs have a default setting that is appropriate.
- Double-space the document.
- Indent the first line of each paragraph.
- Number the pages in the upper right corner.

Follow your teacher's directions for formatting formal research papers. Most papers will have the following features: Title page, Table of Contents or Outline, Works Consulted List.

Crediting Sources

When you credit a source, you acknowledge where you found your information and you give your readers the details necessary for locating the source themselves. Within the body of the paper, you provide a short citation, a footnote number linked to a footnote, or an endnote number linked to an endnote reference. These brief references show the page numbers on which you found the information. Prepare a reference list at the end of the paper to provide full bibliographic information on your sources. These are two common types of reference lists:

A **bibliography** provides a listing of all the resources you consulted during your research. A **works consulted list** lists the works you have referenced in your paper.

The chart on the next page shows the Modern Language Association format for crediting sources. This is the most common format for papers written in the content areas in middle school and high school. Unless instructed otherwise by your teacher, use this format for crediting sources.

MLA Style for Listing Sources

Book with one author	Pyles, Thomas. *The Origins and Development of the English Language.* 2nd ed. New York: Harcourt Brace Jovanovich, Inc., 1971.
Book with two or three authors	McCrum, Robert, William Cran, and Robert MacNeil. *The Story of English.* New York: Penguin Books, 1987.
Book with an editor	Truth, Sojourner. *Narrative of Sojourner Truth.* Ed. Margaret Washington. New York: Vintage Books, 1993.
Book with more than three authors or editors	Donald, Robert B., et al. *Writing Clear Essays.* Upper Saddle River, NJ: Prentice Hall, Inc., 1996.
Single work from an anthology	Hawthorne, Nathaniel. "Young Goodman Brown." *Literature: An Introduction to Reading and Writing.* Ed. Edgar V. Roberts and Henry E. Jacobs. Upper Saddle River, NJ: Prentice-Hall, Inc., 1998. 376–385. [Indicate pages for the entire selection.]
Introduction in a published edition	Washington, Margaret. Introduction. *Narrative of Sojourner Truth.* By Sojourner Truth. New York: Vintage Books, 1993, pp. v–xi.
Signed article in a weekly magazine	Wallace, Charles. "A Vodacious Deal." *Time* 14 Feb. 2000: 63.
Signed article in a monthly magazine	Gustaitis, Joseph. "The Sticky History of Chewing Gum." *American History* Oct. 1998: 30–38.
Unsigned editorial or story	"Selective Silence." Editorial. *Wall Street Journal* 11 Feb. 2000: A14. [If the editorial or story is signed, begin with the author's name.]
Signed pamphlet or brochure	[Treat the pamphlet as though it were a book.]
Pamphlet with no author, publisher, or date	*Are You at Risk of Heart Attack?* n.p. n.d. ["n.p. n.d." indicates that there is no known publisher or date.]
Filmstrips, slide programs, videocassettes, DVDs, and other audiovisual media	*The Diary of Anne Frank.* Dir. George Stevens. Perf. Millie Perkins, Shelly Winters, Joseph Schildkraut, Lou Jacobi, and Richard Beymer. Twentieth Century Fox, 1959.
Radio or television program transcript	"Nobel for Literature." Narr. Rick Karr. *All Things Considered.* National Public Radio. WNYC, New York. 10 Oct. 2002. Transcript.
Internet	*National Association of Chewing Gum Manufacturers.* 19 Dec. 1999 <http://www.nacgm.org/consumer/funfacts.html> [Indicate the date you accessed the information. Content and addresses at websites change frequently.]
Newspaper	Thurow, Roger. "South Africans Who Fought for Sanctions Now Scrap for Investors." *Wall Street Journal* 11 Feb. 2000: A1+ [For a multipage article, write only the first page number on which it appears, followed by a plus sign.]
Personal interview	Smith, Jane. Personal interview. 10 Feb. 2000.
CD (with multiple publishers)	Simms, James, ed. *Romeo and Juliet.* By William Shakespeare. CD-ROM. Oxford: Attica Cybernetics Ltd.; London: BBC Education; London: HarperCollins Publishers, 1995.
Signed article from an encyclopedia	Askeland, Donald R. "Welding." *World Book Encyclopedia.* 1991 ed.

Technology Handbook

WHAT IS TECHNOLOGY?

Technology is a combination of resources that can help you do research, find information, and write. Good sources for research include the Internet and your local library. The library contains databases where you can find many forms of print and nonprint resources, including audio and video recordings.

The Internet

The Internet is an international network, or connection, of computers that share information with each other. It is a popular source for research and finding information for academic, professional, and personal reasons. The World Wide Web is a part of the Internet that allows you to find, read, and organize information. Using the Web is a fast way to get the most current information about many topics.

Words or phrases can be typed into the "search" section of a search engine, and websites that contain those words will be listed for you to explore. You can then search a website for the information you need.

Information Media

Media is all the organizations, such as television, radio, and newspapers that provide news and information for the public. Knowing the characteristics of various kinds of media will help you to spot them during your research. The following chart describes several forms of information media.

Types of Information Media	
Television News Program	• Covers current news events • Gives information objectively
Documentary	• Focuses on one topic of social interest • Sometimes expresses controversial opinions
Television Newsmagazine	• Covers a variety of topics • Entertains and informs
Commercial	• Presents products, people, or ideas • Persuades people to buy or take action

Other Sources of Information

There are many other reliable print and nonprint sources of information to use in your research. For example: magazines, newspapers, professional or academic journal articles, experts, political speeches, press conferences.

Most of the information from these sources is also available on the Internet. Try to evaluate the information you find from various media sources. Be careful to choose the most reliable sources for this information.

HOW TO USE THE INTERNET FOR RESEARCH

Keyword Search

Before you begin a search, narrow your subject to a keyword or a group of **keywords**. These are your search terms, and they should be as specific as possible. For example, if you are looking for information about your favorite musical group, you might use the band's name as a keyword. You might locate such information as band member biographies, the group's history, fan reviews of concerts, and hundreds of sites with related names containing information that is irrelevant to your search. Depending on your research needs, you might need to narrow your search.

How to Narrow Your Search

If you have a large group of keywords and still don't know which ones to use, write out a list of all the words you are considering. Then, delete the words that are least important to your search, and highlight those that are most important.

Use search connectors to fine-tune your search:

AND: narrows a search by retrieving documents that include both terms. For example: ***trumpets AND jazz***

OR: broadens a search by retrieving documents including any of the terms. For example: ***jazz OR music***

NOT: narrows a search by excluding documents containing certain words. For example: ***trumpets NOT drums***

Good Search Tips

1. Search engines can be case-sensitive. If your first try at searching fails, check your search terms for misspellings and search again.
2. Use the most important keyword first, followed by the less important ones.
3. Do not open the link to every single page in your results list. Search engines show pages in order of how close it is to your keyword. The most useful pages will be located at the top of the list.
4. Some search engines provide helpful tips for narrowing your search.

Respecting Copyrighted Material

The Internet is growing every day. Sometimes you are not allowed to access or reprint material you find on the Internet. For some text, photographs, music, and fine art, you must first get permission from the author or copyright owner. Also, be careful not to plagiarize while writing and researching. Plagiarism is presenting someone else's words, ideas, or work as your own. If the idea or words are not yours, be sure to give credit by citing the source in your work.

HOW TO EVALUATE THE QUALITY OF INFORMATION

Since the media presents large amounts of information, it is important to learn how to analyze this information critically. Analyzing critically means you can evaluate the information for content, quality, and importance.

How to Evaluate Information from Various Media

Sometimes the media tries to make you think a certain way instead of giving all the facts. These techniques will help you figure out if you can rely on information from the media.

- ✔ Ask yourself if you can trust the source, or if the information you find shows any bias. Is the information being given in a one-sided way?
- ✔ Discuss the information you find from different media with your classmates or teachers to figure out its reliability.
- ✔ Sort out facts from opinions. Make sure that any opinions given are backed up with facts. A fact is a statement that can be proved true. An opinion is a viewpoint that cannot be proved true.
- ✔ Be aware of any loaded language or images. Loaded language and images are emotional words and visuals used to persuade you.
- ✔ Check surprising or questionable information in other sources. Are there instances of faulty reasoning? Is the information adequately supported?
- ✔ Be aware of the kind of media you are watching. If it's a program, is it a documentary? A commercial? What is its purpose? Is it correct?
- ✔ Read the entire article or watch the whole program before reaching a conclusion. Then develop your own views on the issues, people, and information presented.

How to Evaluate Information from the Internet

There is so much information available on the Internet that it can be hard to understand. It is important to be sure that the information you use as support or evidence is reliable and can be trusted. Use the following checklist to decide if a Web page you are reading is reliable and a credible source.

- ☑ The information is from a well-known and trusted website. For example, websites that end in **.edu** are part of an educational institution and usually can be trusted. Other cues for reliable websites are sites that end in **.org** for "organization" or **.gov** for "government." Sites with a **.com** ending are either owned by businesses or individuals.
- ☑ The people who write or are quoted on the website are experts, not just everyday people telling their ideas or opinions.
- ☑ The website gives facts, not just opinions.
- ☑ The website is free of grammatical and spelling errors. This is often a hint that the site was carefully made and will not have factual mistakes.
- ☑ The website is not trying to sell a product or persuade people. It is simply trying to give correct information.
- ☑ If you are not sure about using a website as a source, ask your teacher for advice. Once you become more aware of the different sites, you will become better at knowing which sources to trust.

HOW TO USE TECHNOLOGY IN WRITING

Personal Computers

A personal computer can be an excellent writing tool. It enables a writer to create, change, and save documents. The cut, copy, and paste features are especially useful when writing and revising.

Organizing Information

Create a system to organize the research information you find from various forms of media, such as newspapers, books, and the Internet.

Using a computer and printer can help you in the writing process. You can change your drafts, see your changes clearly, and keep copies of all your work. Also, consider keeping an electronic portfolio. This way you can store and organize copies of your writing in several subject areas. You can review the works you have completed and see your improvement as a writer.

It is easy to organize electronic files on a computer. The desktop is the main screen, and holds folders that the user names. For example, a folder labeled "Writing Projects September" might contain all of the writing you do during that month. This will help you find your work quickly.

As you use your portfolio, you might think of better ways to organize it. You might find you have several drafts of a paper you wrote, and want to create a separate folder for these. Every month, take time to clean up your files.

Computer Tips

1. Rename each of your revised drafts using the SAVE AS function. For example, if your first file is "essay," name the first revision "essay2" and the next one "essay3."
2. If you share your computer with others, label a folder with your name and keep your files separate by putting them there.
3. Always back up your portfolio on a server or a CD.

Personal computer ▶

Glossary

accurate correct or exact

achieve succeed in doing or getting something as a result of your actions

affect to do something that produces a change in someone or something; influence

alter change in some way

ancient very old

anniversary a day when you remember something special or important that happened on the same date in an earlier year

approach to move closer to someone or something

appropriate suitable for a particular time, situation, or purpose

archaeologist someone who studies very old things and buildings made by people who lived a long time ago

architecture the shape and style of buildings

arrangement a plan or agreement that something will happen

artificial not natural, but made by people

aspect one of the parts or features of a situation, idea, or problem

assassinated murdered, especially for political reasons

assist to help someone do something

athletes people who are good at sports and take part in sports competitions

atomic bomb a very powerful bomb that splits atoms to cause an extremely large explosion

attitude the opinions and feelings that you usually have about someone or something

author someone who writes a book, story, article, play, etc.

average calculated by adding several amounts together and dividing by the total number of amounts

aware realizing that something is true, exists, or is happening

benefit something that gives you an advantage, that helps you, or that has a good effect

bond a feeling or interest that unites two or more people or groups

boundaries lines that divide two places

brief continuing for a short time

campaign a series of actions done to get a result, especially in business or politics

canvases strong cloths that are painted on

canyons deep valleys with very steep sides

category a group of people or things that have related characteristics

cells the smallest living things

ceremony a group of special actions done and special words spoken at an important public or religious event

chaos a state of no order or no control

character traits special qualities or features that someone or something has that make that person or thing different from others

characters people or animals in a novel, story, movie, or play

circumstances the facts or conditions that affect a situation, action, or event

citizen a person who lives in a particular country or city and has special rights there

classical belonging to the culture of ancient Greece or ancient Rome

clues things that help you find the answer to a difficult problem

colorful language words an author uses to make a story, play, or movie sound and look more fun

comment a stated opinion made about someone or something

committee a group of people chosen to do something, make decisions, etc.

communicate express your thoughts and feelings so that others understand them

complex complicated

concept an idea of how something is or how something should be done

conflict disagreement

conservationists people who protect natural things such as animals, plants, or forests

consist to be made up of or contain particular things or people

constant happening regularly or all the time

construct build something large such as a building, bridge, or sculpture

continent one of the large areas of land on earth, such as Africa, Europe, Australia, etc.

conversion the art or process of changing from one form, purpose, or system to a different one

convey communicate a message or information, with or without using words

cooperate to work together with someone else to achieve something that you both want

create make something exist

creature an animal or insect

cultural relating to a particular society and its way of life

damage harm that has been done to something

defendant the person in a court of law who has been accused of doing something illegal

define show or describe what something is or means

democratic organized by a system in which everyone has the same right to vote, speak, etc.

demonstrate protest or support something in public with a lot of other people

deny say that something is not true

destruction the act of breaking or damaging something completely

device a way of achieving a particular purpose or effect

dialect a form of language that is spoken in one area in a different way than it is in another area

dialogue a conversation by two or more characters in a book, play, or movie

disappeared was lost or stopped existing

drama a play for the theater, television, radio, etc.

education teaching and learning

effect a result or a reaction to something or someone

element part of a plan, system, piece of writing, etc.

enormous extremely large in size or amount

environment the land, water, and air in which people, animals, and plants live

establish create

estimate judge the value or size of something

evidence facts, objects, or signs that make you believe that something exists or is true

extinct no longer existing or living

extraordinary very special

fable a story that teaches a lesson

factors several things that influence or cause a situation

fantasy an imagined situation or thing that is not real

feature quality, element, or characteristic of something that seems important, interesting, or typical

figure of speech a word or expression that is used in a different way from the usual one, to give you a picture in your mind

final last in a series of actions, events, or parts of something

finance provide money for something

focus attention to a particular person or thing

forensic relating to methods for finding out about a crime

founders people who establish a business, organization, school, etc.

frontier the area where people are just beginning to explore or live

function the usual purpose of a thing, or the job that someone usually does

generation all the people who are about the same age, especially in a family

genes parts of a cell that decide what traits you will have

gigantic very big

gradual happening or changing slowly

habitats the natural environments in which plants or animals live

height how tall or how far from the ground something is

humor something that amuses people or makes them laugh

hyperbole a way of describing something by saying that it is much bigger, smaller, heavier, etc., than it really is

identify recognize and name someone or something

idioms groups of words that have special meaning when they are used together

illustrate explain or make something clear by giving examples

image a picture that you can see through a camera, on television, or in a mirror; a picture that you have in your mind

impact the effect that something or someone has on someone or something

individual a person, not a group

infinity a space or distance without limits or an end

inherit to get a quality, type of behavior, appearance, etc., from one your parents

inspiration someone or something that encourages you to do or produce something good

instruct to teach someone or show him or her how to do something

intelligent having a high ability to learn, understand, and think about things

interpretation an explanation

intruder someone or something that enters a building or area where they are not supposed to be

legislation a law or set of laws

length the distance from one end of something to the other; how long something is

list of characters a set of names that identify the characters of a play to the reader

mass-produced produced in large numbers using machinery so that each object is the same and can be sold cheaply

medical relating to medicine and the treatment of disease or injury

metaphor a way of describing something by comparing it to something else that has similar qualities, without using the words *like* or *as*. "A river of tears" is a metaphor.

method a planned way of doing something

mood the way that a place, book, movie, etc., makes you feel

moral a lesson about what is right and wrong that you learn from a story or an event

motive the reason that makes someone do something, especially when this reason is kept hidden

mural a very large painting that is painted or placed directly on a wall

myth an ancient story, especially one that explains cultural beliefs or a natural or historic event

narrator someone who tells the story in a movie, book, etc.

natural found in nature, not made by people or machines

numerals written signs that represent numbers

nutrition the process of giving or getting the right kinds of food in order to be healthy

objective something that you are working hard to achieve

occupation job or profession

occur happen

ornithology the scientific study of birds

percent equal to a particular amount in every hundred

period a particular length of time in history or in a person's life

personification a literary device in which nonhuman characters are given human traits

perspective a way of thinking about something that is influenced by the type of person you are or by what you do

philosophy the study of what it means to exist, what good and evil are, what knowledge is, or how people should live

physical relating to the body or to other things you can see, touch, smell, feel, or taste plot the main events that make up the story of a book, movie, or play

point of view the perspective from which a story is written or told

policy a way of doing things that has been officially agreed upon and chosen by a political party or an organization

positive good or useful

precise exact and correct in every detail

predator an animal that kills and eats other animals

procedure the correct or normal way of way of doing something

process a series of actions that someone does in order to achieve a particular result

professional relating to a job for which you need special education or training

published printed and sold

puns amusing uses of a word or phrase that has two meanings, or of words with the same sound but different meanings

pursue chase or follow someone or something to catch him, her, or it

rate the number of times or the speed at which something happens

react to behave in a particular way because of what someone has done or said to you

region a fairly large area of a state, country, etc.

rely on to trust or depend on someone or something

repetition the act of doing or saying something again

require need something

research serious study of a subject that is intended to discover new facts about it

resistance refusal to give in to someone or something

resource something such as land, minerals, or natural energy that exists in a country and can be used in order to increase wealth

respond to react to something that has been said or done

responsibilities things that you have a duty to do or take care of

rhyme scheme a pattern of end rhymes in poems or song lyrics

rhythm a regular pattern of sounds or beats

rights what things are or should be allowed by the law

rituals ceremonies or sets of actions that are always done in the same way

robots machines that can move and do some of the work

role the position, job, or function someone or something has in a particular situation or activity

sacred relating to a god or religion; extremely important and greatly respected

sacrifice to not do something so that you can do something more important

science fiction a type of writing that describes imaginary future developments in science and their effect on life, for example, time travel

section a part of something

sequence a series of related events, actions, or numbers that have a particular order

setting where and when a story or real-life event takes place

setting the scene an author's details about the time and place in a book or play

shift a change in the way people think about something or in the way something is done

simile an expression in which you compare two things using the words *like* or *as*, for example, "Her face was as pale as the moon."

site a place where something is being built or will be built

specific detailed and exact

sphere something in the shape of a ball

spirals shapes that go around and around as they go up

stage directions notes in a play that tell actors what they should do and how they should act

stanzas groups of lines that form part of a poem

statistics a collection of numbers that represents facts or measurements

steep having a slope that is high and difficult to go up

strategies sets of plans and skills used in order to gain success or achieve an aim

stress continuous feelings of worry caused by difficulties in your life

structure the way in which the parts of something connect with each other to form a whole

style a way of doing, making, or painting, something that is typical of a particular period

superintendent a person who is responsible for a place, job, activity, etc.

survive continue to live or exist

suspense a feeling of not knowing what is going to happen next

sustain to make it possible for someone or something to continue to exist over time

techniques special methods of doing something

technology a combination of all the knowledge, equipment, or methods used in scientific or industrial work

theory an explanation that may or may not be true

tolerance willingness to allow people to do, say, or believe what they want

trend the way that a situation is generally developing or changing

tsunami a very large, forceful wave that causes a lot of damage when it hits the land

uniforms particular types of clothing that members of an organization wear to work

unique the only one of its type

volcanoes mountains with holes at the top through which burning rock and fire sometimes rise into the air

weight how heavy something is

welfare health, comfort, and happiness

whorls patterns made out of lines that curl in circles that get bigger and bigger

Index of Skills

Word Study

Writing

Index of Authors, Titles, Art, and Artists

Acknowledgments

UNIT 1

Excerpts from *Chasing Vermeer* by Blue Balliett. Scholastic Inc./Scholastic Press. Copyright © 2004 by Elizabeth Balliett Klein. Used by permission of Scholastic Inc.

Excerpt from *G Is for Googol: A Math Alphabet Book* by David M. Schwartz. Copyright © 1998 by David M. Schwartz, Tricycle Press, Berkeley, CA, www.tenspeed.com. Reprinted with permission.

"Fact or Fiction?" Copyright © Pearson Longman, 10 Bank Street, White Plains, NY 10606.

Teenage Detectives: "The Case of the Defaced Sidewalk" by Carol Farley and "The Case of the Disappearing Signs" by Hy Conrad. Originally appeared on MysteryNet.com. Copyright © 1998, 2005 by Newfront Productions, Inc. Reprinted by permission.

UNIT 2

"Ancient Kids." Copyright © Pearson Longman, 10 Bank Street, White Plains, NY 10606.

"A Cry of Hounds" and "Soap Carving" from *Becoming Namoi León* by Pam Muñoz Ryan. Copyright © 2004 by Pam Muñoz Ryan. Reprinted by permission of Scholastic Inc.

Excerpt from *Later, Gator* by Laurence Yep. Copyright © 1995 by Laurence Yep. Reprinted with permission of Hyperion Books for Children. All rights reserved.

"Amazing Growth Facts." Adapted from *Incredible Comparisons* by Russell Ash, Dorling Kindersley.

"The Old Grandfather and His Little Grandson," an adapted folktale by Leo Tolstoy. Public domain.

UNIT 3

Excerpt from *Run Away Home* by Patricia C. McKissack. Scholastic Inc./Scholastic Press. Copyright © 1997 by Patricia C. McKissack. Reprinted by permission.

"Extraordinary People: Serving Others." Copyright © Pearson Longman, 10 Bank Street, White Plains, NY 10606.

Excerpt from *Zlata's Diary: A Child's Life in Sarajevo* by Zlata Filipović, translated by Christina Pribichevich-Zoric. Translation copyright © 1994 Editions Robert Laffont/Fixot. Used by permission of Viking Penguin, a Division of Penguin Group (U.S.A.) Inc. First published in France as *Le Journal de Zlata* by Fixot et Editions Robert Laffont 1993. Copyright © Fixot et Editions Robert Laffont, 1993. Reproduced by permission of Penguin Books Ltd. and by permission of Editions Robert Laffont.

"Friendships and Cooperation in the Animal Kingdom." Copyright © Pearson Longman, 10 Bank Street, White Plains, NY 10606.

UNIT 4

"Soccer: The World Sport" by Jane Schwartz. Copyright © Pearson Longman, 10 Bank Street, White Plains, NY 10606.

"Casey at the Bat" by Ernest Lawrence Thayer, 1888. Public domain.

"Swift Things Are Beautiful" from *Away Goes Sally* by Elizabeth Coatsworth. Copyright © 1934 by Macmillan Publishing Company, renewed 1962 by Elizabeth Coatsworth Beston. By permission of Paterson Marsh Ltd on behalf of the Estate of Elizabeth Coatsworth.

"Buffalo Dusk" from *Smoke and Steel* by Carl Sandburg. Copyright © 1920 by Harcourt, Inc. and renewed 1948 by Carl Sandburg. Reprinted by permission of the publisher.

"The Hare and the Tortoise" by Aesop. Public domain.

"Going, Going, Gone?" Adapted from *Time for Kids*, January 22, 2002. © 2002 Time for Kids. Reprinted by permission.

"Ivory-Billed Woodpeckers Make Some Noise" by Jill Egan. Adapted from *Time for Kids*, August 5, 2005. © 2005 Time for Kids. Reprinted by permission.

UNIT 5

Excerpt from *The Secret Garden* by Frances Hodgson Burnett and adapted by David C. Jones, from *Plays, The Drama Magazine for Young People*, © 2005. Reprinted with the permission of the publisher PLAYS/Sterling Partners, Inc., PO Box 600160, Newton, MA 02460.

"Kids' Guernica." Copyright © Pearson Longman, 10 Bank Street, White Plains, NY 10606.

Excerpt from *Hoot* by Carl Hiaasen. Copyright © 2002 by Carl Hiaasen. Used by permission of Alfred A. Knopf, an Imprint of Random House Children's Books, a Division of Random House, Inc., and by permission of the author c/o Rogers, Coleridge & White Ltd., 20 Powis Mews, London, W11 1JN.

"A Tree Grows in Kenya: The Story of Wangari Maathai" and "How to Plant a Tree." Copyright © Pearson Longman, 10 Bank Street, White Plains, NY 10606.

UNIT 6

"Life in the Future." Copyright © Pearson Longman, 10 Bank Street, White Plains, NY 10606.

"Southbound on the Freeway" and "Cardinal Ideograms" from *The Complete Poems to Solve* by May Swenson. Copyright © 1993. Used with permission of The Literary Estate of May Swenson.

"Interview with an Astronaut: Dan Bursch." Copyright © 2000 Discovery Communications, Inc. All rights reserved. Reprinted by permission of Discovery Kids.

Excerpt from *The Best New Thing* by Isaac Asimov. Copyright © The World Publishing Company, New York, 1971.

Excerpt from *2095: Time Warp Trio* by Jon Scieszka. Copyright © 1995 by Jon Scieszka. Used by permission of Viking Penguin, a Division of Penguin Young Readers Group, a member of Penguin Group (U.S.A.) Inc., 345 Hudson Street, New York, NY 10014. All rights reserved.

"Genetic Fingerprints." Copyright © Pearson Longman, 10 Bank Street, White Plains, NY 10606.

Credits

ILLUSTRATORS: Ron Himler 218–219, 221, 222–223; Roseanne Kaloustian 296, 298, 300, 303, 304, 306; Dean Klevin 6, 9, 11, 12, 17; Chris Lensch 350-351; Tom Leonard 24, 25; John F. Martin 89, 90, 92, 96; Craig Orback 119; Leah Palmer Preiss 352-353; Arvis Stewart 84, 162, 181; Rick Whipple 140–141, 143, 144, 147, 149, 268, 271, 273, 274–275, 276, 278

PHOTOGRAPHY:
COVER: Background, John Foxx/Getty Images; inset, Stockbyte/Getty Images.

UNIT 1: 2–3 background, Angelo Cavalli/Iconica/Getty Images; 2 top-left, Francis G. Mayer/CORBIS; 2 center-top John Lund/CORBIS; 2 top-right, Art Wolfe/Stone Allstock/Getty Images; 3 top-left, Charly Franklin/Taxi/Getty Images; 2 bottom-left, Todd Gipstein/Getty Images; 2 bottom-right, Werner Forman/Art Resource, NY; 3 bottom-right, Kenneth Garrett Photography; 4 bottom-right, Francis G. Mayer/CORBIS; 13 bottom-right, Photo courtesy of Bill Kline; 15 bottom-right, Judith Miller/Auktionhaus Dr Fischer/Dorling Kindersley; 18 top-left, Martin Cerny/Fotolia, LLC; 18 bottom-right, Stefano Bianchetti/CORBIS; 19 bottom-right, Neil Beer/PhotoDisc/Getty Images; 20 bottom-left, E.A. Kuttapan/Nature Picture Library; 22 top-right, DAJ/Getty Images; 22 bottom, Getty Images; 23 bottom-left, John Lund/CORBIS; 24 center-right, Shutterstock; 25 center, Bert Myers/Mira; 25 center-right, Cosmo Condina/Stock Connection; 25 bottom-right, Photo courtesy of Ed Aiona; 26 center-right, SGM/Stock Connection; 29 center-right, Andy Crawford/Dorling Kindersley; 31 center-right, © Ancient Art & Architecture/Danita Delimont Photography/DanitaDelimont.com; 32 bottom-right, Charles & Josette Lenars/Bettmann/CORBIS; 34 top-right, NASA; 34 bottom-right, Courtesy SPIN-2; 35 top-right, Roger Wood/CORBIS; 35 bottom-left, Mahaux Photography/Image Bank/Getty Images; 36 top-left, Adam Woolfitt/CORBIS; 36 bottom-right, Art Wolfe/Stone Allstock/Getty Images; 37 top-right, Michael Melford/Stone/Getty Images; 37 bottom-left, Time & Life Pictures/Getty Images; 38 top-right, New Zealand Herald/Sygma/CORBIS ; 38 bottom-right, Alamy Images; 39 top-left, Bettmann/CORBIS; 39 bottom-right, Malcolm Chandler/Dorling Kindersley; 40 bottom-right, Morgan, William De (1839–1917)/The Bridgeman Art Library International/The De Morgan Centre, London/The Bridgeman Art Library; 43 center-right, Steve Vidler/SuperStock ; 44 bottom-left, Shutterstock; 45 center-right, Charly Franklin/Taxi/Getty Images; 46 bottom-right, Paul Gilligan/Artville LLC/Getty Images; 47 bottom-right, Dorling Kindersley; 48 top-left, Dorling Kindersley; 48 top-center, Jeffrey Lindberg/Dorling Kindersley; 50 bottom-right, Jeffrey Lindberg/Dorling Kindersley; 51 top-right, Jeffrey Lindberg/Dorling Kindersley; 51 top-right, Jeffrey Lindberg/Dorling Kindersley; 52 top, Jeffrey Lindberg/Dorling Kindersley; 53 top-right, Photo courtesy of Carol Farley; 53 bottom-right, Photo courtesy of Hy Conrad; 54 bottom-right, Dorling Kindersley; 57 center-right, Artists Rights Society, Inc./Giorgio de Chirico, "Melancholy and Mystery of a Street," 1914. Oil on canvas, 24 1/4 x 28 1/2 in. Private Collection. Acquavella Galleries, Inc., NY. © 2008 Artists Rights Society (ARS), New York/SIAE, Rome; 60 top-right, Courtesy Sirchie Fingerprint Laboratories, Inc., Youngsville, NC; 60 bottom-right, Hulton Archive Photos/Getty Images; 62 top-right, Chad Ehlers/Stock Connection; 62 bottom-left, Russ Finley/Finley-Holiday Film Corporation.

UNIT 2: 68–69 background, Jose Luis Pelaez/Iconica/Getty Images; 68 top-left, Andy Crawford/Dorling Kindersley/Courtesy of the Royal Museum of Scotland, Edinburgh; 68 center-top, Viesti Associates, Inc.; 69 top-left, Michael Newman/PhotoEdit; 68 bottom-left, © The Metropolitan Museum of Art/Art Resource; 68 bottom-left, Kraig Scarbinsky/Riser/Getty Images; 69 bottom-left, Ronnie Kaufman/Getty Images; 70 bottom-right, The Granger Collection, New York; 71 bottom-right, © Ancient Art & Architecture/Danita Delimont Photography/DanitaDelimont.com; 72 bottom-right, De Agostini Editore Picture Library/Getty Images; 72 bottom-left, Araldo de Luca/Bettmann/CORBIS; 74 center-right, Nick Nicholls/Dorling Kindersley/© The British Museum; 75 top-right, Lebrecht Music & Arts Photo Library; 75 bottom-left, Nick Nicholls/Dorling Kindersley/© The British Museum; 75 bottom-center, Nick Nicholls/Dorling Kindersley/© The British Museum; 75 bottom-right, Nick Nicholls/Dorling Kindersley/© The British Museum; 76 top-right, Ara Pacis Augustae, Rome/Canali PhotoBank, Milan/SuperStock.; 76 bottom-left, Christi Graham and Nick Nicholls/Dorling Kindersley/© The British Museum; 76 bottom-right, Dorling Kindersley; 77 top-left, Dorling Kindersley/© The British Museum; 77 top-right, Christi Graham and Nick Nicholls/Dorling Kindersley/© The British Museum; 78 bottom-right, Michel Zabe/Dorling Kindersley/© CONACULTA-INAH-MEX. Authorized reproduction by the Instituto Nacional de Antropología e Historia.; 79 top-left, Andy Crawford/Dorling Kindersley/Courtesy of the Royal Museum of Scotland, Edinburgh; 79 top-right, Michel Zabe/Dorling Kindersley/© CONACULTA-INAH-MEX. Authorized reproduction by the Instituto Nacional de Antropología e Historia.; 81 center-right, Morton Beebe/CORBIS; 81 bottom-right, Erich Lessing/Art Resource, NY; 82 bottom-right, Christi Graham and Nick Nicholls/Dorling Kindersley/© The British Museum; 83 center-right, Spencer Grant/PhotoEdit; 84 bottom-right, Viesti Associates, Inc.; 86 bottom-right, Viesti Associates, Inc.; 86 bottom-left, Viesti Associates, Inc.; 93 top-right, EyeWire Collection/Photodisc/Getty Images; 93 bottom-left, Photo courtesy of Pam Muñoz Ryan; 95 bottom, Macduff Everton/CORBIS; 97 center-right, Shutterstock; 98 top-right, EyeWire Collection/Photodisc/Getty Images; 99 bottom-right, Cyril Laubscher/Dorling Kindersley; 100 bottom-right, Elke Van De Velde/Zefa/CORBIS; 107 bottom-right, Prentice Hall School Division; 110 bottom-right, Shutterstock; 112 top-right, Philip Schermeister/National Geographic Image Collection; 112 bottom-right, Adam Jones/Danita Delimont Photography/DanitaDelimont.com; 113 center-right, © Austin J. Stevens/Animals Animals/Earth Scenes; 114 bottom-right, Viesti Associates, Inc.; 115 top-right, A. Riedmiller/Das Fotoarchiv/Peter Arnold, Inc.; 115 bottom-right, Dorling Kindersley; 118 center, Alan Hills/Dorling Kindersley; 119 bottom-right, Bettmann/CORBIS; 121 bottom-right, Michael Newman/PhotoEdit; 123 center-right, Jeff Greenberg/PhotoEdit.

UNIT 3: 134–135 background, Dennis MacDonald/PhotoEdit; 134 top-left, Courtesy of the Library of Congress; 134 top-center, Hulton-Deutsch Collection/Bettmann/CORBIS; 134 top-right, Boulat Alexandra/Sipa; 135 top-left, Dr. Ronald H. Cohn/Gorilla

Foundation/Koko.org; 134 bottom-left, Paula Bronstein/Reportage/Getty Images; 135 bottom-left, Gilles Mingasson/Liaison/Getty Images; 136 bottom-left, J. N. Choate/Bettmann/CORBIS; 138 bottom-right, Lawrence Migdale/Pix; 139 top-right, Colin Paterson/Photodisc/Getty Images; 145 bottom-right, Boston Productions/Prentice Hall School Division; 146 bottom-right, Bettmann/CORBIS; 147 top-right, Courtesy of the Library of Congress; 150 center-right, Martin McEbilly/© New York Daily News, L. P. Reprinted with permission.; 150 bottom-left, Bettmann/CORBIS; 151 bottom-right, JP Laffont/Sygma/CORBIS; 152 bottom-right, Adam Smith/Taxi/Getty Images; 154 center-right, Dagli Orti/The Art Archive; 155 top-right, Bettmann/CORBIS; 155 bottom-right, Hulton-Deutsch Collection/Bettmann/CORBIS; 156 top-right, Bettmann/CORBIS; 156 bottom-right, AP/Wide World Photos; 157 top-right, Francesco Zizola/Magnum Photos, Inc.; 159 center-right, Bettmann/CORBIS; 159 bottom-right, Jean Claude Francolon; 160 bottom-right, John T. Parkinson/Mira; 161 center-right, Bettmann/CORBIS; 164 bottom-left, Ian Shaw/Stone Allstock/Getty Images; 165 top-right, Michael Dinges/Photodisc/Getty Images; 166 bottom-right, Alexandra Boulat/Sipa; 167 bottom-right, Alexandra Boulat/Sipa; 168 bottom-right, Francoise de Mulder/CORBIS; 169 top-right, Alexandra Boulat/Sipa; 170 center-right, Alexandra Boulat/Sipa; 171 top-left, Otto Lang/CORBIS; 171 bottom-right, Les Stone/Sygma/CORBIS; 172 top-right, Nigel Chandler/Sygma/CORBIS; 172 bottom-right, Matthias Schrader/dpa/Landov LLC; 173 bottom, Alexandra Boulat/Sipa; 174 bottom-right, Skjold Photographs; 175 center-right, Courtesy of the Library of Congress; 176 bottom-right, Peter Johnson/CORBIS; 177 center-right, Richard Lewis/Dorling Kindersley; 178 bottom-right, Ron Watts/CORBIS; 179 top-right, Gail Jankus/Photo Researchers, Inc.; 180 bottom-left, Warren Photographic; 181 top-right, Art Wolfe/Danita Delimont Photography/DanitaDelimont.com; 182 bottom-left, Peter Greste/Turtle Pond Publications; 183 center-top, Peter Greste/Turtle Pond Publications; 184 top-right, Hart, G. K. & Vikki/Image Bank/Getty Images; 186 bottom-right, Dr. Ronald H. Cohn/Gorilla Foundation/Koko.org; 187 center-right, EyeWire Collection/Photodisc/Getty Images; 190 center-right, Bettmann/CORBIS.

UNIT 4: 198 background, Bob Thomas/Stone Allstock/Getty Images; 198 top-left, AP/Wide World Photos; 198 center-top, Doran Milich/Allsport Photography/Getty Images; 198 top-right, Hart, G. K. & Vikki/Image Bank/Getty Images; 199 top-left, Arthur A. Allen/Cornell Laboratory of Ornithology; 198 bottom-left, Arthur Tilley/Taxi/Getty Images; 199 center-right, Jeff Foott/Getty Images; 200 top-right, Darren McCollester/Reuters/Bettmann/CORBIS; 201 bottom-right, Max Rossi/Reuters/CORBIS; 202 bottom-right, David Young-Wolff/Stone Allstock/Getty Images; 203 top-left, Jim Zipp/Photo Researchers, Inc.; 203 top-right, Richard Embery/Pearson Education/PH College; 204 bottom-left, Joanna B. Pinneo/Aurora; 205 top-right, Joe Patronite/Image Bank/Getty Images; 205 bottom-left, Hulton Archive Photos/Getty Images; 206 bottom-right, AP/Wide World Photos; 207 top-right, Nicole Bengiveno/The New York Times; 208 top, Nicole Bengiveno/The New York Times; 209 top-right, Nicole Bengiveno/The New York Times; 209 bottom-right, Photo courtesy of Jane Schwartz; 210 top-right, Shutterstock; 211 center-right, AP/Wide World Photos; 213 center-right, Sean Gallup/Getty Images; 214 bottom-left, The Bridgeman Art Library International/A Bison, c.1832 (coloured engraving) by George Catlin (1794–1872) © Bibliotheque Nationale, Paris, France/Lauros/Giraudon/The Bridgeman Art Library; 215 top-right, Hopkins, Edith (fl.1879–98)/The Bridgeman Art Library International/Private Collection/The Bridgeman Art Library; 216 bottom-right, Karl Weatherly/Photodisc/Getty Images; 217 center-right, Tony Freeman/PhotoEdit; 221 bottom-right, Bettmann/CORBIS; 222 top-right, R. C. Frampton/Pearson Education/PH College; 223 top-right, Bettmann/CORBIS; 225 bottom, Tom Leeson/Mira; 227 center-right, Joe Sohm/Chromosohm/Stock Connection; 228 bottom-left, Stockbyte/Getty Images; 229 top-right, Noble, John Edwin (1876–1961)/The Bridgeman Art Library International/Private Collection/The Bridgeman Art Library; 230 bottom, Joe Carini/PacificStock.com; 231 top-right, Cal Vornberger/Peter Arnold, Inc.; 232 full page, Noble, John Edwin (1876–1961)/The Bridgeman Art Library International/Private Collection/The Bridgeman Art Library; 233 bottom-right, Mary Evans Picture Library; 234 top, Fine Art Photographic Library, Ltd.; 235 top-right, The Bridgeman Art Library International/Roger-Viollet, Paris/The Bridgeman Art Library, London/New York; 236 center-right, Hart, G. K. & Vikki/Image Bank/Getty Images; 237 bottom-right, The Bridgeman Art Library International/Louvre, Paris, France/The Bridgeman Art Library; 238 top-right, Adam White/Nature Picture Library; 239 center-right, © Ancient Art & Architecture/Danita Delimont Photography/DanitaDelimont.com; 240 top-right, Schafer and Hill/Peter Arnold, Inc.; 240 center-right, Terry Andrewartha/Nature Picture Library; 240 bottom-right, Doug Gardner/Mira; 241 bottom-right, David Tipling/Nature Picture Library; 242 bottom-right, Robert Fried/robertfriedphotography.com; 243 top-right, Jorg Greuel/Image Bank/Getty Images; 244 background, Peter Anderson/Dorling Kindersley; 244 center, © Academy of Natural Sciences of Philadelphia/CORBIS; 245 background, Peter Anderson/Dorling Kindersley; 245 top-left, Dorling Kindersley; 245 center-right, © Academy of Natural Sciences of Philadelphia/CORBIS; 245 center-bottom © Academy of Natural Sciences of Philadelphia/CORBIS; 246 background, Peter Anderson/Dorling Kindersley; 246 bottom, Arthur A. Allen/Cornell Laboratory of Ornithology; 247 background, Peter Anderson/Dorling Kindersley; 247 top-right, © Academy of Natural Sciences of Philadelphia/CORBIS; 248 top-right, David Peart/Dorling Kindersley; 248 center-right, John Cancalosi/Nature Picture Library; 248 bottom-right, Theo Allofs/Danita Delimont Photography/DanitaDelimont.com; 249 center-right, Prentice Hall School Division; 250 bottom-right, George Holton/Photo Researchers, Inc.; 251 center-right, Joel Sartore/National Geographic Image Collection.

UNIT 5: 262–263 background, Jeff Hunter/Stone Allstock/Getty Images; 262 top-left, Richard Hutchings/PhotoEdit; 262 center-top, © Kids' Guernica International Committee; 262 top-right, Tom Vezo/Nature Picture Library; 263 top-left, William Campbell/Peter Arnold, Inc.; 262 center, Melba Photo Agency/PunchStock; 263 bottom-left, J.H. Pete Carmichael/Image Bank/Getty Images; 264 bottom-left, Jacqui Hurst/Dorling Kindersley; 266 bottom-right, Richard Hutchings/PhotoEdit; 275 center-right,

Bettmann/CORBIS; 275 bottom-right, Plays Magazine; 277 bottom-right, Comstock Images/Alamy Images; 279 center-right, Peter J. Robinson/Photolibrary.com; 280 bottom-right, Peter Byron/PhotoEdit; 281 center-right, Piter Willi/The Bridgeman Art Library International/© 2007 Estate of Pablo Picasso/Artists Rights Society (ARS), New York; 282 bottom-right, Glen Allison/ Mira; 284 background, Christopher Rennie/Robert Harding World Imagery; 284 bottom-right, The Art Archive; 285 background, Christopher Rennie/Robert Harding World Imagery; 285 top, © Kids' Guernica International Committee; 285 bottom-left, The Art Archive; 286 background, Christopher Rennie/Robert Harding World Imagery; 286 top, © Kid's Guernica International Committee; 286 bottom-left, Dallas and John Heaton/Stock Connection; 287 background, Christopher Rennie/Robert Harding World Imagery; 287 top-left, © Kids' Guernica International Committee; 287 top-right, © Kids' Guernica International Committee; 289 bottom-right, Archivo Icongrafico, S.A./ Bettmann/CORBIS; 290 bottom-right, Picasso, Pablo (1881–1973) /The Bridgeman Art Library International/Private Collection/ The Bridgeman Art Library; 291 center-right, Picasso, Pablo (1881–1973)/The Bridgeman Art Library International/Hamburger Kunsthalle, Hamburg, Germany/The Bridgeman Art Library; 292 bottom-left, © Gerlach, John/Animals Animals/Earth Scenes; 293 bottom-right, Mark Richards/PhotoEdit; 294 bottom-right, Jason Laure/Woodfin Camp & Associates, Inc.; 295 center-right, Larry Landolfi/Photo Researchers, Inc.; 303 bottom-right, Jeffery Allan Salter/SABA Press Photos, Inc./CORBIS; 305 bottom-right, Klaus Nigge/National Geographic Image Collection; 307 center-right, Tom Vezo/Nature Picture Library; 308 top-right, Christop Burki/Stone Allstock/Getty Images; 308 bottom, Skip Brown/National Geographic Image Collection; 309 center-right, Novastock/Stock Connection; 310 bottom-right, Shutterstock; 311 top-right, Simon Harris/Robert Harding World Imagery; 312 background, Charlotte Thege/Das Fotoarchiv/Peter Arnold, Inc.; 312 center, Terje Bendiksby/Agence France Presse/Getty Images; 313 background, Charlotte Thege/Das Fotoarchiv/Peter Arnold, Inc.; 313 center-bottom, William Campbell/Peter Arnold, Inc.; 314 background, Charlotte Thege/Das Fotoarchiv/Peter Arnold, Inc.; 314 bottom, De Agostini Editore Picture Library/Getty Images; 315 background, Charlotte Thege/Das Fotoarchiv/Peter Arnold, Inc.; 315 top-right, Mark Winwood/Dorling Kindersley; 316 top-right, © Marc Romanelli/Alamy Images; 317 top-right, Agence France Presse/Getty Images; 317 bottom-right, David Turnley/CORBIS; 318 bottom-right, Marc Moritsch/National Geographic Image Collection; 319 center-right, Dorling Kindersley.

UNIT 6: 330–331 background, Stockbyte/Getty Images; 330 top-left, David A. Hardy/2111 Foundation/Photo Researchers, Inc.; 330 center-top, NASA; 330 top-right, David A. Hardy/ Photo Researchers, Inc.; 331 top-left, Dr. Jurgen Scriba/Photo Researchers, Inc.; 330 bottom-left, Richard Nowitz/National Geographic Society; 330 bottom-center, Rob Atkins/Stone Allstock/Getty Images; 331 center-right, Micheal Simpson/ Taxi/Getty Images; 332 center-right, "Exploration of Mars" by Chesley Bonestell/Black Cat Studios; 332 bottom-left, Mattioli Collection, Milan/Brideman Art Library, London/SuperStock; 333 center-right, Carsten Peter/National Geographic Image Collection; 334 bottom-right, Michael Rosenfeld/Stone Allstock/ Getty Images; 336 top-left, Sony Electronics Inc; 336 top-right, Digital Art/CORBIS; 336 center-left, Patrik Giardino/CORBIS; 336 bottom-left, Geoff Brightling/© Dorling Kindersley/Courtesy of the Department of Electrical and Electronic Engineering, University of Portsmouth; 337 top, Shutterstock; 337 bottom, Richard Davies/Foster and Partners; 338 top, NASA/Photo Researchers, Inc.; 339 top-right, Mike Dunning/Dorling Kindersley/International Automotive Design; 339 bottom-left, The Granger Collection, New York; 340 top, Trek Aerospace, Inc.; 341 top-right, David A. Hardy/2111 Foundation/Photo Researchers, Inc.; 342 top-right, © Forrest J. Ackerman Collection/CORBIS; 343 bottom-right, NASA; 345 center-right, Chris Lyon/Dorling Kindersley; 346 bottom-left, NASA/Science Source/Photo Researchers, Inc.; 346 bottom-right, NOAO/Photo Researchers, Inc.; 347 bottom-right, US Geological Survey/Photo Researchers, Inc.; 348 center-right, Andy Crawford/Dorling Kindersley; 348 bottom-right, Dave King/Dorling Kindersley/Courtesy of the National Motor Museum, Beaulieu; 349 top-right, Dorling Kindersley; 353 bottom-right, Carole Berglie/ Reprinted with the permission of the Literary Estate of May Swenson; 354 top background, European Southern Observatory/ Photo Researchers, Inc.; 354 top, NASA/Goddard Laboratory for Atmospheres; 354 center, NASA; 355 background, European Southern Observatory/Photo Researchers, Inc.; 330 center-top, NASA; 356 background, European Southern Observatory/Photo Researchers, Inc.; 356 top-right, NASA/John F. Kennedy Space Center; 357 top-left, European Southern Observatory/Photo Researchers, Inc.; 357 top-right, NASA/Science Source/Photo Researchers, Inc.; 358 bottom-right, NASA/Photo Researchers, Inc.; 359 top-right, NASA/Science Source/Photo Researchers, Inc.; 361 center-right, AP/Wide World Photos; 362 center, David A. Hardy/Photo Researchers, Inc.; 363 center-right, © Fortean/ Topham/The Image Works; 364 bottom-right, David Young-Wolff/PhotoEdit; 371 bottom-right, James E. Schuck; 373 bottom, Joe Tucciarone/Photo Researchers, Inc.; 374 center-right, Julian Baum/Photo Researchers, Inc.; 375 center-right, NASA/Finley Holiday Films/Dorling Kindersley; 376 bottom-left, Laguna Design/Photo Researchers, Inc.; 377 bottom-right, Courtesy Imaging Forensics, Fountain Valley, Calif.; 378 bottom-right, BananaStock/SuperStock; 379 center-right, Hugh Turvey/Photo Researchers, Inc.; 380 background, Richard Prideaux/Photo Researchers, Inc.; 380 top-right, Tony Cordoza; 380 bottom-right, Michael Dunning/Photographer's Choice/Getty Images; 381 background, Richard Prideaux/Photo Researchers, Inc.; 381 top-right, Tek Image/Photo Researchers. Inc.; 381 bottom-left, James King-Holmes/Photo Researchers, Inc.; 382 background, Richard Prideaux/Photo Researchers, Inc.; 382 top-left, Ron Heflin/AP/Wide World Photos; 383 background, Richard Prideaux/ Photo Researchers, Inc.; 383 top-right, Dr. Jurgen Scriba/Photo Researchers, Inc.; 383 bottom-left, Nathan Benn/Bettmann/ CORBIS; 384 center-right, Scott Camazine/Photo Researchers, Inc.; 385 bottom-right, A. Barrington Brown/Photo Researchers, Inc.; 387 center-right, Jose Luis Pelaez, Inc./Bettmann/CORBIS.

Smithsonian American Art Museum List of Artworks

UNIT 1 Solving the Puzzle of Letters and Numbers

Page 66
Mike Wilkins
Preamble, 1987
painted metal on vinyl and wood
96 x 96 in.
Smithsonian American Art Museum, Gift of Nissan Motor Corporation in U.S.A.
© 1987 Mike Wilkins

Page 67
Robert Indiana
Five, 1984
wood and metal
69⅛ x 26¾ x 18½ in.
Smithsonian American Art Museum, Gift of the artist
© 1984 Robert Indiana

UNIT 2 Capturing Childhood

Page 132
Albert Bisbee
Child on a Rocking Horse, about 1855
daguerreotype
4¼ x 4½ in.
Smithsonian American Art Museum, Museum purchase from the Charles Isaacs Collection made possible in part by the Luisita L. and Franz H. Denghausen Endowment

Page 133
William Holbrook Beard
The Lost Balloon, 1882
oil on canvas
47¾ x 33¾ in.
Smithsonian American Art Museum, Museum purchase

UNIT 3 Respect

Page 196
Jesse Treviño
Mis Hermanos, 1976
acrylic on canvas
48 x 70 in.
Smithsonian American Art Museum, Gift of Lionel Sosa, Ernest Bromley, Adolfo Aguilar of Sosa, Bromley, Aguilar and Associates
© Smithsonian American Art Museum

Page 197
Jacob Lawrence
"Men exist for the sake of one another. Teach them then or bear with them."—Marcus Aurelius Antoninus, Meditations, VIII: 59. From the series Great Ideas of Western Man., 1958
oil on fiberboard
20¾ x 16¾ in.
Smithsonian American Art Museum, Gift of Container Corporation of America

UNIT 4 Baseball in America

Page 260
Mark Sfirri
Rejects from the Bat Factory, 1996
various woods
15⅜ x 36½ in.
Smithsonian American Art Museum, Gift of Fleur and Charles Bresler in honor of Kenneth R. Trapp, curator-in-charge of the Renwick Gallery (1995–2003)

Page 261
Morris Kantor
Baseball at Night, 1934
oil on linen
37 x 47¼ in.
Smithsonian American Art Museum, Gift of Mrs. Morris Kantor

UNIT 5 Dignity Through Art

Page 329
James Hampton
The Throne of the Third Heaven of the Nations' Millennium General Assembly, about 1950–64
gold and silver aluminum foil, Kraft paper, and plastic
180 pieces: 10½ x 27 x 14½ ft.
Smithsonian American Art Museum, Gift of anonymous donors

UNIT 6 Imaging the Future

Page 398
Harry Bertoia
Sculpture Group Symbolizing World's Communication in the Atomic Age, 1959
braised and welded brass and bronze
142¼ x 231¼ x 81 in.
Smithsonian American Art Museum, Gift of the Zenith Corporation

Page 399
Alexander A. Maldonado
San Francisco to New York in One Hour, 1969
oil on canvas and wood
18 x 24 in.
Smithsonian American Art Museum, Gift of Herbert Waide Hemphill Jr. and museum purchase made possible by Ralph Cross Johnson